Luminos is the Open Access monograph publishing program from UC Press. Luminos provides a framework for preserving and reinvigorating monograph publishing for the future and increases the reach and visibility of important scholarly work. Titles published in the UC Press Luminos model are published with the same high standards for selection, peer review, production, and marketing as those in our traditional program. www.luminosoa.org

Egyptian Things

Egyptian Things

Translating Egypt to Early Imperial Rome

———

Edward William Kelting

UNIVERSITY OF CALIFORNIA PRESS

University of California Press
Oakland, California

© 2024 by Edward Kelting

This work is licensed under a Creative Commons (CC BY-NC-ND) license.
To view a copy of the license, visit https://creativecommons.org/licenses.

Suggested citation: Kelting, E. W. *Egyptian Things: Translating Egypt to Early Imperial Rome*. Oakland: University of California Press, 2024.
DOI: https://doi.org/10.1525/luminos.207

Library of Congress Cataloging-in-Publication Data

Names: Kelting, Edward William, author.
Title: Egyptian things : translating Egypt to early imperial Rome /
   Edward William Kelting.
Description: [Oakland, California] : University of California, [2024] |
   Includes bibliographical references and index.
Identifiers: LCCN 2024009329 (print) | LCCN 2024009330 (ebook) |
   ISBN 9780520402188 (paperback) | ISBN 9780520402195 (ebook)
Subjects: LCSH: Rome—Civilization—ƒEgyptian influences.
Classification: LCC DG78.K45 2024 (print) | LCC DG78 (ebook) |
   DDC 937—dc23/eng/20240405

LC record available at https://lccn.loc.gov/2024009329
LC ebook record available at https://lccn.loc.gov/2024009330

Manufactured in the United States of America

32   31   30   29   28   27   26   25   24
10   9   8   7   6   5   4   3   2   1

CONTENTS

List of Illustrations	*vii*
Acknowledgments	*ix*

Introduction: Roman Egypt and Rome's "Egypt"	*1*

PART ONE. INTRODUCING AEGYPTIACA

1. Apion, Roman Egypt, and the Insider-Outsider Problem	*27*
2. Aegyptiaca: Triangulating a Coherently Incoherent Genre	*55*

PART TWO. EGYPT'S ANIMALS: FROM REPRESENTATION TO CULTURAL TRANSLATION

3. From Representation . . . : Anubis, Actium, and the Limits of Exoticism	*87*
4. . . . To Translation: Aegyptiaca, Seth/Typhon, and Human/Animal/ Divine Permeability	*116*

PART THREE. WHAT'S EGYPTIAN FOR "PHILOSOPHER"?

5. Not Dead Yet! Legitimizing Imperial-Period Hieroglyphic Symbolisms	*143*
6. Recuperating the Philosopher-Priest: Embracing a Mixed Intellectual Authority	*169*

Conclusion: Acoreus, Aegyptiaca, and the Question of Cultural Influence	*197*

Works Cited	*209*
Index	*239*

ILLUSTRATIONS

1. The Temple of Dendur, reign of Augustus, with two statues of Amenhotep III (22.5.1, 22.5.2) in the foreground. The Metropolitan Museum of Art, New York   *2*

2. The emperor Augustus offering to the Egyptian gods Horus and Hathor. From the southern wall of the Temple of Dendur, reign of Augustus. The Metropolitan Museum of Art, New York   *3*

3. Statue of the god Anubis-Mercury. From the Villa Pamphili, Anzio, 1st–2nd Century CE. Gregorian Egyptian Museum, Vatican Museums Cat. 22840, Rome. Photo courtesy of the author   *112*

4. Statue of Osiris-Apis. From Hadrian's Villa, Tivoli, reign of Hadrian. Gregorian Egyptian Museum, Vatican Museums Cat. 22807, Rome. Photo courtesy of Marie-Lan Nguyen / Wikimedia Commons   *114*

5. The goddesses Isis and Nephthys preparing a chained and bound donkey, identified with the god Seth, for sacrifice. From the east wall of the first east Osiris chapel of the Temple of Hathor, Dendera, late Ptolemaic to Roman period. Photo courtesy of the author   *127*

6. The god Horus spearing a hippopotamus identified with the god Seth. From the internal east enclosure wall of the Temple of Horus, Edfu, Ptolemaic period. Photo courtesy of the author   *132*

ACKNOWLEDGMENTS

This book pokes around in the interstitial spaces where Aegyptiaca has resided—whether between Egypt and Rome, between Classics and Egyptology, or between ancient and modern forms of cultural mixture. The book itself, like the authors it discusses, reflects the different people, places, and sensibilities between which it is suspended.

I first heard the name "Manetho" as an undergraduate at Brown University, where the core interests that shape this book took root. In Egyptology classes at Wilbour Hall, over the course of my years hanging around Macfarlane House, and during my work-study sorting through David Pingree's collection of astronomical texts, I first got a sense of how ideas moved around the ancient Mediterranean. My mentors in Classics and Egyptology, particularly Jay Reed, Pura Nieto, James Allen, and Leo Depuydt, made it impossible not to try to spend time thinking about Greece, Rome, and Egypt.

This book first saw the light of day as a doctoral dissertation in the Classics Department at Stanford University. Susan Stephens, Grant Parker, and Christopher Krebs all put the pieces on the board that I haltingly began to arrange into something of some coherence. Christopher Krebs helped me learn the ropes of the *FGrH* and put me on to the value of fragmentary authors; Grant Parker made clear the theoretical and political import of the ancient world; and Susan Stephens patiently helped me learn what I actually wanted from my own scholarship. This book was steered by other and more informal conversations at Stanford too, particularly with Stephen Harrison, Alessandro Barchiesi, and Richard Martin. More materially, this book and I have benefited from the generous support of the Ric Weiland Graduate Fellowship and Geballe Fellowship. As I prepared to leave the nest, my colleagues at the Stanford Humanities Center both provided real support at a bumpy time and helped me appreciate the wider stakes that led me to spend so much time with arcane names like Manetho, Apion, and Charemon.

This book became what it now is because of my colleagues at UC San Diego, and there are many to thank: in the Literature Department, my close colleagues Page DuBois and Jacobo Myerston and hallway-mates Lisa Lampert-Weissig and Todd Kontje. I workshopped the introduction with fantastic colleagues—Ameeth Vijay, Amanda Batarseh, Gabriel Bámgbóṣé, and Erin Suzuki. I am especially indebted to friends in the History Department like Mira Balberg, Denise Demetriou, and Ed Watts, who helped me locate my book's authors and their concerns in wider histories of cross-cultural exchange in the eastern Mediterranean. I remain grateful to the Society of Hellman Fellows, which supported research travel and helped this book become a reality.

Many near and far lent this project their time and expertise. I am particularly thankful to the anonymous reviewers, whose attention has helped this book immeasurably. Eric Schmidt and Jyoti Arvey at the University of California Press have good-naturedly endured a first-time author. Colleagues at the Università degli Studi di Firenze, Colorado College, the Society for Classical Studies, and the Classical Association of the Middle West and South have all offered feedback. Any remaining faults are absolutely my own.

Pride of place is owed to friends and family. Friends like Scott Weiss, Stephen Sansom, and Alyson Melzer have been sounding boards and sources of great joy for many years now. I remain in awe of my sister Lily—for many reasons, but especially because she is one of the best writers I know. My mom, Emily, has listened to half-baked ideas, gripes, and good news with love and support. My wife Finn may not have typed up my manuscript, but she has been this book's most incisive and generous interlocutor. This inside joke is meant to acknowledge the difficulty of acknowledging somebody who means so much to me. Finally, I would like to thank my dad, Howard, to whom this book is dedicated.

Introduction

Roman Egypt and Rome's "Egypt"

The Temple of Dendur stands grandly in New York's Metropolitan Museum of Art (fig. 1). Reflecting pools and cool tan-marble floors stylishly evoke the Nile and its surroundings; an enormous semi-translucent ceiling remains a relic of 1970s modernism; a vast wall of glass looks out to Central Park and E. Eighty-Fourth Street. All frame the Egyptian temple's relocation to the former Sackler Wing as a feat so grand that the original temple and its construction look pedestrian. Nominally, the room complements the temple, suggesting an original Egyptian setting. But the soaring space, large reflecting pools, and majestic windows become the object of admiration. We are asked to stand in awe of the imperial project of relocation that allowed an ancient temple to look so small against its modern exhibition. Lyndon Johnson's letter to the museum announcing that it would house the temple, which had been gifted to the United States after its help in the Aswan High Dam Project, proudly concludes that the temple's move to New York "will protect it and make it available to millions of Americans in a setting appropriate to its character."[1]

A setting appropriate to its character, indeed. To most visitors, the Temple of Dendur tidily evokes a transhistorical model of an Egyptian temple. The temporal disjoin between it and the statues of Amenhotep III sitting before it—over 1300 years!—certainly adds to this sense of nebulous timelessness. But the temple is decidedly of Roman-Egyptian origin. It was built in 10 BCE by the emperor Augustus and erected just south of Egypt's southern border. This space, long the frontier of Egypt and Nubia, became a place where Roman power and its cooption of Egyptian iconography of empire were formalized. On its walls (fig. 2), the emperor

---

1. Johnson's letter to the Metropolitan's then-director, Thomas Hoving, is reproduced and discussed in Patch (2018).

FIGURE 1. The Temple of Dendur, reign of Augustus, with two statues of Amenhotep III (22.5.1, 22.5.2) in the foreground. The Metropolitan Museum of Art, New York.

himself, in traditional pharaonic regalia, burns incense for a local Nubian chieftain's deified sons and the pantheon of Egyptian gods—Isis, Osiris, Thoth, Horus, and Hathor—to whom the temple is dedicated.

In the Temple of Dendur, Augustus perpetuates the visual language of Egyptian religion to associate Roman power with the Egyptian forms of imperial self-styling that long preceded it. But precious little of this context has made the trip to the Metropolitan Museum, where the temple's original semantics are now condensed into a bare sign of Egyptian religion that has been improbably and magnificently hauled off to New York. At the Met, the Temple of Dendur inevitably loses much of the spatial and temporal liminality that makes it such an atypical typical Egyptian temple.

That museumgoers in New York can look on Augustus worshipping Isis, Tefnut, Horus, and other animal-headed gods is at first strange. In the *Aeneid*, Virgil had framed Augustus's defeat of Antony and Cleopatra at the Battle of Actium as a victory of the traditional Roman religious order over its vile, monstrous, Egyptian counterpart:

> In the middle the queen Cleopatra calls to her army with native rattle,
> she does not yet look back behind her to the twin snakes.

FIGURE 2. The emperor Augustus offering to the Egyptian gods Horus and Hathor. From the southern wall of the Temple of Dendur, reign of Augustus. The Metropolitan Museum of Art, New York.

> Monstrous forms of every sort of god and the barker Anubis
> hold weapons against Neptune and Venus and against Minerva.[2]

Augustus's apparent distaste for Egyptian religion, one of many tools through which civil war against Antony was recast as a war between a Roman self and a barbarous, effete, Egyptian Other, took firm root. Cassius Dio tells us that Augustus patently refused to visit the Apis bull: "And for this same reason he also didn't want to meet with the Apis bull, claiming that he was wont to worship gods, not cattle."[3] The *Aeneid*, not quite finished when disseminated after Virgil's death in 19 BCE, and the temple, completed in 10 BCE, alternatively depict Augustus defeating and worshipping the same set of Egyptian gods.

---

2. *Aen.* 8.696–700: regina in mediis patrio vocat agmina sistro, / necdum etiam geminos a tergo respicit anguis. / omnigenumque deum monstra et latrator Anubis / contra Neptunum et Venerem contraque Minervam / tela tenent. Text is that of Mynors (1969). Where unnoted, translations are my own.

3. Dio Cass. 51.16.5: κἀκ τῆς αὐτῆς ταύτης αἰτίας οὐδὲ τῷ Ἄπιδι ἐντυχεῖν ἠθέλησε, λέγων θεοὺς ἀλλ' οὐχὶ βοῦς προσκυνεῖν εἰθίσθαι. Text is that of Boissevain (1895–1901).

4   INTRODUCTION

This is an odd disjunction: Egyptian religion is simultaneously vilified in Rome and, in Egypt, used to advertise Roman power. It is all too easy to write off this disconnect as situational. What happens in Egypt, stays in Egypt (until it is carted off to New York or Paris or London or Madrid). Augustus's activity in Egypt is incommensurate with the "Egypt" denigrated by Virgil and Cassius Dio.[4] In the Temple of Dendur, Egyptian priestly elite expediently underline a continuity of rule central to the ideology of Egyptian kingship. By barbarizing Egyptian religion, Roman authors create a schematic Rome-Egypt binary to stress the continuity of a *Romanitas* that had been undergoing constant rearticulation in the socio-political upheaval of the first centuries BCE and CE.[5]

In emphasizing the herculean task of relocating the temple, the Metropolitan Museum unwittingly perpetuates an imperial sleight of hand that had begun with Augustus himself. The Temple of Dendur is one entry in a millennia-long history of robbing Egypt of its big, heavy stuff. Augustus, who took Egypt's obelisks to decorate Rome, looms large in this history of looted antiquities. Pliny the Elder, the famous encyclopedist, brags about the ships that Augustus had built to bring obelisks from Egypt to Rome: "More than anything, there was the problem of carrying obelisks to Rome by sea. The ships were quite the spectacle. Augustus the divine had memorialized the boat that carried the first obelisk in permanent docks in Pozzuoli because of this miraculous deed."[6] The act of transport outshines the original creation of the obelisks, a shift of emphasis that redefines the value of objects that had long coordinated royal power with solar religion. As for Rome's obelisks, so too for Dendur.

Pliny's celebration of the transport of Egypt's obelisks exemplifies the ways that Rome's control of Egypt incentivized and gave shape to the movement of people and goods across the Mediterranean.[7] Exchange between Egypt and Rome puts paid to the "what happens in Egypt, stays in Egypt" narrative used to cleave off the Temple of Dendur from the antipathy to Egypt promoted by Virgil and Cassius Dio. Exoticism, barbarization, and Orientalism have for some time been invoked to justify this separation between Egypt in Rome and Roman Egypt.[8] The obelisk may travel from Egypt to Rome, but the cultural attachments that make an obelisk a significant object to Egyptians do not travel along with it. So long as Romans

4. For Augustus's (and other emperors') building activity in Egypt, see Klotz (2012, 227–45).

5. This barbarizing line of argumentation has been made by Smelik and Hemelrijk (1984), Sonnabend (1986), Pfeiffer (2015, 50), and Gasparini (2017, 399).

6. Plin. *HN* 36.70: super omnia accessit difficultas mari Romam devehendi, spectatis admodum navibus. divus Augustus eam, quae priorem advexerat, miraculi gratia Puteolis perpetuis navalibus dicaverat. Text of Pliny is that of von Jan and Mayhoff (1967).

7. For these imports, see Roullet (1972), Malaise (1972a, 1972b), and Vittozzi (2006).

8. Pearson (2021, 193–94) pushes back against a dichotomy of full incorporation or complete exoticism when approaching Egyptian culture's presence in Rome. In chapter 1, I address the limits of Orientalism (see Said 1978) as a theoretical frame used to justify the schism between Roman Egypt and Egypt in Rome.

project their own significance onto Egyptian objects, landscapes, languages, priests, and animals, the Egypt on display in Roman literature and material culture can be held apart from the historical realities of Roman Egypt.[9] But this separability, built on the relative independence of Rome's Egypt from Egypt itself, fails to capture a vibrant process of cultural translation that surrounded the movement of goods and people from Egypt to Rome.[10]

This book sets out to recapture one of these processes of cultural translation: a literary tradition in which culturally mixed Egyptian authors wrote about Egypt for a Greek and Roman audience. This literary tradition's popularity in Rome has been masked by a perceived gulf between Rome's Egypt and Egypt's Egypt that is far from ubiquitous or inevitable. Orientalism has often been retrojected back into the ancient world to justify this chasm, but it is better suited to modernity and the academy.[11] It calls attention to the different disciplinary trajectories of Classics and Egyptology. A divide has emerged between those who study Roman views of Egyptian animal worship, or the hieroglyphic script, or priestly wisdom, from those who read Egyptian-language texts on those very traditions. Arguments for the isolation of Rome's own projected "Egypt" and the historical Egypt stand firmly at odds with a reality of travel, of people and ideas, from Egypt to Rome. Egyptian traditions hitched a ride with the culturally mixed Egyptian authors who made the trip from Egypt to Rome on paths carved by Rome's newly formed Principate. In this book, I want to document their whole trip, starting from Egypt and Egyptology and ending in Rome and the cultural history of the imperial period.

The Temple of Dendur is so exciting because it makes clear that the Egypt with which Rome came into contact was—far from an empty signifier of exoticism—a complex mixture of cultural traditions. Whenever I can dragoon family, friends, in-laws (anyone, really) to visit the temple with me, I cannot help but dwell on everything that makes it idiosyncratic. This starts with the cartouches in which Augustus's power is literally spelled out. The titulature is simultaneously Greek, Egyptian, and Roman while being none of these things exclusively. Sometimes, Augustus is simply called "Pharaoh" (*pr-ꜥ*), a label for the institution of kingship rarely used as a stand-alone title in pharaonic titulature. In other cartouches

---

9. This separation extends across the two key groups discussing Romans' views of Egypt—those who work on material culture and on literature. For the latter, see Sonnabend (1986), Manolaraki (2013), Leemreize (2016), and Merrills (2017). For the former, see most recently Swetnam-Burland (2015), Barrett (2019), Pearson (2021), and Mazurek (2022, 59–87), who emphasizes the deterritorialization of Egyptian religion and its reinvention as a Greco-Roman fantasy.

10. Guldin (2018, 18–21) underlines the reciprocal influence of physical movement across space and metaphors of translation.

11. Parker's comparison of the Lateran obelisk and Diocletian's stele cautions that appropriation as a theoretical frame risks "reifying cultural boundaries" (2018, 138), a caution that could extend to Orientalizing approaches to Roman interest in Egypt. See Swetnam-Burland (2015, 187n2) for a similar note of caution.

6   INTRODUCTION

(fig. 2), Augustus is "the Autocrator, Caesar, alive forever" (𓀀𓁹𓊃𓊃) (𓍹𓁹𓋹𓌀𓏏𓆓𓍺)
(ʾwttrtr qysrs ʿnḫ ḏt). Both on the lexical level and in the cultural semantics of
power, the title is a creative amalgam. It translates into Greek (Καῖσαρ) and then
Egyptian (qysrs) Augustus's self-advertised position as Caesar's heir and adopted
son; Augustus is an Autocrator, a Greek term for sole rule transliterated into Egyptian. As an Autocrator, Augustus adopts a label for kingship typical of Ptolemaic
Egypt and its mixture of Greek and Egyptian idioms of power. The traditional
royal tag "alive forever" (ʿnḫ ḏt), here abbreviated in later hieroglyphic spelling,
continues an Egyptian ideology of royal immortality that was part and parcel of
pharaonic conceptions of kingship, but was just finding its footing in Rome with
Julius Caesar's postmortem divinization. In one title, a multimodal expression of
power looks back to Egyptian traditions of the pharaonic past, remakes them in
conversation with a mixed Greco-Egyptian argot of Ptolemaic power, and then
leverages both Egyptian pasts (the one pharaonic, the other Ptolemaic) to incorporate Rome into Egyptian religious culture.

This mixture of traditions is what I find exciting and want to call attention to
in this book. What is true of cartouches can be extended to the interconnected set
of Egyptian religious themes on Dendur's walls. The hieroglyphic script, animal-
shaped gods, scribal priests—they too are idiosyncratic and speak to the liminal
moment of the early-imperial period. How did Egyptians of this period present
these "Egyptian things," and how did Romans receive those explanations? What
strategies did Egyptians use to explain the hieroglyphic script to Romans who
were keen to see in it either the secrets of the universe or (as in the Augustus
example) a potent means of expressing power? When faced with a barbarizing
rhetoric demonizing cow-gods, how did Egyptians go about underlining the systems of significance surrounding a beetle-headed divinity? By spending time with
these questions, I hope to put center stage Egyptian culture of the imperial period
and the ways that Egyptians presented it to a Roman audience. In the process,
I will be arguing both that Rome's imagined Egypt was meaningfully shaped by
what Egyptians had to say, and that what imperial-era Egyptians had to say about
Egypt is a meaningful continuation of the pharaonic-era traditions on display in
the Egyptian-language texts and monuments studied by Egyptologists.

DEFINING "EGYPTIAN THINGS"

To Rome went both objects associated with Egypt and Egyptians who strategically
translated those objects' original semantics to a Greek and Roman audience. Shin-
ing a light on these Egyptians and their interpretations of Egyptian objects and
traditions reveals intercultural exchange, agency, and dialogue where exoticization, barbarization, and cultural projection have been assumed.[12] In part, this shift

---

12. Smelik and Hemelrijk (1984) and Sonnabend (1986) (on Egypt in Roman literature) and Versluys (2002) and Swetnam-Burland (2015) (on Egypt in Roman material culture) have emphasized
Rome's barbarizing or exoticizing portrait of Egypt.

INTRODUCTION   7

in focus is meant to balance the story of Egyptian material culture's presence in Rome with Egyptians' creative explanations of that material culture. Many more people have written about the cult of Isis and Rome's Egyptianizing objects than about Egyptian authors who both wrote about Egypt and traveled from Egypt to Rome.[13] The fate of the term *Aegyptiaca* is exemplary. Miguel John Versluys, like others before him, chose "Egyptian things" (*Aegyptiaca*) to describe Egyptian and Egyptian-looking things in Italy. In 2007 Molly Swetnam-Burland continued the trend, explicitly defending the value of Aegyptiaca as a category for Egyptian-looking—and not just Egypt-originating—material culture in Italy. She, and Versluys before her, gravitated toward Aegyptiaca because it blurs the line separating Egyptian objects imported to Italy from Egyptian-looking objects made in Italy.[14]

Versluys and Swetnam-Burland used the term for material culture, but in antiquity Aegyptiaca was applied to texts. Like its sister-terms *Babyloniaca* and *Romaica*, Aegyptiaca was an open-ended term for Greek-language texts about the history and culture of a non-Greek community.[15] These different terms speak to the efflorescence of autoethnographic writing in the Hellenistic world. Babylonians, Egyptians, and Romans wrote about their own traditions for a wide Greek-speaking audience.[16] The Egyptian Manetho, Babylonian Berossus, and Roman Quintus Fabius Pictor leveraged their positions as priests or senatorial elite to present an authoritative version of their own people's history. The specific contours of that cultural self-presentation were flexible. The term Aegyptiaca, like its other ethnic counterparts, was deliberately blurry. As a blank neuter plural adjective, "Egyptian things" offered plenty of wiggle room.[17]

Long before Augustus or the Temple of Dendur, the Hellenistic period gave rise to an Egyptian presentation of Egypt that was read by a Greek-speaking audience. After Alexander, Egyptians began writing about Egypt in Greek. As yet, this has been commonly understood as a brief blip restricted to Manetho, its first

---

13. The cult of Isis has been a central object of scholarly attention, not least because of regular international conferences, published in Bricault (2004), Bricault, Versluys, and Meyboom (2007), Bricault and Versluys (2010, 2014), and more recently Gasparini and Veymiers (2018). Italy's Isis temples as archaeological sites are studied by Tran-tam-Tinh (1964), Dunand (1973), Lembke (1994), and Versluys, Clausen, and Vittozzi (2018). Isiac epigraphy was investigated by Vidman (1969). The Isis cult's presence in Book 11 of Apuleius's *Metamorphoses* is discussed by Egelhaaf-Gaiser (2000) and Assmann (2002).

14. Swetnam-Burland (2007, 119), anticipated in Versluys (2002), picked up in Swetnam-Burland (2015), and used widely in Barrett (2019, 10–17) and Mazurek (2022, 4–6). For the history of the label "Egyptianizing," see Pearson (2021, 8–14). See too Malaise (2005, 201–20), who sets out to disambiguate *Aegyptiaca, Pharaonica,* and *Nilotica*.

15. Dillery (2002) positions Quintus Fabius Pictor, Manetho, and Berossus as kindred third century BCE auto-ethnographers. Josephus's *Contra Apionem* and *Antiquitates Iudaicae* are texts working in a similar vein, but in the early imperial period.

16. For the concept of auto-ethnography, see above all Hayano (1979).

17. Dench (2013, 259–60) notes the importance of auto-ethnography, though she repeats the common assumption (see too the Manetho/Berossus pairing in Kuhrt 1987; Verbrugghe and Wickersham 1996; and Dillery 2015) that Manetho and Berossus were its only real practitioners and that the third century BCE was its *floruit*.

8   INTRODUCTION

practitioner. His list of Egyptian kings arranged into dynasties gave birth to an Egyptian presentation of Egyptian history indebted to, but positioned against, Herodotus.[18] Manetho translated Egyptian historiographic sensibilities in unequal dialogue with a new Ptolemaic regime keen to naturalize its control of Egypt. In the process, he wrested for himself the precarious agency to define and defend Egyptian conceptions of kingship to the Ptolemies, who elevated Greek as an unequally valued language, cultural tradition, ethnic affiliation, and tax and legal category. Manetho has finally received scholarly attention that places him at the intersection of Greek and Egyptian intellectual traditions.[19] The finesse of this cultural negotiation—the way that Manetho brings Egyptian historiographic traditions of the kings list and *Königsnovelle* into a form legible to a Greek audience—had long been lost in a data-oriented approach that utilized the dynastic history of Manetho's Aegyptiaca without appreciating the cultural conditions of its production. John Dillery and Ian Moyer, in particular, have reemphasized through Manetho's text the continued vibrancy—rather than senescent posteriority—of Egyptian intellectual culture of the Ptolemaic period.[20]

Manetho has yet to be seen as a point of origin for a tradition that stretches into and is critical to Rome and the imperial world. There is a much longer list of Egyptians who continued in the literary form of Aegyptiaca begun, but not circumscribed, by Manetho.[21] With Aegyptiaca as a dynamic, diachronic tradition, the domains in which Manetho and his successors insinuated themselves expand well beyond the dynastic history of Egypt for which Manetho is most famous. Manetho will, then, be the hulking presence whose shadow adumbrates those latter-day authors of Aegyptiaca who are the subjects of this book. To give these authors their due, one must approach Manetho's formation of Aegyptiaca from a new perspective. In part, this is to see strands of Manetho's intellectual production that have been drowned out by the reputation, in antiquity and modernity, of his dynastic history of Egypt's kings. Manetho's philosophical presentation of Egyptian religion, texts on pharmacology and astrobotany, and etymologies of Egyptian gods'

---

18. For Herodotus's influence on Hellenistic auto-ethnography, see Murray (1972, 208–10). Dillery (2016) emphasizes Manetho's participation in a wider habit of syncing Greek and non-Greek events; Moyer (2011, 84–141) underlines Manetho's conversance with Egyptian historiographic conventions and his Egyptian sensibility around the past's connections to the present.

19. Gruen (2017, 307–10) approaches Manetho's (and Berossus's) intercultural negotiation from the perspective of Hellenistic court patronage of ethnographic writing. Aufrère (2014) locates Manetho's authorial production in the cultural history of Ptolemaic Alexandria.

20. Above all, Moyer (2011, 84–141) and Dillery (1999, 2015); cf. Redford (1986, 201–332) for an Egyptological perspective. I do not mean to diminish the work of Egyptologists who take a more data-oriented approach to Manetho's kings list, such as Helck 1956.

21. Burstein (1996) comes closest to a review of Aegyptiaca as a tradition, though see too Escolano-Poveda (2020, 92–115), who coordinates Manetho's and Chaeremon's representation of Egyptian priests; and Dickie (2001, 205–8), who discusses Apion and Pancrates.

names open a much larger terrain of the Egyptian *topoi* and generic traditions that constitute Aegyptiaca.

The autoethnographic tradition of Aegyptiaca is the subject of this book, about which I make two interconnected arguments: first, that this is a literary tradition that extends beyond Manetho, its first and best-known practitioner; second, that the popularity of literary Aegyptiaca outside Egypt exemplifies a process of translation of Egyptian traditions from Egypt, through a blended Greco-Egyptian medium, to Greeks and Romans. This story of translation is one worth telling, precisely because it challenges prevailing narratives that focus either on the exoticism of Egyptian-looking goods in Rome or the barbarism and archaism that Egypt connotes in Roman literature. These translations of Egyptian culture were certainly precarious and metamorphic. Aegyptiaca bent to the mundane social realities of Rome's political control of Egypt and its continuation of Ptolemaic governance. But as I will show, that does not diminish the impact and agency of Egyptians who helped shape Romans' views of Egypt.

Aegyptiaca as a tradition has been sidelined for reasons both benign and malign. Part of the problem is pragmatic. Until recently, these authors' fragments resided in the monumental, but user-unfriendly (and German-language) *Fragmente der griechischen Historiker*.[22] Jacoby's text has now been digitized and republished as *Brill's New Jacoby*, but the prohibitive expense of accessing the new database continues to marginalize these authors. The disciplinary terrain surrounding Roman Egypt is also at issue. I am positioning these authors of Aegyptiaca as bridges between Egypt and Rome. These authors took cultural traditions discussed in the Egyptian language, wrote about them in Greek, and had as their audience Romans who wrote in Latin. By using a framework of cultural translation, I connect authors of Aegyptiaca both with Greek and Latin imperial literature and with Demotic texts, the dominant language of Roman Egypt. The realities of disciplinary boundaries and language training have made it difficult to trace the movement of ideas across these three languages.

Another part of the problem is methodological. The authors I discuss in this book are preserved only indirectly, when they and their texts are mentioned by authors whose texts do survive. There is a set methodology for fragmentary authors that has made post-Manetho authors of Aegyptiaca unappealing subjects when discussed individually. But my main focus is on the tradition itself, rather than the specific authors who comprise that tradition. The distinction matters. Manetho has been given more attention than his string of successors partially because he leaves a more substantial number of fragments. A reconstructive approach to fragmentary texts, the one traditionally taken to write about the authors I discuss in this book, demands that one take the available fragments and piece together

---

22. Jacoby (1923–1958).

from them an (admittedly fuzzy) picture of the original work.[23] If that is the goal, most post-Manetho authors of Aegyptiaca are not worth one's time. That helps explain why there has yet to be any synthetic account of such Egyptians and their contributions to the Roman view of Egypt.[24] But by abandoning reconstruction and instead stitching together kindred topological points across authors, I offer a pointillistic portrait of Aegyptiaca. Even as the exact contours of specific authors' works remain murky, Aegyptiaca's vibrancy, popularity, and impact on the imperial world can take center stage.

Imperial authors of Aegyptiaca reside at a crossroads. To recover them, one must wade into fragmentary literature, source criticism, and prosopography, long the foundations of Classics' methodological rigor. But these authors have been hidden for so long precisely because, as culturally mixed figures bridging Egyptian and Greek identities and spanning the Roman and Roman-Egyptian worlds, they have been of only marginal interest to those scholars best trained in that methodological skill set. They are both uniquely suited to, but long shortchanged by, the normative (but certainly hotly contested) definition of Classics as an academic discipline. By using the traditional skills of philology to center authors of Aegyptiaca, I would like to make a methodological argument alongside a substantive one: that the old-fashioned philological and historiographic tools that have traditionally bolstered a narrow vision of Greek and Roman literature can instead promote an expansive Mediterranean world characterized by cultural pluralism.

Aegyptiaca is a literary tradition in which Egyptians wrote about Egypt for an external audience. Each of those three elements is productively elastic: the variety of subjects that fall under the "about Egypt" umbrella; just who counts as an Egyptian in a culturally mixed Roman-Greek-Egyptian world; and an imperial-era audience that straddles the divide between imperial Greek and Roman social milieux. I do not want to resolve totally any of these three tensions. The audience for Aegyptiaca is Roman, broadly defined.[25] In a culturally mixed environment, the term Egyptian should be capacious. The heterogeneous traditions that cohere

---

23. For a methodological overview of studying fragments, see Ginelli and Lupi (2021a, 1–12). Gumbrecht (1997) etiologizes this reconstructive approach to fragmentary texts. The two main conference volumes that thematize fragments (Most 1997; Ginelli and Lupi 2021b) confirm the typically author-centered, rather than topological, approach to fragmentary texts (though cf. Berardi 2021, who prioritizes genre over author).

24. The most important recent work on such authors is van der Horst (1981, 1982, 1984, 2002), Burstein (1996), Dillery (2003), Damon (2008, 2011), Keyser (2015), and Escolano-Poveda (2020, 92–115, *passim*).

25. That is to say, the audience for Aegyptiaca were those who lived either in the city of Rome or in one of Rome's provinces. In this way, I take a capacious definition both of Aegyptiaca's authors and of its audience. A Roman subject like Plutarch can meaningfully be called "Roman," for the purposes of discussing Aegyptiaca's audience outside of Egypt but within the network of the Roman empire. On Plutarch's (and other imperial Greeks') navigation of Greek identity and Roman subject position, see Kemezis (2019), Monaco Caterine (2019).

through the label "Egyptian things" should not be lost under the well-founded but often misleading category "history writing."[26]

Aegyptiaca as a genre was open-ended. The neuter plural adjective ("Egyptian things") encapsulated a wide range of subjects that Egyptians wrote about, not just dynastic history. Some traditions loom particularly large. Aegyptiaca was shaped, for example, by the intellectual antagonism between Jews and Egyptians surrounding the history of the Exodus. The Exodus narrative had real stakes in the world of Alexandria in the first century CE. When Aegyptiaca occurs as a generic label concatenating a succession of Egyptian authors, it is in this vein. The late-antique Alexandrian Cosmas Indicopleustes proves as much: "Those writing Aegyptiaca, namely Manetho and Chaeremon and Apollonius Molon and Lysimachus and Apion the Grammarian, mentioned Moses and the exodus of the sons of Israel from Egypt."[27] Cosmas Indicopleustes certainly suggests that the Exodus is a central theme binding these authors together, but already in antiquity no one subject had exclusive ownership of the term Aegyptiaca. There is no set hierarchy that makes a given subject a more or less central "Egyptian thing." As I proceed through Aegyptiaca's disparate subjects, I prioritize those narrative threads that pose the most forceful challenge to a disciplinary model of cultural representation that makes assumptions about what Romans and Greeks thought about Egypt without taking into account what Egyptians themselves had to say on the subject. In this rubric, Aegyptiaca's treatment of animal-shaped gods (chapter 4), the hieroglyphic script (chapter 5), and the interconnection of religious and philosophical inquiry (chapter 6) gain in size, so they occupy a central position in the chapters that follow.

The same push-and-pull between heterogeneity and coherence applies to just who counts as an Egyptian author. Manetho is such a felicitous anchor for Aegyptiaca because his Egyptian identity is so secure. He wrote in the early days of the Ptolemaic period, with the imprimatur of his Heliopolitan priesthood vouching for his authority regarding pharaonic history.[28] But as time went on, things got messier. Several hundred years of cultural mixture made tidy distinctions between the identity categories Greek and Egyptian blurrier. Even in the more cut-and-dried domain of citizenship status, deme affiliation, taxation, and law courts, the slipperiness between statuses combines with name changing and lacunose

---

26. By which I mean, the general category of ancient historiography and its cognate genres, like ethnography, geography, and paradoxography.

27. *Christ. Top.* 12.4 = *BNJ* 618 T 5b: οἱ δὲ τὰ Αἰγυπτιακὰ συγγραψάμενοι, τουτέστι Μανεθὼν καὶ Χαιρήμων καὶ Ἀπολλώνιος ὁ Μόλων καὶ Λυσίμαχος καὶ Ἀπίων ὁ Γραμματικός, μέμνηται Μωυσέως καὶ τῆς ἐξόδου τῶν υἱῶν Ἰσραὴλ τῆς Αἰγύπτου. For these authors, see *BNJ* 609 and Waddell (1940) (Manetho); *BNJ* 618 and van der Horst (1984) (Chaeremon); *BNJ* 728 (Apollonius); *BNJ* 621 (Lysimachus); and *BNJ* 616 (Apion).

28. Manetho's connections to Sebennytos and position as Heliopolitan priest are widely accepted (e.g. Moyer 2011, 86), even if the latter is only mentioned in a far from ironclad source, a pseudonymous letter quoted by Syncellus (*BNJ* 609 F 25).

12   INTRODUCTION

evidence to make any clear boundaries around the category Egyptian difficult to maintain.[29]

This is particularly acute in the case of Aegyptiaca and auto-ethnography, where identity and cultural expertise are often invoked to circularly reinforce each other. Manetho's Egyptianness explains, and is itself vouchsafed by, his dynastic history of Egyptian kings. But for culturally mixed Greco-Egyptian authors whose self-identification mixed together Greek and Egyptian signaling, that same circularity works to opposite effect. Scholars invoke these authors' culturally mixed presentation of Egyptian traditions—blending together Homeric tidbits with explanations of the scarab's cultural significance—to make clear that latter-day authors of Aegyptiaca were not "really" Egyptian.[30] In the coming chapters, I coordinate post-Manetho authors of Aegyptiaca with Egyptian-language texts—like the Demotic Book of Thoth or the Edfu temple inscriptions—that also reflect cultural mixture occurring in Ptolemaic and Roman Egypt. In doing so, I will show how imperial Egyptian culture—whether accessed via Demotic literature, hieroglyphic inscriptions, or Aegyptiaca—continued to be Egyptian culture even as it incorporated Greek intellectual traditions practiced in Alexandria and Egypt's other city-states.

ALEXANDRIA AND THE EGYPT-(GREECE)-ROME BINARY

Turning the spotlight to Manetho's successors is not just an exercise in advancing the timeline of Ptolemaic cultural mixture. It is also to see how things in Egypt look from a Roman perspective. Cultural translation, through which I will be framing Egyptians' presentation of Egyptian traditions to an external audience, ends up in the Roman imperial world.[31] With that end destination in place, the history of contact between Egypt's Greek and Egyptian residents joins up with very different dynamics of Rome's self-positioning against Egypt. That interplay provides much of the conceptual difficulty surrounding later authors of Aegyptiaca, who begin in Egypt and end up in Rome. To contextualize these authors, I have to keep my eyes trained on two very different binaries. First, Roman poets like Virgil and Propertius leaned heavily on a Rome-Egypt binary in the years after Augustus's victory

---

29. For name-changing and demography, see Clarysse and Thompson (2006) and Coussement (2016); for taxation, Wallace (1938); for law, Katzoff (1980) and Wolff (2002).

30. For example, Fowden (1986) presents Chaeremon's philosophical portrait of Egyptian priests as evidence of the "long-drawn out senescence" (65) of Egyptian learning.

31. My own phrase "cultural translation" borrows from two distinct theoretical traditions. First is a postcolonial understanding of "cultural translation" first developed in Bhabha (1994, 212–35), and summarized by Trivedi (2007). Second, see Reiß and Vermeer (1984) for a *skopos* theory of translation, which prioritizes texts' social function in originating and target cultures. In both cases, I add "cultural" to indicate the way that translation events are bicultural rather than bilingual, to paraphrase Reiß and Vermeer (1984, 26).

over Antony and Cleopatra at Actium. Second, a Greek-Egyptian binary dictated how those within Egypt navigated language, status, and taxation.[32]

For the domain of Aegyptiaca, it is important to see how the latter binary, and the mutual influence of Greek and Egyptian culture in Ptolemaic Egypt, changes when Rome enters the picture. Intellectual opportunities in Rome incentivized authors of Aegyptiaca to have their cake and eat it too; they sought to be jacks of all trades who represented to a Roman audience both an authoritative source for traditional Egyptian *topoi* and a typically well-educated Alexandrian, who could teach Romans the hallmarks of Greek literary, grammatical, and philosophical culture. Romans and mainland Greeks viewed the intra-Egyptian legal divisions separating ethnic Greeks and Egyptians only dimly and imperfectly, a fact that culturally mixed authors of Aegyptiaca capitalized on for their own social advancement.

Alexandria is the point where these two binaries intersected. The history of Alexandria and of Aegyptiaca are intertwined. By prioritizing post-Manetho authors of Aegyptiaca, I also aim to place the intellectual, cultural, and social history of first-century CE Alexandria on its own footing, outside the shadow of early-Ptolemaic Alexandrian intellectual culture.[33] Alexandrian history of the early-imperial period puts Aegyptiaca and the social conditions of its creation into context. This is true both for the topics discussed in Aegyptiaca and for the social and economic advantages that authors of Aegyptiaca hoped to gain through their work. The latter is a key thread through which I tie together Aegyptiaca into a coherent tradition. Apion, one important author of Aegyptiaca, was an ethnic Egyptian who was able to gain Alexandrian citizenship.[34] That mattered, both because it bestowed tax advantages and because it was a key stepping-stone to Greece and Rome.[35] Authors of Aegyptiaca, like their material counterparts, took a road to Rome that traveled via Alexandria.

Apion and other authors of Aegyptiaca were, quite literally, ambassadors of Alexandria for a Roman audience. Apion was chosen to represent Alexandrian

---

32. A raft of scholarship of the past several decades has sensitively navigated the contact and mixture of Greek and Egyptian culture in Ptolemaic Egypt, whether via documentary papyri (Clarysse and Thompson 2006), religious and scribal texts (Jasnow and Zauzich 2005; Dieleman 2005; Papaconstantinou 2010; Kidd 2011; Quack 2021 [to cite only one piece of his prolific scholarship]), city-specific analysis (Thompson 1988; Vleeming 1995), epigraphy (Daumas 1952), or Alexandrian literature (Stephens 2003; Ryholt 2012).

33. Of work on Alexandria (especially Fraser 1972, but also the collections of Ruffini and Harris 2004; Hirst and Silk 2004; Méla et al. 2014), more attention is paid to the Ptolemaic than to the Roman period (though cf. Lembke, Minas-Nerpel, and Pfeiffer 2010 and Vandorpe 2019, who focus on Roman Egypt specifically).

34. As Delia (1991, 29, 56, 164) makes clear, and as I discuss in chapter 1.

35. Delia (1988 and 1991) focuses on the dynamics of Alexandrian citizenship in the Roman period. Jördens (2012) offers a good introduction to Roman-Egyptian citizenship. Relevant too is the issue of Jews' status, which is a key context for the riots of 38 CE, as Bilde (2006) and Gambetti (2009, 57–76) demonstrate.

14 INTRODUCTION

citizens to the emperor Caligula; Chaeremon and Tiberius Claudius Balbillus, two other authors of Aegyptiaca, joined a committee of Alexandrians asking for certain political rights from the new emperor Claudius.[36] In all three cases, these figures were both the faces of Egyptian intellectual traditions and advocates for the city of Alexandria, personages whose elite social position brought them to Rome and the emperor. This ambassadorial role anchors Aegyptiaca's textual representation of Egypt in its authors' literal representation of Alexandria before the Roman emperor.

These authors of Aegyptiaca all represented Alexandria amid the fallout from Alexandrian Greeks' violent attacks against Alexandrian Jews in the early first century CE.[37] Romans' control of Egypt, and particularly Caligula's apparent aspirations to godhood, upset the delicate balance through which Jews living in Alexandria had secured the right to property and tax exemption.[38] There were very real stakes surrounding this unrest—Alexandrian Greeks risked losing their rights to political assembly because they instigated the communal violence; more seriously, Jews had been terrorized and had lost their right to own property altogether. The relationship between Egyptian and Greek identity categories in Alexandria was bound up in these riots. The riots of 38 CE vividly demonstrate the social stakes that gave shape to Alexandrian Egyptians' and Jews' mixture of Greek and non-Greek intellectual traditions. Both Philo and Apion, the Jewish and Alexandrian ambassadors to Caligula, came to embody a Greco-Jewish and Greco-Egyptian intellectual authority specific to the city of Alexandria.[39]

This history of social unrest spills over into the best-attested subject of Aegyptiaca. Almost every author of Aegyptiaca, beginning with Manetho, wrote an account of the Exodus story that exculpated Egyptians and denigrated Jews. Josephus's painstaking rejection of these arguments is the best through-line for Aegyptiaca as a durative tradition. Writing in the first century CE, Josephus arranged the Egyptian authors whom he rebuts into a discrete lineage on which Felix Jacoby drew in his still authoritative aggregation of these authors. The canon formation surrounding Aegyptiaca, in antiquity via Josephus and in modernity via Jacoby and *Brill's New Jacoby*, is a blessing and a curse. It makes clear at the outset that already in antiquity, Aegyptiaca was an identifiable tradition that extended beyond

36. For the former, see Philo's *Legatio ad Gaium* and Smallwood (1961); for the latter, see Claudius's letter to the Alexandrians (published in Smallwood 1967, no. 370), with Stuart Jones (1926, 18).

37. The best source is Philo's *In Flaccum*, on which see Alston (1997) and van der Horst (2003). An overview of the riots is widely available, in, e.g., Collins (2005, 86–90) and Gambetti (2009, 167–93).

38. For an overview of the history of Jews in Egypt, see Mélèze-Modrzejewski (1991); for Jews in Alexandria, Gruen (2002, 54–83).

39. For Philo's intellectual position as philosopher and Jewish thinker, see Niehoff (2018) (especially part 3). For a broader treatment of Greco-Jewish intellectual cross-pollination in Alexandria, see Niehoff (2011).

Manetho. Later authors like Chaeremon and Apion—the target of Josephus's *Against Apion*—were also essential contributors to Aegyptiaca. But this Jewish context, and its indirect impact on boundaries that Jacoby drew around "Egyptian things," unduly limits Aegyptiaca to one social context and generic tradition that admittedly looms large over, but should not circumscribe, the way that Egyptians wrote about Egypt for a Greek and Roman audience.

In sum, I want to emphasize that the success of authors of Aegyptiaca as literal and metaphorical ambassadors of Alexandria and its intellectual culture was due to, not in spite of, the way they blurred Greek and Egyptian traditions into a mixed form. The Stoic philosopher-cum-scribal priest Chaeremon, the most famous exegete of the hieroglyphic script for a Roman audience, was the head of the Alexandrian Library before becoming Nero's tutor. Pancrates gained membership in the Museum by composing an epyllion in honor of Hadrian's lover Antinous, by putting on a typically Egyptian magic show for Hadrian himself, and finally by writing a biography of the Egyptian king Bakenrenef.[40] Even the rarefied institutions of Alexandrian society were sites of cultural mixture and polyvalent authority. That figures like Apion and Chaeremon and Pancrates were connected to such institutions, that they were Alexandrian citizens, does not disqualify them from the Manethonian legacy of Aegyptiaca or from the label "Egyptian." Early-imperial authors of Aegyptiaca developed a culturally mixed authority that spanned both the Greek and Egyptian cultural traditions that were being practiced in Egypt. Their success in the former, their reputations as Homerists and Stoics and panegyrists, does not delegitimize their expertise in the latter. I find these authors of Aegyptiaca so valuable precisely because they challenge our assumptions about what an authentic Greek-language presentation of Egyptian culture looks like in the early-imperial world.

FRAMING AEGYPTIACA

The authors I discuss in this book have not been Egyptian enough for most Egyptologists or Greek enough for most Classicists. They make scattered appearances in work on Romans' representation of Egypt and Egyptians.[41] They, like Alexandria of the early-imperial period, have resided on several different disciplinary

---

40. Van der Horst (1984) collects Chaeremon's fragments and Frede (1989) offers a biography. For Pancrates, see Dickie (2001, 198, 205) and Burstein (2016), with Ogden (2004 and 2007, 231–70).

41. Most frequently, historicizing readings of Lucan's *Bellum Civile* (Manolaraki 2013, 107, and Tracy 2014, 260) see in Caesar's Egyptian interlocutor Acoreus the author of Aegyptiaca and tutor of Nero Chaeremon. Other key work on Egypt in Roman literature deals with Aegyptiaca only rarely, e.g. Iversen (1961) (hieroglyphic), Smelik and Hemelrijk (1984) (animal worship), Meyer (1961), Sonnabend (1986), and Leemreize (2016) (poly-thematic surveys of Republican and early-imperial literature), Merrills (2017) (the Nile across media), and Erler and Stadler (2017) (Egypt in Platonic philosophy).

16   INTRODUCTION

margins. In the domain of Hellenism, they are too late for the Hellenistic period and too early for the Second Sophistic. Their Alexandrian status and Greek-language texts make them important, but peripheral, presences in Egyptological work on Demotic literature of the imperial period. They have featured as only supporting actors in the economic and social history of Roman Egypt, which prioritizes papyrological over indirectly transmitted evidence.[42]

That in-betweenness, however, is what makes these figures so important. Their Egyptian identities reflect a Mediterranean world defined by mixture and contact. Collective interest in recovering a broader Mediterranean typified by exchange and contact hits up against the methodological barriers that have kept Aegyptiaca as a rich cross-cultural intellectual tradition out of view. Scholars who have discussed the movement of ideas and traditions between Egypt and Greece have shown just how much can be gained by centering these authors and their work.[43] To pick just one example, authors of Aegyptiaca were the ones who broadcast Egyptian myths of Osiris and Seth to those like Plutarch and Apuleius who were keen to promote the common ground shared between Egyptian religion and Platonic philosophy.[44]

I have been emphasizing the role that authors of Aegyptiaca should play in Rome's reception of Egypt, but they also show how pharaonic traditions—like the Osiris myth—continue into the Roman period and a Greco-Egyptian milieu. Pharaonic traditions were changed, but not erased, by processes of cultural mixture occurring in Ptolemaic and Roman Egypt. Latter-day Aegyptiaca, as a bridge between Egypt and Rome and as an act of cultural translation, offers a valuable perspective from which to view both how Greeks and Romans made sense of Egypt *and* how Egyptian traditions continued to be Egyptian traditions, even as they were influenced by Greek and then Roman control of Egypt.

For a long time, fidelity to Egyptian cultural traditions and to Alexandrianism has been a zero-sum game. To identify authors of Aegyptiaca with Alexandrian intellectual culture is to mark out their distance from a pure Egyptian culture practiced elsewhere in Egypt. This book is animated by my desire to push back against a wrong-headed dichotomy of cultural mixture and cultural authenticity. To center the mixture of Greek and Egyptian traditions in Aegyptiaca is not to erase

---

42. Chaeremon's presentation of priestly life has been cited by Demotists like Jasnow (2011, 315–16), Escolano-Poveda (2020, 105–16, 214–17), and Quack (2021, 75), who all use Chaeremon as a *comparandum*—whether "borderline" (Quack 2021, 75) or "Greco-Egyptian" (Escolano-Poveda 2020, 115)—for Demotic texts about Roman-Egyptian priestly life. For the social history of Roman Egypt, interest has been paid to Apion's Alexandrian citizenship (Delia 1991) and the administrative careers of figures like Thrasyllus and Tiberius Claudius Balbillus (Cichorius 1927; Krappe 1927; Schwartz 1949).

43. Griffiths (1969, 1970, 1975) and Burstein (1996). For Greek-Egyptian contact in general, see Rutherford (2016).

44. That is a topic I pick up in chapter 4, where I address Plutarch's and Apuleius's reliance on Aegyptiaca (e.g. Plutarch's debt to Manetho and Apion, per Griffiths 1970, 75–100; see too Porphyry's partial debt to Chaeremon, per von Lieven 2017, 287).

INTRODUCTION   17

any possibility of a legitimate exposition of Egyptian culture for a non-Egyptian audience after Manetho. I set out to rebut that misconception by tracing a thread of cultural translation that begins in imperial-era, Egyptian-language intellectual traditions, continues through Aegyptiaca, and ends up in Greek and Roman literature.[45] The mixture of Greek and Egyptian intellectual traditions in Aegyptiaca was a creative strategy of translation that sought to make available to Greeks and Romans those aspects of Egyptian culture that were critical to the original social function of objects hauled off from Egypt to Rome. It is decidedly not a black mark against these authors' Egyptian bona fides.

Both Greek and Egyptian intellectual traditions practiced in Egypt by Egyptians are Egyptian. That is true across Egypt: it holds for those residing in Alexandria, in Egypt's regional capitals (the nome *metropoleis*), and in the countryside.[46] This is a seemingly straightforward, but unexpectedly thorny, clarification for cultural production rooted in Egypt but presented to Rome. One can acknowledge the prerogatives of Alexandrian citizenship—to say nothing of Egypt's other city-states (*poleis*), or the other interlocking status markers surrounding the *gymnasium*, tribal affiliation, and the *metropoleis*—without completely severing Alexandria from the conceptual map of Egypt and Egyptian traditions.[47] Wrestling with that surprisingly complex claim, that a cultural tradition can be both Alexandrian and Egyptian, will sustain the presentation of Aegyptiaca that follows in the next six chapters.

Ambiguity and multiplicity are all well and good, but at the end of the day I need to land on a label, be it Egyptian, Alexandrian, Greek, or Greco-Egyptian.[48] In an ideal world, I could denote these authors with a label like Alexandrian*. That new version of Alexandrian* could encompass both the very real systems of inequality delineating Alexandrian versus Egyptian citizenship and the broad and multicultural traditions practiced in Alexandria in the first century. To Romans

45. This complements work that offers source criticism of Romans' and Greeks' discussions of Egypt, most notably Plutarch's *On Isis and Osiris* (Parmentier 1913; Griffiths 1970; and Hani 1976) and Apuleius's *Metamorphoses* (Griffiths 1975; Egelhaaf-Gaiser 2000; and Finkelpearl 2012).

46. For the culturally mixed milieu of Greco-Egyptian metropolitan elite, see Tacoma (2006, 126–27). Bowman and Rathbone (1992) provide an essential overview of status and Roman administration; they note (113) the precipitous disappearance in Roman Egypt of the ethnic identification that had been widely used in Ptolemaic Egypt, on which see generally Mélèze-Modrzejewski (1985), reprinted in Mélèze-Modrzejewski (1990).

47. Van Minnen (2002 350–51), focusing on *metropolites* and the gymnasial order (cf. Ruffini 2006), also notes well the push-and-pull between ethnically oriented gatekeeping around gymnasial and metropolitan status and the reality of ethnic Egyptians' participation in institutions like the *ephebate* and *gymnasium*.

48. It is telling that many avoid these labels more or less entirely. Escolano-Poveda (2020, 105–13) slots Chaeremon into the "Greco-Egyptian" chapter alongside Manetho, but her biographical overview focuses mostly on Chaeremon's occupational (philosopher, sacred scribe) versus identity (Alexandrian, Egyptian, Greek) labels. Dillery (2003, 383–84) introduces Apion but avoids any identity label (though see 388 for discussion of *Ap.* 2.28 and the phrase "Apion the Egyptian").

18   INTRODUCTION

like Pliny the Elder and Greeks like Plutarch, Alexandria's mixture of Greek and Egyptian intellectual traditions was just as important a hallmark of Alexandrianism as Alexandria's restricted citizenship and Alexandrians' privileged status. The limited evidence available suggests that most Romans were not very quick to distinguish the specifics of Alexandrian versus Egyptian citizenship. Pliny the Younger had no idea that his masseur Harpocras needed Alexandrian citizenship before he could become a Roman citizen.[49] But Romans very readily identified a culturally mixed Alexandrian religious and intellectual culture that was present, via Isis temples, wall paintings, and immigrants alike, in the city of Rome.[50] This tempered Alexandrianism would be complementary, rather than dichotomous, to the label "Egyptian." To be sure, "Egyptian" as a technical citizenship label referred to all those—ethnically Egyptian *or* Greek—who were neither Roman citizens nor citizens of Egypt's four *poleis*: Alexandria, Ptolemais, Naucratis, and later Antinoöpolis. Legally speaking, Egyptian and Alexandrian are mutually exclusive. But for the purposes of this book and for authors of Aegyptiaca, Alexandrian and Egyptian labels alike need to hew a middle ground between their technical meaning and the broader cultural connotations that were primary points of reference among Aegyptiaca's external Greek and Roman audience.

I cannot, however, use something as woefully clunky as Alexandrian*. There is no perfect way to capture the intersecting valences that define the social position of latter-day authors of Aegyptiaca. That is what makes them interesting. They are slippery, demanding a new frame of reference for the identity labels Alexandrian, Greek, and Egyptian. So, to refer to the identities of these authors, I use the simple term "Egyptian." When Rome enters the picture, Egyptian as a cultural tag was readily applied to those who also could be called Alexandrian, or even Greek. To return to the domain of citizenship, Romans considered all those who were neither Romans nor polis-citizens "Egyptian," be they ethnically Greek or Egyptian or some combination of the two. Romans use the simple term "Egyptian" where scholars typically prefer the useful but anachronistic label Greco-Egyptian.[51] If "Egyptian" has yet to be used in this way, whether because of an overemphasis on a static image of pharaonic Egyptian culture or because of the dictates of Roman-Egyptian social history, this book tries to prove that it can.[52] The Egypt imagined

49. Per Plin. *Ep.* 10.6–7, where Pliny unknowingly makes a mistake by procuring Roman citizenship for his physical therapist without first getting him Alexandrian citizenship, a fact which Trajan (passive aggressively) rebukes in 10.7.

50. As Savvopoulos (2010) argues, Isis religion was inextricably connected to the city of Alexandria; this is clear already in Manetho (Plut. *DIO* 28, 361f–362a = *BNJ* 609 T 3), who is one of the purported "founders" of a Sarapis statue whose arrival in Alexandria forms an etiology of the Isis cult.

51. Per Rowlandson (2013, 221–24). I do not mean this in a derogatory way. I will use "Greco-Egyptian" as a shorthand for cultural mixture practiced in Egypt, even as I am arguing that, in the domain of identity labels, Aegyptiaca and its authors are still "Egyptian."

52. Where work on the social history of Roman Egypt (e.g. Bowman and Rathbone 1992) focuses on citizenship status, membership in a gymnasium, or metropolitan residency and stresses that ethnic

INTRODUCTION   19

by Romans was of precisely this mixed form, precisely because of the impact of authors of Aegyptiaca.

This messiness around identities is nothing new. Colonizations ancient and modern led to processes of mixture dependent on and productive of systems of inequality. Different colonial contexts developed different terms for mixture, each of which has its own history. The Caribbean's and Latin America's creole, North America's métis, New Spain's mestizo, and lusophone South America's mestiço are all particular, even as they reflect overlapping processes of colonial mixture from which emerged mixed groups on which national identities were founded.[53] In what follows, I prefer creole and creolization as frames for authors of Aegyptiaca. This owes less to the historical peculiarities of the places from which "creole" originated.[54] It is, instead, because I admire the Martinican poet and philosopher Édouard Glissant's enunciation of creolization's ecumenical reach and unending diachrony.[55] But no matter the term chosen, reembracing cultural mixedness must coexist with a healthy awareness of those who were violently excluded from these purportedly capacious groups.[56] That same balance must be struck for imperial authors of Aegyptiaca. It is important both to accept on its own terms Aegyptiaca's unique mixture of Greek and Egyptian traditions and to appreciate that these authors' mixed Greco-Egyptian identity is particular to social positions—like scribal priests, grammarians, and philosophers—that were in large measure defined through exclusivity and elitism. That ambivalence is an important reason why postcolonial discussions of culturally mixed intellectual production can enrich, and themselves be enriched by, the history of Aegyptiaca and the social trajectories of its authors.

This all assumes that I can call Rome's control of Egypt colonial, or use the theoretical apparatus of cultural change of colonized peoples to make sense of

---

affiliation falls out of use in the Roman period, I am trying to create space for "Egyptian" as a label that can felicitously characterize culturally mixed intellectual production practiced in Egypt (including Alexandria).

53. In the case of the term "creole," that history is well traced by Baker and Mühlhäusler (2007), and Stewart (2007) generally.

54. Laird (2010, 167–68) describes histories of the pre-Columbian past written by the creole historians of New Spain. That colonially framed impetus for claiming literary authority over a past only partially one's own is, as I continue to discuss in chapter 1, a productive frame for this book's subjects: culturally mixed authors of Aegyptiaca who benefited from their self-advertised knowledge of the pharaonic past.

55. Britton (1999), Wiedorn (2018), and Drabinski (2019) offer an overview of Glissant's work and thinking, which was (unsurprisingly, given his emphasis on the unpredictable and dynamic) heterogeneous. I am particularly indebted to the formulation of creolization offered in Glissant (1996 and 1997), whose utility for Aegyptiaca I defend in chapter 1.

56. Per Palmié (2007, 76): "Self-perceived, and self-declared, 'creoledom' we might conclude is a decidedly 'modern' project—in all senses of the word, including those pertaining to uniquely 'modern' forms of exclusion." For creolization, see also the pioneering but historically ungrounded defense offered by Hannerz (1987).

20   INTRODUCTION

Aegyptiaca. This question of colonization in ancient Egypt is yet another way that Roman Egypt is overshadowed by Ptolemaic Egypt.[57] The arguments made against using colonization—arguments that are well made but that I will push back against—focus mainly on the Ptolemies' internal rather than external control of Egypt and respond more or less directly to scholarship that sought to draw a straight line between Egyptian resentment of Ptolemaic rule and twentieth-century, anti-colonial wars of independence.[58] Moving from Ptolemaic to Roman Egypt and engaging with scholarship on indigenous elites in colonial societies change the picture.[59] Rome's external control of Egypt sets it apart from the Ptolemaic situation; postcolonial scholarship has analyzed well the kind of nuanced negotiation of colonizer and colonized that Roger Bagnall thought was lacking in the work of Édouard Will and Barbara Anagnastou-Canas.[60]

More substantively, though, there is the threat of universalizing the contingent dynamics of European colonialisms by uncritically retrojecting postcolonial concepts back into the ancient world. In what follows, I frame the Hellenistic and imperial-era mixture of Greek and Egyptian culture through contemporary work on creolization and colonization. But Rome's control of Egypt and its relationship to Egypt's previous occupiers are idiosyncratic and cannot easily be collapsed into European colonization. To my mind, the converse is not without its risks: studiously sealing off ancient imperialisms to avoid any whiff of anachronism forecloses conversations with colleagues who work on the contemporary world, conversations that would benefit ancient and modern scholarship alike. I am not the first to try to navigate that balance. I am particularly indebted to Ian Moyer and Paul Kosmin, who have argued that Dinesh Chakrabarty's "historical translation" can allow for a discussion of ancient systems of occupation that is in conversation with, without being circumscribed by, more modern instantiations of these dynamics.[61]

57. Work using colonization and imperialism as frames within Egypt generally focuses on Ptolemaic Egypt, e.g. Anagnostou-Canas (1989–1990, 1992) and Cohen (1983). Work on Roman imperialism that asks fundamentally postcolonial questions of identity under external occupation generally looks elsewhere in the empire, as Woolf (1994, 1998) (on Gaul) and van Dommelen (1998) (on Sardinia) make clear.

58. This case against colonization is made by Bagnall (1997). More recently, Moyer (2022, 162–63) has cautioned against the limited utility of modern frames of colonization for indigenous responses to and anger towards Ptolemaic rule.

59. Vasunia (2013, 223–24) notes the opportunities gained by Indians who managed to enter the colonial Indian Civil Service but emphasizes the barriers to entry they faced. Derchain (2000, 34–35) notes the spirit of collaboration with the Ptolemaic court on display in Egyptian scribal priests' inscribed autobiographies.

60. In other words, Bagnall (1997) promotes a vision of "colonial" readings of Egypt that relies on a model of strict antagonism between colonizer and colonized, in the mold of Will (1979, 1985) and Anagnostou-Canas (1989–1990, 1992).

61. Moyer and Kosmin (2022, 10–11) cite Chakrabarty (2008) to set out a "parallax view" of ancient and contemporary forms of indigenous resistance. That is a comparative orientation I hope to continue, even as I will push more strongly for the felicity of modern theorizations of mixture for post-Manetho authors of Aegyptiaca.

Aegyptiaca, then, sits at the intersection of two equally vital frameworks. First, Aegyptiaca is a culturally mixed tradition; like all processes of colonially inflected mixture, Aegyptiaca was not a teleological march that began with the disparate inputs of Egyptian and Greek traditions and ended with a singular and static mixture of the two. My comparison of different authors' areas of expertise will show that Aegyptiaca, from its inception under Manetho to later practitioners writing under Hadrian (my chronological endpoint), developed a web of cultural traditions that was dynamic. Aegyptiaca, like the mixed identities of its authors, was heterogeneous and fluid.

But by the same token, authors of Aegyptiaca created a culturally mixed identity within finite social and economic boundaries. The creative mixture of traditions characteristic of Aegyptiaca did not happen in a vacuum. Authors of Aegyptiaca wrote what they wrote in the way that they wrote it because it helped them take advantage of the new roads that connected Rome and Roman Egypt.[62] To put it plainly, Aegyptiaca helped them get paid. The traffic in ideas, like the traffic in goods, traveled along paths that followed the dictates of imperial control and systems of inequality that arranged Roman citizenship, Alexandrian citizenship, and Egyptian citizenship hierarchically. I need to be honest about that social and economic hierarchization and its real effect on Aegyptiaca while still adopting a theoretical perspective that can highlight the creativity of post-Manetho authors of Aegyptiaca, rather than bemoan their mixed Greco-Egyptian texts as proof of the death of Egyptian culture. Threading that needle is easier said than done, but it is the only way to discuss the traffic in ideas between Egypt and Rome with the nuance that authors of Aegyptiaca deserve.

OUTLINE OF THE BOOK

I approach Aegyptiaca in three parts. The first surveys the tradition as a whole, underlines the heterogeneous cultural traditions it comprised, and discusses the social and economic position of its authors. The second uses the specific *topos* of Egypt's sacred animals to demonstrate that a singular focus on Romans' representation of Egyptian animal worship has masked processes of cultural translation in which authors of Aegyptiaca, Greeks, and Romans all participated. The third asks how we should position the translations of Egyptian traditions in Aegyptiaca against an Egyptian-language background with which Aegyptiaca has often been unfavorably compared. By recuperating Aegyptiaca's symbolic presentation of hieroglyphic and its philosophical portrait of the Egyptian priest, I push back against one of the most frequent scholarly responses to post-Manetho authors of

---

62. Robinson (2016) shows how imperial networks of control structure translational activity; in the process, he also charts a middle ground between a theory of "cultural translation" in postcolonial anthropology—where translation is a broad term for cultural mediation—and in translation studies, which generally uses translation in a stricter sense.

22   INTRODUCTION

Aegyptiaca: that they were not "really" Egyptian and did not "really" know about Egyptian culture.

Part 1, "Introducing Aegyptiaca," views Aegyptiaca synoptically. The first chapter focuses on Apion, a key author of post-Manetho Aegyptiaca. I start by asking whether Apion was an Egyptian or a Greek. This admittedly tendentious but heuristically valuable question brings to the fore the competing hierarchies of language, citizenship status, place of birth, and cultural expertise that have made the question so vexing. As a Greek-speaking ethnic Egyptian who was given Alexandrian citizenship and then traveled to Rome, Apion reveals the pitfalls of a longstanding tendency to divide Egypt into an interior where pharaonic traditions endured, and an exterior where Greek culture thrived in cities like Alexandria. Apion's intellectual authority is that of a mixed insider-outsider: he was an expert on Homer who offered close grammatical readings long associated with Alexandria, but he also discussed the worship of the scarab beetle and plant medicine. I juxtapose two postcolonial lenses, Édouard Glissant's creolizing "roots" and Anna Tsing's colonially circumscribed "roads," to appreciate rather than bemoan Apion's mixed identity and then locate that identity against a backdrop of Roman imperial control of Egypt.

Chapter 2 expands Aegyptiaca beyond Apion through three successive case studies of Chaeremon, the Balbilli, and Pancrates. In doing so, I shine a light on the underlying social context that gives coherence to a genre that I am defining by its heterogeneity. Each author wrote cross-cultural texts rooted in both the Greek and Egyptian intellectual traditions practiced in Egypt. But their different areas of expertise speak to a truly wide-ranging set of Greek (philosophy, praise-poetry, epigram) and Egyptian (astronomy, magic, historiography) subgenres that constitute Aegyptiaca. By the same token, these authors all shared a direct connection to the Roman emperor. By attending to these authors' connections to institutions like the Library of Alexandria and the Museum, I argue that expertise in Egyptian culture constituted a much more central part of imperial-era Alexandrianism than has been appreciated.

Part 2, "Egypt's Animals: From Representation to Cultural Translation," zeros in on one important strand within Aegyptiaca—sacred animals in Egyptian religion. Through a two-step reevaluation of Romans' views of Egypt's sacred animals, I recenter authors of Aegyptiaca and shift scholarly discussion away from Orientalism and toward cross-cultural translation. Chapter 3 shows that Romans' interest in Egypt's sacred animals was more variegated and less unilaterally negative than has been assumed. A frequently repeated narrative in which Julio-Claudian antipathy toward Egypt gave way to Flavian acceptance loses track of the different strategies of representation that shaped different authors' engagement with the animal *topos*. In one case, Roman authors like Tibullus, Ovid, and Statius used metamorphosis and syncretism to make comprehensible the canine Anubis and bovine Apis. In another strategy, Romans conducted remarkably even-handed debates about the risks and rewards of conceptualizing the divine in anthropomorphic (human) versus zoomorphic (animal) form.

Recentering these discussions of zoomorphism makes space for Aegyptiaca. As I show in chapter 4, authors of Aegyptiaca guided these philosophical discussions of Egypt's animals. The bulk of the chapter focuses on the Egyptian god Seth, his Greek counterpart Typhon, and the animals with which they were associated. As a hated god who opposed religious order, Seth's animal identification has been hidden by the artificially narrow term "animal worship." I trace Seth's path of translation from Egypt to Rome. I begin with the pharaonic myth of Horus and Seth, which regularly featured a set of wild animals—hippopotami, crocodiles, asses—into which Seth metamorphosed. Authors of Aegyptiaca strategically presented Seth's metamorphoses in the Greek traditions of enigma and symbol. As such, Seth's identification with wild animals encapsulated larger philosophical systems of order and chaos. When presented in these terms, Greek and Roman authors like Plutarch and Apuleius were quick to endorse these philosophical presentations of Egyptian culture.

Part 3, "What's Egyptian for 'Philosopher'?," takes up Egyptian authors' use of symbolism and the questions of authenticity that it introduces. Two specific hallmarks of Egyptian culture loop Aegyptiaca into conversations around the cultural projection of Greek concepts onto non-Greek traditions. In chapter 5 I focus on the hieroglyphic script, which was often discussed in symbolic terms. The prevalence of these symbolic explanations speaks to the liminal status of hieroglyphic, which was slowly falling out of use in the early-imperial period. Even as there were fewer new hieroglyphic inscriptions, the philosophical significance of written Egyptian was a mainstay across cultural contexts. Thus, the emperor Domitian emphasized his family's dynastic status by writing their names in cartouches on a Roman obelisk. Plutarch's philosophical presentation of Egyptian religion included an Egyptian-language etymology of the god Amun. Authors of Aegyptiaca touted their access to hieroglyphic inscriptions. These presentations of hieroglyphic lead to a much larger question of authority: did authors of Aegyptiaca actually *know* the hieroglyphic script? I return to the Egyptian Chaeremon, who wrote a treatise on hieroglyphs that emphasized their philosophical significance. To many, this has been a sign that Chaeremon had no idea what he was talking about. But I look at Egyptian-language discussions of hieroglyphic symbolism to provide context for Chaeremon's philosophizing presentation of hieroglyphic.

Chapter 6 continues with Chaeremon, whose other main work presented Egyptian priests as philosophers. This served Chaeremon well, since he advertised himself as both an Egyptian priest and a Stoic philosopher. As with his symbolic explanations of hieroglyphs, Chaeremon's "philosophification" of Egyptian priestly life has led many to emphasize his unreliable, outsider, and Greek approach to Egyptian cultural activity. But Glissant's theory of creolization offers a persuasive argument against this dichotomous view of authority. I evaluate this

24   INTRODUCTION

creolization of the philosopher-priest from both Greco-Roman and Egyptian perspectives. First, Greek and Roman authors of the imperial period regularly claimed that Greek philosophers like Pythagoras, Plato, Eudoxus, and Solon trained with Egyptian priests. Second, Egyptian-language priest manuals from the Ptolemaic and imperial periods also present a mixed philosopher-priest. One, the Demotic-language *Book of Thoth*, draws a striking equivalence between the Greek term "wisdom-lover" (*philosophos*) and the Egyptian term "knowledge lover" (*mr-rḫ*). This translation forms a powerful response to any apparent inauthenticity of Chaeremon's self-presentation as a philosopher. The specific constellation of the philosopher-priest thus speaks to a creolizing world that produced new modes of cultural authority that authors like Apion and Chaeremon could claim.

In a brief conclusion, I reapproach Aegyptiaca through two frames. First, I turn to Lucan's *Bellum Civile*. Its final book contains a dialogue between Julius Caesar and an Egyptian philosopher-priest, Acoreus. Through a reading of their conversation, I show that authors of Aegyptiaca undergird Lucan's representation of this Egyptian sage and his arbitration of Egyptian cultural wisdom. Acoreus, faced with an intellectually and imperially insatiable Roman audience of one, offers a precis of the core themes I have associated with Aegyptiaca.

Zooming out from this one-on-one conversation between Roman and Egyptian, I end by making a broader point about Egypt's influence on the Greco-Roman world. I place Aegyptiaca against the backdrop of Martin Bernal's pioneering, if controversial, *Black Athena*. Aegyptiaca and its intermingling presentation of Greek and Egyptian pasts can continue questions of cultural contact poorly served by an isolationist approach to Greek and Roman culture. A mix of benign and malign neglect that has marginalized the mixedness one sees in Apion, Chaeremon, and the other subjects of this book offers a more nuanced explanation of Egypt's hidden influence on the Greco-Roman world. Post-Manetho Aegyptiaca thus makes clear that the classical has been, and continues to be, an object of constant reinvention. Rather than chase back an ever-receding moment of cultural influence of Egypt on Greece, we might better see how Egypt, its imperially framed relationship with Rome, and its mixed peoples and traditions were (and should continue to be!) a central site in the making and remaking of the classical.

PART ONE

Introducing Aegyptiaca

1

Apion, Roman Egypt, and the Insider-Outsider Problem

Was Apion, the first-century CE Homeric critic, ethnographer of Egypt, and eponymous target of Josephus, a Greek or an Egyptian? Asked another way, is Apion's work on Egypt and its peoples ethnographic or auto-ethnographic?[1] When he writes about Egypt, does he do so from the outside looking in, a so-called "etic" perspective; or does he offer a picture of Egypt from within, an emic account of a culture in which he is enmeshed?[2]

However frustrating, the answer to these either/or questions is "yes." In what follows, I will qualify this "yes." Emic/etic and ethnography/auto-ethnography binaries can be productive precisely because of their inadequacy. They cannot really do justice to texts written by Apion and others like him. It will become clear that the culture in which Apion is embedded and over which he claims authority has been hidden by anachronistic classical and pharaonic connotations of "Greek" and "Egyptian." As soon as the question of identity is posed on those terms, Apion's specific Egypt is lost. City-states like Alexandria and Naucratis, and the cultural traditions associated with them, turn into an inside "outside." In this spatialized rubric, when Apion gains expertise in Alexandrian intellectual culture, he turns

---

1. Dench (2013, 259–60) calls attention to the importance of auto-ethnographers like Manetho and Berossus, the standard examples of Greek-language historiography written by non-Greeks (on which see Dillery 2015).

2. The emic/etic heuristic (derived from phon-emic and phon-etic) has a long pedigree (for a summary see Headland, Pike, and Harris 1990). Pike (1967) first developed the pair for anthropology, to change an epistemological question of objectivity and subjectivity in ethnographic observation into a methodological question of interior (emic) versus exterior (etic) explanations of systems. Hall (2002, 44–45; 2003) and Tober (2017, 479–80 for "self-ethnography") use emic/etic as a frame for the ancient world.

28   INTRODUCING AEGYPTIACA

Greek and leaves behind an "interior" perspective on Egypt. The peculiar and still lacunose dynamics of citizenship and status in Roman Egypt—the tripartite system of Roman citizenship, citizenship in a city, and general residency in Egypt—have exacerbated this over-schematized separation of insider and outsider perspectives on Egyptian culture. Greek and Egyptian traditions that had become indissociably intertwined are instead juxtaposed as alternatives that are respectively allotted to so-called "Greek cities" and to the rest of Egypt.[3] An insider-outsider approach promotes a dichotomous image of culture that erases what makes the Egypt of Apion so fascinating.

WHO WAS APION? WHAT MAKES
AN EGYPTIAN EGYPTIAN?

Choosing a label for Apion is not an idle matter. Apion scholars have had real difficulty naming Apion. Isidore Levy, Pieter van der Horst, and Hugo Willrich have defined their own work on Apion through this prism of identity, writing articles entitled "is Apion Alexandrian?" or "is Apion Egyptian?"[4] Implicitly or explicitly, these questions of citizenship status entail a secondary attempt to frame his discourse on Egypt as Greek or Egyptian—whether he is an outside ethnographer or an inside auto-ethnographer. There is no way to discuss fully what Apion wrote about without appreciating the position from which he was writing about it.

Whatever the identity label, Apion cut a broad swath across the Mediterranean. He went on lecture tours around Greece and eventually moved to Rome, where he set up shop as a teacher and grammarian. Apparently, he knew how to market himself and was a shameless self-promoter. Even Aulus Gellius, the second-century Roman author of the wide-ranging, twenty-book-long *Attic Nights*, said that Apion was too loquacious: "Apion might perhaps be too talkative out of a wrongful passion for ostentatiousness—he is very much a seller of himself in publicizing his erudition."[5] Apion's authority is *not* Gellius's. Gellius's text is a masterclass in how to perform reading and research, against which Apion's proclivity to ostentation and self-promotion stands in such stark relief.[6] In other words, Apion's intellectual profile was outsized and splashy and not at all

---

3. The basic distinction between these three classes—Romans, Alexandrians and citizens of a "Greek city," and *perigrini Aegyptii* (everybody else) is lucidly summarized in Jördens (2012). See Marotta (2017, 175) for a discussion of Apion and evaluation of Egyptians' access to higher citizenship statuses. Bowman and Rathbone (1992, 113–14) contextualize issues of status against the backdrop of Roman administrative changes of the Ptolemaic system.

4. Levy (1900b, 188) (section VIII of Levy 1900a); van der Horst (2002, 207); Willrich (1895, 172).

5. Gell. *NA* 5.14.3 = *BNJ* 616 T 10a: fortassean vitio studioque ostentationis sit loquacior—est enim sane quam in praedicandis doctrinis sui venditator. Translations of Apion are my own; text is from Keyser (2015).

6. Howley (2018, 157–203) traces Gellius's performance of reading and research, which is regularly contrasted with predecessors (like Pliny and Apion) whose methods he finds fault with.

"bookish." He claimed to have summoned Homer's ghost, which Pliny the Elder viewed with not unexpected suspicion.

Apion's fantastic tales about Egypt circulated widely and were prone to hyperbole.[7] The broad popularity of his work paved the path that he took toward Rome and fame. It also piqued the scorn of fellow thinkers like Pliny, Gellius, and Seneca, who all thought his successes were built on lies and pseudo-intellectual posturing. They gave Apion the nickname "Quarrelsome" (*Pleistoneikês*) to help make this point.[8] Like Gellius, Pliny the Elder uses Apion's brash personality—which even the emperor Tiberius criticized—as a foil against which to present his own modesty: "Indeed Apion the grammarian—whom Tiberius Caesar used to call the world's cymbal, although he could come off as the drum of his own renown. . . ."[9] Apion's brand of intellectual display opened doors and alienated many.

Apion the Egyptian, Apion the Greek

Few people from antiquity disliked Apion quite as intensely as Josephus, who devoted a whole text, *Against Apion*, to tearing apart his reputation.[10] Josephus remains, alongside Pliny, one of the best—though extremely biased—sources for Apion. The tension between Jews and Egyptians underlying Josephus's polemic provides essential background for Apion and his work. Jewish and Egyptian authors wrote contrasting portraits of Moses and the Exodus: Egyptians claimed that Jews fleeing Egypt were in fact leprous Egyptians. Both Jews and Egyptians wrote these dueling portraits amid a larger quest for Roman support, which could only be secured at the other group's expense. This competition for Roman favor helps explain Josephus's insistently dichotomous view of Greek and Egyptian identities. To discredit Apion's representation of Egypt's Jews, Josephus attacks Apion's claim to Greekness:

> And why must one be amazed if Apion tells lies about our ancestors, saying that they were Egyptians by birth? *He himself made the opposite lie about himself! Born in the Oasis of Egypt, and, one might say, the first of all Egyptians, he swore off his true homeland and birth and, by falsely claiming to be from Alexandria, conceded the wickedness*

---

7. A complicating factor is that Pliny the Elder looms so large as an evaluator of Apion's miraculous claims about Egypt and the natural world. His generally suspicious attitude to Apion's claims, summed up by the terse and dismissive "incredible to say" (*incredibile dictu*), is discussed by Damon (2008, 350–51, and 2011) (cf. Manolaraki 2018).

8. Damon (2011) outlines Pliny's, Seneca's, and Josephus's general suspicion toward Apion. Luke (2016, 290–92) notes Pliny the Elder's low opinion of Apion's scholarly method. His nickname "Quarrelsome" was confused for a patronymic in the Suda and later metamorphosed into "victor" (Πλειστονίκης), as Jacobson (1977) has discussed.

9. Plin. *HN* praef. 25 = *BNJ* 616 T 13: Apion quidem grammaticus—hic quem Tiberius Caesar cymbalum mundi vocabat, cum propriae famae tympanum potius videri posset.

10. Apion stands in here for the whole tradition of Aegyptiaca, which Josephus criticizes along similar lines. For Josephus's characterization of Apion, see Jones (2005), and for the text generally see Barclay (1998) and Goodman (1999).

30   INTRODUCING AEGYPTIACA

of his own birth. . . . The high-born Apion seems to want to offer his slander of us Jews to the Alexandrians as a sort of payment for the citizenship given to him. He knows how they hate the Jews who live in Alexandria, and he makes a show of insulting them and looping in all the others, in both cases telling shameless lies.[11]

The quote is a lot to digest. First and foremost, it is the evidence on which Apion's standard biography is based: Apion was an Egyptian by birth, later given Alexandrian citizenship. In this regard, Apion seems to have accomplished a rare feat. Ethnic Egyptians did not often attain Alexandrian citizenship, with its attendant privileges.[12] Jacoby's *Fragmente der griechischen Historiker*, the authoritative source for Apion's life and work, relies on Josephus for Apion's heading ("Apion von Oasis und Alexandria"). This double characterization—Apion of the Oasis and Alexandria—spatializes Apion's ethnic and cultural reinvention as a Greek. In this geographic scheme, inland Egypt becomes emblematic of Apion's former Egyptian identity, and Alexandria his newfound Greekness.

The Byzantine encyclopedia the Suda constructs an alternative biography for Apion that outlines the same entrance into Alexandrian culture. According to the Suda, Apion was born as a house-slave of the famously prolific Alexandrian scholar Didymus "Bronze Guts"—so called for the intestinal fortitude necessary to author the four thousand texts he reputedly wrote. Didymus first developed an intellectual persona rooted in Alexandria but presented squarely to Rome, thus creating a template that Apion and others would adopt.[13] It remains uncertain whether Apion actually was a "house-slave" (*threptos*) or, as Cynthia Damon and others have suggested, was instead a "pupil."[14] Either way, the same biographical trajectory takes root. Apion was born an Egyptian but made his way into Alexandria and its Greek intellectual milieu.

There are good reasons to link Apion's Alexandrian citizenship and his possible participation in Greek culture. The barriers to citizenship that were erected in Roman Egypt, but that Apion apparently skirted, were deliberately located in institutions like the gymnasium whose primary function was the transmission of Greek cultural knowledge. But this spatialization of culture and the particular way that it associates identity (Greekness) and place (Alexandria) is neither inevitable

11. Joseph. *Ap.* 2.28–9, 31–2 = *BNJ* 616 T 4a: αὐτὸς γὰρ περὶ αὐτοῦ τοὐναντίον ἐψεύδετο, καὶ γεγενημένος ἐν Ὀάσει τῆς Αἰγύπτου, πάντων Αἰγυπτίων πρῶτος ὤν, ὡς ἂν εἴποι τις, τὴν μὲν ἀληθῆ πατρίδα καὶ τὸ γένος ἐξωμόσατο, Ἀλεξανδρεὺς δὲ εἶναι καταψευδόμενος ὁμολογεῖ τὴν μοχθηρίαν τοῦ γένους . . . For accessibility and economy, here and throughout I only print the italicized excerpts of extended Greek passages.

12. According to Delia (1991, 29, 56, 164), Apion was the *only* ethnic Egyptian to be awarded Alexandrian citizenship.

13. Didymus (*BNP* 4.396–8) was a prolific commentator and compiler of his predecessors' work, particularly that of the earlier librarian of Alexandria Aristarchus. For Didymus's place in the grammatical tradition, see Pfeiffer (1968, 274–79).

14. Damon (2008, 338).

nor inherently true. Josephus's spatialized strategy is designed to help him make a point: Apion's repudiation of his own identity helps explain his misguided slander of Jews. When this spatialized rubric of culture leaps from Josephus to Jacoby, from antiquity to modernity, one risks losing sight of just how tendentious this one-to-one matching of ethnicity and place is. It implies that different cultures in Egypt are sealed-off bubbles that can be discussed in isolation. This is particularly true for Alexandria, where it is easy to lose sight of a broader, multiethnic Alexandrian population when emphasizing the restrictions that barred many ethnic Greeks and Egyptians alike from citizenship. As a result, a falsely static vision of a Greek Alexandrian culture extends unchanged from the time of Callimachus or Theocritus for hundreds of years, into the early-imperial period.[15]

To Josephus, Apion's Alexandrian identity is secondary. At heart, Apion is an Egyptian. He uses the wordy periphrasis "being the first of all Egyptians" to ensure that the point comes across clearly.[16] Apion may have illegitimately gained Alexandrian citizenship, but he is not *really* Alexandrian, because he is Egyptian. Josephus uses the tension of Greco-Egyptian identity as a tool by which to delegitimize Apion's reliability and skewer his betrayal of his own heritage. A common strategic ethnic fluidity practiced in Egypt becomes a type of "passing." Apion's Alexandrian citizenship is a disingenuous attempt to cover up his true self, which will always be tethered to his birth in the Oasis, an unimpeachably Egyptian part of Egypt. The language of betrayal imagines that ethnic identity is a zero-sum game. To become an Alexandrian citizen is to become more Greek; to become more Greek is to become less Egyptian.

Pliny the Elder, the wide-ranging encyclopedist and the other main source for Apion, also identifies Apion as an Egyptian by birth.[17] In his section on beetles, Pliny cites Apion's allegorizing interpretation of the scarab beetle's importance in Egyptian theology: "The scarab beetle that rolls balls of dung. For this reason most of Egypt worships scarab beetles among the gods, in Apion's elaborate interpretation, in which he gathers that the labor of the sun is similar to this animal's, to make excuses for the rites of his own people."[18] Labelling Apion's interpretation "elaborate" is far from complimentary. To Pliny, Apion's explanation is merely an attempt to smooth out Egyptian cultural practices to which he is tethered but for which he wants to provide a cross-cultural interpretation. This plays into Pliny's wider discrediting of Apion's scholarship. As Cynthia Damon has noted of Pliny and others, "their trenchant criticisms of the quality of his [Apion's] scholarship

---

15. Stephens (2003) has emphasized Egypt's impact on these poets.

16. Joseph. *Ap.* 2.29 = *BNJ* 616 T 4a: πάντων Αἰγυπτίων πρῶτος ὤν.

17. Damon (2011) catalogues Pliny's quotations and discussions of Apion.

18. Plin. *HN* 30.99 = *BNJ* 616 F 19: . . . scarabaeum, qui pilas voluit. propter hunc Aegypti magna pars scarabaeos inter numina colit, curiosa Apionis interpretatione, qua colligat solis operum similitudinem huic animali esse, ad excusandos gentis suae ritus. On this quote, and on Pliny's generally familiarizing portrait of Egypt, see Manolaraki (2018, 356–58).

32   INTRODUCING AEGYPTIACA

may reflect chagrin at the flimsy foundation of so sparkling an edifice."[19] But among the general motivations for Pliny's criticism of Apion discussed by Damon, I would like to underline just how central identity is to these critiques. Identity is reduced once again to a static and inescapable point of origin. It is the crucible with which to assay intellectual output.

As in Josephus, "birth" is the true source of one's identity. Both Pliny and Josephus use the same root word—*genos* in Greek, *gens* in Latin—to denote the "people" to whom Apion is tied. This is a natural word for both authors to use. Its semantic range covers both people groups with a common descent and animal species.[20] The overlap between natural species and human community inbuilt into the term enables Josephus and Pliny to claim that Apion's Egyptian identity is inalienable. Perhaps unsurprisingly, *genos* was instrumental in the later formulation of race.[21] As in processes of racial identification, Josephus and Pliny use *genos* and *gens* to bind Apion to a people and suggest that this connection is immutable and essential. One's birth is an ineluctable anchor that other markers of identity like language, education, or citizenship cannot erase.

But to many, Apion was a Greek.[22] Seneca represents knowledge of Greek culture in the language of filiation: "Apion the grammarian, who under Gaius Caesar (Caligula) circulated throughout Greece and was adopted into the ranks of Homerists by all the towns."[23] Knowledge of Homer allows Apion to be "adopted" into a realm of cultural expertise. Homer turns into an ersatz citizenship test that facilitates Apion's movement within Greek spaces. As in Josephus, there is a coordination of identity and movement. But where Josephus sets out to delegitimize Apion's Greekness and entrance into Alexandria, Seneca emphasizes his conversance with Greek literature to explain his smooth circulation around mainland Greece. These assignations of Greek and Egyptian identities are not easy to reconcile or explain away. Pliny's and Seneca's different labels for Apion cannot be written off as the product of alternatively reliable and unreliable sources; Seneca was a closer contemporary of Apion than either Josephus or Pliny the Elder.

---

19. Damon (2008, 361).

20. Denoted by *LSJ*, *s.v.* γένος subsections III and V, respectively.

21. Race is the first definition of γένος offered in the *LSJ* and of *gens* in *Lewis and Short* and the chosen translation in the Loeb editions of Josephus's *Against Apion* (Thackeray 1926, 303) and of Pliny's *Natural History* (Jones 1963, 343). For γένος and (proto/early) racial thought, see Isaac (2006, 113–14) and McCoskey (2012, 29–31).

22. Other authors fall into this camp. For example, the Christian world-historian Julius Africanus (*Chron.* 70 = *BNJ* 616 T 3b), who studied in Alexandria and wrote in the late-second and early-third centuries CE, classes Apion among Greeks, together with Posidonius and Herodotus. He adds (*Praep. Evang.* 10.10.16 = *BNJ* 616 T 3a) that Apion's father was a certain other Ποσειδώνιος, which suggests a Greek ethnicity but could certainly mask mixed Greco-Egyptian ancestry.

23. Sen. *Ep.* 88.40 = *BNJ* 616 T 5a: Apion grammaticus, qui sub C. Caesare tota circulatus est Graecia et in nomen Homeri ab omnibus civitatibus adoptatus. . . .

Aulus Gellius puts it the most bluntly. He calls Apion a "Greek man" (*Graecus homo*, 7.8.1), defining Apion above all by his expertise in Greek literary culture. Before offering up the criticism of Apion's ostentatiousness quoted above, Gellius explains his attribution of Greekness to Apion: "Apion, nicknamed 'Quarrelsome,' was a learned man endowed with a deep and varied knowledge of Greek culture. They say his books are famous, they recount a history of all the amazing things that are seen and heard in Egypt."[24] As in Seneca, Apion's mastery of Greek literature is a primary point of reference. Rather than his specific bona fides as a Homerist, Gellius prefers to note Apion's knowledge of the broad categories denoted by "literature" (*litterae*) and "knowledge" (*scientia*). Gellius is an author whose cultural worldview is filtered through his bookishness, so this coordinated assignation of Greekness and erudition makes good sense. He often deploys these buzzwords. Versions of the phrase "gifted in wisdom/arts/authority" ripple across the *Attic Nights* and apply equally to Greeks and Romans: Herodes Atticus, Solon, Scipio Africanus, the Elder Pliny, and many others.[25]

Beyond cultural fluency, the perspective Apion adopts toward Egypt is particularly important. Gellius segues from Apion's general mastery of Greek culture to his representation of Egypt. By prefacing Apion's Egyptian work with praise of his Greek erudition, Gellius suggests that the perspective through which Apion views Egypt supports, rather than undermines, his claims to Greekness. Apion's Egypt is thoroughly exoticized and prone to exaggeration. Like Herodotus, the famous "father of lies," Apion's work was always perceived to play with the reasonable limits of veracity, a fact to which the putative title of Apion's text, the "true history," points.[26] Through this emphasis on unbelievability, Gellius implies that Apion's work was Herodotean—an etic, outsider's perspective on Egypt's marvels solidly in the Greek historiographic vein. This Herodotean paradoxographic framework helps explain the tonal bivalence of Gellius's description of Apion's work. An attribution of wisdom and Greek cultural expertise ("gifted in the various matters of Greek knowledge") gives way to a critique of Apion's truth-bending ostentatiousness.[27]

---

24. Gell. *NA* 5.14.1–2 = *BNJ* 616 T 10a: Apion, qui Plistonices appellatus est, litteris homo multis praeditus rerumque Graecarum plurima atque varia scientia fuit. eius libri non incelebres feruntur, quibus omnium ferme quae mirifica in Aegypto visuntur audiunturque historia comprehenditur.

25. This constant evaluation of others' "learning" is well-discussed by Howley (2018, 118–19, regarding Pliny, and 204–52, regarding the reader as "expert on experts"). These phrases (*praeditus* with an ablative noun like *facundia, sapientia, artibus, auctoritate*) occur sixteen times in the *NA*. For these specific figures, see respectively 1.2.1, 2.12.2, 6.12.1, and 9.4.13.

26. Damon (2011, 142–44) (cf. Keyser 2015 *ad* T 13 for a more cautious interpretation of the title). The "father of lies" label comes from, but is never actually used in, Plutarch's *On the Malice of Herodotus*. There, Plutarch catalogues Herodotus's sustained, malicious belittlement of the Greeks and their accomplishments.

27. Howley (2018, 112–56) shows that Gellius criticizes the Elder Pliny in similar fashion.

34   INTRODUCING AEGYPTIACA

Moving beyond Seneca and Gellius, Apion broadcast Greek identity by participating in a range of traditionally Greek intellectual domains. As the Suda's reference to Didymus makes clear, Apion fit comfortably in the line of Alexandrian grammarians who delved into the minutiae of Greek texts.[28] In fact, the label "grammarian" outpaces all other identity labels—Egyptian, Alexandrian, Greek—ascribed to him.[29] Within this broad tradition, Apion was particularly well known for his work on Homer. He wrote the *Homeric Glosses*, a text firmly in the tradition of the editions and commentaries on the Homeric corpus published by other Alexandrian grammarians.[30] This work must partially explain Seneca's anecdote that Apion went on a lecture tour of Greece in his capacity as a Homerist. The slippage between identity and intellectual authority comes into focus. Apion's status as a Greek or Egyptian is bound up in what he writes about—Homer, Exodus—and how he writes about it, whether as an Alexandrian textual critic or as a Herodotean-style storyteller.

38 CE and the Alexandria Issue

Apion's success as a grammarian points to a tension between Alexandrian as a citizenship status and Alexandrianism as an intellectual tradition. In the domain of social history, Diana Delia emphasizes that Apion was exceptional—an ethnic Egyptian given Alexandrian citizenship.[31] But in the realm of intellectual culture, Apion's work on Homer is entirely typical of the Alexandrian grammatical tradition. A dissonance arises between Apion's exceptional citizenship status and very standard grammatical expertise, even as both Alexandrian identities facilitated Apion's move to Rome. It is especially difficult to resolve this tension between Apion's social and intellectual Alexandrian identities when the different authors who cite Apion—Josephus, Philo of Alexandria, Pliny—understand the label "Alexandrian" differently.

Apion's deputation to Rome on behalf of Alexandria provides some clarity when confronting these different valences of "Alexandrianism." Apion was chosen to represent Alexandrian Greeks after the anti-Jewish riots of 38 CE, which erupted when the Roman Prefect of Egypt Flaccus summarily denied Alexandrian Jews their long-established rights of Alexandrian citizenship and residency.[32] In the

---

28. So says Suda α 3215, s.v. Ἀπίων = *BNJ* 616 T 1, which claims that he took over the position formerly held by Theon and that he was the student both of Apollonius son of Archibius and of Euphranor. For discussion of the apparent timing of this succession, see Damon (2008, 338–39).

29. He is called a grammarian by eight different sources (the Suda, Clement, Jerome, Seneca, Pliny the Elder, Julius Africanus, and Tatian); an Egyptian by three sources (Josephus, Clement, Pliny the Elder); a Greek by two sources (Gellius and Julius Africanus); and an Alexandrian by two (Athenaeus and Jerome, and technically Josephus as well).

30. The *Homeric Glosses* is collected and edited by Neitzel (1977).

31. Delia (1991, 29, 56, 164).

32. The most thorough discussion remains that of Gambetti (2009), whose analysis of the events is often at odds with Philo's version in the *in Flaccum*.

aftermath of this controversial edict and Alexandrians' violent enforcement of it, both Alexandrian Greeks and Jews sent delegations to Caligula to represent their side.[33] Alexandria's Jewish population chose the Greek-educated Jewish thinker Philo, and Alexandrian Greeks chose Apion. Whether chosen for the anti-Jewish sentiment apparent in his work or as a result of his recent Alexandrian citizenship, Apion's speech denigrating the case of Alexandrian Jews apparently hit the mark. Perhaps because Apion insinuated that Alexandrian Jews did not worship the cult of the imperial family, Caligula gave Philo an icy reception and soon dismissed him. As Philo bemoans in his *Legatio*, Caligula was busy with home renovations during their meeting. While Philo was making his case to restore Jews their rights, Caligula kept halting the meeting to choose colored glass and criticize room fittings.[34]

Within the context of this riot, Apion became the face of Alexandrians for a Roman audience. As a citizen, Apion may have deviated from a normative definition of an Alexandrian. But in Rome, Apion was quite literally a representative Alexandrian. In other words, Apion should be the yardstick through which one measures what Alexandrianism looks like for Romans of the early first century CE. Apion's ability to move fluidly between Greek and Egyptian culture and his success as an ambassador to Caligula provide some clarity around just what constitutes an Alexandrian in the early-imperial period—both legally and culturally. The political upheaval that brought Jews, Alexandrians, and Egyptians into conflict for Roman favor forms the backdrop against which Josephus's dogged emphasis on Apion's aberrant and inauthentic Alexandrianism becomes intelligible. It is precisely the events of 38 CE that motivate Josephus's diatribe against Apion with which I opened. Josephus later makes explicit the irony of Apion's citizenship, given recent events in Alexandria. He juxtaposes Apion's own illegitimate claim to Alexandrian citizenship with the expropriation of Jews' entirely legitimate citizenship:

> *If Apion swears off this type of honorary citizenship, let him stop calling himself an Alexandrian! Since he was, as I said before, born in the deepest depths of Egypt, how could he be an Alexandrian when honorary citizenship does not count, as he himself claims in our case.* And yet it is the Egyptians alone that Romans, masters of the inhabited world, refuse to allow a share of any citizenship whatsoever. He is so noble that he claims to have a share of rights which he was prevented from possessing while attempting to sycophantically criticize those who have lawfully received them.[35]

---

33. Joseph. *AJ* 18, 257, 259–60 = *BNJ* 616 T 6. The circumstances of the riots are also laid out by Smallwood (1961, 11–24). She adheres to Philo's version of events much more closely than Gambetti (2009), who emphasizes Caligula's role in precipitating the violence.

34. Smallwood (1961, 24–27) summarizes the embassy. For Philo's complaint about Caligula's attention to contractors during their (main, second) meeting, see *Leg.* 358–59, 364.

35. Joseph. *Ap.* 2.41 (cf. Gambetti 2009 210): εἰ δὲ τούτου ἀφαιρεῖται τὸν τρόπον τῆς πολιτείας Ἀπίων, παυσάσθω λέγων αὑτὸν Ἀλεξανδρέα· γεννηθεὶς γάρ, ὡς προεῖπον, ἐν τῷ βαθυτάτῳ

36   INTRODUCING AEGYPTIACA

In brief, Alexandrian status is as bitterly contested as it is ill-defined.[36] Josephus sets out to prove that Egyptians have no business claiming Alexandrian rights; that they are, as a group, uniquely disenfranchised within the Roman empire. The rationale for this emphasis on Apion's Egyptian origins and ill-gotten status is relatively clear, given Apion's popularity as a Hellenist. Josephus only feels compelled to make this argument because Apion was such a success as an ambassador to Caligula. He pulls out all the stops to discredit Apion because he feels the need to do so. But even laying aside these explanations of Josephus's motivations, the paucity of evidence and scholarly disagreement about the meaning of said evidence counsel caution: one should not rush to claim that Apion is an outlier against some other apparently widespread, but evidentiarily unavailable, definition of Alexandrian.

Nor should one assume that Romans—to whom Apion was first a literal, and then a cultural ambassador of Alexandria—cared much about the technical distinctions between an Alexandrian, a "townsman" (*astos*), a "demesman" (*dêmotês*), an "enrolled ephebe" (*ephêbos*), and a "citizen" (*politês*) that Josephus and Philo discuss. To Alexandrian Jews, for whom these distinctions made a material difference in status and residency rights, these categories were extremely important. They were similarly important for citizens of Egypt's *poleis*, like Athenaeus. A citizen of the city Naucratis and a resident in Alexandria, Athenaeus is one of the few authors besides Josephus who specifies that Apion was an Alexandrian.[37] Athenaeus and Josephus, authors writing from a position within the Roman empire in which citizenship and status were precarious, are the exceptions that prove the rule.

Romans had a different perspective when navigating the lines separating Greek and Egyptian culture in Egypt. They could just as readily see Apion as an arbiter of Alexandrianism and the ways that Egyptian and Greek intellectual traditions there were co-constituted. There is little evidence that Romans like Pliny the Elder cared much about whether Apion had been an ephebe or had a deme affiliation—that is, whether an asterisk should be placed on Apion's "honorary" citizenship. In fact, Pliny, like other Romans of the imperial period, rarely uses "Alexandrian" as an identity label at all.[38] In other words, Josephus's trenchant criticism reveals that the specific legal category of "Alexandrian" was of immense economic and social consequence in Egypt. But by the same token, Pliny's discussions of Apion reveal that this specific legal definition does not circumscribe the ways that Romans made

---

τῆς Αἰγύπτου πῶς ἂν Ἀλεξανδρεὺς εἴη τῆς κατὰ δόσιν πολιτείας, ὡς αὐτὸς ἐφ' ἡμῶν ἠξίωκεν, ἀναιρουμένης.

36. Delia (1991, 54) names only 273 secure attestations of Alexandrians listing a deme affiliation in Roman-Egyptian documentary evidence. "Alexandrian" *tout court* also occurs in documentary evidence, with uncertain meaning (El-Abbadi 1962 claims it was used interchangeably with a deme affiliation, though this interpretation remains heterodox).

37. Ath. *Deipn.* 1.29.16 = *BNJ* 616 T 4b, F 36.

38. Only once (*HN* 35.146), of Polemon.

sense of the label "Alexandrian" and the ways that ethnic Egyptians like Apion wielded it as they charted a path to Rome.

Muddying the Cultural Waters

Apion's representation of Alexandria extended beyond his role as ambassador. Apion's work in the *Homeric Glosses* shows that he also exemplified Alexandria's intellectual culture. His close philological engagement with the Homeric corpus signals the claims he made to forms of Greek erudition long associated with the Alexandrian grammarians. He plays a number game commonly deployed in Greek symposia to broadcast learning.[39] As he observes, the opening word of the *Iliad*, μῆνιν, signals the total combined books of the Iliad and Odyssey: "μ" represents the number forty, and "η" represents eight, providing in the first two letters the number 48.[40] To cement his status as an Alexandrian grammarian, Apion also gained fame (or at least notoriety) for the textual emendations that constitute the *Glosses*. So, for example, Apion emends the line "until in Ortygia the golden-throned sacred Artemis" into "until in sacred Ortygia the golden-throned Artemis," changing "sacred" from a nominative modifier of Artemis into a dative modifier of Ortygia, presumably to better distribute the adjectives.[41]

Apion's stature as a Homerist was prominent enough that even Josephus acknowledged it: "And concerning the poet Homer, though himself a grammarian, Apion wasn't able to say with assurance what Homer's homeland was; the same goes for Pythagoras, though he was born only yesterday and the day before."[42] Josephus's remark has some bite. He uses the specific figures of Homer and Pythagoras as tools with which to undercut Apion's claims to Greek cultural erudition via the hallowed term "grammarian."[43] As in his earlier argument that Apion's Alexandrian citizenship was ill-gotten, Josephus here implies that Apion's knowledge of Greek intellectual culture is hollow and inauthentic. As a final flourish, Josephus

---

39. For examples of such number play, see Plut. *Quaest. Conv.* 9.5, 740e–f and the "Cattle Problem" discussed by Leventhal (2015).

40. On this number symbolism, see van der Horst (2002, 210). Seneca cites it as an example of the useless liberal arts that his addressee Lucilius ought to avoid.

41. Schol. *HPQ* 5.123 = *BNJ* 616 F 41: "ἦος ἐν Ὀρτυγίηι χρυσόθρονος Ἄρτεμις ἁγνή (*Od.* 5.123)." Ἀπίων τὸ "ἁγνή" περισπᾶι κατὰ δοτικήν, ἀκούων ἐν Ὀρτυγίηι ἁγνῆι.

42. Joseph. *Ap.* 2.14 = *BNJ* 616 F 33: καὶ περὶ μὲν Ὁμήρου τοῦ ποιητοῦ γραμματικὸς ὢν αὐτὸς οὐκ ἂν ἔχοι τίς αὐτοῦ πατρίς ἐστι διαβεβαιωσάμενος εἰπεῖν, οὐδὲ περὶ Πυθαγόρου μόνον οὐκ ἐχθὲς καὶ πρώιην γεγονότος. For the precise tenor of the phrase ἐχθὲς καὶ πρώιην see Dillery (2003, 385).

43. Dillery (2003) cogently argues that Josephus felt the need to undermine Apion's widely recognized reputation as a grammarian to fully rebut the latter's representation of Jews in his Aegyptiaca. Dillery traces (385–88) all passages in which Josephus criticizes Apion's status as grammarian (which occurs four times in the *Contra Apionem*, all in reference to Apion). Josephus's ironizing use of "grammarian" not only satirizes Apion's inability to date Homer, but also his reliance on disreputable sources for Moses (2.12, 14), his misdating of the Exodus (2.15), and his incorrect, Egyptian etymology of the term "sabaton" (sabbath) (2.21).

38   INTRODUCING AEGYPTIACA

makes a joke about the transmigration of souls to emphasize that Apion's ignorance of Pythagoras is even more unforgiveable, given the latter's never-ending
rebirth into the world.

Josephus's critiques were designed to hit Apion where it would hurt. Apion
actively promoted his privileged knowledge of Homer's biography. Pliny the Elder
recalls a lecture that Apion gave when Pliny was a young man.[44] After discussing an herbal remedy, Apion pivoted to Homer: "(Apion) also said that he had
summoned a ghost to insistently ask Homer where he was from and from which
parents he was born, but that he did not dare to declare publicly what answer the
ghost gave."[45] At first glance, Apion's ghost-conjuring is odd, to say the least.[46] To
Pliny, it is proof that Apion, long considered prone to exaggeration, does not let
scholarly rigor get in the way of self-promotion.[47] But Apion's interest in Homeric
ghostly visitation has some precedent. Ennius, the progenitor of Latin epic poetry,
famously proclaimed in his *Annales* that Homer's ghost visited him in a dream and
told him the secret workings of the universe.[48] Relying on the Pythagorean transmigration of souls, Ennius claimed that, after a brief time as a peacock, Homer's
soul passed on into him. Ghosts and the transmigration of Homer's soul allow a
non-Greek, Ennius, to strengthen his apparent connection to Greek literary history through the language of reincarnation.[49] At least according to Pliny, Apion
promoted similar avenues of access to Homer and the Greek cultural cachet he
provided. Apion's ghost-summoning helps bolster an authority over Greek cultural history that his Egyptian origin risks undermining.

The ghostly summoning of Homer begins to reveal the interconnected evidence
that different authors used to call Apion a Greek or Egyptian. Apion's work on
Homer and on Egypt were not sealed off from each other.[50] He sometimes inserted

44. Here I follow the argument made by Dillery (2003, 385–87), that these passages from Josephus
and Pliny "dovetail" (385).

45. Plin. *HN* 30.18 = *BNJ* 616 F 15: Apion prodiderit . . . seque evocasse umbras ad percunctandum
Homerum, quanam patria quibusque parentibus genitus esset, non tamen ausus profiteri, quid sibi
respondisse diceret.

46. Dickie (2001, 207) connects it (and Apion) to a longer tradition of magical self-performance
in the Roman provinces.

47. Pliny's scorn of Apion's self-promotion is Damon's (2011, 134–35) main point of emphasis in her
reading of this anecdote. She is less attuned to the Ennian pedigree, which I am suggesting is necessary
context for Apion's claims to be a Homerist despite his Egyptian background.

48. Skutsch (1985) places the dream relatively early in the *Annales*, at 1.iii–x, with the peacock
transformation at ix. For later authors who mentioned the dream and its Pythagorean underpinning,
see Skutsch (1985, 147–67). Ennius's southern Italian origins are often invoked to explain his interest in
Pythagoreanism, given Pythagoras's connections to Croton (on which Diog. Laert. 8.3).

49. The general role of Pythagoreanism here has been debated. Aicher (1989, 230–31) sees Pythagorean metempsychosis as metaphor for and defense of the efficacy of stylistic translation between Greek
and Latin. Delatte (1915, 109) has drawn on the importance of Homer for Pythagoreans. Skutsch (1968,
6–9) provides earlier models of literary-philosophical soul transmigration.

50. This is partially demonstrated by Josephus's critiques of Apion's work on Egypt, which necessarily includes Josephus's delegitimization of Apion's expertise as a Greek-language glossator

APION, ROMAN EGYPT, AND THE INSIDER-OUTSIDER PROBLEM   39

flags of his own Egyptian identity into his interpretations of Homer. According to the Homeric commentator Eustathius, Apion insisted that the Elysian fields and isles of the blessed mentioned in the *Odyssey* were located not in the far West, but in the Egyptian Delta, around the Canopic branch of the Nile. Apion's justification lies in a traditionally Greek etymological expertise: he derives Elysian from ἰλύς, the word for alluvial soil long connected with the Nile inundation.[51] In this instance, typically Alexandrian grammatical knowledge is invoked to serve an Egyptian-centric reinterpretation of Homer. Apion's etymology of Elysium is the tip of the iceberg. Apion was a prolific etymologizer. As Susanne Neitzel has emphasized, the interpretations one sees in the *Homeric Glosses* were as influential as they were roundly criticized by fellow grammarians.[52]

Besides Homer, Apion also uses medicine to insinuate Egypt into the domain of Greek culture. The herbology lecture that Pliny heard provides a good example: "When in my adolescence I saw Apion the grammarian assert that *cynocephalia* ('dog-head'), which in Egypt is called '*osiritis*,' was a divine herb effective against all poison. If the whole plant is uprooted, he claimed that he who uprooted it would die immediately."[53] Apion first gives two names for the same plant and then makes fantastic claims about the properties of said plant. The gloss *osiritis* is revealing, in two directions. Methodologically, it points up a difficulty inherent in authors who have been indirectly preserved. It is unclear whether this gloss of *cynocephalia* as *osiritis* is an interpolation that Pliny himself is making—whether this coordination belongs to Pliny the Elder—or whether one can include it in the broad "assertion" that Pliny is attributing to Apion.[54] Here, certainty is never guaranteed. Arguing fervently for one or the other option would inevitably hit a dead end. I would instead emphasize that Pliny is looping Apion in on a cross-cultural translation that is, in important ways, co-authored by them both. This model of co-authorship is one I will return to in coming chapters when facing this slippage of authority between cited and citing author.

Beyond exemplifying a methodological challenge, this translation is significant on its own grounds. Through *osiritis*, Apion, and by extension the citing author Pliny, demonstrate their ability to move between Greek and Egyptian terminology. Apion offers both Greek and Egyptian words for the same plant, thus using

---

(by emphasizing, per Dillery (2003, 389–90), Apion's "deviant" and "idiosyncratic" interpretations in the *Homeric Glosses*).

51. Eust. *Od.* 4.563 = *BNJ* 616 F 11a. Damon (2008, 350n45) reveals that this is, as is typical of Apion, idiosyncratic. Elysian was more typically derived from "lightning-struck" (ἐνηλύσιος).

52. Neitzel (1977, 208). Josephus (*Ap.* 2.3) calls him a "crowd pleaser" (ὀχλαγωγός). Neitzel (1977, 207–9) and Damon (2008, 344–47) make clear that other etymologizers of Homer like Apollonius single out Apion's interpretation and either explicitly (κακῶς) or implicitly (ὁ δὲ Ἀπίων) criticize it.

53. Plin. *HN* 30.18 = *BNJ* 616 F 15: . . . cum adulescentibus nobis visus Apion grammaticae artis prodiderit cynocephalian herbam, quae in Aegypto vocaretur osiritis, divinam et contra omnia veneficia; sed si tota erueretur, statim eum, qui eruisset, mori . . .

54. Keyser (2016, 455) tries to reconstruct Apion's original pharmacological work from Pliny's obviously tendentious citations of Apion's tall tales.

40 INTRODUCING AEGYPTIACA

translation to bolster his authority, which spans the Greek and the Egyptian. Interestingly, Apion and Pliny claim that *cynocephalia* and *osiritis* belong to separate languages, even as both are denoted in Latin in Pliny's text. The gloss gestures to multilingualism while remaining monolingual.[55] This sneakily complicated use of language thus relies on a distinction between the semantics of transliterated (*osiritis*) and translated (*cynocephalia*) terms to carve out authorial cachet. Beyond the literal translation it offers, the reference to Osiris in the name *osiritis* opens up much broader processes of cultural equivalence-drawing that tie together Egyptian religion, Greek and Egyptian pharmacology, and botany.[56] Through one plant, one can broach much larger issues of how cultural translation of intellectual traditions is undertaken, the socio-economic motivations that frame these translations, and the questions of authority that culturally "in between" figures like Apion pose.

Apion's fragmentary status is of course frustrating; the basic features of Apion's work, its narrative texture, remain out of reach. The questions of attribution—is the *osiritis* gloss Pliny's or Apion's?—are as aporetic as they are unavoidable. On a more basic level, it makes Apion harder to find. The difficulty of access to the places where citations and quotations of Apion are compiled has hindered work on a literary tradition that defies generic labels and moves fluidly between Greek and Egyptian domains of expertise. This material is collected in editions of fragmentary authors that are necessarily imperfect and often cost-prohibitive.[57] These different editions carve Apion into distinct component parts in ways that necessarily mask the cultural cross-pollinating that mixes together Egyptian and Greek traditions. Apion's work is bifurcated and presented both in the *Fragmente der griechischen Historiker* (for his work on Egypt) and in Neitzel's *Apions Glossai Homerikai* (for his activity as grammarian).[58] The task of collecting fragmentary authors and creating generic canons through which they are lumped together is fraught with difficulty. The editors of such collections have expressed well the inevitable limitations of this process.[59] As a result, one loses sight of Apion.

---

55. There remain two potential complications: first, that the phrase "is called in Egypt" refers to a Greek-language Egyptian regionalism; second, that Apion would have originally denoted the plant with its actual Egyptian name. I find these two options less likely. To the first, the syntax seems to replicate the lingual equivalence-drawing one sees in Herodotus; second, there is very little evidence for direct translation between Egyptian and Latin that does not pass through a Greek intermediary.

56. For evidence on the Osiris-poison connection in Demotic magical papyri, see column xix.10 (text published by Griffith and Thompson 1921), an anti-poison spell that invokes the cup of Osiris (*p w n nb n Wsr*). See also the plant poultices in column xiv.22, which mentions an Anubis-plant. The Crocodilopolis manual P. Vindob. D. 6257 (with Reymond 1976, 39) offers similar evidence of translation between Greek and Egyptian pharmacology.

57. Most (1997) grapples with this imperfection. Among the contributions, Bowersock (1997) is apposite, since he uses case studies from Jacoby's *FGrHist* to discuss the limits of fragmentary framing.

58. Keyser (2015) (the update of the original *FGrHist* 616) and Neitzel (1977), respectively.

59. Schepens (1997) summarizes the editorial process to discuss the necessary imperfections of the historiographic and nationalist (*genos*-based) approach that Jacoby took.

But difficulty of access notwithstanding, the methodological questions necessitated by indirect transmission have long deserved answers. Focalizing Apion through the network of different Greek and Roman authors who cite him illustrates just how unstable and flexible the relationship between ethnic identity and literary production is. The perspective of the observer, their own motivations and cultural position, provides essential context for the way they represent Apion. When assigning an identity to Apion, citing authors differently hierarchize his place of origin, citizenship, cultural expertise, or language. To the Elder Pliny, a first-century CE Roman and near contemporary, Apion was, in spite of his *interpretatio Graeca*, an Egyptian by "birth" (*gens*). To Josephus too, another chronologically proximate source, Apion is Egyptian, regardless of citizenship. But to Aulus Gellius, Seneca, and more chronologically far-flung authors like Julius Africanus, Apion was a Greek, defined as such by his conversance with the fundamentals of Greek intellectual culture. His work on Homer and his seemingly etic, Herodotean representation of Egypt mount a case for a Greek identity label. The different components of identity (place of birth, religious affiliation, intellectual output) are contestable, and unable to be collapsed into a single "Egyptian" or "Greek" standpoint.

APION AND AEGYPTIACA UNDER
MANETHO'S LONG SHADOW

A tacit bias underlies all of this. To many modern readers, Apion is not *really* Egyptian. *Osiritis* notwithstanding, there is not enough in Apion's work that looks like what Egyptologists actually study. It does not help Apion's case that there is a ready point of comparison who overshadows him. Manetho remains the paradigmatic model of an Egyptian who wrote about Egypt for Greeks (if not yet Romans).[60] Occupying a privileged position as a Heliopolitan priest in the early third century BCE, Manetho wrote the "Egyptian Matters" (*Aegyptiaca*), which presents a dynastic history of Egypt. His text, which lists Egyptian kings and lumps them into a set of dynasties, is indebted to Egypt's historiographic traditions of "annals" (*gnwt*) and "accomplishments" (*nḥtw*) and evidences a clear continuity with other, much earlier kings lists.[61] Manetho's text is similar in form to canonical pharaonic-era annals like the Palermo Stone, the Abydos King List, and the Turin Royal Canon.[62]

An expertise in this type of Egyptian historical memory was just one component of Manetho's authoritative Egyptian intellectual identity. He also garnered religious bona fides through his connections to Heliopolis (Egyptian *jwnw*), a predynastic

---

60. So, for example, Dench (2013, 259–60) cites Manetho and Berossus as the clear examples of auto-ethnographic writing. They are discussed in the same vein in Dillery (1999, 112, and 2015).

61. For *gnwt*, see Redford (1984, 65–96); for *nḥtw*, see Galán (1995, 41–100).

62. The broader tradition of the kings list and Manetho's connections thereto are laid out in Redford (1986, 201–30). Wilkinson (2000) deals specifically with the Palermo Stone, and Ryholt (2004) with the Turin Royal Canon.

42   INTRODUCING AEGYPTIACA

site, Old-Kingdom cult center for Atum, and the birthplace of Egypt's solar religion. Beyond Heliopolis, testimonia speak to Manetho's general access to temples and their libraries. His ability to publicize in Greek information that otherwise resided in gated-off repositories of pharaonic knowledge became a primary point of reference for Greeks and Romans discussing his work. Thus, Manetho and his Babylonian contemporary Berossus have come to fossilize a set auto-ethnographic pattern: Manetho and Berossus translated Egyptian and Babylonian knowledge traditions into Greek. They did so under the shadow of newly arrived Ptolemaic and Seleucid dynasts who increasingly leveraged these knowledge traditions for their own benefit.[63] Even when translated into Greek, Manetho is still working within a recognizably Egyptian vein.

Through his Greek-language, yet unambiguously Egyptian text, Manetho thrust emic, consummately "insider" auto-ethnography into the Greek-language discourse on Egypt. Manethonian scholarship—particularly the work of Ian Moyer and John Dillery—has debated just what position Manetho takes in relation to Egyptian and Greek discourses on Egypt and its past. They have asked whether Manetho replicates the hallmarks of a Greek, Herodotean tradition against which he is largely positioning his own text.[64] But this debate aside, he nonetheless possesses an Egyptian authority vouchsafed by his access to, and mastery over, pharaonic-Egyptian knowledge. On this Dillery and Moyer agree. Manetho knows, can represent, and can translate Egyptian written in hieroglyphic; his *Aegyptiaca* delves into Egyptian literary forms like the "king's novel" and hymns.[65]

The modern disciplinary importance of Manetho's text is itself significant. His kings list is essential to the reconstruction of pharaonic history; his dynastic organization is still used today. Manetho's importance to Egyptology operates as a circular, ex post facto imprimatur of legitimate Egyptianness: Egyptians are the people studied by Egyptologists.[66] However many problems there are in his dynastic organization—and anybody interested in the political history of the First Intermediate Period can speak to these problems—Manetho's text is still invaluable. In the face of all these indices of Manetho's authority, how can Apion—with his glosses of Homer and paradoxographic stories about Egypt—really be emic and auto-ethnographic? Apion is no Manetho.

These comparisons unnecessarily undermine Apion's claims to an authentic Egyptian identity. They suggest that there was a narrow window for Aegyptiaca,

63. Even though it is overly schematic in its treatment of politics and religion, Huss (1994, 123–29 for Manetho) presents valuable evidence for the relationship between the Ptolemies and Egyptian priests.

64. Dillery (2015, 301–47), and Moyer (2011, 84–141).

65. The "king's novel" is a specific subgenre of royal *res gestae* outlined by Loprieno (1996, 281–82 for problems of definition) and typologized by Hofmann (2004).

66. For an Egyptological reconstruction of Manetho's core political history, see Redford (1986, 231–332).

the title for Manetho's work and an umbrella term for texts written about Egypt by Egyptians but presented to Greeks and Romans.[67] To most, Aegyptiaca begins and ends with Manetho. It turns into a brief, early-Ptolemaic efflorescence. Apion does not enter into the conversation. That is why the comparison does so much damage. It delimits the space in which Aegyptiaca is allowed to operate. It implies that only Egyptians with an ill-defined ethnic and cultural purity should be of interest for the way that they represent Egypt and claim an intellectual authority over it. It separates Aegyptiaca and Alexandrian intellectual culture into alternately Egyptian and Greek traditions. Most importantly, it ignores the ways in which cultural contact between the constituent Greek and Egyptian parts of Ptolemaic Egypt produced a new face of Egyptian intellectual authority with which Rome came into contact.[68]

Even Manetho himself, at first blush the representative of Aegyptiaca in its strict guise of emic annalistic history, wrote broadly and synthetically. The canonized Egyptological Manetho I just outlined misses much of his intellectual activity. Besides his king list, Manetho is credited with a text called *On the Preparation of Kyphi*, a medical-cum-religious incense (Egyptian *kʾp.t*) used in temples and for fumigation. Plutarch repeats a recipe for *kyphi* in *On Isis and Osiris*, a Platonic interpretation of the Osiris myth that drew heavily on Manetho for reliable information on Egyptian religion.[69] Manetho's interest in a religio-magical incense inaugurates a mixed religious and technical presentation of Egypt that Apion's *osiritis* continues. A combination of Greek and Egyptian traditions is inbuilt into Aegyptiaca from its foundation.

Recentering Cultural Mixedness

Comparisons between Manetho, the first identifiable practitioner of Aegyptiaca, and latter-day practitioners of this genre like Apion need not inevitably conclude that Manetho's Egypt is the only one worthy of the name. A comparison of Manetho and Apion can help carve out a new space in which the new intellectual culture practiced by fluid and difficult-to-pin-down figures like Apion can be appreciated on its own terms. Apion's interest in both things Greek like Homer and things Egyptian like scarab beetles does not make him less Egyptian than Manetho. It does make clear that the meaning of "Egyptian" has changed from Manetho to Apion. What has been a specific issue of what to call Apion balloons out into a

---

67. The term Aegyptiaca has been used by scholars as a generic label, as is clear in Burstein (1996, 598–604) and Dillery (2003, 383).

68. This cultural contact has been increasingly well-discussed by historians of Ptolemaic Egypt, with volumes like Rutherford (2016) and Papaconstantinou (2010) (multilingualism specifically) devoted to the subject.

69. Manetho is cited for his "On Preparation of Kyphi" in Suda μ 142, s.v. Μάνεθως = *BNJ* 609 T 1 (cf. F 16a). Plutarch, implicitly (per Jacoby) but not explicitly citing Manetho, repeats the recipe in *DIO* 52, 372c and 80, 383e–384b.

much larger question about how one can discuss Egyptian culture in a world characterized on the one hand by an increasingly blurry Greek-Egyptian cultural milieu and on the other by the rise to preeminence of Roman hegemony in the Eastern Mediterranean. Apion opens a vantage onto something new: a culture born of contact between Egyptians and Greeks but that is neither Egyptian nor Greek in the way that those two cultures have normally been understood.[70] It is this literary tradition, and these Egyptians, that this book will recuperate.

Postcolonial scholarship has long focused on cultures changed by imperial occupation. To discuss Apion and Roman Egypt more broadly, one must navigate through two opposite dangers. On the one hand, one cannot simply conclude that colonization effects the "death" of an indigenous culture.[71] This kind of thinking has been implicit in work on Roman Egypt, where Persian, Greek, and then Roman occupations contributed to the supposed death of Egyptian culture. Work on Roman-Egyptian culture often trades in rhetorics of decline, whether in the "stagnation" of temple architecture or in the "long-drawn-out senescence" of scribal and religious learning.[72] In this decline model, Apion and others like him are fallen characters irreparably separated from an original, better Egyptian culture.

But on the other hand, one cannot pretend that colonization can be ignored. In the practice of anthropology in the nineteenth century, this led to a dogged quest to root out the "pure" parts of colonized cultures and ignore the places and people that were no longer unimpeachable examples of timeless indigeneity. This too occurs in Egypt, amid claims that in the hinterland Egyptian culture continued unchanged by Ptolemaic and Roman occupations. Too often, inscriptions in Ptolemaic- and Roman-Egyptian temples are presented as tidy evidence of much earlier pharaonic religion.[73]

To properly see Apion and his texts, one needs to look both to the endurance of Egyptian traditions and to the changes that Ptolemaic and Roman occupations

---

70. To paraphrase the "third space" of Bhabha (1990).

71. Bagnall (1997) is loath to discuss the Ptolemaic occupation of Egypt in the language of colonization. More recently, Moyer (2022, 173–74) cautions against an uncritical application of modern decolonization struggles to the ancient world; as he notes, this theoretical retrojection risks masking the moral frameworks that animated Egyptian resistance to Ptolemaic rule.

72. Arnold (1999, 228) for the "stagnation" of Roman-Egyptian temple architecture, Fowden (1986, 65) for the "long-drawn-out senescence" of scribal and religious traditions. See also the language of "neglect, decline, and abandonment" in Bagnall (1993, 322), forcefully rebutted by Frankfurter (1998, 12–13, 28–30), who emphasizes instead the resilience of local Egyptian religion. In the case of Hermeticism, Bull (2018, 370, 465) deftly rebuts an overuse of "decline" when confronting the changes in Roman-Egyptian temple and cult practice.

73. Much of our knowledge of key mythic cycles derives from temples of the Roman and Ptolemaic periods. Restricting oneself to Edfu, this reconstructive impulse is laced throughout Chassinat (1931) and Blackman and Fairman (1942, 1946). In this regard, the critique offered by Finnestad (1985, 5–6), to situate the temple in its Ptolemaic moment, is salutary. For Philae, see also Dijkstra (2008, 15–18), which despite its title ("the end of Egyptian religion") emphasizes transformation over decline.

made to life in Egypt. A theoretical framework built on cultural mixture can best capture this dual vision. As I have been suggesting, it is unproductive to force Apion into Greek or Egyptian frames and bemoan the Egyptian culture of which he is emblematic. His own embodiment of a mix of cultural forms and traditions offers a middle way that captures the processes of contact and creative connection characteristic of Roman Egypt.

This reevaluation of mixedness has been an important development within modern communities reflecting on colonially mediated cultural contact. So, for example, the *creolité* movement of the French Caribbean has been animated by a desire to acknowledge and celebrate, rather than ignore or bemoan, the mixed cultures produced by colonialism—even as such movements emphasize that this mixture was the product of colonizers' systematic violence. A label that creates space for mixedness is the only real answer to my opening, tendentious question about Apion's identity. Apion's Egyptianized Homer (or Homeric Egypt) is untidy. Discussions of Apion should not trade in disjunctive either/ors. Apion's authority as auto-ethnographer is derived from, and not in spite of, the blending of Greek and Egyptian in his testimonia and fragments. To call Apion an Alexandrian is not to deny that he is an Egyptian.

Terms like creolization, hybridization, and the various cognates of "mixedness" (*métissage, mestizaje*) have been differently applied and arise from different contexts, but they all, at their heart, try to recuperate designations of mixed people. The early history of labels such as creole, métis, or mestizo points to an attempt to individuate a person of mixed-race background. That this mixture is embodied is critical to the semantics of these terms, even after they widened into broader theoretical frames for mixed cultures. In other words, a diversity that consists of distinct cultural entities that reside alongside each other is not really diverse. Whether via hybridization or creolization, there has been a sustained interest in combating this juxtaposed diversity and the maintenance of cultural purity which it enables.[74] Turning from modernity to antiquity, the processes of cultural exchange and contact that took hold in Ptolemaic Egypt have been an object of focus for many who have underlined this very point.[75]

Despite these recent efforts, many discussions of Egypt in the Roman world still trade in this view of juxtaposed, but otherwise pure, Greek and Egyptian cultural domains. In this rubric, the Greek and Egyptian components of Egypt are

---

74. Among these different terms, I will use creolization and its application by Glissant. But this is not to deny the value of other theorizations, like the defense of hybridity offered by Bhabha (1994, 25 for political hybridity and 57–60 for linguistic hybridity), which also seeks to combat false narratives of purity. This differs from the narrower, teleological definition of hybridization critiqued by Glissant (1996, 18–21, and 2009, 64).

75. This has become a dominant theme in work on Ptolemaic Egypt, with too long a bibliography to list here. Of particular importance is Thompson (1988), Stephens (2003), Dieleman (2005), Jasnow and Zauzich (2005), Clarysse and Thompson (2006), Moyer (2011), Ryholt (2012), Quack (2021).

co-existing solitudes that exist alongside, but across a chasm from, each other. The traditional view of Alexandria as next to, but not within, Egypt has engraved this isolated purity. Apion's representation of Alexandria troubles this image of a sealed-off Greek city. The spaces that Apion traverses are brought into connection and collectively constitute an inherently diverse Egypt. This inextricable inter-connection of Alexandria and the rest of Egypt sets the stage for Apion's intellectual production. Apion mixed together a spectrum of intellectual traditions that cannot be completely separated into Greek and Egyptian component parts.

Apion benefits from, and is himself a benefit to, these broader theoretical discussions of cultural mixedness under systems of imperial power. Apion can enrich modern discussions of cultural mixture just as much as he is enriched by them. This starts with his unapologetic opportunism.[76] Apion was a loud promoter of his own expertise; in a very material way, Apion's ability to promote different identities opened doors that brought him fame and repute. The socioeconomic realities that shaped Apion's own culturally plural intellectual authority are important context. Apion's shameless opportunism points up a social cachet gained from cultural mixture that can add nuance and social context to wider discussions of creolized intellectual traditions.

Creolization is just one thread in this broad "mixedness" movement, but it can help recenter Apion and the tradition of Aegyptiaca.[77] Like many previously pejorative terms for mixture, the term creole has a long history. It has bounced from a historical designation to individuate those born in the New World vs. the Old, to the plank of elite "creole nationalists" during the decolonizations of the late-eighteenth and nineteenth centuries, to a linguistic term for language contact, into a broader postcolonial term to celebrate the mixed.[78] Amid this swirl of interconnected usage, the Martinican novelist, poet, and philosopher Édouard Glissant offers a defense of creolization that reveals how discussions of Apion have gone awry.[79]

> The argument that I will put before you is that the world is creolizing: that is, the world's cultures today, brought into contact with each other at lightning speed, in an absolutely conscious manner, change through exchange with each other, by

---

76. As I discuss in the Introduction, this mirroring of ancient and modern holds particularly true for the exclusivity inbuilt in elites' arrogation of a mixed identity, both by authors of Aegyptiaca like Apion and Chaeremon and by early-modern creoles.

77. Hannerz (1987) reintroduced creolization into cultural anthropology, taking it as a linguistic term. This fails to see creole's earlier usage, as a way of individuating Europeans born in the colonies from those born in Europe.

78. Baker and Mühlhäusler (2007) offer an overview of the term's movement into linguistics. Anderson (1991) developed the label "creole nationalists"; his broad application of "creole" is critiqued by Palmié (2007, 69).

79. Glissant's work belies any simple description, but Britton (1999) remains the best synopsis of his intellectual trajectory.

way of inexorable clashes, pitiless wars, but also of advances in consciousness and hope, which enable us to claim—without being utopian, or rather, by embracing utopianism—that today's human communities are engaging in the difficult process of giving up something to which they have obstinately clung for a long time: *that is, the conviction that the identity of a being is valid and recognizable only if it excludes the identity of all other possible beings.*[80]

Glissant singles out this last change of perspective—moving from a narrow to a capacious and plural identity formation—as creolization's goal. Only with this kind of identity can one push past Josephus's zero-sum critique of Apion's Greekness to a fuller appreciation of Apion's many identities. Josephus argued that Apion's Egyptian identity, itself inalienable and unalterable, necessarily excludes and delegitimates Apion's Alexandrianism and Greekness. I would argue that one does not need to accept the presentism highlighted by Glissant to appreciate the correction he is offering to zero-sum identity formation.[81] Apion reveals that this plural and non-exclusive sense of self has always been there, even as some claim it is the preserve of contemporary globalization.

The shift from creole to creolization highlights that cultural mixture is a process rather than an achieved state. It is constantly ongoing and does not reach a fixed or predetermined end. This is why Glissant stresses the "chaos-world" and its constant, unpredictable, and non-teleological contact.[82] Glissant's chaotic and unending view of cultural contact was heavily influenced by rhizomatic philosophy.[83] Rhizomes underline decentered, unending, "chaotic" collaborative processes that stand in contrast to a center-expansion, individualist model entailed by tree-based imagery. Glissant latches onto this idea to emphasize that a proper vision of cultural mixture is decentered and ongoing. In other words, Apion is not the end result of a fixed combination of Greek and Egyptian inputs that started under Ptolemy Soter. Apion's Aegyptiaca is not a predictable, set outcome when pure "Greek" and "Egyptian" cultures are mixed together. A "chaotic" vision of creolization is designed to oppose this static and fixed view of cultural connection.

Put simply, no matter when one looks in the ancient Mediterranean, mixing is already underway.[84] The pharaonic-Egyptian and classical-Greek cultures that

---

80. Glissant (2020, 6), translated from Glissant (1996, 15). Emphasis my own.

81. Apion's transit around the Mediterranean and diversity of expertise also help to rebut the different "speeds" of ancient and modern creolization proposed by Glissant (1996, 27–28).

82. As Glissant grew older, he increasingly underlined a processual and ongoing theorization of "relation." His "chaos world" borrows from scientific chaos theory to emphasize the random, ongoing quality of creolization (on which see Glissant 1996, 81–107).

83. Promoted in Deleuze and Guattari (1980, 9–37) and discussed by Glissant (1997, 195–96) and Britton (1999, 17–18).

84. In this respect, creolization's insistence on the processual and the ongoing borders on the "always-already given" formulation of Althusser (2001, 119), who stresses how we are, from our birth, already subjects in ideological systems.

48   INTRODUCING AEGYPTIACA

overshadow Apion's novel combination of Greek and Egyptian traditions were not themselves pure or born in isolation. An appreciation of the ongoing process of exchange provides welcome caution in two directions. It helps mitigate the sense that Alexander the Great's conquests were a "big-bang" moment that inaugurated cultural exchange between Greeks and Egyptians. The histories of material and intellectual exchange between Egypt and Greece extend thousands of years before Alexander.[85] The unendingness of cultural mixture also obviates the language of death and decay that haunts work on the intellectual culture of Roman Egypt. Despite its remarkable conservatism, Egyptian culture was always changing. Egypt's combination of an elasticity that admits cultural exchange and a deep cultural conservationism is what makes the later periods of Egyptian history so remarkable.

Even when cultural exchange is a process without beginning or end, the pace at which exchange takes place can accelerate. Cultures were put into contact because of the political and demographic changes of the Hellenistic and early-imperial world distinctly from, and to a greater degree than, the periods which immediately preceded them. Even though cultural exchange and mixture is a permanent fixture of the ancient Mediterranean, one can still justifiably note the new set of legal and socioeconomic frames for that mixture. A combination of Greek and Egyptian traditions is not new.[86] That said, the extent of that mixture in Apion's work and its orientation toward Rome *are* new. The introduction of Rome as a third node adds a critical ingredient that makes Apion's specific embodiment of cultural exchange, mixture, and movement even more deserving of a theoretical point of view that can accommodate it.

Movement is the operative word. Apion moved from the Oasis, through Alexandria, to Rome. In doing so, he followed a path carved by the dictates of an imperial apparatus predicated on the exchange of goods. Alexandria was the intermediary for the movement both of people and of stuff—one could only become a Roman after he or she became an Alexandrian. The geographer Strabo's opening salvo on Alexandria claims: "It is the greatest emporium in the inhabited world."[87] Keeping an eye on the imperial apparatus that facilitated movement brings together two different Aegyptiacas, the one a culturally mixed literary tradition and the other the broad label for material culture exported from Egypt to Rome. They were complementary exports. People, ideas, cults, cereals, and stones moved from Egypt to Rome through Alexandria.[88] Like Apion's auto-ethnography and the mixture of

---

85. See, for instance, the lengthy bibliography provided by Pfeiffer (2013).

86. Work on the early-Ptolemaic world makes clear that this creative combination of cultural forms has a long life. See, e.g., Stephens (2003) for Alexandrian literature, and the Greek and Demotic variants of both Greek and Egyptian literature (e.g., the Dream of Nectanebo and the Alexander Romance) discussed by Ryholt (2012).

87. Strabo 17.1.13: μέγιστον ἐμπόριον τῆς οἰκουμένης ἐστί.

88. While he focuses on the high empire, Haas (2007, 41–44) notes the economic importance of Alexandria. For a broader perspective on Rome's international trade and Egypt's importance thereto, see Tomber (2012).

Greek and Egyptian traditions it promoted, the objects that moved from Egypt to Rome were invested with a swirl of different cultural significations that is poorly served by a disjunctive and sequential (first Egyptian, then Greek, then Roman) approach to meaning and identity.[89]

Both of these Aegyptiacas must be viewed from two competing perspectives. The hybrid and dynamic identities of both author and object are best framed through creolization and its rhizomatic imagery.[90] This helps undermine the prioritization of birth used by Josephus to discredit Apion. To Josephus, movement becomes cultural erasure—Apion attempts to abandon an Egyptian identity when he moves to Alexandria. The same zero-sum game of value extends to Egypt's material culture. Obelisks become purely a sign of imperialism and exoticism as soon as they leave Egypt. In response, it is worth appreciating these objects' polyvalency and combating essentialist views of identity. But still, one must appreciate that the paths that Apion and obelisks took to Rome were well-worn. Networks of exchange are both facilitated and circumscribed by processes of imperial occupation. Roman control of Egypt is no different.

In her 2005 book, the anthropologist Anna Tsing developed the term "friction" to capture this interplay of facilitation and circumscription of exchange. She uses the metaphor of the "road" to highlight this tension: "Roads are a good image for conceptualizing how friction works: Roads create pathways that make motion easier and more efficient, but in doing so they limit where we go. The ease of travel they facilitate is also a structure of confinement. Friction inflects historical trajectories, enabling, excluding, and particularizing."[91] Both types of Aegyptiaca, the set of objects exported from Egypt and the literary genre inaugurated by Manetho, traveled to Rome on precisely this kind of road.

Since Droysen coined the term "Hellenism," there has been a belief that Hellenism could change other cultures without itself being changed.[92] With Alexander's conquest, Greek culture expanded into newly emptied spaces, and the resulting process ran only in one direction. Friction offers a welcome corrective, one that shifts away from a unidirectional and one-sided view of cultural contact. Per Tsing, "cultures are continually co-produced in the interactions I call 'friction:' the awkward, unequal, unstable, and creative qualities of interconnection across difference." In an interconnected world, cultures are co-produced. In other words, Greek culture is implicated into this image of exchange. Cultural mixture goes in both directions, if not equally.

---

89. Discussing material culture, Barrett (2019, 34–35) cautions against "dismissing Egyptian meanings, uses, and values as a priori irrelevant to Roman Aegyptiaca."

90. I use the term "identity of objects" intentionally, to put their own status on an equal level with authors of Aegyptiaca. This revaluation of nonhuman objects (so-called object-oriented ontology) is developed by Harman (2018).

91. Tsing (2005, with the two quotes at 4 and 6 respectively).

92. Droysen (1836–43). For review and analysis of its impact, see Momigliano (1994, 147–61). Chrubasik and King (2017) (particularly King 2017 and Paganini 2017) reevaluate Hellenism in the context of Ptolemaic Egypt.

Centering the cultural mixedness of the Hellenistic and imperial periods does not just help validate Apion's Egyptian identity, which is enriched, rather than problematized, by his interest in Greek intellectual culture. It also makes clear that canons of Greek literature were not shielded from the cultural contact that is a defining feature of the Eastern Mediterranean world. To Romans, Apion became an authority over intellectual traditions that are reliably Greek. For Pliny the Elder, he was the one who discussed Homer and Pythagoras. To reach further afield, Apuleius was a North-African who was one of *the* authorities over Middle Platonism.[93] Apion thus shines as bright a light on imperial Greek culture as he does on imperial Egyptian culture. His own biography particularizes a general anxiety of certain Greeks of the imperial period, that Greek culture was no longer tethered to the traditional places where it had been practiced.[94] Ethnic Egyptians could legitimately claim Greek traditions as their own. It is only amid this broad, inexorable, and constantly evolving relocation of Greek culture that the fence-building, gate-keeping, and general cultural conservatism of authors like Plutarch, Athenaeus, and Philostratus gain coherence.

Tsing and Glissant use different metaphors—road and root—to imagine the ties that connect across difference. Glissant's "roots" prioritize decentralization to promote a fundamentally "relational" and nonhierarchical creation of meaning.[95] Tsing uses the road to grapple with an interconnection that is both enabled and delimited by colonial and neocolonial systems of exchange. Apion contributes to both perspectives on cultural production under systems of power. Especially when framed against Glissant's theory of creolization, Apion is a Greek/Egyptian/Alexandrian who reconfigures and, ultimately, broadens culturally plural intellectual authority. Once we leave behind a litmus of purity and primordial authenticity, emic presentations of Egypt born under creolization emerge from Manetho's considerable shadow. Manetho's stature has kept hidden the long history of Egyptians articulating Egyptian culture in a mixed cultural vocabulary. In the chapters that follow, I will reemphasize that Aegyptiaca was not a static blip located in the early Ptolemaic period; it was instead a dynamic, "chaotic" process in dialogue with the social and economic exigencies that dictated its production. This development

93. So, for example, he wrote a handbook titled the *De Platone*. For Apuleius as Middle Platonist, see Dillon (1997, 306–38).

94. Or, to use terminology developed by Deleuze and Guattari (1980, 16–19), there is a process of deterritorialization and reterritorialization, where Greek cultural systems are dislocated from their original localities in mainland Greece and introduced to Egypt, where they are then incorporated into Egyptian systems of thought.

95. Glissant (2009) emphasizes the ethical value of "relation." It is worth noting that, like Tsing, Glissant is also keenly aware of the systems of control that shape creolization—his constant interest in the Middle Passage (discussed in Drabinski 2019) is the most obvious example of this kind of colonially controlled movement.

of Aegyptiaca is decidedly not the story of declining authority, of the death of true Egyptianness.

But even among this ongoing intellectual creativity, Apion followed a road to Alexandria and Rome that was created by systems of power and control. One can only arrive at an honest image of Apion's cultural production by seeing the unequal systems of control that put Egyptian, Greek, and Roman traditions on different footings. Whether Manetho or Apion, authors of Aegyptiaca were forced to navigate an imperial apparatus. Apion helps advance that conversation into the Roman period. Discussions of Apion's co-production of Greek and Egyptian cultures must not only account for Ptolemaic systems of inequality within Egypt, but must also keep an eye on a wider background of Roman imperial control of the Eastern Mediterranean that created new "roads" on which Apion traveled.

Apion and the other practitioners of Aegyptiaca I will go on to describe forged a new identity to best articulate Egyptian culture in (unequal) dialogue with Orientalizing Roman projections of Egypt and Egyptians. The role that such authors of Aegyptiaca had in presenting Egyptian culture to a Roman audience only emerges in a theoretical framework that gives space to their own agency. In this regard, I am deliberately leaving aside Orientalism as a theoretical strategy.[96] This is not to dispute its utility for Greek or Roman projections of an Egyptian other. It is merely to point out that Orientalism, by definition, cannot discuss people like Apion and the way they move between Orient and Occident.[97] Said ably proves that his subjects do not listen to, or have any meaningful awareness of, emic articulations of the spaces onto which the West projects Orientalizing fantasies. The same lack of awareness has been implicitly brought along with Orientalism into the ancient world. But this assumption speaks more to modern disciplinary codification—Apion resides in between Classics and Egyptology—than to the reality of the ancient world.

Mapping Aegyptiaca

Apion and others who arrogated a new, mixed Egyptian identity reveal the importance of changing Aegyptiaca from a single designation for Manetho's work to a broader, ongoing literary discourse. This wider Aegyptiaca was practiced by a range of Egyptians deploying a range of different intellectual authorities for social advancement among Ptolemaic and then Roman dynasts. Apion's specific synthesis of Homer and Egyptian paradoxography was one of many different ways that

---

96. Said (1978).

97. Parker (2011, 6–7) notes the incommensurability between actual movement of Egyptians to Rome and the quite different mechanics of Orientalism, which do not incorporate this type of human interaction.

authors of Aegyptiaca carved out authority for themselves through a mixture of Greek and Egyptian intellectual traditions. What does the terrain encompassed by Aegyptiaca look like? Who practiced it, and what did they talk about? Under what emperors? How did they represent Egypt?

The slipperiness of Apion's identity applies more broadly to the full spectrum of authors writing on Egypt. Creolization and Glissant's "root" metaphor of ongoing intercultural contact warn that policing boundaries between Greek, outsider representations of Egypt and authoritative, Egyptian auto-ethnography is untenable. There is no one set template of mixture for Greek and Egyptian contact. This spectrum of Greco-Egyptian authorial identity must also account for time. Creolization as an unbounded process helps chart a path from the early Ptolemaic period, when exogenous Greeks followed socioeconomic opportunity and migrated to the court of the Ptolemies, down into the early-imperial period and Apion.

Different authors, then, offer different definitions of what an Egyptian might be. Some of these definitions might be too loose. Hecataeus of Abdera, an exogenous ethnic Greek who moved to Alexandria and wrote a history of Egypt copied by Diodorus, is not Egyptian in the same way—or even to the same extent—as an indigenous Egyptian like Manetho.[98] The substance of their texts bear this out: Hecataeus hews more closely to Herodotean storytelling, and Manetho to Egyptian annalistic history. But that said, both authors lived in Egypt; they both blended Egyptian and Greek elements in their texts; they both wrote about Egyptian history and had reliable access to Egyptian temple archives. A comparison of Hecataeus and Manetho provokes contradictory and equally important responses: drawing firm lines around and thus making meaningful the category "Egyptian;" and appreciating Glissant's creolization, which proves that such boundary-policing is treacherous.

But no matter how you slice it, Aegyptiaca is still a substantial literary tradition: Ptolemy of Mendes, Charon of Naucratis, Lyceas of Naucratis, Asclepiades of Mendes, Chaeremon, Hermaeus, Lysimachus, Thrasyllus of Mendes, Pancrates, Seleucus of Alexandria, and Amometus all wrote on and resided in Egypt between Ptolemy Soter and Hadrian.[99] These places of origin, largely restricted to locations in the Delta, speak to the ambiguous ways in which locales in Egypt are tethered to specific identities.[100] As in Apion's Alexandrianism, the wider tradition of Aegyptiaca will reemphasize that "Greek" cities like Naucratis in fact represent a productive mixture of Greek and Egyptian culture. They are decidedly not bulwarks of unmixed and unchanging Hellenism. As a crude mechanism, such lists of now-fragmentary authors can reveal a background of cultural mixture

---

98. For Hecataeus's fragments, Lang (2012). For Diodorus's use of Hecataeus, Murray (1970) (*pace* Muntz 2008).

99. These are the toponyms assigned to these authors by Jacoby.

100. I note the tension between the fluidity of cultural mixedness and the rigidity of citizenship statuses in Roman Egypt in the Introduction.

that contextualizes a blinkered definition of Greek cultural purity endorsed by Athenaeus and other mainstays of imperial Hellenism.[101]

APION BETWEEN ROOT AND ROAD

Apion is an Egyptian who is both Egyptian and Greek. That messiness is what makes him such a productive introduction to a discourse on Egypt called Aegyptiaca. Through Apion, one can push Aegyptiaca beyond and outside the confines of Manetho. It is a tradition in part defined, rather than undercut, by its authors' propensity to participate in Alexandrian intellectual culture—in Apion's case Homeric textual criticism. These authors' dual role, both in imperial Greek intellectual history and in the presentation of Egyptian traditions, is an asset of, and not a flaw in, the definition of Aegyptiaca I will flesh out in the next chapter.

The path that Apion took to Alexandria and then Rome points in two directions simultaneously. Like grain, stone, and other material culture that were exported from Egypt, Apion followed a road to Rome that had been charted by processes of imperial occupation. Tsing's imagery of the road and of friction begin to show how the cultural co-constitution of traditions one sees in Apion's work is simultaneously enabled and circumscribed by imperial systems of control. But at the same time, Glissant's discussion of creolization challenges what has been a Venn diagram-like approach to cultural mixture in Roman Egypt. There remains an insistent belief that Greece and Egypt are circles with a delimited area of intersection. Apion's cross-cultural, synthetic work redraws that conceptual map.[102] It instead points to a new domain of Greco-Egyptian culture that created a new range of intellectual authorities. The literary tradition of Aegyptiaca was characterized by a cultural "web," in which disparate traditions were connected to each other in a constantly evolving network of exchange, contact, and mixture. This dual vision—imperial circumscription and creative, non-hierarchical cultural entanglement—is a defining feature of Aegyptiaca, which I am arguing is an identifiable literary tradition situated at the intersection of these two competing frames.

Apion's embassy on behalf of Alexandrians brought him face-to-face with the emperor Caligula. Josephus's critiques of Apion yoked together his intellectual output—particularly his views on the Exodus—and his social trajectory to Rome via Alexandria. Rome and its self-positioning against the preexisting *polis* system thus inflected the practice of Aegyptiaca. This extends well beyond Apion. All the authors of Aegyptiaca I will discuss in the following chapters also had a direct relationship with the Roman emperor, whether Caligula, Nero, Domitian, or Hadrian. This relationship between emperor and author structured Greeks' and

---

101. Thompson (2003) emphasizes the value that Athenaeus places on the Hellenism of Egypt's Greek *poleis*.

102. Glissant (2009, 64–66) critiques "hybridization" for precisely this reason.

Romans' interpretations of the texts that these authors wrote. The reverse is also true. Thus, not only was the tradition of Aegyptiaca shaped by Roman systems of power; Aegyptiaca itself helped shape those systems of power in the first place. This reciprocal interconnection of Greco-Egyptian intellectual culture and Roman justifications of imperial power is a central component of Aegyptiaca and Alexandrianism, to which I turn in the next chapter.

2

Aegyptiaca

Triangulating a Coherently Incoherent Genre

Through Apion, I have introduced the Egyptian discourse on Egypt called Aegyptiaca and suggested that it was an identifiable tradition extending beyond its first practitioner Manetho. Apion opened the door onto a broad auto-ethnographic genre—Egyptians writing in Greek about Egyptian culture for a non-Egyptian audience—whose vibrancy and importance extended into the imperial period. As a tradition that combined various genres, Aegyptiaca is difficult to pin down. The flexibility and cultural mixture that characterize Apion and his work were constitutive features of Aegyptiaca and its authors.

Apion's own brand of literary expertise thus gives way to Aegyptiaca's much wider terrain. In the interconnected web of creolizing intellectual traditions through which I am defining Aegyptiaca, different authors occupied different coordinates. Chaeremon, the Balbillus family, and Pancrates—the subjects of this chapter—brought together a different mix of Egyptian and Greek genres in different ways. The literary heterogeneity exemplified by these authors' works, and fundamental to Aegyptiaca, has been poorly served both by the boundary-setting around "historian" in Jacoby's *Fragmente der griechischen Historiker* and by the very literal separation of these authors into multiple versions of themselves along the fault lines that separate their Greek and Egyptian intellectual activity.[1]

Two competing themes arise when Aegyptiaca is viewed synoptically, rather than through individual exemplars like Manetho or Apion. On the one hand, there

---

1. Of the authors discussed in this chapter, Chaeremon (618), Thrasyllus (622), and Pancrates (625) receive entries in *FGrH* (and its update *BNJ*), and Tiberius Claudius Balbillus and Julia Balbilla do not. Thrasyllus's astrological fragments are excluded from his entry in *FGrH*, as are the Pancrates discussed in Lucian and the magical papyri. The different Balbilluses identified in the *PIR* (discussed below) are the clearest example of this separation.

56   INTRODUCING AEGYPTIACA

was no one set template to write Aegyptiaca. There is more to Aegyptiaca than Apion's Egyptianized Homer, or Manetho's annalistic history, or even the entire succession of Egyptian authors contained in Jacoby. Aegyptiaca brought several different Egyptian knowledge traditions together: Egyptian religion, presented in both natural-philosophical and mythological terms; Alexandrian intellectual culture, of which Apion, Chaeremon, and other authors of Aegyptiaca were mainstays in the imperial period; Egyptian history, variously investigated through pharaonic annalistic genres, paradoxography, epic poetry, and religious history; and technical genres like astronomy, pharmacology, and mathematics, which were born of the cultural mixture of Egypt's Hellenistic period. Grammatically and substantively, Aegyptiaca is plural.

But on the other hand, there is some coherence here. All of the Egyptians discussed in this chapter shared a direct—if sometimes transitory—connection with the Roman emperor. Aegyptiaca as a mixed literary tradition became symptomatic of the processes of social change that Egyptians capitalized on for advancement, but traditionalist Romans frequently bemoaned. Biographical trajectories that brought these authors to positions of bureaucratic prominence and to the emperor's inner circle adumbrate the way that their texts were viewed. These authors strategically presented Egyptian culture—its astrological knowledge, its priestly learning, its history of kingship—in a way that served the purposes of Rome's emperors, who increasingly relied on Egypt for ideological justification of sole rule. In this respect, the Hellenistic backdrop of Aegyptiaca prefigures imperial-era authors. Manetho navigated how best to tell Egypt's story to a new Ptolemaic regime keen to take advantage of Egyptian forms of imperial self-expression. This same dynamic continues in the work of Chaeremon, the Balbilli, and Pancrates, all of whom presented their own texts under the same set of motivations. The tension between these two facets of Aegyptiaca—its wide-ranging subject matter and the consistency of its authors' biographies—is the "coherent incoherence" I discuss in this chapter.

CHAEREMON THE EGYPTIAN PHILOSOPHER

The questions of identity that Apion posed continue as one moves on to other authors of Aegyptiaca. Chaeremon, the tutor of Nero, Stoic philosopher, and Egyptian sacred scribe, benefits from the same indeterminacy of identity.[2] Just like Apion, one can ask whether he should be called a Greek or Egyptian or Alexandrian, because like Apion different scholars have variously applied these labels to him. Jonathan Tracy calls Chaeremon an ethnic Greek, Elena Manolaraki calls him

---

2. To paraphrase the list of Chaeremon's identifiers offered by Moyer (2011, 242n136). Chaeremon is frequently cited, but rarely discussed. For the most recent scholarship on Chaeremon, see van der Horst (1982, 1984), Barzanò (1985), Frede (1989), and Rodríguez (2007).

Egyptian, and both identify him as an Alexandrian.[3] This ambiguity lays bare, once again, the difficulty of hierarchizing the different elements—citizenship, language, place of birth, education—that constitute identity labels like Greek, Alexandrian, and Egyptian. Chaeremon's slippage across different cultural domains extends to the texts that he wrote, which have a threefold interest in Greek, Egyptian, and blended Greco-Egyptian knowledge traditions. Chaeremon is most frequently cited for his *Hieroglyphica*, an explanation of the hieroglyphic script that highlights the philosophical and cosmological concepts built into hieroglyphic signs. Such a text would certainly have been popular for a Roman audience, given the ubiquity of hieroglyphic-inscribed Egyptian and Egyptianizing objects across Italy.[4]

But in addition to claiming Egyptian authority via the *Hieroglyphica*, Chaeremon also wrote about Greek language and literature. His treatise on Greek expletive conjunctions (think "certainly" or "indeed") does not sound like the most scintillating text.[5] But like Apion's textual criticism, it rubber-stamped Chaeremon's position of authority as a grammarian in the Alexandrian mold. The Suda, a Byzantine encyclopedia, is admittedly not the most reliable source, but it still claims that Chaeremon ran the Alexandrian libraries, embassies, rescripts, and letters.[6] While the historical accuracy of this claim is debatable, the assignation of so many core Alexandrian responsibilities proves that Chaeremon successfully cemented an association with Alexandrian administration and intellectual culture that stood the test of time.

There is more promising evidence for Chaeremon's Alexandrian connections. He appears in one of the best documentary sources for Rome's relationship with imperial Alexandria. The papyrus in question (P. Lond. 1912) contains the emperor Claudius's letter to the Alexandrians, written in 41 CE. In it, he responds to a series

---

3. Tracy (2014, 260), where he specifies that Chaeremon is an ethnic Greek based on his name. Elsewhere (9, 43, 174) he opts for "Alexandrian polymath." Manolaraki (2013, 107) calls Chaeremon "Egyptian" (ditto Moyer 2011, 242n136; cf. the "Memphite" of Frankfurter 1998, 225), though Manolaraki later (108) fleshes that out with the label "Alexandrian Stoic philosopher."

4. I discuss Chaeremon's explanation of hieroglyphic in detail in chapter 5. Swetnam-Burland (2015, 41–53) analyzes hieroglyphic inscriptions created *de novo* in Italy and calls attention to the Egyptians in Italy—Chaeremon included—who facilitated their creation.

5. Per *BNJ* 618 F 9. Chaeremon's work on conjunctions is mentioned by the famous Alexandrian grammarian Apollonius Dyscolus in his definitive work *On Syntax* (p. 515 in the Bekker numeration derived from the *Anecdota Graeca* v. 2, though better consulted through the standard edition, Schneider 1878, 248).

6. Per Suda δ 1173, s.v. Διονύσιος Ἀλεξανδρεύς = T 4, which claims that Dionysius succeeded Chaeremon as head of libraries, department of letters, embassies, and rescripts. For the Suda as source for testimonia and fragments, see Vanotti (2010), and particularly the discussion of Jacoby's use of the Suda in Schepens (2010, 9–11). Unless otherwise noted, I use van der Horst (1984) for text and numeration of Chaeremon's testimonia and fragments, and translations are my own. Where important, I will compare the numeration of Keyser (2014) (*BNJ* 618).

of requests made by Alexandrian ambassadors.[7] After solicitously offering golden statues, a holiday, and a temple to honor Claudius's ascension to power, the Alexandrian petitioners had tried to pin all responsibility for the ongoing Alexandrian riots on Jews, rather than themselves. In the bulk of the letter, Claudius thanks the Alexandrians for the honors, but denies their request for a *boulê* and refuses to clear them of all blame in causing the riots. Claudius's diplomatic response includes Chaeremon's name among the list of Alexandrian ambassadors who authored the original petition.[8]

Here again, Chaeremon checks the same box as Apion, who had also represented Alexandrians to Claudius's predecessor Caligula during the riots of 38 CE. As in that case, Chaeremon's standing as an Alexandrian ambassador seems to be connected to his activity as an author, particularly his pro-Egyptian history of the Exodus. Chaeremon's Exodus account also receives vitriolic criticism from Josephus in the *Against Apion*.[9] The social unrest in imperial Alexandria, where the struggle for Roman support led to tension and violence, creates similar templates for Apion and Chaeremon, who wrote texts disparaging Jews of the Exodus and represented Alexandrian citizens in an embassy to the emperor.

Where Apion broadcast culturally mixed Alexandrian expertise through an Egyptianized Homer, Chaeremon made a name for himself as a Stoic philosopher and exegete of Egyptian priestly life.[10] His central position in Alexandrian intellectual culture, bolstered through his grammatical knowledge and his repute as a philosopher, helped him move to Rome in 48 CE, when he became Nero's tutor at the request of Nero's mother Agrippina.[11] This privileged position brought Chaeremon even greater renown and solidified his epithet "the Stoic." When the Roman epigrammatist Martial cracked a joke at Chaeremon's expense, he used this moniker (*Chaeremon Stoice*, 11.56.1) to help his punchline land: given the miserable, poor life that Chaeremon had led (poor bedding, gnats, unwarmed hearth, black

---

7. For text, see Smallwood (1967, n370). Łukaszewicz (1998) explains Claudius's response through his familial connections to Egypt.

8. Most (Stuart Jones 1926, 18; van der Horst 1984, ix; *ad* T 5; and Osgood 2011, 65) agree that the Chaeremon listed is the same as Chaeremon the philosopher-priest. Several (Rodríguez 2007, 56; Keyser 2014, *ad loc.*) hedge their bets. The letter (P. Lond. VI 1912) mentions Chaeremon at line 17. Bilde (2006, 199) situates the letter in the social unrest that spanned from 38 CE (Apion's deputation) to 41 CE (Chaeremon's deputation).

9. Joseph. *Ap.* 1.288–93 = F 1, who suggests that Chaeremon closely followed Manetho's account, locating the Exodus under Amenhotep and his son Ramesses, which is a creative, but historically incorrect, lineage.

10. Chaeremon is a *philosophus*, and specifically a Stoic, in T 9, F 10, F 11. For Chaeremon's self-positioning as a philosopher and priest who performs to Roman expectations of Eastern wisdom, see Moyer (2011, 269–70).

11. Note that, as Barzanò (1985, 1987–88) and Frede (1989, 2075–76) make clear, Chaeremon was primarily a philosophical tutor. See also the discussion of Rodríguez (2007, 54–67), which takes the appointment as a point of departure for a larger account of Chaeremon's biography and Nero's connections to Egypt.

bread), Chaeremon's Stoic acceptance of death was far less impressive.[12] Porphyry and Eusebius, who also call Chaeremon a Stoic, are more generous. Porphyry ranks Chaeremon as a preeminent Stoic, and Eusebius claims that Chaeremon and Cornutus were the key sources of Greek allegoresis from whom the Alexandrian Christian Origen drew inspiration.[13]

Chaeremon actively leveraged his reputation as a philosopher to strengthen his claims to privileged knowledge of Egyptian priests. That composite expertise was critical to his intellectual authority and is indirectly reflected by the variety of titles ascribed to him. Chaeremon is variously called a Stoic, a philosopher, and a sacred scribe (*hierogrammateus*), the last an upper-level priestly position.[14] This mixture of philosophical and priestly knowledge continues in his extant fragments, which present Egyptian priests in a deliberately philosophical vocabulary to harmonize Greek and Egyptian wisdom-seeking. There are questions about Chaeremon's cultural authority that crop up when he tries to naturalize a mixed philosopher-priest. One is forced to ask whether Chaeremon's philosophical portrait of Egyptian priestly life is an outsider, and ultimately Greek, image of an Egyptian knowledge tradition. That is something I will return to in chapter 6; for now, it is important to see how Chaeremon's domain of intellectual authority, as a Stoic philosopher and exegete of hieroglyphs and priestly wisdom, broadens the intellectual ambit of Aegyptiaca.

Astrology and Aegyptiaca's Other Cultural Exports

Chaeremon's specific interest in the mixed philosopher-priest broadens the areas of expertise associated with authors of Aegyptiaca like Manetho and Apion. When Chaeremon's work is kept in view, Egyptian priests shift from a shorthand for emic authority to real practitioners of a technical knowledge that Chaeremon suggests is equally central to Greek philosophical and Egyptian religious wisdom traditions. Jerome provides a valuable view onto Chaeremon's characterization of that technical knowledge: "Chaeremon the Stoic, a most eloquent man, says about the life of the ancient Egyptian priests that, laying aside all the business and cares of the world, they were always in the temple and they surveyed the nature and causes of things, and also the calculations of the stars."[15] Chaeremon segues from the general contiguity of philosophers and priests to one specific intellectual tradition where they converge. Per Chaeremon, priests broadly contemplate "the nature and origin of the world" (*rerum naturas causasque*). But at least in Jerome's recapitulation,

---

12. Mart. 11.56 = T 10.

13. Porph. *Abst.* 4.8 = F 10; Euseb. *Hist. Eccl.* 6.19.8 = T 9.

14. He is called a sacred scribe in T 6, F 4, F 12, F 13. Note that in Josephus's recapitulation of Chaeremon's Exodus account, Joseph and Moses are called *hierogrammateis*, which is meant to connote magical and prophetic expertise, on which see Catastini (2010).

15. Jerome *Jov.* 2.13 = F 11: Chaeremon stoicus, vir eloquentissimus, narrat de vita antiquorum Aegypti sacerdotum, quod omnibus mundi negotiis curisque postpositis semper in templo fuerint et rerum naturas causasque ac rationes siderum contemplati sint.

60 INTRODUCING AEGYPTIACA

this broad and (in the case of Lucretius's *De Rerum Natura*) generic title for philosophical investigation narrows into the contemplation of the stars. Even as one should not invest too much in Jerome's exact phrasing, this sequence is illustrative.

Within the general mixture of "contemplation" that allows Chaeremon to centralize the "philosopher-priest," astronomy is the specific discipline where Egyptian and Stoic technical traditions coalesce. This point of connection expands the intellectual domains that I have claimed belong to Aegyptiaca. The stars can provide a solid foundation on which to trace the interconnectedness of Egyptian and Greek approaches to technical knowledge.[16] As one moves across the Hellenistic and imperial periods, this interconnection evolves into an entirely mixed tradition over which authors like Chaeremon exercised authority.

Astronomy and astrology loop in a wider set of Egyptians who wrote about Egypt's knowledge traditions.[17] Authors of Aegyptiaca wielded an astrological expertise that guaranteed them popularity in Rome, where everyone from Tiberius to cheating housewives demanded accurate horoscopes.[18] Two names in particular, the legendary and historically nebulous Nechepso and Petosiris, became synonymous with this kind of Egyptian astronomical authority. Their reputations were well established in the Roman-imperial world: Pliny cites them as informants in his discussion of astronomy; the epigrammatist Lucillius presents Petosiris as the yardstick against which subsequent astrologers measured themselves; Juvenal, in a fit of not uncharacteristic hyperbolic indignation, complains that Romans refused even to leave their houses unless Petosiris's text permitted it.[19] Nechepso's and Petosiris's fame as Egyptian king and priest, respectively, lent them pharaonic bona fides on which their authority and popularity were built. In Porphyry's introduction to Ptolemy's *Apotelesmatica*, Petosiris is one of the "elders" (*presbuteroi*) who were foundational authors of astrology.[20] But the actual text that circulated under his name, the second-century BCE *Astrologoumena*, is clearly the product of a Hellenistic, Greek-language, culturally mixed tradition.[21]

---

16. The section of Méla et al. (2014) on the sciences (395–535, Marganne and Aufrère 2014 especially) is a good introduction to the intercultural scientific production of Alexandria.

17. Especially in Hellenistic Egypt (per Neugebauer 1975, 5), astrology and astronomy were closely connected, with the former as a practical application of the latter. Accurate horoscopes depended on geometric astronomy and the measurement of planetary movement, on which see Evans (1998, 343–44).

18. Cumont (1937) remains a helpful introduction, with a structure that connects the key astrological traditions with relevant source texts. His introduction (13–21) traces astrology's dissemination from Egyptian sources to its Greco-Egyptian practitioners in Alexandria.

19. Pliny: *HN* 2.88, 7.160; Lucillius: *Anth. Pal.* 11.164; Juvenal: 6.575–81.

20. On Porphyry's reconstruction of the astrological tradition, see Gundel (1966, 214).

21. Such is convincingly argued by Moyer (2011, 228–48), who locates the Petosiris and Nechepso material at the intersection of a longstanding indigenous astronomical tradition and intensifying contact between Babylonians, Egyptians, and Greeks in the Late, Ptolemaic, and early imperial periods. For dating of the Nechepso-Petosiris material, see Cramer (1954, 17–18). For an overview of Nechepso and Peto-

The Suda's entry on Petosiris gets the point across: "Petosiris, Egyptian, philosopher. Just like the Greeks and Egyptians he arranged *Selections on the Gods from the Sacred Books, Astrological Matters,* and *Concerning the Mysteries among the Egyptians*.[22] This last text, which promised to publicize privileged knowledge kept hidden in Egypt, is the stuff of Aegyptiaca. It hews closely to the authority over Egyptian arcana that Manetho and Chaeremon claimed. The pithy label "Egyptian philosopher" dovetails with Chaeremon's own self-presentation as a Greek philosopher who had access to restricted spaces of Egyptian priestly knowledge.

Shifting to the stars moves Aegyptiaca outside and beyond the traditional boundaries imposed by the dictates of modern scholarship. Jacoby's collection of fragmentary historians is an invaluable repository for authors like Manetho, Apion, and Chaeremon. But its designation of Aegyptiaca depends in large part on Josephus and the specific context of intellectual antagonism between Jews and Egyptians of the imperial period. That is important background for Aegyptiaca, one that has shaped my own discussion of Apion and Chaeremon so far. But it is far from the only thematic mainstay for Aegyptiaca. Straying outside Jacoby brings in new mixed intellectual traditions that were integral to Aegyptiaca. Particularly through this frame of astrology, it is easier to see the wider list of Egyptian authors whose multiculturism undergirded their intellectual output.

THE BALBILLI AND THE GREEK FACE
OF EGYPTIAN AEGYPTIACA

Juvenal hates the weight that Romans assign to Egyptian astrologers. Amid the long-winded, misogynistic screed of his sixth satire, he singles out astrology for criticism:

> Be mindful to avoid meeting the kind of woman . . . who will not go along when her husband seeks camp and home, *should she be recalled by Thrasyllus's numbers*. When it's her pleasure to be carried to the first milestone, the appropriate hour is chosen from a book. If the corner of her little eye itches when rubbed, she demands salves upon consultation with her horoscope. Should she be lying sick in bed, *no time is more fit for food than the one which Petosiris has given*.[23]

---

siris more generally, see Gundel (1966, 27–36) (with astrological filiation at fig. 2), and for fragments, Riess (1892). See too Ray (1974), Neugebauer (1975, 567–68), Keyser (1994), and Zucker (2014, 417).

22. Suda π 1399 = T 1 *Nechepsonis et Petosiridis reliquiae* ed. Riess: Πετόσιρις, Αἰγύπτιος, φιλόσοφος, καθὰ Ἕλληνες καὶ Αἰγύπτιοι τὰς περὶ θεῶν διετάξατο ἐπιλογὰς ἐκ τῶν ἱερῶν βιβλίων, Ἀστρολογούμενα, καὶ Περὶ τῶν παρ' Αἰγυπτίοις μυστηρίων. Note that there are textual problems in the passage, and Adler's (1928) edition of the Suda is preferable to Riess's (1892) edition of the Petosiris and Nechepso fragments.

23. Juv. 6.572–81: illius occursus etiam vitare memento / . . . quae castra viro patriamque petente / non ibit pariter numeris revocata Thrasylli. / ad primum lapidem vectari cum placet, hora / sumitur ex libro; si prurit frictus ocelli / angulus, inspecta genesi collyria poscit; / aegra licet iaceat, capiendo nulla videtur / aptior hora cibo nisi quam dederit Petosiris. Text is that of Clausen (1992).

62   INTRODUCING AEGYPTIACA

To make his point, Juvenal names two astrologers popular among Romans. I have already mentioned Petosiris, *the* authority on horoscopes for Greeks and Romans.

The other name, Thrasyllus, opens up new terrain. Thrasyllus, like Chaeremon and Apion, was an Alexandrian elite whose expertise helped him advance to Rome, where he became the personal astrologer of the emperor Tiberius.[24] His reputation grew especially because, though Tiberius had long since banished the practice of astrology in Rome, Thrasyllus's cozy relationship with the emperor had shielded him from this blanket proscription.[25] He and Tiberius were attached at the hip after their meeting in Rhodes, where Thrasyllus finally persuaded Tiberius of his own ability as a prophetic astrologer. Suetonius, with his typical flair for the dramatic, tells of their meeting at Rhodes during Tiberius's self-imposed exile:

> At that time Tiberius very much tested the astrologer Thrasyllus, whom he had attached to his retinue as a teacher of wisdom. Thrasyllus affirmed that when a ship was spotted good news was being brought—at the very moment when Tiberius had made up his mind to hurl Thrasyllus into the sea while they were taking a walk together, on the grounds that Thrasyllus was a liar and rash confidant in his secrets, what with things turning out adversely and against predictions.[26]

The anecdote was popular enough that both Tacitus and Cassius Dio also mention the same basic story, even if the prophetic moment by which Thrasyllus saved himself differs across accounts.[27] As a bilingual inscription from Smyrna reveals, the subsequent friendship was close enough that Thrasyllus received Roman citizenship and became Tiberius Claudius Thrasyllus.[28] Thrasyllus charted a path that began in Alexandria, progressed through Greece, and ended in Rome. Like Apion's movement around Greece as a Homerist, Thrasyllus cemented an Alexandrian expertise that offered him paths of movement around Greece. But unlike Apion, Thrasyllus's Roman enfranchisement highlights the concrete importance of citizenship status for Alexandrians hoping to make a move to Rome.

Thrasyllus was a more prominent figure than many realize. According to Frederick Cramer, the preeminent scholar of Greco-Roman astrology, "Thrasyllus the Alexandrian must be considered not only as one of the most versatile, but also one

---

24. For background, see Gundel (1966, 148–51) and Tarrant (1993, 7–11).

25. On Tiberius's expulsion of 16 CE, see Tac. *Ann.* 2.27–32. Ripat (2011, esp. 122–23 on Thrasyllus and his son Balbillus) cautions against this traditional narrative (laid out by, e.g., Cramer 1954, 232–48) of blanket expulsion of astrologers. This is fair, though one might push back against her rigid distinction (123) between professional and amateur astrologer.

26. Suet. *Tib.* 14.4: Thrasyllum quoque mathematicum, quem ut sapientiae professorem contubernio admoverat, tum maxime expertus est affirmantem nave provisa gaudium afferri, cum quidem illum durius et contra praedicta cadentibus rebus ut falsum et secretorum temere conscium, eo ipso momento, dum spatiatur una, praecipitare in mare destinasset. Text is that of Kaster (2016).

27. For the anecdote, see Tac. *Ann.* 6.21 and Dio Cass. 55.11, with Krappe (1927) and Oliver (1980).

28. *CIL* 3.7107, and Tarrant (1993, 9).

of the most profound scholars of his era."[29] Thrasyllus's intellectual authority as an astrologer was rooted in an Egyptian self-presentation. His own work imitated the Nechepso/Petosiris material. The scholia to the above Juvenal passage call Thrasyllus "another Petosiris" to make explicit his Egyptian intellectual lineage.[30] Per the corpus of Greek astrological papyri: "Also regarding the seven-zoned planetary system Thrasyllus divides it according to the *paradosis* of Nechepso and Petosiris, as he himself says."[31] This technical language easily distracts from Thrasyllus's Egyptian cultural signaling. Seven-zoned systems and *paradosis* are alienatingly technical. But this should not mask the ways in which Thrasyllus leverages an association with the exemplars of an Egyptian astrological tradition for social advancement in Rome.

Beyond astrology, Thrasyllus wore many hats. Plutarch offers evidence that is tantalizing and murky in equal measure. He mentions a Thrasyllus—from the Egyptian town Mendes—who wrote an Aegyptiaca that included fun facts about the Nile's stones:[32] "Other stones are also produced in it that are called *kollôtes*. Swallows collect them at the time the Nile rises, and build the so-called Swallow Wall, which restrains the rush of the water and does not allow the land to be destroyed by the flood, as Thrasyllus records in his *Aegyptiaca*."[33]

This is strange stuff.[34] It is challenging to square a swallow-oriented Thrasyllus with the astrological Thrasyllus I have been discussing so far. Stanley Burstein's entry in *Brill's New Jacoby* treats this Thrasyllus independently from and without reference to the astrologer. When faced only with the Plutarch anecdote, Burstein doubts the historicity of this Thrasyllus of Mendes.[35] Plutarch's specific ascription of the swallow anecdote to Thrasyllus is certainly uncertain. But when it is looped into the evidence available for the astrologer Thrasyllus, I am inclined to agree with Richard Tarrant, who suggests that an interest in the Nile was likely a part of the astrologer Thrasyllus's wide-ranging expertise.[36]

---

29. Cramer (1954, 93).

30. Riess (1892, F 4).

31. *CCAG* VIII.3.100, ll. 19–20: διαλαμβάνει δὲ καὶ περὶ τῆς ἑπταζώνου κατὰ τὴν Πετοσίρεως καὶ Νεχεψώ, ὡς αὐτός φησιν, παράδοσιν. The astrological fragments of Thrasyllus are also available in Tarrant (1993, 242–49).

32. This is the Thrasyllus discussed in *BNJ* 622 (Burstein 2015). Burstein doubts the historicity of this Thrasyllus.

33. Plut. *De Fluv.* 16.2 = *BNJ* 622 F 1 (Burstein 2015 for text and translation): γεννῶνται δὲ καὶ ἄλλοι λίθοι κόλλωτες καλούμενοι. τούτους κατὰ τὴν ἀνάβασιν τοῦ Νείλου συλλέγουσαι χελιδόνες, κατασκευάζουσι τὸ προσαγορευόμενον Χελιδόνιον τεῖχος, ὅπερ ἐπέχει τοῦ ὕδατος τὸν ῥοῖζον, καὶ οὐκ ἐᾷ κατακλυσμῷ φθείρεσθαι τὴν χώραν, καθὼς ἱστορεῖ Θράσυλλος ἐν τοῖς Αἰγυπτιακοῖς.

34. Interestingly, it is not totally coming out of left field. Swallows that block up the Nile occur already in Pliny (*HN* 10.94), who does not cite a source.

35. Burstein (2015), who adduces as evidence the tenuous historicity of *all* authors cited in the *De Fluviis* (on which see Cameron 2004, 127–34).

36. Tarrant (1993, 7n11).

64   INTRODUCING AEGYPTIACA

Pliny the Elder offers evidence that bridges Thrasyllus's otherwise *outré* river-rock interests in Plutarch with his more securely attested astrological expertise. A passage on sea snakes and their poisonous bites in Pliny's *Natural History* includes the opinions that Thrasyllus had on the matter: "Thrasyllus reports that nothing is as good against snake bites as crabs, and that pigs bitten by snakes heal themselves by eating crabs, and that snakes are in torment when the sun is in Cancer."[37] This is even stranger, if wonderfully typical of Pliny. But odd claims about snake torture notwithstanding, this citation of Thrasyllus is more difficult to dismiss as a fabrication. The pivot toward Cancer and the zodiac connects up this discussion of crabs and snakes with the world of astrology, for which Thrasyllus was better known and more widely cited. The shared interest in animals and aquatic life puts the Plutarch and Pliny citations of Thrasyllus in the same general area. At the end of the day, the risk of circularity (using Pliny's Thrasyllus to confirm Plutarch's Thrasyllus, which bolsters Pliny's Thrasyllus) necessarily makes any mutual identification of these different Thrasylluses tentative.

But both Pliny's and Plutarch's citations of Thrasyllus are important nonetheless. There is risk on both sides—in rashly connecting these Thrasylluses together *and* in insistently isolating different Thrasylluses according to their area of expertise. Pliny shows just how messy and interconnected intellectual traditions like pharmacology and astrology were. Thrasyllus's astrological expertise was multifaceted enough to range into the specifics of crab remedies and snake torture. Plutarch's confident subsummation of the swallow-wall story under the generic category of Aegyptiaca is illustrative, even if its Thrasyllan authorship has been debated. The Plutarch passage reveals the heterogeneous anecdotes and intellectual domains that ancient authors arrayed under Aegyptiaca's aegis. In other words, Plutarch's loose use of Aegyptiaca as a post hoc, catch-all term is precisely the point. Even if they were not originally a part of a text called *Aegyptiaca*, swallows and Nile rocks came to be two among many staves that propped up the generic label "Egyptian things."

To return to surer ground, Thrasyllus is most famous as a philosopher. As Juvenal's mention of "Thrasyllus's numbers" suggests, his expertise lay in between areas typically denoted by astrology and philosophy. His knowledge of the predictive power of numbers is owed to Pythagoreanism, a philosophical school whose interest in number theory was well-known in antiquity. In a similar vein, Thrasyllus canonized the works of the atomist Democritus and helped establish Democritus's debt to Pythagoreanism.[38] But Thrasyllus's most famous "canonization" stems from his expertise as a Platonist. He divided the Platonic corpus into groups of

---

37. Plin. *HN* 32.55: Thrasyllus auctor est nihil aeque adversari serpentibus quam cancros; sues percussas hoc pabulo sibi mederi; cum sol sit in cancro, serpentes torqueri.

38. Tarrant (1993, 95–107 for his specific tetralogies, 148–77 for Neopythagoreanism), though see also Cramer (1954) for intersections with his career as astrologer.

four. While this legacy might not sound impressive, Thrasyllus's tetralogies laid the foundation for the renaissance of Platonic philosophy in the early-imperial period. In short, Thrasyllus helped create the Platonic corpus we know today.[39] As in his astrological work, Thrasyllus's impact on the intellectual development of imperial philosophy is significant.[40]

The heterogeneity of Thrasyllus's expertise across philosophy and astrology and (potentially) astro-pharma-herpetology has flown under the radar. He reveals two issues that have undercut the prevalence and recognizability of Aegyptiaca. First, different scholars focus on different elements of Thrasyllus's intellectual portfolio. As with Chaeremon, Thrasyllus ably moved between his philosophical and astrological expertise. But unlike Chaeremon, these two facets of Thrasyllus's authority have been discussed in two different disciplinary contexts that prioritize two different versions of Thrasyllus. The one is rooted in a Greco-Egyptian astrological tradition that reaches back to Petosiris. In the other, Thrasyllus's importance as a Platonic and Pythagorean philosopher puts him squarely in the domain of imperial Greek culture. The results of these two very different discussions of Thrasyllus and his work are unfortunate. While those who approach Thrasyllus solely from the perspective of the history of philosophy should not be expected to parse the cultural semantics of astrology, the partition of Thrasyllus's Alexandrian origins, astrological expertise, and contributions to Platonism has hidden the places where the multiculturalism and intellectual history of the imperial period intersect.

Thrasyllus is the first of three generations of Balbilli that leveraged a creolized Egyptian identity for both advancement up the ranks of Roman power and intellectual cachet as authors of Aegyptiaca. First Thrasyllus, then his son Tiberius Claudius Balbillus, and finally his great-granddaughter Julia Balbilla all deployed a mixed Greek and Egyptian identity, and all became personal confidants of the Roman emperor. There has been a stark disciplinary divide that has separated them from Manetho, Apion, Chaeremon, and others canonized by Jacoby. But both sides are equally important examples of how Aegyptiaca operated, the way it wove together cultural traditions, and the social advancement that it facilitated for its authors.

Like Father, Like Son: Tiberius Claudius Balbillus

Tiberius Claudius Balbillus, likely if not definitively Tiberius Claudius Thrasyllus's son, followed in his (putative) father's footsteps.[41] The need for this string of

---

39. Here, I follow Tarrant (1993), who argues for Thrasyllus's impact on the Platonic corpus. Tarrant (11–17) defends Thrasyllus's potential role in establishing the tetralogies (per Diog. Laert. 3.56) in the face of scholarly arguments to the contrary.

40. The scholia to the above-quoted Juvenal passage (*ad* 6.576, Wessner 1931, 111) identify Thrasyllus as a preeminent Platonic philosopher.

41. I take a "monist" approach (following Cichorius 1927; Cramer 1954, 95; and Gundel 1966, 151) and identify one Balbillus out of the four different attestations listed in Stein et al. (1933–2015,

66   INTRODUCING AEGYPTIACA

caveats is telling. The methodological nitty-gritty of piecing together a person's single biography from disparate attestations has erased multicultural identities and heterogeneous authority. Only those with a real stomach for imperial proso-pography, where one argues about whether Balbillus "a" is the same as Balbillus "b," have waded into the different facets of Balbillus's biography and intellectual output. This has, quite literally, created different "Balbilli," whose careers and texts have been separated out from each other. So, for example, the authoritative compendium for such work, the *Prosopographia Imperii Romani*, lists four different Balbilli for the period between 40–60 CE, each of which emerges from a different cultural and political context.[42] One was a prefect of Egypt. A different Balbillus was well-known for his astrological work. A third Balbillus had a diplomatic career as procurator under Claudius. Yet another Balbillus participated in the same Alexandrian deputation to Claudius as Chaeremon did.

The criteria that scholars have used to stitch together (or ravel out) these different Balbilluses minimize his heterogeneous expertise. Arthur Stein, the editor of the Balbillus entry in the *PIR*, argues that the bureaucrat of Egypt Balbillus cannot be the same as the astrologer Balbillus, largely because he thinks dabbling in astrology would be unseemly for a Roman official.[43] But as Hans-Georg Pflaum has shown, this denial of multivalent authority is entirely modern.[44] It is far from uncommon that somebody who was a bureaucrat in Egypt, with a position in the Library of Alexandria, would draw on those bona fides to write astrology. There is certainly good reason to be cautious before claiming that all attested Balbilluses of the 40s, 50s, and 60s CE are one and the same. But methodological caution easily slips into disciplinary value judgments (like Stein's) that erase multicultural authority.

It is important at the outset to clarify that, even if some elements of Balbillus's life are sketchy—whether our Balbillus is the son of Thrasyllus; whether the chronology allows our Balbillus to be the same as the Alexandrian ambassador of 41—there is a core and uncontested biography that locates him solidly in the domain of Aegyptiaca. According to both Tacitus and a dedicatory inscription from Ephesus, he was an official in Egypt in charge of "the sacred groves and all sacred locations in Alexandria and in all Egypt, and in charge of the museum and library in Alexandria, and high priest to Hermes of Alexandria."[45] The laundry list

---

PIR B 38, C 813). Even if one is more conservative and admits only that Balbillus was both an astrologer and prefect of Egypt (the argument preferred by Schwartz 1949, 46–47 and Pflaum 1960–1961, I.40), Balbillus would still be a participant in Aegyptiaca, as an author on Egypt with a biographical connection to Alexandria.

42. Stein et al. (1933–2015, *PIR* B 38, C 813). Note that this excludes the now common datum (included in his *OCD* entry, Scullard and Levick 2012) that Balbillus was Thrasyllus's son, on which see Tac. *Ann.* 6.22.4, below.

43. See also Stein (1933, 126–27), a standalone article that makes the same argument.

44. Pflaum (1960–1961, I.38–39).

45. Tac. *Ann.* 13.22 names Balbillus as the prefect of Egypt under Nero. For his posts in Alexandria listed in the dedicatory monument of Ephesus (I. Eph 3042), see the reconstruction of Smallwood

of appointments not only speaks to the power that a prefect of Egypt had as the representative of Rome. It also, like Manetho's, Apion's, and Chaeremon's similar appointments in the library and temples, became the basis for Balbillus's intellectual output. In this regard, it is essential to know that, other ambiguities notwithstanding, the same person was a prefect of Egypt and used that position to strengthen his legitimacy as an astrologer.

So this is what a biography of Balbillus likely looks like: some evidence for his early life in Alexandria appears in the same letter from Claudius to the Alexandrians that had mentioned Chaeremon.[46] In the letter, which is dated to 41 CE, Balbillus appears as an Alexandrian delegate who single-handedly received approval from a hesitant Claudius to erect a gold statue of the "Claudian August Peace."[47] The promise of a gold statue apparently launched Balbillus into a successful career and Claudius's good graces. As the Ephesus inscription outlines, he was awarded the illustrious *hasta pura* during Claudius's invasion of Britain in 43 CE and then took up an important position handling the various appeals that squabbling Greek city-states constantly made to Rome. Then came the final coup. Balbillus returned to Egypt, where Nero appointed him prefect from 55–59; the *praefectus Aegypti* was the head of Roman rule in Egypt and one of the most important positions in Roman administration. Because of the implicit threat that the position posed, the prefecture was restricted to equestrians and was tightly controlled by the emperor. Augustus had executed Gallus, the first Roman to oversee Egypt, after his power in Egypt threatened to eclipse Augustus's.

Balbillus apparently owed this extremely remunerative post to Agrippina, Claudius's wife and Nero's mother. Tacitus (*Ann.* 13.19–22) suggests that Agrippina gave Balbillus the post because he had helped smooth things over after Agrippina's first fight with Nero. Beyond his overarching position as prefect of Egypt, Balbillus advertised other key positions in Alexandrian intellectual culture: he was a high priest of Hermes and he oversaw the Library of Alexandria and Museum. Through this mélange of positions, the political and intellectual begin to blend together: Balbillus was the face of an external Roman administration

---

(1967, n261a). There is a lacuna in the dedication, but the posts in Alexandria are secure. For a restoration of the text that includes "Balbillus, son of Thrasyllus," see Cichorius (1927, 104).

46. P. Lond. VI 1912. Due to dating issues, Schwartz (1949, 47) and Pflaum (1960–1961, I.40) prefer to identify this Alexandrian ambassador as an identically named father of our Balbillus. They do not believe that Balbillus could be a representative of Alexandria in 41 CE and the grandfather of Julia Balbilla, whose poems are firmly dated to 130 CE. I follow Rosenmeyer (2018, 142), and find this timeline possible, if Balbillus was relatively young as an ambassador and Julia Balbilla was roughly contemporary in age to her travel companions Hadrian and Vibia Sabina (and thus born sometime in the 70s or 80s CE).

47. P. Lond. VI 1912 lines 35–7 (Smallwood 1967, n370). Balbillus is mentioned (as Τιβέριος Κλαύδιος Βάρβιλλος) in the opening list of ambassadors in line 16 and is later singled out for the statue-request in line 35.

68   INTRODUCING AEGYPTIACA

to Egyptians; to Romans, his connections to the library and to Egyptian temples explained his mastery of Egyptian astrological knowledge.[48]

Just as his biography overlaps with the curriculum vitae of Chaeremon, his intellectual career imitated Thrasyllus's. He too gained fame as an astrologer. Tacitus touts the similarity of Thrasyllus and Balbillus. After his description of Thrasyllus's attachment to Tiberius, Tacitus concludes by remarking that Thrasyllus's son is a chip off the old block: "Naturally, that the reign of Nero was predicted by the son of this same Thrasyllus will be recalled in due course, lest I stray too far now from the present undertaking."[49]

Balbillus was able to provide timely advice to Nero when a comet seemed to predict Nero's impending demise. Suetonius's sensationalist account of the episode implicates Balbillus in Nero's "creative" solution to this astrological conundrum: "Nero, anxious about that fact [that the comet presaged his death], decided on death for every particularly high-born person after he learned from the astrologer Balbillus that kings commonly averted such portents and cast them off of themselves onto the heads of nobles by slaughtering some illustrious person."[50] Balbillus provides an astronomical justification for Nero's tyrannical purge of Rome's elite. Through this justification, he leverages the practices of Hellenistic kings for the benefit of Nero and the still inchoate foundations of the principate. Balbillus, like other Alexandrian Egyptians, was able to deploy an expertise particularly well suited to the precarious position of the emperor. The practices of Ptolemaic dynasts provide the solutions to the problems faced by an emperor widely resented by senatorial elite. The same had been true with Thrasyllus and Tiberius, whose relationship was predicated upon Thrasyllus's ability to provide an Egyptian and celestial justification for the rule of an otherwise quite unpopular emperor. A clear connection emerges between Balbillus's particular skill set (using the stars to justify sole rule in Egypt) and Nero's famous devolvement into paranoid tyranny.

There is intriguing, if scanty, evidence that Balbillus's intellectual activity ventured beyond astrology. According to Seneca, Balbillus also discussed the wonders that he saw in Egypt. In the *Naturales Quaestiones*, a Stoic account of nature that includes a lengthy description of the Nile, Seneca cites Tiberius Claudius Balbillus as witness and chronicler of an unbelievable fight between dolphins and crocodiles. The incredibility of the episode (a pitched battle between species) continues the animal wonders that had been the stock in trade of Apion. Apion's Greek perspective on Egypt's wonders was proof, in Gellius's eyes, of Apion's mastery of

---

48. Cumont (*CCAG* VIII.4.234 n. 1, ll. 3, 10, 233) makes precisely this argument, presenting Balbillus's reliance on Egyptian months as evidence of his attempts to cement his position as an expert in the Egyptian astrological tradition.

49. Tac. *Ann.* 6.22.4: quippe a filio eiusdem Thrasulli praedictum Neronis imperium in tempore memorabitur, ne nunc incepto longius abierim. Text is Heubner (1994).

50. Suet. *Ner.* 36.1: anxius ea re, ut ex Balbillo astrologo didicit, solere reges talia ostenta caede aliqua illustri expiare atque a semet in capita procerum depellere, nobilissimo cuique exitium destinavit.

Greek culture.[51] The same is true in the case of Balbillus. When Seneca cites Balbillus's story, he calls him "Balbillus, the best of men, singularly expert in every type of study."[52] The obvious flattery should not mask Seneca's ascription of polymathy to Balbillus. However fleeting, this animal anecdote creates a connection between Balbillus and Apion that recenters animal paradoxography as yet another stave supporting Aegyptiaca.

Through Balbillus, one begins to see how Egypt was both an intellectual font of astrology and a politically important site for the ideological defense of the emperor.[53] This combination of the political and the intellectual is secure, even if some elements of Balbillus's biography are subject to disagreement. The hazards of prosopography and the asterisks it requires us to place on reconstructed biographies should not hide that which the available evidence *does* illustrate: that Balbillus was both a bureaucrat who occupied important posts in Alexandria and the inheritor of a culturally mixed intellectual tradition whose Egyptian prestige was vouchsafed by Nechepso and Petosiris. These two facets of Balbillus's career undergird the wider importance of Aegyptiaca as a politically motivated, colonially framed, multicultural intellectual tradition.

Memnon in Creolization: Julia Balbilla and the Poetics of Aegyptiaca

Tiberius Claudius Balbillus's granddaughter, the Hadrianic poet Julia Balbilla, also offers valuable (if biased) proof of her grandfather's intellectual achievements. In one poem, she refers to her grandfather as "Balbillus the wise." The medium is more important than the message. The reference to her grandfather comes from the set of four epigrams she—like so many other visitors to the statue—carved onto the base of the statue of Memnon.[54] The inscribed epigrams were made during the visit of Hadrian and his wife Vibia Sabina to Thebes in 130 CE. Julia Balbilla, like her grandfather and great-grandfather, was closely tied to the emperor and his wife, with whom she traveled as they made their way around the empire. She is an imperial Greek poet whose high valuation of archaism and the classical past fit in well with Hadrian's noted philhellenism.[55] Writing in the second century CE, she binds the Greco-Egyptian mixture constitutive of Aegyptiaca to the prac-

---

51. Most notably, his tales of Androcles and the lion (*BNJ* 616 F 5) and of the boy and the dolphin (F 6). For Gellius's discussion of Apion's learnedness, see chapter 1.

52. Sen. *Nat. Quaest.* 4a.2.13: Balbillus, virorum optimus perfectusque in omni litterarum genere rarissima. . . . Text is Oltramare (1961).

53. My own emphasis on this Egyptian astrological tradition and its popularity in Rome is not meant to discount the importance of the other cultures (the Chaldeans/Babylonians, most notably) whose astronomical traditions influenced Egyptian, Hellenistic, and Roman astronomy.

54. For cultural and literary analysis of the epigrams (including their panegyric of Hadrian, debt to the epigrammatic tradition, and exemplification of imperial-era classicism), see above all Rosenmeyer (2018, 141–69). See too Edmonds (1925), Ippolito (1996), Brennan (1998), and Sonnino (2016).

55. Rosenmeyer (2018, 155–57) (cf. 2008, 347–52) collocates these archaisms and Aeolicisms.

70   INTRODUCING AEGYPTIACA

tice of imperial Hellenism and the ever-widening territory denoted by the term Second Sophistic.[56]

Balbilla offers a face of Hellenism that cannot be disassociated from the range of other eastern Mediterranean traditions with which it is bound up. Her ancestry is Commagene on her father's side and Egyptian through her maternal line, which stretches back to Balbillus. In both her Egyptian and Commagene heritage, there is a thoroughly blended Greekness. The Hellenistic kingdom of Commagene, in southeastern Asia Minor, was a site of mixture between Greek, Syrian, and Parthian cultures.[57] As in Ptolemaic Egypt, Numidian North Africa, and so many other places in the Hellenistic Mediterranean, Commagene upper elite adopted a Greek cosmopolitanism. They looped themselves into the Hellenistic world through "glocal" Hellenizing material culture and marriage with other mixed Greek elite.[58] Balbilla stands at the end of a long process through which Greece was embedded into and coextensive with a range of other cultural contexts. As such, she helps reveal that creolization is not a teleological synthesis that produces one set type of mixed identity. Her adroit use of her Greek, Egyptian, and Commagene backgrounds—and the way those backgrounds support her own elite social position—reflect well the double-edged history of creolization, which is a type of cultural mixture wielded specifically by elites. Balbilla's identity is indissociably Greek and Egyptian, even as it is distinct from her grandfather's similarly indissociable combination of Greek and Egyptian backgrounds.

Balbilla sits atop the porous boundary separating Aegyptiaca from cognate genres. Balbilla's Egyptian identity is secure, even as she was likely a visitor to rather than resident of Egypt. Her poetry, inscribed on Memnon, is at once very deliberately not available to a wide external readership and composed with a targeted non-Egyptian audience of two in mind—Hadrian and Vibia Sabina. Her only partial participation in the definition of Aegyptiaca I have defended so far provides real stakes to the otherwise abstract challenges posed by a coherently incoherent tradition. Through Balbilla, one must hold onto, but not grip too tightly, the categories Egyptian, Egyptian traditions, and external audience that constitute Aegyptiaca. Balbilla is an Egyptian positioning herself as a translator addressing Memnon on behalf of a non-Egyptian audience. She arrogates authority via a performance of emic knowledge of Egyptian geography and religion. She thus

---

56. Philostratus, the originator of the term (*VS* 1 pref. 481), was denoting the rise of epideictic oratory, on which see Schmitz (1997, 13–14) and Whitmarsh (2001, 41–44; 2005, 4–5). But the term has come to describe almost all imperial Greek intellectual culture (cf. Johnson and Richter 2017).

57. This mixing of Greek and local cultural traditions is also evident in Antiochus I and his funerary and religious program at Nemrud Dağ, discussed by Versluys (2017b, 108–84).

58. The collected essays in Quinn and Prag (2013) (particularly Fentress 2013 and Quinn 2013) shine a light on this dynamic. For "glocal" as a denotation of the mixture of the local and the globalizing, see the defense of the term by Robertson (1995).

continues in the spirit of Aegyptiaca, while still interweaving elements of inscribed verse epigram that cannot be easily folded into the practice of Aegyptiaca.

The four poems she left on the statue offer rare evidence for inscribed verse epigram written by a woman. She deploys Aeolicisms and invocations of the Muses to put her own elegiac stamp on Sapphic poetry and the tradition of classical lyric.[59] She trades in similar tropes of the immortality of subject and poet through poetry. Her reuse of the poetry-as-monument theme plays on the poem's placement on the statue of Memnon, the eternal monument par excellence. This reception of Sappho and lyric poetry by imperial-era women like Julia Balbilla is a fascinating story well-discussed by scholars like Emily Hemelrijk and Patricia Rosenmeyer.[60]

The poem also displays how Julia Balbilla uses the figure of Memnon to celebrate a constellation of Greek and Egyptian cultures that is central to her own sense of self as granddaughter of a mixed Greco-Egyptian person. One poem, written for Vibia Sabina, draws this in clear colors:

> When I was beside Memnon with the Lady Sabina:
> Memnon, son of Dawn and old Tithonus,
> Sitting opposite Thebes, Diospolis,
> Or alternatively Amenoth, Egyptian king, as Egyptian priests
> who know ancient lore name him,
> Hello! In singing may you eagerly welcome her,
> The august wife of the emperor Hadrian.
> A barbarian cut off your tongue and ears,
> That godless Cambyses; with a baneful death
> He paid the penalty, struck by the tip of the same sword
> With which he pitilessly slew the divine Apis.
> But I don't believe that this statue of yours could be destroyed,
> And I henceforth keep in my mind a soul forever immortal.
> For my parents and grandparents were reverent,
> Balbillus the wise and king Antiochus,
> The former the father of my kingly mother,
> And king Antiochus, father of my father.
> From them I too obtained noble blood,
> And these verses are my own, Balbilla the reverent.[61]

---

59. The specific coordination of Aeolic Greek and elegiac distichs is a rare combination whose significance Rosenmeyer (2008, 351–55) has investigated. She demonstrates that Balbilla's debt to Sappho is far from straightforward.

60. Hemelrijk (1999, 113–14, 157–63) and Rosenmeyer (2008 and 2018, 159–68). Cf. also Bowie (1990, 61–66).

61. 29 (ed. Bernand and Bernand 1960, 86–92): Ὅτε σὺν τῇ Σεβαστῇ Σαβείνηι ἐγενόμην παρὰ τῷ Μέμνονι. Αὔως καὶ γεράρω, Μέμνον, πάι Τιθώνοιο, / Θηβάας θάσσων ἄντα Διὸς πόλιος, / ἢ Ἀμένωθ, βασίλευ Αἰγύπτιε, τὼς ἐνέποισιν / ἴρηες μύθων τῶν παλάων ἴδριες, / χαῖρε, καὶ αὐδάσαις πρόφρων ἀσπάσδε[ο κ]αῦτ[αν] / τὰν σέμναν ἄλοχον κοιράνω Ἀδριάνω. / Γλωσσαν μέν τοι τμᾶξε [κ]αὶ ὦατα βάρβαρος ἄνηρ, / Καμβύσαις ἄθεος· τῶ ῥα λύγρῳ θαγάτῳ / δῶκέν τοι ποίναν τὤτωι ἄκ[ρῳ] ἄορι πλάγεις / τῷ νήλας Ἄπιν κάκτανε τὸν θέϊον. / Ἀλλ᾽ ἔγω οὐ δοκίμωμι σέθεν τόδ᾽ ὄλεσθ᾽ ἂν ἄγαλμα, /

72   INTRODUCING AEGYPTIACA

The epigram opens with a creative mixture of mythological and historical background that is the bread and butter of Aegyptiaca in its narrower, history-writing valence. She names Memnon first in his Greek mythological guise, as the heroic son of Eos and Tithonus who went off to fight in Troy in the now-lost *Aethiopis*. She then pivots to an Egyptian historical frame, naming Memnon as Amenoth, an Egyptian king. Memnon thus bridges Egyptian-historical and Greek-mythological realms and binds them together into one identity. A classicizing Memnon cedes the floor to a flexible mythological system that naturalizes multiple identities.[62] From the outset of the poem Julia proves that traditional mechanisms of appropriating Greekness—like using stylized dialecticisms—exist alongside, rather than compete against, the poem's celebration of a specifically Egyptian form of archaism.[63]

The poem's opening puts this cultural pluralism front and center. The first sentence offers up two different names for the same person, one Greek and one Egyptian. In doing so, Julia Balbilla poeticizes polyonymy. The social reality of Egypt incentivized name-changing among its population. Egyptians took on Greek names for social advancement into Greek positions. Similarly, Greeks moved between names to navigate the different legal and tax systems that had been set up for the Greek and Egyptian inhabitants of Egypt.[64] Julia Balbilla repurposes polyonymy from a quotidian part of social life in Egypt into a tool for broad mythological and cultural translation. Memnon, like authors of Aegyptiaca who move between Egyptian and Greek cultural frames, yokes together different traditions. Julia Balbilla's inclusion of both Memnon and Amenoth underlines her authority over both Greek and Egyptian reference points.

Memnon/Amenoth is the first example of a poetics of translation that runs throughout the poem. This translation takes place on multiple levels. Most basically, Balbilla offers different words that denote the same person or place. So, for example, she provides both an emic and an etic name for Thebes. First she chooses the etic term "Thebes," a name that had no traction within Egypt but was commonly used outside it. She soon provides an emic gloss, using the internal and administratively accurate name Diospolis. The latter is a closer Greek translation of the city's Egyptian name, "The city of Amun" (*njwt-Jmn*). Through Diospolis, the Egyptian semantics of city (*njwt*) are translated into Greek (*polis*) and a god's identity is translated from Egyptian (Amun) to Greek (Zeus/Dios). Even if

---

ψύχαν δ' ἀθανάταν λοῖπϙν ἔσωσϙα νόϙ. / Εὐσέβεες γὰρ ἔμοι γένεται πάπποι τ' ἐγένϙντο, / Βάλβιλλος τ' ὁ σόφος κ' Ἀντίοχος βασίλευς, / Βάλβιλλος γενέταις μάτρος βασιλήϊδος ἄμμας, / τῶ πάτερος δὲ πάτηρ Ἀντίοχος βασίλευς· / κήνων ἐκ γενέας κἄγω λόχον αἷμα τὸ κᾶλον, / Βαλβίλλας δ' ἔμεθεν γρόπτα τάδ' εὐσέβε[ος].

62. In this regard, I am building on the observation of Rosenmeyer (2008, 350) that Balbilla's mixed background colors her otherwise typically Second-Sophistic penchant for mastering genealogies and mythologies.

63. For example, Αὔως, τὼς, and πάι Τιθώνοιο. Rosenmeyer (2018, 158) notes the interconnection of linguistic archaism and this Egyptian genealogy of Memnon.

64. A phenomenon well discussed in Coussement (2016), who restricts herself to the Ptolemaic period.

Diospolis is in some ways "authoritative" within Egypt, this denotation of Diospolis as "emic" might rankle: even the Egyptian version of Thebes is Greek. It is worth acknowledging the changing terrain on which I am positioning "emic" and "etic." Julia Balbilla, residing in the second century, shows the limits of categories like "interior" and "exterior" and "emic" and "etic." Balbilla's poetry provokes competing desires. On the one hand, I want to acknowledge that an emic and culturally authoritative explanation can use a Greek word. On the other, it is important to admit that Diospolis points to an act of erasure, through which the Egyptian term (*njwt-Jmn*) is given no space in Balbillla's specific alternation between an Egyptian (but Greek language) Diospolis and a non-Egyptian (but *still* Greek language) Thebes. Balbilla's act of translation is messy, but a translation nonetheless.[65]

The alternation of Memnon and Amenoth also represents a redrawing of "authoritative" and "exterior." I mentioned the broad cultural translation between historical/Egyptian and mythological/Greek. But the specific denotation of "Amenoth" deserves attention.[66] As in the Thebes/Diospolis pair, the interior and "Egyptian" alternative is rendered in Greek. The Egyptian Amenoth and Greek Memnon are both written in Greek, even as Memnon is "etic" and imposed from outside and Amenoth is emic and marked out as an authoritative Egyptian identification. But where Diospolis translates, Amenoth transliterates. The transliterated Amenoth allows the Egyptian referent, its Egyptian sound, to remain intact in ways distinct from the thoroughgoing translation between Amun's town and Zeus's polis. Transliteration is an elusively simple translational strategy. Amenoth, like transliteration more broadly, is an asymptote that approaches but never fully crosses the boundaries delineating inherited pharaonic culture. The placement of the poem on an object which so obviously *did* include Egyptian-language texts amplifies this interplay between the emic authority of names transliterated from Egyptian to Greek (Amenoth), that transliteration's role in cross-cultural syncretism (Memnon/Amenoth), and that syncretism's distance from the pharaonic presentation of a king's name in hieroglyphic in a cartouche (*Nebmaatre Amenhetep*).

In a basic sense, Balbilla's Egyptian identification of Memnon as Amenoth is correct, however troublesome that word might be. The statue in question was originally a funerary monument for the Eighteenth-Dynasty king Amenhotep III (Greek *Amenôphthis*, Egyptian *nb-mȝ't-r' Jmn-ḥtp*) that stood in front of his now-lost mortuary temple on the west bank in Thebes. Balbilla's ability to elucidate this background and identify the statue as this Egyptian king is more impressive than it looks. Very few references to any Amenhotep exist in Greek literature.[67] None comes before Manetho, who first names him as a king of the Eighteenth Dynasty.

---

65. It thus shares in the same dynamics of translation that animate Pliny's *osiritis-cynocephalia* gloss (chapter 1).

66. Rosenmeyer (2018, 18n48) notes the authors who make this identification. In poem 31.2, Balbilla switches to Phamenoth (Φαμένωθ), likely confusing king with month.

67. References are rare; Pausanias makes the link after Julia Balbilla. Other mentions (Dorotheus of Sidon, Thessalus, and Plutarch) are for the Egyptian month Φαμένωθ, not the king.

74 INTRODUCING AEGYPTIACA

Then Chaeremon and Josephus pick him up, when the Exodus story was often slotted into the Eighteenth Dynasty.[68] But these are the only references until Julia Balbilla. The type of knowledge that is associated with Manetho's Aegyptiaca and learned expositions of Egyptian traditions are on display in Julia Balbilla's poetry, even as she is never associated with Manetho or with the authoritative exposition of "rubber-stamped" Egyptian history accessed via Egyptian priests.[69] Balbilla's ability to identify Amenhotep as Amenhotep rather than Memnon substantiates these claims to authoritative sources.

After this initial display of translation between Greek and Egyptian frames, the poem uses the language of barbarism to align Greece and Egypt on one side against the Persian Cambyses. Balbilla reemphasizes a tradition that reaches back to Herodotus, where Cambyses's invasion of Egypt is folded into the larger narrative of Greece's fight with Persia. An Egyptian/Persia antipathy that contrasts an impious, Apis-bull-slaughtering, Memnon-defacing barbarian Cambyses with norms of Egyptian religiosity bleeds into a different binary, one between a Greek self and a Persian other.[70] The structure of Herodotus's Histories yokes these two different Persian barbarisms together: Persia is simultaneously the reviled invader of Egypt and of mainland Greece. Greece and Egypt blur into each other through their common enemy.

In other words, when Cambyses defaces the statue and cuts off its ears and nose, he is committing a sacrilege against both the Egyptian Amenhotep and the Greek mythological Memnon. An external barbarian cements the interconnection of Greek and Egyptian identities that is applicable to Memnon and Balbilla alike. Balbilla reapproaches a very classical theme (Persia as a foil through which to define Greekness) and underlines its potential for a world in creolization. Cambyses's barbarism paves the way for the poem's denouement. Balbilla reassures Memnon that she is reverent in all the ways that Cambyses, who murdered Egypt's sacred cow and defaced Memnon, was not. She vouchsafes her reverence through the broad and culturally plural background that she proceeds to cite. Not least, she is uniquely appreciative of Memnon because of her grandfather Balbillus. This reverence, in the confines of the poem, is suitably fuzzy. It is narrowly a declaration of piety, a rejection of Cambyses's cruelty. But her piety is introduced by, and then leads to, the culturally plural background of addressee and author alike. As Patricia Rosenmeyer has persuasively argued, Balbilla's arrogation of nobility and reverence emerges directly from her appreciation of Memnon's and Thebes's different names.[71]

---

68. Joseph. *Ap.* 1.288–93 = Chaeremon F 1.

69. 29 ed. Bernand and Bernand: τὼς ἐνέποισιν / ἴρηες μύθων τῶν παλάων ἴδριες.

70. Depuydt (1995) seeks to move beyond a Herodotean view of Cambyses as Apis-slaughtering madman (3.27–33) to Egyptian evidence, most of which paints him as a fine inheritor of pharaonic practices, including properly burying (rather than murdering) the Apis bull. That does not erase his legacy in Greek literature as an external ruler who aligned himself against, rather than naturalized his power through, Egyptian culture.

71. Rosenmeyer (2018, 158–59).

The address, then, represents a broad mandate of cross-cultural appreciation. Memnon, as half-ruined monument grandly standing near Thebes, becomes the patron god of mixture and of interconnected Greek and Egyptian intellectual traditions.

PANCRATES'S MANY FACES: TOWARD A METHODOLOGY OF CREOLE AEGYPTIACA

Julia Balbilla is not the only author of Aegyptiaca to deploy Egyptian culture to praise Hadrian. Per Athenaeus, Pancrates was "a poet, one of the inhabitants of Alexandria."[72] Like Chaeremon and Tiberius Claudius Balbillus, Pancrates had a position in the Museum that he was able to secure by flattering the emperor. The successful bit of flattery is preserved in Athenaeus: when walking with Hadrian in Alexandria, Pancrates pointed out a red lotus. He then claimed that the red lotus grew out of the ground because of the blood spilled by a lion killed by Hadrian and his lover Antinous in a hunt they had undertaken the previous year. Pancrates suggested the flower be named "Antinoeis" in honor of Hadrian's beloved, which charmed Hadrian and secured Pancrates a comfortable job. Pancrates's typically Alexandrian mode of learned sycophancy complemented his other work, which mixed together Greek and Egyptian traditions.

Athenaeus's different citations of Pancrates bear out this mixture.[73] In two different passages Athenaeus names two texts written by Pancrates: one is an epic poem on Bakenrenef, a famed Egyptian king.[74] Bakenrenef was one of the last pharaonic kings before the Persian occupation, a position that explains both his reputation among later Egyptians as a paragon of good rule and the pessimistic prophecies of coming destruction that are associated with his reign.[75] The other text is an epyllion that narrates Hadrian's apparently well-known Libyan lion hunt. Both poems were indebted to both Greek and Egyptian perspectives. His epic poem on Bakenrenef further combined authentically Egyptian annalistic history with an Herodotean discourse on Egyptian kings.[76] His lion-hunt epyllion participated both in a slender aesthetic long associated with Alexandrian poetry and in pharaonic traditions of royal hunts.

---

72. Ath. *Deipn.* 15.21 = *BNJ* 625 T 1: Παγκράτης τις τῶν ἐπιχωρίων ποιητής.

73. Athenaeus's Alexandrian and Hellenizing portrait of Pancrates builds on his similar treatment of Apion, which I discuss in chapter 1.

74. Markiewicz (2008) lays out the different (and often contradictory) associations Greek and Roman authors made with Bakenrenef.

75. Most famously, the Prophecy of the Lamb alluded to both in Manetho and in a different Greek-language Egyptian annalistic history (P. Lips. Inv. 590 and 1228, with Popko and Rücker 2011). For text and translation, see respectively Zauzich (1983) (cf. Chauveau's 2017 reedition and discussion) and Simpson (2003, 445–49). For introduction, see Quack (2009, 176–78), and for more in-depth discussion, see Thissen (1998 and 2002), who situates it in the pessimistic and apocalyptic literary traditions.

76. Bakenref is mentioned (as Βόκχωρις/Βόκχορις) four times by Diodorus (1.45.2, 65.1, 79.1, 94.5, with Markiewicz 2008, 313–14) and four times by Plutarch (*Vit. Demetr.* 27.11, 13, *DIO* 354b, *De vit. pud.* 529e).

76   INTRODUCING AEGYPTIACA

Very little from either work survives. A traditional interest in now-fragmentary authors would dictate that scholars try to systematically reconstruct now-lost work from the fragments that are extant.[77] That is nearly impossible with Pancrates, given the absolute paucity of surviving fragments. But that does not mean that Pancrates is unimportant. Pancrates's individual texts might be sketchy in their details, but his cross-cultural intellectual output is still securely attested. This fact of culturally plural polymathy can be a complementary object of scholarly focus for fragmentary authors poorly served by the "here's how his work would have looked like" approach.

Pancrates amplifies a central argument of this chapter: that an otherwise dry prosoprographic process of linking attestations is a necessary prerequisite for a broader reevaluation of the breadth and range of expertise of culturally mixed Alexandrians. The latter requires the former. Juxtaposing the different cultural traditions signposted by different fragments plays to the strengths of these authors' haphazard state of preservation in ways that a reconstructive approach cannot. Aegyptiaca's importance as an ongoing literary tradition only comes to the fore by synoptically surveying the generic range of its authors' literary activity. One might not know with absolute precision the details of any one of these activities. But one *can* know that Pancrates's authority circumscribed them all.

The Pancrates discussed by Athenaeus wrote an epyllion in honor of Hadrian and Antinous and an epic poem on a famed Egyptian king. That is all that is included in the Pancrates canonized in Jacoby.[78] But there are other contexts for Pancrates: he is mentioned both by the humorist Lucian and in the corpus of magical texts collected under the label "Greek Magical Papyri" (*PGM*). The magician Pancrates who appears in the *PGM* shares many of the same features of the Pancrates discussed by Athenaeus.[79] Purely on the basis of dating, the magician Pancrates is a very near contemporary of Athenaeus's Pancrates. Pancrates's encounter with Hadrian in Athenaeus is firmly dated to 130 CE; the specific text—the Paris Magical Papyrus—that mentions the magician Pancrates is a compendium that is excerpting from an original work reliably dated to the mid-second century CE.[80] Even more convincingly, the magician Pancrates also fields a meeting with Hadrian in Egypt, which would sync up the two Pancrateses to the year.

---

77. This has been called a "bio-bibliographic approach," whose origins are well outlined by Dionisotti (1997). Gumbrecht (1997, 316–18) traces this scholarly trend back to c. 1800 and the romanticization of ruins, which provide a material foundation to complementary processes of imagination and "restitution" (323) of fragments' original whole.

78. Burstein (2016), who only includes these two passages—one as testimonium, one as fragment.

79. Stanley Burstein (2016 *ad* T 1) argues for the "probable identification" of Athenaeus's Pancrates with three other attestations.

80. For *Quellenforschung* on the Paris Magical Papyrus, see Preisendanz and Henrichs (1973–1974, 64–65) and LiDonnici (2003, 144, esp. n10). Kuster (1911) first proposed a second century CE original on which the surviving codex was based.

The relevant section of the larger magical compendium discusses a spell of attraction. As the text promises, the spell "inflicts sickness excellently and destroys powerfully, sends dreams beautifully, accomplishes dream revelations marvelously and in its many demonstrations has been marveled at for having no failure in these matters."[81] In the narrative flow of the text, Pancrates is a practitioner who proves the spell's potency and accuracy in a demonstration to Hadrian:

> ... Pachrates, the prophet of Heliopolis, revealed the power of his own divine magic to the emperor Hadrian. For the spell attracted in one hour; it made someone sick in two hours; it destroyed in seven hours, and sent the emperor himself dreams as he thoroughly tested the whole truth of the magic within Pachrates's power. And marveling at the prophet, he ordered double fees to be given to him.[82]

The opening phrase contains two striking differences from Athenaeus's Alexandrian Pancrates. First, the name itself is spelled differently: this magician is Pachrates, not Pancrates. The change is a subtle but nevertheless illustrative tweak in transliteration. The Egyptian name that is typically transliterated as Pancrates is *pȝ-ḥrd*, "the one who belongs to the (Horus) child."[83] To make the name legible to a wider audience, the Greek spelling "Pancrates" opted for a much looser adaptation: the Egyptian definite article *pȝ* becomes the unrelated, but well-known Greek prefix "pan;" the Egyptian sound "*ḥ*" turns into a kappa to render the well-known and semantically attested suffix -krates. In other words, social comprehensibility is the priority. The translation to Pancrates moves the name further from its Egyptian equivalent, but fits in more naturally as a Greek name with Greek semantics: to put it crudely, it is a name that means something in its Greek version. The magical papyri transliterate, rather than translate, the Egyptian name. "Pachrates" directly transliterates the definite article *pȝ* and more accurately denotes the Egyptian sound *ḥ* with the more phonically accurate suffix -chrates. In the cultural context of magical papyri, which like astrology were a mixed Greco-Egyptian tradition, Pachrates can be referred to with a name that is Greek in spelling but still Egyptian in meaning. Pancrates/Pachrates is a small variation that speaks volumes about the socio-linguistic work at play in rendering Egyptian people's names in different Greek versions in different cultural contexts.

---

81. Translation from Betz (1986). Text and numeration from Preisendanz and Henrichs 1973–1974. *PGM* IV.2443–6: κατακλίνει γενναίως καὶ ἀναιρεῖ ἰσχυρῶς, ὀνειροπομπεῖ καλλίστως, ὀνειραιτητεῖ θαυμαστῶς καὶ ἐν πλείσταις ἀποδείξεσιν ἐθαυμάσθη οὐδεμίαν ἔγκλισιν ἔχουσα τούτων.

82. *PGM* IV.2449–55: Παχράτης, ὁ προφήτης Ἡλιουπόλεως, Ἀδριανῷ βασιλεῖ ἐπιδεικνύμενος τὴν δύναμιν τῆς θείας αὐτοῦ μαγείας. ἦξεν γὰρ μονόωρον, κατέκλινεν ἐν ὥραις β΄, ἀνεῖλεν ἐν ὥραις ζ΄, ὀνειροπόμπησεν δὲ αὐτὸν βασιλέα ἐκδο<κ>ιμ<ά>ζοντος αὐτοῦ τὴν ὅλην ἀλήθειαν τῆς περὶ αὐτὸν μαγείας· καὶ θαυμάσας τὸν προφήτην διπλᾶ ὀψώνια αὐτῷ ἐκέλευσεν δίδοσθαι.

83. For this change, see Preisendanz (1942, 2072); cf. Lüddeckens (1983, 211; 1986, 411). As they note, this variation between Pancrates and Pachrates is relatively common in Ptolemaic and Roman Egypt.

78   INTRODUCING AEGYPTIACA

Second, different toponyms connect Pancrates to different places to underline different areas of expertise. To denote Pancrates's bona fides as a magician, the magical papyrus claims he is from Heliopolis, a city in the Delta synonymous with inherited traditions around Egyptian religion ever since its importance as the cult center of Old-Kingdom solar religion.[84] To denote Pancrates's status as a Greek poet, Athenaeus claims he is from Alexandria. This distinction speaks more obviously to the way that places of origin (Heliopolis, Alexandria) are used as fungible frames through which to view an author's authority and expertise. The same was true for Manetho, who was a resident of Alexandria but whose expertise in Egyptian culture was underlined by his position as a priest of Heliopolis.[85] These places of origin and areas of authorial expertise reinforce each other. Pancrates's residency in Alexandria (in Athenaeus) and Heliopolis (in the magical papyri) are invoked to highlight his Greek and Egyptian expertise, respectively. But these different areas of expertise also are used to reconfirm circularly that Alexandria should be associated with Greek culture and Heliopolis with Egyptian culture. This choice of Pancrates's origin is not a static or stable historical fact. It is a signifier of identity that was flexible and responsive to generic context: a thumb pin on Glissant's conceptual map of creolization.

Beyond the different vantages onto Pancrates offered by these variations in name and place of origin, the spell hews remarkably closely to the biographical precis that Athenaeus offered. According to Athenaeus, Pancrates's offer to name a red lotus after Antinous had impressed the emperor enough to secure Pancrates a comfortable position in the Museum. In the spell, Pancrates's prophetic magic is impressive enough that Hadrian grants him "double fees." As Daniel Ogden has noted, there is an obvious syntactic similarity between Athenaeus's anecdote and the magical papyrus.[86]

These two attestations of Pancrates—one by the collector of Greek culture Athenaeus and the other in the magical papyri—speak more readily to the intellectual flexibility of Egyptian authors of Aegyptiaca than to an improbable coincidence of two different Egyptian advisers of Hadrian named Pancrates. Suggesting that the two passages refer to the same person is not to deny that they are either (a) not independent of each other or (b) only marginally truthful accretions onto the same historical persona. But the broad verisimilitude of the anecdotes is more important than legislating their strict historicity. Pancrates could reasonably appear to win over Hadrian both through a traditional display of magic and through

84. That history is laid out succinctly in Kákosy (1977).

85. He is referred to as a priest and resident of Heliopolis in *BNJ* 609 F 25.

86. Ogden (2004, 107–10; 2007, 250). Respectively "Pancrates the poet, one of the inhabitants . . . to the emperor Hadrian" (Παγκράτης τις τῶν ἐπιχωρίων ποιητής . . . Ἀδριανῶι τῶι αὐτοκράτορι) and "Pachrates the Heliopolitan prophet to the emperor Hadrian" (Παχράτης, ὁ προφήτης Ἡλιουπόλεως, Ἀδριανῷ βασιλεῖ).

typically Alexandrian praise poetry.[87] As with Thrasyllus's swallows, the variation that emerges in these two post hoc discussions of Pancrates is not a problem. It is exactly the point I am trying to underline about the cross-cultural authority for those writing about "Egyptian things," whether those "things" are lotus plants or magical spells. Even in very different generic contexts, there is a sustained interest in the way that Pancrates wields his expertise to impress an emperor and secure advancement.

Pancrates is also mentioned by Lucian, a mixed Assyrian-Greek satirist. Like Julia Balbilla's paternal line, he hailed from the kingdom of Commagene, which had become Roman Syria in the first century CE. Lucian was attuned to and quick to satirize culturally mixed people who laid claim to a Greek identity. He includes himself in this group: in one of his dialogues, a character refers to a thinly vailed version of Lucian as "the Syrian" and "still a barbarian in accent and wearing a kaftan like a Syrian."[88] Lucian's preoccupation with cultural mixture spans Syria and Egypt, where he had spent some time during his career.[89] In a different dialogue, the *Lover of Lies*, Lucian paints Pancrates with the same brush he had applied to himself.

Lucian's Pancrates seems to overlap with the Pancrateses mentioned by Athenaeus and the magical papyri. As Daniel Ogden concludes, "they are, in short, best seen as different faces of the same tradition."[90] In this light, Ogden has suggested that Lucian's Pancrates is patterned on the Pancrates of the magical papyri.[91] Within the *Lover of Lies*, Pancrates is a magician who mentors the narrator Eucrates. Eucrates's description of Pancrates's curriculum vitae echoes the positions and titles of other authors of Aegyptiaca. Specifically, Pancrates is called "one of the sacred scribes," a position also held by Chaeremon.[92] To Eucrates, Pancrates's status as sacred scribe builds toward a much more substantial claim: "He is amazingly wise and knows all of Egyptian culture."[93] Eucrates's compliment links Pancrates to a much longer-lived kind of intellectual authority, in which authors like Seneca and Gellius underlined the polymathy of authors

---

87. P. Oxy. 1085, though in a fragmentary state of preservation, contains a sizable fragment of the poem.

88. *Bis Acc.* 27: βάρβαρον ἔτι τὴν φωνὴν καὶ μονονουχὶ κάνδυν ἐνδεδυκότα εἰς τὸν Ἀσσύριον τρόπον. Text is Macleod (1972–1987).

89. On which see Swain (1996, 321n77–323n87).

90. Ogden (2007, 252). Dickie (2001, 205) also identifies as one person the Pachrates of the Paris Magical Papyrus, Lucian's Pancrates, and Athenaeus's Pancrates. Escolano-Poveda (2020, 181–82) lays out, but does not fully endorse, the links between these different Pancrates attestations.

91. Ogden (2004, 107–10) (redeveloped in 2007, 248–52), Burstein (2016, *ad* T 1), Preisendanz (1942, 2072–73).

92. For Chaeremon's position as sacred scribe, and the strategies of translation surrounding the *hierogrammateus*, see chapter 6.

93. Lucian *Philops.* 34: . . . Μεμφίτης ἀνὴρ τῶν ἱερῶν γραμματέων, θαυμάσιος τὴν σοφίαν καὶ τὴν παιδείαν πᾶσαν εἰδὼς τὴν Αἰγύπτιον.

80   INTRODUCING AEGYPTIACA

of Aegyptiaca—Balbillus and Apion, respectively. This cultural ambassadorship is encyclopedic. It is denoted in Lucian by the loaded word *paideia* to amplify a catholic intellectualism.

The magic performed by Pancrates mixes Greek representations of an exoticized, miracle-filled Egypt and traditionally Egyptian descriptions of magicians. As Eucrates narrates: "I did not recognize who he was at first, but when I saw him performing many other wondrous deeds whenever we moored the boat—especially riding on crocodiles and swimming together with beasts, and those animals crouching and wagging their tails—I knew that he was a holy man."[94] The heavy exoticism would seem to preclude any legitimately Egyptian representations of magic. But Dedi, the famous magician from a Middle Kingdom tale contained in Papyrus Westcar, has the same ability to tame otherwise wild beasts: "He knows how to make a lion go behind him."[95] Animal-taming is a cultural commonplace that naturalizes a mixture of Greek and Egyptian sensibilities around magic.[96] Eucrates concludes that these magical feats prove Pancrates's bona fides as "a holy man," a label through which "priest" shades into a generally exoticized wonder-worker.

As with Apion and Chaeremon, Pancrates's Egyptian priestly training blends into Greek philosophical self-presentation. The two frames are complementary traditions that co-constitute the authority claimed by Chaeremon and Pancrates. In Lucian, Pancrates's Egyptian knowledge bleeds into his concomitant expertise as a Pythagorean philosopher. Pancrates gained his magical prowess only after training with Isis for twenty-three years, all while underground. This echoes Pythagoras himself, who had also trained with Egyptian priests. Another historical character in the *Lover of Lies* makes Pancrates's apparent Pythagoreanism even clearer. Within the dialogue, Pancrates trained not only the narrator Eucrates, but also the interlocutor Arignotus. This character Arignotus is historically well-known as a Pythagorean philosopher. By casting Pancrates as Arignotus's teacher, Lucian conjures a plausible but nevertheless fictitious scenario in which authors of Aegyptiaca help train Pythagorean philosophers.

Arignotus may have been trained by Pancrates, but he is, like Lucian himself, cruel in his description of Pancrates's cultural mixture: "'You're talking about my teacher Pancrates,' said Arignotus, 'a holy man, completely shaved, always

---

94. Lucian *Philops.* 34: καὶ τὰ μὲν πρῶτα ἠγνόουν ὅστις ἦν, ἐπεὶ δὲ ἑώρων αὐτὸν εἴ ποτε ὁρμίσαιμεν τὸ πλοῖον ἄλλα τε πολλὰ τεράστια ἐργαζόμενον, καὶ δὴ καὶ ἐπὶ κροκοδείλων ὀχούμενον καὶ συννέοντα τοῖς θηρίοις, τὰ δὲ ὑποπτήσσοντα καὶ σαίνοντα ταῖς οὐραῖς, ἔγνων ἱερόν τινα ἄνθρωπον ὄντα.

95. P. Westcar 7, 5 (ed. Blackman and Davies 1988, tr. Simpson 18): *jw-f rḫ(.w) rḏjt šm m'j ḥr-s'-f sšd-f ḥr t'*.

96. Frankfurter (1998, 227–28) juxtaposes Pancrates's magical display and Papyrus Westcar to emphasize imperial-era lector priests' deliberate use of the magician persona for social advancement in Rome. Escolano-Poveda (2020, 183–84) connects Pancrates' crocodile riding to imagery on Horus cippi.

thoughtful, speaking Greek impurely, lanky, snub-nosed, with lips that jut out and pretty thin in the legs."[97] Pancrates's flexible and mixed identity, emblematic of the wider tradition of Aegyptiaca, is recast into a grotesque body. Some of the typical fascinations of cultural mixture that Lucian had developed in his self-satirization reappear here. Lucian described himself as "a barbarian in accent," just as he singles out Pancrates's accented Greek. This laser-like focus on accent amplifies core issues of creolization, which is a postcolonial theorization rooted in language contact.[98] Literally, Lucian claims that Pancrates "hellenizes impurely." In the prestige economy of the imperial Greek world, this is a damning insult. Language purity had long been wielded as a litmus test by which to establish the legitimacy of one's claim to Greekness. In Arignotus's list of insults, impure speech is a bridge between a comic stereotype of the Egyptian priest—linen clothes, shaved head—and a racialized description through which Pancrates's body precludes any legitimate Greek identity. His lips and legs and nose are a dead giveaway that Pancrates is and always will be an Egyptian.

AEGYPTIACA IN REVIEW

Lucian is such a fascinating note to end on because he juxtaposes two competing visions with which to view authors of Aegyptiaca. Pancrates is the idealized image of cultural competency and intellectualism. He is an authority on magic and Egyptian culture on the one hand, and Pythagorean philosophy and Greek culture on the other. But this creolizing intellectual expertise soon gives way to a racializing portrait of accented speech and grotesque body that suggests that any attempts at "Greekness" will always be betrayed by a body that can never not be Egyptian.

This delegitimization of Pancrates's claim to a mixed identity brings me full circle. I opened this part of the book with a quote from Josephus, in which he trots out Apion's birth in the Oasis and Egyptian origins to discredit his status as an Alexandrian Greek. Lucian also satirizes a creolizing identity to suggest that, try as Pancrates might, he will never "really" be Greek. Lucian's and Josephus's criticisms prove the historical power and prevalence of such mixed figures. These criticisms emerge from very different contexts: Arignotus's criticisms of Pancrates' impure Greek, like Lucian's self-satirization of his own accent, humorously comment on the cultural cachet of pure Atticism.[99] Where Lucian is playful when he cuts Pancrates down to size, Josephus is serious. His delegitimization of Apion's Alexandrian citizenship reflects the tension surrounding first-century CE multiculturalism under Roman power. Like Apion, the Pancrates discussed by

---

97. Lucian *Philops.* 34: Παγκράτην λέγεις, ἔφη ὁ Ἀρίγνωτος, ἐμὸν διδάσκαλον, ἄνδρα ἱερόν, ἐξυρημένον ἀεί, νοήμονα, οὐ καθαρῶς ἑλληνίζοντα, ἐπιμήκη, σιμόν, προχειλῆ, ὑπόλεπτον τὰ σκέλη.

98. As emphasized by Baker and Mühlhäusler (2007).

99. On Atticism, see canonically Schmid (1887–1897), and the social framing of language purity in Schmitz (1997, 67–96).

Athenaeus was an Alexandrian Greek. Both Pancrates and Apion are ambassadors of Alexandrianism whose ability to represent Greek culture piques the ire of other culturally mixed people—Josephus and Lucian. Whether seriously or playfully, the latter two cannot help but reemphasize the fact that, when push comes to shove, both Apion and Pancrates are really just Egyptians.

Chaeremon, the Balbilli, and Pancrates brought together increasingly wide-ranging intellectual traditions under one authorial identity. Aegyptiaca was a tradition and an ongoing creolizing process, not a Manethonian flash in the pan. If one thing has become clear, it is that there was no one set pattern through which these figures created their intellectual authority or coordinated Egyptian and Greek traditions. This variegated and networked image of cultural combination makes rigid distinctions between an insider's emic presentation of Egypt and an external Greek mode of representation untenable. Astrology—practiced by Chaeremon, Thrasyllus, and Tiberius Claudius Balbillus—is so fruitful because it offers a paradigmatic example of a creolizing intellectual tradition in which a combined Greco-Egyptian perspective is "emic." This mixture extends well beyond astrology. Julia Balbilla addressed Memnon as an archetype of the blended Egyptian and Greek persona through which she defined her own identity as poet and epigrammatist. Memnon's mythic antiquity helps Julia Balbilla imagine a world where creolizing processes had never not been underway.

Alexandria was the site where this blending took place. Chaeremon, the Balbilli, and Pancrates occupied positions in temples, the Library of Alexandria, and the Museum. These different posts bridge the religious and literary, Greek and Egyptian, to create a new intellectualism that should not be masked by Alexandria's long-standing association with Greek literary culture and position near, rather than in, Egypt. The heterogeneous, cross-cultural literary production of these authors was the Alexandrian culture that Rome encountered. Authors of Aegyptiaca like Chaeremon, Tiberius Claudius Balbillus, and Apion were, quite literally, ambassadors of Alexandria for a Roman audience.

Aegyptiaca as a genre was consistently read through the biographical proximity of author with emperor. Balbillus used astrological know-how to help Nero kill off his senatorial competition and avoid a fated death. Pancrates impressed Hadrian either through an epyllion or through a display of magic. Julia Balbilla played the intermediary between Memnon and the emperor and his wife. These encounters between Egyptian and emperor reflect the mutual influence and attraction through which the intellectual traditions embedded in Aegyptiaca were increasingly politicized, shaped into a form that could best serve the emperor and justify his position of authority.

The historical and social context that makes these authors of Aegyptiaca so important has taken shape. But as yet I have only hinted—via swallows and crocodile fights—at the substance of these texts. One can appreciate *that* these Egyptians blended together Greek and Egyptian cultural perspectives: that Chaeremon was both a source for privileged priestly knowledge and a well-known Stoic philosopher; that Apion bridged Greek and Egyptian perspectives on animals. But it is also necessary to show *how* they did so. This will help position Aegyptiaca as a bridge between long-standing traditional Egyptian cultural forms discussed by Egyptologists and Roman authors like Virgil and Juvenal discussed by Classicists. In the next section, I trace how one widely recognized cultural commonplace—Egypt's sacred animals—traveled across that bridge.

PART TWO

Egypt's Animals

From Representation to Cultural Translation

3
———

From Representation . . .

Anubis, Actium, and the Limits of Exoticism

The ekphrasis of Aeneas's shield in Book 8 of the *Aeneid* looks forward to the cataclysmic conflict between Octavian and Antony. To reimagine the civil war between two Romans as a fight between Octavian and Cleopatra, between Roman order and foreign chaos, Virgil turns to Egypt's gods:[1] "In the middle the queen Cleopatra calls to her army with native rattle, she does not yet look back behind her at the twin snakes. Monstrous forms of every sort of god and the barker Anubis hold weapons against Neptune and Venus and against Minerva."[2] Monstrous Egyptian animal gods oppose august Roman divinities. Over a century later, the satirist Juvenal took up the same theme: "Volusius of Bithynia, who doesn't know what sort of monsters mad Egypt worships? . . . Whole towns venerate cats there, here freshwater fish, a dog there—but none worships Diana."[3] The abhorrence for Egyptian religion displayed by Virgil and Juvenal suggests that Rome had no place for Egypt and its strange practices. Even as the role of Egypt in the Roman empire

---

1. I here emphasize that Virgil soldered Egyptian zoomorphism onto dichotomizing Egypt-Rome battle imagery, rather than falling into the trap of critiquing, but simultaneously reinscribing, the debate about the *Aeneid*'s optimistic or pessimistic view of Augustan rule and Roman imperialism, a pattern noted by Thomas (2001, 20–24). For the shield's use of triumphal imagery, see McKay (1998, 210–11) and Pandey (2018, 194–201).

2. Virgil *Aen.* 8.696–700: regina in mediis patrio vocat agmina sistro, / necdum etiam geminos a tergo respicit anguis. / omnigenumque deum monstra et latrator Anubis / contra Neptunum et Venerem contraque Minervam / tela tenent.

3. Juv. 15.1–8: Quis nescit, Volusi Bithynice, qualia demens / Aegyptos portenta colat? . . . / illic aeluros, hic piscem fluminis, illic / oppida tota canem venerantur, nemo Dianam.

had changed drastically between Virgil and Juvenal and the reigns of Augustus and Hadrian, there is a shared reliance on barbarizing rhetoric.

When we look at material culture, the opposite picture emerges. The cult of Isis spread throughout the Roman empire. In many ways, Isis's trajectory is similar to Apion's. Originally Egyptian, in the Ptolemaic period Isis became a central figure in Alexandria and bridged Greek and Egyptian religious traditions. This cultural pluralism facilitated her movement around the Mediterranean: Isiac inscriptions can be found from Spain to Syria.[4] The trappings of Egyptian religion—and animal gods like Anubis and the Apis bull—were scattered across Italy. There were well-known Isis temples in Pompeii and Rome's Campus Martius, the former still standing to this day.[5] The elegist Propertius spends a poem complaining that his girlfriend's adherence to the cult of Isis keeps them from spending time together.[6] During Isis festivals like the "discovery of Osiris" (*inventio Osiridis*) and the "navigation of Isis" (*navigium Isidis*), so-called Anubophores would don the dog-faced mask of Anubis. Their public commitment to Anubis worship forms a very different response to Egypt's animals than one sees in Virgil.[7] Isis and animals were thus closely intertwined. In the years after Actium, they jointly reflected a new kind of Roman multiculturalism that elicited divergent responses. Augustus himself forced Rome's Isis temple to move outside the *pomerium*, Rome's sacred boundary. Tiberius destroyed the Campus Martius temple after a Roman magistrate donned an Anubis mask to sexually assault the Isis devotee Paulina.[8] Both emperors tried to create space within the city for a Roman religious identity that could be free from Egyptian religion's obviously significant influence.[9]

Back to Rome

If one follows authors of Aegyptiaca on their journeys to Rome, what reception did they receive? When the scene changes from Roman Egypt to Egypt in Rome, the

---

4. Mazurek (2022) focuses on the cult of Isis in imperial-era Greece. Of particular note is her interest (88–119) in the materiality of Isis cult in Greece, which skews toward Greek stylistic paradigms to facilitate connections between Isis and goddesses like Aphrodite, Demeter, and Athena.

5. The Isis temple in the Campus Martius is well discussed by Lembke (1994) and Versluys, Clausen, and Vittozzi (2018); for Isis at Pompeii see Tran-tam-Tinh (1964) and Swetnam-Burland (2015, 105–41).

6. In 2.33a, Propertius directs a tirade against Isis because his girlfriend is off celebrating a festival in her honor. As Miller (1981, 105, 108) notes, Propertius, like Virgil, presents all of Rome as a unified front opposed to Isis. But, in doing so, Propertius offers a self-aware performance of the lover's outsized and mock-epic response to a personal annoyance.

7. For background on visual and literary evidence for these Anubophores, see Bricault (2000–2001). Gasparini (2018, 726–27, 743) (cf. Gasparini 2017, 396–98) integrates the Anubophores into the larger theatricality of Isiac performance. For cult worship of Anubis, see Sfameni Gasparro (2018).

8. On this episode, see Gasparini (2017) and chapter 6 in this book.

9. Orlin (2010, 211–12) (cf. Orlin 2008, 243–45, for Augustus's use of the *pomerium* as an essential ideological boundary) argues that this marginalized, but did not ban outright, the cult of Isis.

contours of cultural contact change with it. It is no surprise that Greek and Roman authors were fascinated with Egypt, whether because of the Nile, hieroglyphs, Isis, or the like. Amid that variety of themes, this and the next chapter take up the role of animals in Egyptian religion. As I will show, Egypt's sacred animals do a particularly good job reflecting larger disciplinary patterns through which Egyptologists' versus Classicists' perspectives on a given *topos*'s Egyptian origin and Greco-Roman reception drift apart from each other. Whether embraced alongside Isis or rejected by Virgil and Juvenal, it is all too easy for Egypt's animals to become a foil for the complexities of Romanness under empire, one of several Egyptian mirrors through which Romans made sense of themselves. The alterity of Egypt's animals helps crystallize an author's relationship to the emperor, or an Anubophore's public commitment both to a citizenship status and a religious community, or a Roman banqueter's reaction to the exotic fauna of a Nilescape.[10] To be sure, these Romans' creative conceptualization of Egypt should be evaluated on its own terms. But all the same, this insistent individuation of Rome's fictive Egypt continues to push out of frame the actual systems of significance surrounding animals in Egyptian culture.[11]

In this chapter, I chart a path to authors of Aegyptiaca and their own role in the animal/religion *topos* via the heterogeneous strategies of cultural representation through which Greek and Roman authors explained Egypt's sacred animals. Those strategies of representation partially (but only partially) track a frequently cited transition from Julio-Claudian antipathy to Flavian patronage of the cult of Isis.[12] I proceed through three main modes of representation. The first, the rhetoric of barbarization associated with Virgil and Actium, is a strategy of non-translation. In the aftermath of the civil war, Roman authors refused to see a cow as anything other than a cow. In the second strategy, Roman authors leveraged patterns of mutual identification—of Io with Isis, or Osiris with Apis—to connect Egypt's animals with cognate stories of human/animal/god fluidity in the Greek mythological tradition. In a third strategy, Greek and Roman authors took a step back to weigh the pros and cons of zoomorphic versus anthropomorphic gods. As will become clear over the course of this chapter, the cult of Isis and dynastic change in Rome are undoubtedly central frames for these three different strategies and the way

---

10. For an exoticizing interpretation of Egyptianizing material in Rome, see Versluys (2002, 354–55, 375–76) and Swetnam-Burland (2015, 18–19) (though Pearson 2021, 194 pushes back against exoticism's explanatory utility).

11. Malaise (2005), Swetnam-Burland (2015, 30), and Versluys (2017a, 276) have all sought to individuate Romans' fictive Egypt. Barrett (2019, 34–35, 58–59) reframes the "authentic" vs. "fictive" debate in terms of Romans' selective and eclectic engagement with and transformation of earlier Egyptian models.

12. For the Flavian recuperation of Egypt, see (on the literature side) Manolaraki (2013, 13–14, 125–32, and 2018); for Pompeian imagery, Barrett (2019, 21–28); and for the cult of Isis, Mazurek (2022, 64–65).

90   EGYPT'S ANIMALS

they appear in authors like Lucan or Statius. But by prioritizing the strategies that different authors used, I argue that these two frames also have their drawbacks: a rigid periodization oriented around an emperor's support for or opposition to Isis overburdens the concept of "imperial ideology" and flattens out tonally ambivalent engagement with Egypt. Once I have emphasized Romans' multifaceted interest in Egypt's animals, the threads of cultural translation woven by authors of Aegyptiaca can be spliced in with a larger domain of cultural representation under empire that is of broad interest to Classicists.

A COW IS NOT A GOD: JULIO-CLAUDIAN BARBARIZATION

I have been cautioning against overusing barbarism and exoticism, but it is easy to see why they are such attractive explanations of Romans' responses to the role of animals in Egyptian religion.[13] It is important not to dismiss barbarism outright, but instead to locate barbarizing descriptions of Egypt in a specific social and historical context. The rhetorical strategies that Virgil and Propertius crafted after Actium inaugurated a Roman self-definition against Egypt designed specifically around the challenges that had accompanied the civil war.[14] Actium kicked off a new kind of discourse well suited to the post hoc reconstruction of Augustus's consolidation of power, whose fulcrum was regularly located at Alexandria with the death of Cleopatra and Antony. For the alienation of Antony and Cleopatra from Roman and Greek identities to be effective, Virgil's portrait of Isis and her retinue of animals had to reject the culturally mixed iconography in her Roman temples. Egyptian religious traditions around animal-formed gods are roundly criticized to distance those, like Cleopatra, whose iconographic self-presentation changed between Greek and Egyptian idioms.

The need to demonize Cleopatra thus ensured that Egyptian sensibilities around animals and the divine were cut to size to fit the procrustean bed constructed by elite male authors of the post-Actium decades.[15] Virgil was not the only such author.[16] Propertius also gives space to this systematic comparison of Rome

---

13. For barbarizing explanations, see Smelik and Hemelrijk (1984) and Maehler (2003). Pfeiffer (2015) notes the ethnic Greeks in Egypt who participated in animal cult, but still contrasts (50) intra-Egyptian acceptance with a version of Roman interest in Egypt's sacred animals circumscribed by the Actium moment.

14. Pandey (2018, 197) underlines these two authors' "intergeneric dialogue" vis-à-vis Nile scenes.

15. Hornung (1982, 100–42) surveys the range of those Egyptian sensibilities.

16. The shield of Aeneas looms large in Virgil's antagonistic arrangement of Rome and Egypt, but note too the presence of Osiris in the Trojans' climactic fight with the Rutulians in *Aen.* 12.458–61, through which (per Reed 1998, 403) Actium rhetoric seeps into the Trojans' fight against native Italians.

and Egypt via divine bodies.[17] Propertius begins a poem situating his own enslavement (his words) to his girlfriend through a list of historical and mythological exempla of men's dangerous subservience to their lovers. Cleopatra is the central figure in this catalogue. Propertius's poem mirrors Virgil's approach: "Assuredly, whore queen of foul Canopus, the one branded mark of Phillip's blood, you dared to place barking Anubis against our Jupiter."[18] Like Virgil, Propertius uses barking to underline Anubis's animality, undercut the legitimacy of Egyptian religion, and mark out Cleopatra as guilty by association. The poem's emphasis on captivating women suggests that Octavian's real antagonist is not his fellow Roman Antony, but is instead Cleopatra, by whom Antony had been perversely ensnared.

Over time, a set narrative took hold in which Augustus personally inaugurated the demonization of Egyptian animal gods one sees in Virgil and Propertius. There is some evidence in the series of coins he minted in 28–27 BCE to mark the annexation of Egypt. These coins and their legend *Aegypto Capta* not only signal the rearticulation of civil war as imperial annexation, they also use a lone crocodile to underline Egypt's exoticism.[19] More promising evidence long postdates Augustus's actual life. Cassius Dio, the hellenophone Roman historian, points out that Augustus himself found animal worship irredeemably misguided. During Augustus's tour of his new province, Dio notes that Augustus studiously avoided traditional modes of Egyptian worship: "And for this same reason Augustus also didn't want to meet with the Apis bull, claiming that he was wont to worship gods, not cattle."[20] Like the "barker" motif, Dio's bon mot elevates the animality of the Apis bull to create a rhetorically effective contrast between the bestial and the divine. It is important to clarify that this cannot be taken as tidy evidence of Augustus's own beliefs. Dio is likely populating the anecdote—where Augustus shows deference to Alexander and Sarapis but dismisses the Ptolemies and the Apis bull—with his own view of a paradigmatically moderate conqueror. This is especially true when Dio is writing some two hundred years after the events in question and is clearly fashioning Augustus as a model for the contemporary Severan emperors.[21] This rejection of the Apis bull might be an idiosyncrasy of Dio's tendentious representation of Augustus, but the literary convention of Egyptian religious barbarism is

---

17. Relevant are Propertius's emphasis on a chained Nile in 2.1—which takes up rivers' metonymic importance in triumphal imagery—and his comments (2.31) on the portico of the Danaids in the Palatine complex, discussed by Pandey (2018, 94).

18. Prop. 3.11.39–41: scilicet, incesti meretrix regina Canopi, / una Philippei sanguinis usta nota, / ausa Iovi nostro es latrantem opponere Anubim. Text from Heyworth (2007) (whose reading departs from the manuscripts).

19. *RIC* I Augustus 275A and B, 544, 545 (cf. 546).

20. Cass. Dio 51.16.5: κἀκ τῆς αὐτῆς ταύτης αἰτίας οὐδὲ τῷ Ἄπιδι ἐντυχεῖν ἠθέλησε, λέγων θεοὺς ἀλλ᾿ οὐχὶ βοῦς προσκυνεῖν εἰθίσθαι.

21. See Rich (1990), Reinhold and Swan (1990), and regarding the Severans, Gabba (1984, 73–75).

still notable in its longevity. In this entrenchment of Egyptian religious deviance and its importance to the Egyptianization of the civil war, the convenience of the Apis bull needs little elaboration.

As the scene shifts from Augustus and Actium to the later Julio-Claudians, authors continued to locate the origins of Rome's turn toward empire and the principate in Pompey's, Cleopatra's, and Antony's deaths in Egypt. Even as times changed, the rhetorical convenience of animals-qua-gods remained the same. The epic poet Lucan is a particularly loud voice in this continuation of the barbarizing template. Lucan's engagement with Egypt is certainly multifaceted. He simultaneously underlines Egypt's culpability in Pompey's death and draws natural-philosophical inspiration from the Nile and its inundation. Jonathan Tracy and Eleni Manolaraki have taken up Lucan's combination of Egypt's political and natural-philosophical import and the light that the fictional priest Acoreus shines on that combination. That is an angle of approach I will return to in the Conclusion.[22] For present purposes, I want to flag Lucan's easy use of barbarizing rhetoric around Egypt's sacred animals.

Like Virgil, Lucan returns to Anubis to denigrate Egypt and bemoan its corruption of Roman cultural practices. After Lucan recounts the death of Pompey in Egypt, he complains that Egyptian gods have marched into Rome even though Pompey remains ignominiously buried in Egypt: "Into Roman temples we've received your Isis and half-divine dogs."[23] Egypt's sacred animals help Lucan defamiliarize the goddess Isis, an otherwise anthropomorphic and culturally mixed Greco-Egyptian divinity. The more vehemently Lucan keeps Egypt's gods at a distance, the clearer their popularity in Rome becomes. Lucan thus juxtaposes Egypt's culpability in Rome's fall into sole rule with its detrimental effects on Roman religious practices. He connects a "capital P" political resonance of Egypt—as site of the death of the Republic—with a "lower-case p" political emphasis on the negative impact of Isis religion on Roman cultural norms. Caesar's embrace of Ptolemaic luxury and Rome's embrace of Egyptian gods go hand in hand.[24]

In a similar spirit, Lucan humorously blurs the lines separating Egypt's gods from its food. Lucan cannot help but crack a joke to that effect in Book 10, when Caesar first meets Cleopatra at a banquet in Alexandria: "They served up many birds and beasts, Egypt's gods."[25] It is a felicitous joke. Lucan's gibe about Egypt's

---

22. Tracy (2014, 3–8) sets up this dichotomy and maps it onto Lucan's endorsement of pharaonic Egypt and criticism of Ptolemaic Egypt. Manolaraki (2013) contrasts a politicized Nile of the Pompey episode (ch. 2) with the philosophized Nile of the Nile digression (ch. 4).

23. Luc. *Bell. Civ.* 8.831–2: nos in templa tuam Romana accepimus Isim / semideosque canes . . . Text is Bailey (1997).

24. Manolaraki (2013, 80–117) emphasizes the political stakes of the Nile digression in Book 10, where Caesar implicates himself into a succession of Nile-conquering dynasts which begins with Sesostris and proleptically anticipates Nero.

25. Luc. *Bell. Civ.* 10.158–9: multas volucresque ferasque / Aegypti posuere deos.

barbaric "taste" in gods does double duty; it riffs on the bestiality versus divine dynamic inbuilt into the barker Anubis while also looping in a related critique of Eastern luxury and banqueting, which had long been used to criticize Cleopatra in Actium literature. To cap it off, Lucan's joke reemphasizes the vector of this combined cultural and political degradation, which travels from Cleopatra to her co-banqueter Caesar and, by extension, on to Nero.[26]

In both passages, I would emphasize just how much animal gods are to Lucan a rhetorical convenience. They form a readymade object of outrage that can be trotted out at key narrative moments like the death of Pompey. By echoing Anubis in particular, Lucan uses Egyptian gods as yet another way to position his own epic against Virgil's. In a poem whose stylistic hallmark is sustained expressions of pessimism—whether via parodic subversion or rhetorical questions—Egyptian religion's barbarity is both rhetorically effective and widely legible because of Virgil's precedent.

IO WAS TURNED INTO A COW: EXPLANATION VIA SYNCRETISM AND METAMORPHOSIS

There was, then, a keen desire to work through Rome's own transitions, its increasingly multicultural and widespread empire, through Egypt's sacred animals. Simmering in the background, as in Lucan's condemnation of Isiac religion and its coterie of animal gods, is a frustration that these Egyptian practices have become a part of Rome. That is what animates Juvenal's condemnation of Egyptian animal worship in *Satire* 15, which is only coherent when read against his critiques of Egypt's presence in Rome—via the figure Crispinus—in earlier satires.[27]

I am not arguing against the fact of the Actium script and its fossilization of a binary between Roman anthropomorphism and Egyptian zoomorphism. But even if that Actium script loomed large, it should not completely overshadow contemporary discourses that do not fit the pattern it set. Actium rhetoric around Egypt's animals thus reflects the larger problems of the term "Augustan ideology," which too easily becomes a freestanding monolith against which all culture must be measured.[28] I am far from the first to caution against this overamplification of Augustan exceptionalism and oversimplification of the term "political."[29]

---

26. Per Feldherr (2021, 140–42) (cf. Tracy 2014, 95–96), Lucan traces Roman luxury (particularly Neronian excess) back to Cleopatra and Egypt.

27. For example, his frustration with Isiac religion in *Satire* 6 (6.526–9, 13.93) and his diatribes against the Egyptian Crispinus in *Satires* 1.26–9 and 4.1–36.

28. Galinsky (1996, 12–14), on the reciprocity of Augustus's "authority" (*auctoritas*), shows that this puts the cart before the horse. Roman authors and artists produce, rather respond to, the cultural dynamics which are called "Augustan."

29. Habinek (1997) notes this false exceptionalism and Farrell (1998) the dangers of collapsing political readings of literature into a pro- or anti-Augustan dichotomy.

94   EGYPT'S ANIMALS

In other words, the Actium script is dangerous because, when it overshadows other Roman representations of Egypt's animal gods, it changes the color of those same representations.[30] Passages that are taken as an Orientalizing representation of Egyptian practices concordant with Virgil's, Propertius's, or Lucan's general critiques might, when viewed in their own light, reveal a more complex reaction to the ways in which Egyptian and Roman religious traditions were comparable.

The Flavian poet Statius is a good example. He writes a send-off poem (propempticon) that wishes the Roman administrator Maecius Celer well as the latter heads off on a military assignment in Syria.[31] Celer follows the standard route, traveling to Syria via Alexandria. In that vein, Statius asks Isis to welcome Celer and teach him about a range of Egyptian traditions, which Statius proceeds to catalogue. Among the set of topics Isis ought to cover for Celer, Egyptians' mode of religious worship is central: "With you there to guard him, let him learn why they equate lowly animals and the great gods."[32] There is an unambiguous rhetorical similarity connecting this line with Dio's rejection of the Apis bull. Statius, like Dio's Augustus, draws a contrast between the "low" (*vilis*) and the "great" (*magnus*) to amplify the misguidedness of treating beast and god as equals.

But the structure of the poem promotes a different reading. In the first place, Statius asks Isis to be a guide who not only teaches Celer, but also keeps him safe. This tutelary Isis, as protector of travelers, stands apart from the antagonistic role assigned to her by Virgil and Lucan.[33] As Eleni Manolaraki has argued, Statius includes Isis's sistrum and paints a triumphal atmosphere to first raise the image of an Augustan-era, inimical Isis leagued with Cleopatra and then to subsume that threatening Isis into a new and entirely supportive role.[34] That new role loudly announces the new politics of Isis under the Flavians. Statius is writing with the support of Domitian, an emperor who—unlike Augustus—actively contributed to the temple of Isis in Rome.[35] Celer, both because he stands in for the Egyptophile Domitian and because he spent his youth in Egypt, facilitates a suitable response to

---

30. Virgil *Aen.* 8.685–700, Prop. 3.11, and Hor. *Ep.* 9 are the examples cited most typically, for example by Maehler (2003, 205–10) and Smelik and Hemelrijk (1984, 1854, 1928–29) (who do not mention Horace).

31. The poem is the first of three (3.2–4) Statius addresses to those in the imperial and military bureaucracy, as Newlands (2002, 232–33) notes in her discussion of the risks of service under bad emperors.

32. Stat. *Silv.* 3.2.107–13: te praeside noscat / . . . vilia cur magnos aequent animalia divos. Text from Bailey (2015). See also Smelik and Hemelrijk (1984, 1960–61).

33. That tutelary function aligns well with Isis's soteriological role in inscriptions dedicated by seafaring merchants, collected by Vidman (1969).

34. Manolaraki (2013, 191–92). See too Putnam (2017, 117–19), who notes allusions to Virgil in Statius's description of Isis (3.2.101–7).

35. As proven most obviously by the original placement of Domitian's obelisk (now in the Piazza Navona) in the Isis temple of Rome, on which see Lembke (1994, 69–70) and, on Domitian's activity in Egypt, Klotz (2008).

a long lineage of political antagonism between Egypt and Rome. Where to Lucan Egypt is guilty in Pompey's death, in the propempticon Isis more than delivers on Statius's request for Celer's safe transit.[36]

Beyond Isis's supportive rather than antagonistic relationship to Celer, Statius leans heavily on the long-standing Io/Isis pairing. Statius, like many before him, identifies Isis with Io: "Isis, formerly stabled in the caves of Phroneus."[37] Io's metamorphosis into a cow in Argos (where these caves were located) and then journey to Egypt were regularly invoked as a cross-cultural origin story for the Egyptian goddess Isis.[38] This equivalence-drawing thus locates Isis in a specifically Greek mythological and literary context absent in Virgil and Lucan.

The long pedigree of the Isis-Io syncretism thus paves the way for the explanatory role Statius assigns to Isis in the poem.[39] Io's metamorphosis into a cow provides an answer to the question Isis is supposed to answer for Celer: why Egyptians think animals can be gods. Io's time as a cow suggests that humans and gods alike can lurk beneath an animal exterior. Through Io, it begins to become clear that the cow-god identification inbuilt into Apis worship is also reflected in the Greek and Roman tradition of human-god-animal metamorphosis—where gods, demigods, and mortals regularly change shape. Statius had already tipped his hand earlier in the poem, when he introduced the Greco-Egyptian shape-shifter Proteus.[40]

Statius's willingness to loop Isis into a propempticon for his friend Celer certainly reflects the new political climate of the Flavians. But Statius is still building on earlier authors who connected their patrons with, rather than contrasted them against, Egyptian practices.[41] The Roman elegist Tibullus shows that this warmer approach to Egypt took hold even during Augustus's rule. After stints supporting the assassins Brutus and Cassius and then Antony, the famous literary patron Marcus Valerius Messalla Corvinus had eventually aligned with Augustus and took part in the latter's victory at Actium. Among his public works, Messalla rebuilt a

---

36. Per Manolaraki (2013, 193–94).

37. Stat. *Silv.* 3.2.101: Isi, Phoroneis olim stabulata sub antris.

38. Herodotus 2.41 makes the identification. Relevant too are the interconnected Io tales in Ovid and Valerius Flaccus, both of which (*Met.* 1.747, V. Fl. 4.416–18) position the myth as a prelude to contemporary Isis cult, on which see Manolaraki (2013, 144).

39. In this and in what follows, I am indebted to the defense of "syncretism" offered by Frankfurter (2018, 15–20), who defines syncretism as "an assemblage of symbols and discourses" and *not* "the weaving together of two theological systems" (16). Where Droge (2001, 376) claims that syncretism is "devoid of explanatory utility," I maintain that it can help locate Aegyptiaca's modes of cultural mixture in the specific domain of religious transformation.

40. Manolaraki (2013, 199) notes that Io-Isis's biform and multilocal identity answers Statius's questions. Statius is far from alone in using Proteus in this way. So, for example, Philostratus's *Life of Apollonius* (1.4) includes a mention of Proteus of a similar type (on which see Miles 2016).

41. In this regard, I am pushing back a bit against Manolaraki (2013, 215–16), who explains Statius's warmer view of Isis through the Flavians' new attitude to Egypt. Tibullus's endorsement of the peaceful Osiris suggests that this alignment of Egyptian god with poetic addressee precedes (and thus cannot be wholly explained by) the Flavians.

96   EGYPT'S ANIMALS

road through Tusculum that occasioned a poem of praise from Tibullus, whose poetry Messalla sponsored. In Ode 1.7, Tibullus honors Messalla in a surprising way. Before offering explicit praise of the road in question, Tibullus develops a lengthy comparison of Messalla and the god Osiris.[42] As the logic goes, Messalla, like Osiris and his syncretic partner Dionysus/Bacchus, is a bringer of peace and of civilization.[43] Analogizing a confidant of Augustus to an Egyptian god is perhaps surprising, since Actium rhetoric deliberately associated Egyptian religion with Cleopatra and the forces opposed to Augustan order. But the identification is there to be seen. Tibullus's praise for his Roman patron via Osiris points to a cross-cultural framework of religious identification that is contemporary with, but ideologically distinct from, the Actium template.[44]

Tibullus uses the Nile and then the Apis bull to effect an otherwise delicate transition from praising Messalla's war valor to singling out Osiris's value as paradigm of peace: "Father Nile, barbarian youth, taught to mourn the Memphite bull, sing of you and marvel at you as their Osiris. Osiris first made a plow with expert hand. . . ."[45] Tibullus thus triangulates the Nile, its identification with Osiris, and the contiguity of that pair to the practice of mourning the dead Apis bull. To be clear, this leaves aside the identification of the living Apis bull as the embodiment or visual manifestation of a range of different Egyptian gods—particularly the patron god of Memphis, Ptah, and the later syncretic funerary god Ptah-Sokar-Osiris.[46] In a pharaonic cultural context, identifying the dead Apis bull with Osiris as a divinized "Osiris-Apis" (*Wsr-Ḥp*) is far from remarkable.[47] It is only with the development of the Hellenistic god Sarapis (developed from the Greek transcription "*Osor-apis*") that the Apis/Osiris pairing rises to a particular position of prominence.[48] The importance of Isis cult elsewhere in Tibullus's poetry points to a potential vehicle of cultural explanation: a set of Egyptian practices around the

---

42. While less essential as a critical reading of the poem, the Egyptological perspective on 1.7 offered by Koenen (1976, 135–57) remains valuable.

43. For the identification of Messalla and Osiris, see Bowditch (2011, 109–11), and earlier Gaisser (1971, 225–28). For the interconnection of the Messalla/Osiris and soldier/farmer pairs, see too Konstan (1978, 174–75) and Moore (1989, 424).

44. I find unpersuasive subversive readings of the poem, where the Osiris identification is meant to feign praise while substantively undercutting that praise via the Egyptian referent. With Moore (1989, 428), I think Tibullus uses Osiris to bring Messalla as violent *triumphator* into his own vision of rural peace.

45. Tib. 1.7.27–9: te canit utque suum pubes miratur Osirim / barbara, Memphiten plangere docta bovem. / primus aratra manu sollerti fecit Osiris. . . . Text is from Luck (1998).

46. For the Apis bull as ba of a range of divinities, see Kessler (1989, 56–90).

47. That said, the presence of the personal name "Osorapis" in the documentary record speaks to the Egyptian importance of the Osiris-Apis pair, on which Coussement (2016, 90, cat. 84) and Clarysse (2009, 213–17).

48. As demonstrated by the proliferation of Sarapis worship across the Roman world, on which see Tran-tam-Tinh (1983) and Takács (1995).

Apis bull and its funerary cult is refracted—albeit with distortions—into a Roman cultural context.

Hellenistic versus pharaonic Apis worship notwithstanding, it is still significant that Tibullus contextualizes god, animal, and river through each other. There remains a translation of a god-animal pair from Egypt, through Isis cult, into Tibullus's poetry. In the process, Tibullus reveals the divergent positions taken to Egypt even under the Julio-Claudians: Egyptian gods can be identified with, rather than foils for, elite Romans; they can facilitate a delicate conversation on the merits of peace versus war in the years after Actium. The presence of barbarizing language—"the barbarian youth" (*barbara pubes*, 27–28)—in this otherwise surprisingly amiable approach to Osiris is doubly valuable: it helps push back against a sense that any poem that does not hew fully to the Actian template is by definition anti-Augustan; and it shows that "barbarian" as a designation for non-Romans does not foreclose any possibility for substantive engagement with Egyptian religion.[49]

Ovid's *Metamorphoses* is an essential entry in this tradition of mythological explanations of Egypt's sacred animals. Like Statius's Io/Isis and Tibullus's Osiris/Bacchus pairs, Ovid's worldwide story of change is constructed by syncing up, rather than schematically contrasting, different cultural traditions. Its manifold tales of humans, gods, and animals constantly offer up origin stories for flora and fauna that connect the natural world with the divine realm. The *Metamorphoses'* focus on "bodies changed into new forms"[50] makes it the perfect place for an etiology of deities who take on a nonhuman animal form. The song of the Pierian muses includes just such an etiology of Egypt's sacred animals:[51]

> . . . she says how Typhon, sent out from earth's darkest depths, scared the heavenly gods. How they all fled, until the land of Egypt and the Nile with its seven mouths welcomed them in their exhaustion. How the earth-born Typhon came there too and the gods hid themselves in false shapes: 'Jupiter,' she said, 'became the leader of the flock, whence derives Libyan Ammon, even now represented with curving horns; Delian Apollo hid in a crow, the son of Semele in a goat, the sister of Phoebus in a cat, Juno in a snow-white cow, Venus in a fish, and Mercury in an ibis bird.'[52]

49. To build on Manolaraki (2013, 34–35).

50. Ov. *Met.* 1.1–2: In nova fert animus mutatas dicere formas / corpora.

51. See also the similar story in Diodorus 1.86.3, which attributes it entirely to Egypt and thus lacks the cross-cultural explanatory framework inbuilt into Ovid's version. Buxton (2009, 162) positions the anecdote (and divine escape generally) as one among several of the gods' motivations for animal metamorphosis (cf. Bremmer 2021, 199n124).

52. Ov. *Met.* 5.321–31: emissumque ima de sede Typhoea terrae / caelitibus fecisse metum cunctosque dedisse / terga fugae, donec fessos Aegyptia tellus / ceperit et septem discretus in ostia Nilus. / huc quoque terrigenam venisse Typhoea narrat / et se mentitos superos celasse figuris: / "dux"que "gregis" dixit "fit Iuppiter, unde recurvis / nunc quoque formatus Libys est cum cornibus Ammon; / Delius in corvo, proles Semeleia capro, / fele soror Phoebi, nivea Saturnia vacca, / pisce Venus latuit, Cyllenius ibidis alis. Tarrant (2004) for text.

98   EGYPT'S ANIMALS

The *Metamorphoses* as a project highlights the presence of animal-shaped gods in the Greco-Roman mythological canon. The gods associated with these animals may be subjected to an *interpretatio Graeca*—Mercury stands in for Thoth, Typhon for Seth, Juno for Hathor, Diana for Bastet (and perhaps Sekhmet). But even still, Ovid is perfectly comfortable offering a narrative around animal gods that connects rather than separates Egyptian and Roman religious attitudes.[53] I do not want to minimize the nagging sense that Ovid subsumes Egyptian traditions into a fundamentally Greek story; the sense that this is an act of cultural projection of the Greek onto the Egyptian rather than of cultural translation of Egyptian mythology for a Greek and Roman audience. That is a question I will return to in chapter 6. For now, these explanations of Egypt's animal gods demonstrate that a cross-cultural connective model rooted in metamorphosis had its own footing even under Augustus.

The earlier authors on whom Ovid depends for this Typhon story wrote during a time of increased cultural contact. Ovid's Typhonic etiology of Egyptian animal worship builds on Nicander's *Heteroioumena*, a Hellenistic text whose fourth book contained the Typhon myth.[54] Nicander's text, like Callimachus's *Aetia* and so much fragmentary literature of the fourth century BCE, reveals how the movement of people around the Mediterranean was reflected in literature that synthesized Greek and non-Greek aetiological traditions in new ways.[55] The poor state of preservation of these texts makes it easy to lose sight of the Hellenistic origins of Ovid's cross-cultural aetiologizing.

The location of the Typhon story within the *Metamorphoses* adds a wrinkle. The Olympians' flight to Egypt is part of the warped era of the Typhonomachy, when the titan Typhon battled with the Olympian gods. Ovid places this etiology in the mouths of the Pierides, whose contest with the Muses maps onto Typhon's quarrel with the Olympians. In the Pierides' anti-Muse account, Typhon is the surprise hero of a narrative that is deliberately contrary to Olympian values. Within this overarchingly pro-Typhon story, this etiology could be an attempt by the Pierides to ridicule the Olympian gods by connecting them with Egypt's animals. The otherwise august Olympian gods are guilty by association with Egypt's lowly animal gods. This interpretation, persuasively outlined by Gianpiero Rosati, is appealing.[56]

---

53. See, on this connective function, the discussion of Aston (2017) (chapter 5, 3.2), who situates the passage against the wider backdrop of Greek theriomorphism.

54. The now lost section was epitomized by Antoninus Liberalis, who relates the Typhon myth in §28. It is also present in pseudo-Apollodorus 1.6.3, another imperial-era compilation.

55. Even as I am claiming something new in the combinatory impulse of Nicander, I do not want to discount the cross-cultural identifications already present in, e.g., Herodotus's *Histories* Book 2. Callimachus's *aetia* of Argos's fountains and of Berenike's victory, like the Io myth, helped link Argos and Egypt. As Acosta-Hughes and Stephens (2012, 168–70) note, this vouchsafes the legitimate Greekness of the otherwise ethnically marginal Macedonians.

56. Rosati (2009, 272–74 for theriomorphism as an anti-Olympian ridiculing strategy; 276–78 for the cultural battle of priority of syncretized gods). Richter's (2001, 213–36) reading of Plutarch's *DIO*,

FROM REPRESENTATION 99

The other main example of divine metamorphosis into animals occurs within the similarly subversive speech of Arachne, who cites (6.115–28) the greatest-hits catalogue (Leda and the swan, Europa and the bull) of gods seducing women while in animal shape.

But an emphasis on shock value and subversion—even when persuasively argued—risks putting the cart before the horse. In the race to a ridiculing message, readings of the passage focused on the Pierian narrators have elided the unified cosmogony created by this etiology. An argument for rivalry and ridicule still requires that religious systems—including Egypt's animal-shaped gods—are synced. For the ridicule to land, there needs to be an accepted premise in which gods can transform into animals and can travel between Greece and Egypt. That cross-cultural premise is further strengthened by the speech of Pythagoras in Book 15, in which metempsychosis provides a philosophical justification for human-animal metamorphosis.[57] The Pythagorean coda to the *Metamorphoses* adds a complexity that has not been fully appreciated in the subversive readings of this passage.

The Pierian context cannot wholly explain away the identification of the Olympian gods with the Egyptian habit of worshipping animals, not least because Egypt's animals reappear outside the Pierides-Muses contest, during the story of Iphis's gendered metamorphoses in Book 9.686–94.[58] Telethusa had been told by her husband Ligdus that, because of their poverty, they could not afford to have a daughter.[59] Once pregnant, Telethusa—a devotee of Isis—was at a loss about what to do. One night Telethusa fell asleep and was visited by Isis, who encouraged her not to expose the daughter to whom she was soon to give birth. It is important to note that the Iphis story, and Isis's salvatory role in it, lack any negative frame. In the dream, Isis is accompanied by her standard retinue, which includes the *latrator* Anubis, Bastet (called Bubastis by Ovid), Osiris, and the Apis bull. The specific representation of Egypt's gods in Book 9 is thus bound up in the cult of Isis and the sacred animals that were associated with it—most notably the Apis bull

---

which emphasizes Plutarch's belief in Greek philosophy's priority and superiority to Egyptian religion, is a valuable *comparandum*.

57. The speech of Pythagoras runs for 404 lines in the final book of Ovid's *Metamorphoses*. The intended tone of Pythagoras's speech has been divisive. Some see it as a parody of philosophical discourse (Segal 1969, 278–92, and van Schoor 2011, 129–35, the former opposed by Little 1974), others a wonder-filled, unphilosophical philosophical discourse (Myers 1994, ch. 4, and Beagon 2009, 297–98), and yet others a speech that hearkens back to earlier philosophical poetry (Hardie 1995, 210–12, and Oberrauch 2005). Lévi (2014, 295–305) offers a measured review of the issue.

58. One can add to this list of non-Pierian-framed Egyptian passages the tale of Erysichthon in *Met.* 8.731–7, where Achelous cites Proteus, the Egyptian shape-shifter, as an archetype of unbridled metamorphosis.

59. Not unsurprisingly, most critical attention (especially Pintabone 2002 and Kamen 2012) has focused on Iphis's gendered metamorphosis and the episode's representation of same-sex desire.

and Anubis. In this regard, Ovid anticipates the presentation of Egypt's animals in Statius, who similarly coordinated Isis-as-counselor, the Apis bull, and Anubis.

By repeating the *latrator* epithet and turning Isis from a sistrum-rattling Cleopatra-partisan into an agent of sound advice, Ovid directly responds to Virgil. As Rosati has argued, Ovid recontextualizes *latrator* Anubis and the Isiac retinue to counterbalance Virgil's eristic representation of them in the shield of Aeneas.[60] The rarity of the phrase *latrator Anubis* (these are the only two passages in which it appears) makes it clear that Ovid is intentionally contraposing his own and Virgil's interest in the most iconic example of animals in Egyptian religion. So too is it clear that Isis religion is a dominant frame through which that alternative barbarization of and engagement with Anubis is deployed, both here and elsewhere in Ovid's poetry.[61] But the scope and ambition of the *Metamorphoses* is reflected in the heterogeneous ways Ovid engages with Egypt's animals across Book 5 and Book 9. Juxtaposing his own view of Isis and Anubis with Virgil's is certainly one of those modes of engagement. But Ovid's interest in the Typhon story shows his debt to a Greek tradition that long precedes him and that falls outside the domain of Isis cult.

In the cases of Statius, Tibullus, and Ovid, it is important to make space for Roman discussions of Egypt's sacred animals that avoid complete exoticization or demonization. Through the coordination of Greco-Roman (specifically Olympian) and Egyptian religious systems, Ovid, Tibullus, and then Statius make creative connections between Egypt and Greco-Roman sensibilities. Thus Tibullus offers protreptic praise of his patron Messalla as a mixed Osiris-Bacchus figure to emphasize the value of peace and agricultural prosperity as against martial violence, a theme that recurs throughout his corpus.[62] This praise of Osiris's pacifism can naturally loop in the Apis bull and its death, whose connections to Osiris were promoted via the cultural export Sarapis. Ovid can trot out the same stereotyped vision of Isiac and Egyptian worship presented in Virgil—including the deliberate emphasis on the bestial barker Anubis and the bovine Apis—but tie it into a broader tapestry of stories about bodies that change shape and move between cultures. To Ovid, the fluidity of gods' animal and anthropomorphic exteriors helps him tell the larger story of metamorphosis and its cosmogonic primacy.[63] It is essential to note that this push-and-pull is inflected, but not entirely

---

60. Rosati (2009, 286–87) sees this passage as a correction of Actium-inflected propaganda and the poets who participated in its propagation. This helpfully correlates the poetic contraposition Ovid takes to Virgil with a similar contraposition on Egyptian animals.

61. *Amores* 2.13.7–14 (cf. Rosati 2009, 285–86) provides a perfect example. An embedded prayer to Isis for Corinna's wellbeing frames a catalogue of Egyptian gods that includes Anubis (with animality suppressed) and the Apis bull.

62. See, e.g., the similar valorization of peace over war in 1.10, which repeats the same peace/viticulture nexus facilitated by Osiris/Bacchus in 1.7.

63. For Ovid's cosmogony, see Myers (1994). She references the etiology only briefly (viii).

circumscribed, by the on-the-ground debate about Isis-worship's popularity in the city of Rome.

A COW IS LIKE A STATUE:
THE NTHROPOMORPHISM/ZOOMORPHISM DEBATE

Even before Actium implicated Egypt into Romans' self-reflection on the principate, Romans were struck by the central position of animals in Egyptian religion. Cicero is a good example. The condemnatory language he deploys seems to connect directly with the critiques made by Virgil, Propertius, and Lucan. In the *Tusculan Disputations*, Cicero bemoans Egyptian animal worship in obviously pejorative language: "Who doesn't know the customs of the Egyptians? Their minds are steeped in perverse mistakes and would undergo any sort of torture before committing violence against an ibis or snake or cat or dog or crocodile."[64] The language of perversion creates a wedge that separates Egyptian and Roman habits. The catalogue—whose length is exaggerated through the polysyndeton of "or" (*vel*)—runs through the cast of beastly characters typically associated with Egypt's sacred animals.

But underneath the eye-catching vocabulary, this condemnation of Egypt's misplaced religiosity is surprisingly nuanced. As I quoted him, Cicero bemoans Egyptians' "perverse" (*pravus*) religious practices. In the context of the speech, though, Egyptian religious practices are being praised. In Book 5 of the *Tusculan Disputations*, Cicero presents a Stoic argument that criticizes the deleterious effect of the emotions and defends the singular importance of virtue for the happy life. In this condemnation of the emotions, fear of pain receives its own repudiation.[65]

To help make his point, Cicero offers a list of miraculously pain-tolerant peoples. As a part of this exoticizing catalogue, Egyptians are a ready point of comparison through which Cicero criticizes Romans' enervation and the pain intolerance brought on by excessive luxury. Egyptians' fortitude in the face of adversity—their willingness to suffer torture rather than commit sacrilege—compares favorably with the moral dissolution in Rome about which Cicero is grumbling. Their religious missteps notwithstanding, Egyptians appear in a catalogue of non-Romans who practice a Stoic fortitude that the text is in fact endorsing. This is certainly a broadly drawn exoticization of Egyptian practices. Cicero's Egyptians are thin foils in a discussion which focuses on Rome. But it is still important to note that Egypt's animals help him mount a broader philosophical argument about religious practices and the emotions.

64. Cic. *Tusc. Disp.* 5.78: Aegyptiorum morem quis ignorat? quorum inbutae mentes pravitatis erroribus quamvis carnificinam prius subierint quam ibim aut aspidem aut faelem aut canem aut crocodilum violent. Text from Pohlenz (1982).

65. For this overarching argument about fear of pain and the best way of overcoming it, see Woolf (2015, 214–24).

Cicero points to a strain in Roman literature where Roman and Egyptian habits are weighed against each other. In the *Tusculan Disputations*, that discussion was contrastive. But elsewhere, Cicero makes an assimilatory argument that opposes the schematic separation seen in Virgil. In the *De Legibus*, Cicero leverages the same "worshipping animals" motif to make a universalizing argument: "nor, if among different peoples there are different beliefs, is it the case that those who worship a dog and cat as gods are not afflicted by the same superstition as other peoples."[66] Even where the outward expression of worship is different, Egyptians and Romans experience the same underlying drive to superstition. Egypt's sacred animals help Cicero prove cultural universals to the dialogue's interlocutors Atticus and Quintus. Cicero encourages his audience to look past the superficial difference of worshipping animals or statues to appreciate that the impulse to worship is the same for Romans and Egyptians alike.

These two Cicero examples are, then, not the concordant examples of "deviant worship" they at first seem. Egypt's animals defy that kind of summarization. Their utility to Cicero is heterogeneous. In one case, animals are woven into an assimilatory argument that connects Roman and non-Roman superstition. In another, animals are used to opposite effect: they prove a dissimilatory argument that separates Roman and non-Roman pain intolerance and tolerance. In both cases, Cicero's interest in the motif defies the poles of imperial assimilation or barbarization. So too does Cicero—as a late Republican author—help show that Romans' interest in the question is not a simple rubric through which an author advertises their stance vis-à-vis an emperor's accepted approach toward Isis.

The ambivalence on display here—eye-catching denigration of monstrosity overshadowing the more nuanced contextual argument being made with Egyptian animal worship—pops up frequently in Roman discussions of Egyptian religion. Pliny the Elder is a particularly important example, as a post-Actium Roman author. When excerpted, his criticism is obvious: "some peoples treat animals as gods, even some repulsive ones, and many things even more shameful to speak of, swearing by rotten food and other such stuff."[67] This is damning. But once again, it helps Pliny make an argument about a larger failing that Egyptians and Romans share equally. As Eleni Manolaraki has noted, Pliny's criticism of Egyptian animal worship in 2.16.5 is only a small part of a larger criticism of religious representative

---

66. Cic. *De Leg.* 1.32: nec si opiniones aliae sunt apud alios, idcirco qui canem et felem ut deos colunt, non eadem superstitione qua ceterae gentes conflictantur. Text from de Plinval (1968). For the role of superstition in Cicero's articulation of the "correct" practice of religion, see Wynne (2019, 76–78).

67. Plin. *NH* 2.16: gentes vero quaedam animalia et aliqua etiam obscena pro dis habeant ac multa dictu magis pudenda, per fetidos cibos, alia et similia iurantes. Smelik and Hemelrijk (1984, 1959–60) note Pliny's suspicion toward anthropomorphism too, but still emphasize his overarching criticism of animal worship.

strategies.[68] To Pliny, anthropomorphism, with its attendant insistence on divine adultery and intranecine rivalry, is just as grave a misstep as animal-shaped zoomorphism. His criticism of anthropomorphism is even more forceful:

> That people even believe in marriages among the gods and that, in such a long lifespan, nobody is born from them, and that some gods are eternally aged and grey, others young men and boys, dark-complexioned, with wings, limping, hatched from an egg and living and dying every other day—that is pretty much the stuff of puerile nonsense (*puerilium prope deliramentorum*).[69]

There is a real risk of stripping examples of animal worship from quotes like this. When viewed holistically in Pliny's larger Stoic argument about the divine, all "morphic" representations of the gods have their problems. Anthropomorphism is just as foolish and puerile as zoomorphism is shameful.

The Pliny anecdote has begun to shift gears, from a critique of Egyptian animal worship to a comparison of human- and animal-shaped gods. When one pauses to reintegrate these passages into their original context, there emerges a sustained interest in the different merits (or pitfalls) of representing the gods as humans (anthropomorphism), as animals generally (zoomorphism), or as wild animals specifically (theriomorphism).[70] Pliny's equal frustration with anthropomorphism and zoomorphism reflects both the Stoic frame that unifies the *Natural History* and his larger attempts at analogization between Egyptian and Roman cultural practices.[71]

To pivot toward this "morphic" discussion, I need to reevaluate the basic framing I have been using so far. Moving from the cult of Isis—where devotees would readily worship Anubis and Sarapis—to Pliny begins to show the limits of the phrase "animal worship." There is a good deal of damage done when discussions of Greco-Roman interest in Egypt begins with the premise "Egyptians worshipped animals" rather than the premise "Egyptians worshipped *with* animals."[72] Persevering with an underdefined phrase "animal worship" necessarily tips the balance

---

68. Manolaraki (2018, 353–59) frames Pliny's comparative approach to the twin pitfalls of anthropomorphism and zoomorphism through the "Vespasianic reconstruction of Egypt," which made earlier strategies of barbarization untenable.

69. Plin. *NH* 2.17: matrimonia quidem inter deos credi tantoque aevo ex <i>is neminem nasci et alios esse grandaevos semper canosque, alios iuvenes atque pueros, atri coloris, aligeros, claudos, ovo editos et alternis diebus viventes morientesque, puerilium prope deliramentorum est.

70. This is one vein in a larger issue of squaring the divine's immanence on earth and transcendence, an issue discussed by Vernant (1986, 40–45). Kindt (2019) brings this balance of anthropomorphic familiarity and transcendent ontology to bear on Greek gods' temporary zoomorphisms.

71. To reiterate an argument made by Manolaraki (2018).

72. Egyptologists have long called for this distinction and cautioned against the skewed picture painted by the animal-cult template. See particularly Hornung (1982, 137–38) and Kessler (2005, 35–37).

104   EGYPT'S ANIMALS

toward the conclusion that to Romans Egypt's sacred animals were a free-floating signifier of nebulous strangeness or cosmopolitan modishness.[73]

As a first step toward an Egyptian perspective on the issue, I would build on those who, like Eleni Manolaraki and Julia Kindt, have used zoomorphism rather than animal worship to frame the issue of Egypt's sacred animals.[74] As they note, many Romans appreciated that a scarab-headed god is less a matter of animal cult, and more a matter of representing a god in animal form. This is distinct from "animal worship" (theriolatry), which focuses on the direct worship of wild animals rather than their utility as a form of identification of the divine. To be sure, the line separating form (envisioning a god in the shape of a falcon) and essence (said falcon *is* divine) is blurry at best. But the difference of approach still bears fruit.[75] When rephrased as a question of representation, the difference between a living animal and a piece of wood carved into a statue is less stark.

Even as he predates Pliny, Cicero even more fully developed this strain of equivalence-making between anthropomorphic and zoomorphic representations of the gods. In the *De Natura Deorum*, Cicero uses the dialogue form to compare the different approaches to the divine taken by Epicurean, Stoic, and Skeptic philosophies. Cotta represents Academic skepticism and serves as the mouthpiece for Cicero's own philosophical point of view. He opposes Velleius, who espouses an Epicurean, anthropomorphic divinity that is eternal, changeless, and uninvolved. To Cotta, this makes an Epicurean god pretty much useless. To make the point, he notes that even the Egyptians worshipped animals like the ibis because of their utility. He leverages a common utilitarian explanation of Egyptian animal worship that stretches through Diodorus back to Herodotus.[76] Cotta points to this decidedly quotidian and function-oriented approach to divinity to emphasize the pitfalls of Epicureanism's eternal, aloof, and ultimately unhelpful divinity.

The Epicurean Velleius and the Skeptic Cotta disagree about the divine's anthropomorphism. Where Velleius sees god's anthropomorphic form as natural and "true," Cotta insists it is merely conventional and culturally specific. In this refutation, Cotta highlights the variety of forms in which different cultures conceptualize the divine:

> Ever since we were little we recognize Jupiter, Juno, Minerva, Neptune, Vulcan, Apollo, and the other gods by the appearance with which painters and sculptors have

---

73. Smelik and Hemelrijk (1984) (cf. the even-handed, but still exoticizing reading of Kindt 2021b). I use "floating signifier" to indicate a "symbol in its pure state, therefore liable to take on any symbolic content whatever," per Lévi-Strauss (1987, 63–64).

74. This is a central premise of Kindt (2019, 2021b) and is discussed by Manolaraki (2013, 198–206 on Statius, 301–2 for Philostratus; 2018, 353–59, on Pliny the Elder).

75. Hornung (1982, 137–38) notes the ways that different bodies of evidence amplify or blur this distinction between god and animal manifestation.

76. This strain begins with Herodotus (e.g., his utilitarian explanation of ibis-worship at 2.75) and extends, via Hecataeus of Abdera (following Murray 1970), to Diodorus 1.87, and then to Plutarch *DIO* 74, 380f.

wanted to depict them—not only by their appearance but even by their attire, age, and clothes. But not so for the Egyptians, Syrians, and pretty much all other barbarians; for you would see that their respect for certain animals is stronger than ours is for the most sacred temples and statues of the gods. We've seen many temples that have been laid waste to and many statues of gods that have been carried off from the most sacred shrines by our own countrymen, but nobody has ever heard, even by hearsay, of a crocodile or ibis or a cat being harmed by an Egyptian. So what do you think? That the Egyptians don't consider the Apis a god, that bull sacred to the Egyptians? As much as you do that Juno the savior of yours. You never see her—not even in your dreams!—except with goat-skin pelt, spear, shield, and slippers with pointed toe. But that isn't how Argive or Roman Juno looks.[77]

Cicero deploys Egyptian divine animals in a context that hinges on the medium in which the divine is conceptualized. Within this domain, Cicero, and Academic skepticism more broadly, are much more willing to accept zoomorphism as a strategy for imagining the divine; an animal form is no less viable than the highly localized portraits of, say, an Argive or Roman Juno. The specific way that god and form are linked illustrates this preoccupation with the media with which humans and divine can face each other. The verb *videri* links the subject Apis and the predicate *deum*. While casual translation suggests "seem," a more formal translation of "is seen as" or "appear as" better fits the passage and recenters visualization as against the connotations of incredulity in "seems."[78]

Vision and conceptualization are the dominant motifs of the passage. To advance a Skeptic argument about a god's true form, Cotta emphasizes that a generic "you" can only recognize gods in a specific and localized guise. The mention of clothes and ornament helps Cotta make his relativizing argument for seeing the divine: it is no sillier to believe that animals represent the divine than to imagine that one's own highly regional cult imagery is *the* true form of that god. This focus on vision subtly, but insistently, introduces issues of mediation that shift the tone of the passage away from the distancing effect between Egyptian and Roman habits animating Actium rhetoric.

When the question is rephrased on these terms, Cotta's attitude becomes quite different from the stereotypical befuddlement with which Romans wonder why Egyptians treat a cow as a god. Zoomorphism is considered an effective

---

77. *Nat. D.* 1.81–82: a parvis enim Iovem Iunonem Minervam Neptunum Vulcanum Apollinem reliquos deos ea facie novimus qua pictores fictoresque voluerunt, neque solum facie sed etiam ornatu aetate vestitu. at non Aegyptii nec Syri nec fere cuncta barbaria; firmiores enim videas apud eos opiniones esse de bestiis quibusdam quam apud nos de sanctissimis templis et simulacris deorum. etenim fana multa spoliata et simulacra deorum de locis sanctissimis ablata videmus a nostris, at vero ne fando quidem auditumst crocodilum aut ibin aut faelem violatum ab Aegyptio. quid igitur censes Apim illum sanctum Aegyptiorum bovem nonne deum videri Aegyptiis? tam hercle quam tibi illam vestram Sospitam. quam tu numquam ne in somnis quidem vides nisi cum pelle caprina cum hasta cum scutulo cum calceolis repandis. at non est talis Argia nec Romana Iuno. Text from Ax (1980).

78. This is a standard use of the passive of *video*, which often appears in divine revelation (e.g., Ennius's dream in F 3 of the *Annales*).

106   EGYPT'S ANIMALS

explanation of another Egyptian religious *topos*, the extremity of its piety. Cotta explains Egyptian piety, versus Rome's moral decline, through their choice of animate, versus inanimate, sacred objects.[79] Insofar as the media of the divine are necessarily imbued, at least partially, with the essence of the divine, an animate being could be a more suitable medium than an inanimate object.

Cicero's engagement with Egypt's sacred animals is, then, far from condemnatory. His comparison of clothed statues and animals reveals a new impetus for comparative discussion for the conceptualization of the divine. To focus on select words like *barbara* and *bestia* is to misconstrue the wider point Cicero is making about the distance between divine image and essence. As in metamorphosis literature that prioritized the points of connection between Egyptian and Greco-Roman myth, the zoomorphism-anthropomorphism debate allowed Roman authors to juxtapose different cultures' approaches to divine icons in ways that avoid the poles of barbarizing alienation and domesticating familiarity.[80]

PLUTARCH'S *ON ISIS AND OSIRIS*: PHILOSOPHIZING EGYPT'S ANIMALS

Plutarch's *De Iside et Osiride* (*DIO*) brings together cross-cultural syncretism and the zoomorphism/anthropomorphism debate. Plutarch here lays out a philosophical reading of the myth of Osiris, the Egyptian god-king who was murdered by his brother and would-be usurper Seth (in Plutarch, syncretized with and referred to as Typhon), reanimated by his sister Isis, and later avenged by his son Horus.[81] Plutarch then segues into a broader defense of the similarities shared between Greek philosophy and Egyptian religion. Plutarch's retelling of the myth suggests that the struggle of Osiris and Isis against Seth/Typhon is an example of the dualist metaphysics of the good and the bad that was a foundation of Plutarch's Platonism.[82] Isis's victory over Seth/Typhon is a felicitous myth for a metaphysical primacy of the good over the bad.

Plutarch offers a sustained engagement with Egypt's sacred animals only matched in scope by Diodorus.[83] The *DIO* is a text long central to Egyptological reconstructions of the Osiris myth, which is as important to ancient Egyptian cosmology as it is lacunose in Egyptian-language evidence. Alongside the *Memphite Theology* and the more playful and literary rendition of the myth in the Late-Egyptian *Contendings of Horus and Seth*, Plutarch provides critical evidence

79. Sonnabend (1986, 123–24).
80. For "domesticating the foreign," see Manolaraki (2018), Barrett (2019, 20, 141–42), and Mazurek (2022, 183).
81. When referring to Plutarch's discussion of the Osiris myth, I will use the admittedly clunky phrase Seth/Typhon. For the goals, sources, and content of the *DIO*, see Griffiths (1970).
82. Summarized at *DIO* 46, 369d. On Plutarch's dualism, see Dillon (1988, 107–13).
83. Diodorus discusses Egyptian animal worship at 1.83–90 (cf. Smelik and Hemelrijk 1984, 1895–1905).

of the narrative's core components.[84] Even more germane to my goals in this book, it has long been the point of departure for those, like J. Gwyn Griffiths, interested in showing the joins connecting Greco-Roman and Egyptian literary and intellectual culture.[85] Both narrowly for the Osiris myth and broadly for Greek and Egyptian intellectual contact, the *DIO* is *the* text.

Plutarch's discussion of Egypt's sacred animals synthesizes the different explanations offered by Greek and Roman authors. Much of Plutarch's account harkens back to Herodotus, whose utilitarian approach to Egypt's animals continued to shape authors in the imperial period. I have argued elsewhere that Juvenal's condemnation of Egyptians' worship of wild animals subtly loops in the Herodotean explanations—totemism, utilitarianism—which makes that worship intelligible.[86] But unlike Juvenal's subtle incorporation of these explanations, Plutarch addresses them head-on. Plutarch rips apart many of the popular explanations of zoomorphism. He rejects Ovid's etiology of animal gods, in which Typhon chased the Olympians to Egypt, where they hid in animal shapes: "The notion that the gods transformed into these animals because they were afraid of Typhon, as if concealing themselves in the bodies of ibises, dogs, and hawks, exceeds any and all fairy tales and mythology (*muthologian*)."[87] Unlike Ovid, Plutarch sees "mythology" (*muthologian*) not as a wellspring for poetic innovation, but as childish nonsense. Like Pliny, Plutarch worries that any assignation of fear and subterfuge to the Olympians attributes too much emotional volubility to the divine.

Plutarch is no kinder to the other popular origin stories for sacred animals. He presents, and then brushes aside, the political etiologies found in Diodorus: that the animals sacred to Egyptian communities were originally military standards by which to totemically organize the army.[88] This germinated into a wider range of social theorizations of animal worship. There was a related explanation that

---

84. Griffiths (1970, 78–81), Hani (1979, 469–70), and Smelik and Hemelrijk (1984, 1961) have all underlined Plutarch's ability to engage with Egyptian religious material reliably, even granting that Platonism impacts his narration and interpretation of the Osiris myth. For the core components of the Osiris myth, see Assmann (2001a, 123–47).

85. This is of course evident from Griffith's commentary on the *DIO* (Griffiths 1970). But it ripples throughout his work, whether on allegory (Griffiths 1967, 1969) or on Isis/Osiris (Griffiths 1960a, 1960b, 2012).

86. Kelting (2019). Diodorus (1.90) mentions that Egyptian communities expressed their collective identity through animal totems.

87. *DIO* 72, 379e: τὸ μὲν γὰρ εἰς ταῦτα τὰ ζῷα τοὺς θεοὺς τὸν Τυφῶνα δείσαντας μεταβαλεῖν, οἷον ἀποκρύπτοντας ἑαυτοὺς σώμασιν ἴβεων καὶ κυνῶν καὶ ἱεράκων, πᾶσαν ὑπερπέπαικε τερατείαν καὶ μυθολογίαν . . . Text from Griffiths (1970).

88. Diod. Sic. 1.86.4, 1.90.1. The predynastic and early-dynastic use of sacred animals has sometimes been interpreted totemically, in ways not very different from the explanations dismissed by Plutarch. Core evidence includes predynastic standards with zoomorphic images connected to a king's local base (e.g., standards displayed in the Scorpion and Narmer maceheads), the choice of the Seth-animal in the serekh of the Second Dynasty king Peribsen, and the changing serekhs of Kasekhem/Khasekhemy, his successor. For an overview, see Wilkinson (1999, esp. 69, on the political implications of serekh choice, and 168–70, on standards and their symbolism).

108   EGYPT'S ANIMALS

animal masks were royal insignia and evolved into the worship of said animals.[89] In a later political variant, kings used animal worship to keep the Egyptian populace pitted against each other and thus easily governable.[90] This divisive function of animals—acting as a community's totem or organizing principle—became the key for Juvenal's communalist approach to sacred animals in Satire 15.

After moving briskly through these alternate explanations, Plutarch decides in favor of utilitarian and symbolic explanations of animal worship. Of these, the purely utilitarian explanation is rooted firmly in the Greek tradition and spans the length of Greeks talking about Egypt, from Herodotus through Diodorus. In this logic, animals were worshipped for the useful things they did. Plutarch clearly echoes this tradition, repeating Herodotus's and Diodorus's utilitarian explanations for the worship of the snake-eating ibis, crocodile-killing ichneumon, wool-giving sheep, and plow-bearing oxen.[91]

Plutarch's general survey of Egyptian worship of animals includes a specific comparison that caps a dual-reading dynamic I have been promoting in this chapter. His discussion of Egyptian practices first looks like a direct critique of Egyptian theriolatry. In its excerpted form, Plutarch's opening salvo on Egyptian animal worship seems to reject Egyptian behavior and endorse a Greek sensibility:

> Egyptians have experienced this a great deal concerning their sacred animals. In this the Greeks correctly state, and believe, that the dove is the sacred animal of Aphrodite, the serpent the sacred animal of Athena, the raven of Apollo, and the dog of Artemis—as Euripides says, 'Dog, you will be the glory of light-bearing Hecate.' *But most Egyptians, in worshipping the animals themselves and treating them as gods, have not only filled their religious services full of ridicule, but this is the least of the evils of their stupidity.*[92]

First and foremost, Plutarch brings to the surface a distinction whose importance I have been trying to underline: that worshipping an animal is distinct from identifying an animal with a god. Plutarch endorses zoomorphism but lambastes in no uncertain terms a mistaken identification of these animals *as gods*.

The above quote certainly seems to differentiate (bad) Egyptian theriolatry from (good) Greek zoomorphism.[93] But once again, this is a passage that looks different when divorced from its original argument. The opening pronoun "this" hints at key context which has been omitted. It is clunky to quote long passages.

---

89. Diod. Sic. 1.62.4. While masks themselves are not attested as royal insignia in battle, Diodorus's actual examples—snake and lion imagery—were constituent elements of a king's iconography.

90. Isoc. *Bus.* 25–6, Diod. Sic. 1.89.5.

91. *DIO* 74, 380f; Diod. Sic. 1.87.

92. Note especially the play on ἄγαλμα, which combines the sense of "pet/delight" and "statue (esp. of the gods)." *DIO* 71, 379d–e: Αἰγυπτίων δ' οἱ πολλοὶ θεραπεύοντες αὐτὰ τὰ ζῷα καὶ περιέποντες ὡς θεοὺς οὐ γέλωτος μόνον οὐδὲ χλευασμοῦ καταπεπλήκασι τὰς ἱερουργίας, ἀλλὰ τοῦτο τῆς ἀβελτερίας ἐλάχιστόν ἐστι κακόν.

93. That is the reading offered by Smelik and Hemelrijk (1984, 1961–62).

But in the present case, the full passage redraws an Egyptian/Greek contrast into a new form of comparison:

> So, for instance, there are those of the Greeks who haven't learned or grown accustomed to calling bronze and painted and stone works as statues and honorary dedications of the gods, but simply call them gods, and they then dare to say that Lachares stripped Athena naked, and Dionysius gave a buzz cut to Apollo of the golden locks, and Capitoline Zeus was set on fire and destroyed during the civil war. These people unknowingly follow along with and take up wicked ideas that are in keeping with the names.
>
> Egyptians have experienced this a great deal concerning their sacred animals. In this the Greeks correctly state, and believe, that the dove is the sacred animal of Aphrodite, the serpent the sacred animal of Athena, the raven of Apollo, and the dog of Artemis—as Euripides says, 'Dog, you will be the glory of light-bearing Hecate.' But most Egyptians, in worshipping the animals themselves and treating them as gods, have not only filled their religious services full of ridicule, but this is the least of the evils of their stupidity.[94]

The passage takes on a completely different complexion. No longer is there a comparison between Greeks and Egyptians in which Greeks are right and Egyptians are wrong. There are misguided views to be corrected among both groups.[95] Even more importantly, there is the same comparison of statues and animals. Plutarch and Cicero both equate worshipping animals and statues. They become kindred media through which to honor and display reverence for the gods. To undress the statue is not to undress the god. Thus not only are Greek and Egyptian practices brought into alignment, but Plutarch is criticizing idolatry (with statues) just as forcefully as theriolatry (with animals). In other words, Plutarch's authorial and philosophical cachet emerges from his keen desire to show that medium is not the same as essence. The quote becomes a general criticism of confusing how you worship (with statues or animals) with what you worship (the divine). Egyptian practices become symptomatic of a larger problem rather than uniquely at fault. Plutarch, by saying "not least have Egyptians experienced this," underlines the equivalency of Greeks and Egyptians who fall into errant ideas about divine representation. The dividing line is one of expertise, wisdom, and (implicitly) elite status, not of cultural difference.

Plutarch's description of the Apis bull is a good example of his persistent distinction between zoomorphism and direct animal worship. As Plutarch styles it, "The Apis, with a few other animals, seems to be the sacred image of Osiris."[96] The grammatical construction—literally, "is the sacred object of Osiris" (ἱερὸς εἶναι τοῦ Ὀσίριδος)—repeats the syntax used in the Aphrodite-dove pairing (ἱερὸν

---

94. *DIO* 71, 379c–e: ὥσπερ Ἑλλήνων οἱ τὰ χαλκᾶ καὶ τὰ γραπτὰ καὶ λίθινα μὴ μαθόντες μηδ᾽ ἐθισθέντες ἀγάλματα καὶ τιμὰς θεῶν, ἀλλὰ θεοὺς καλεῖν . . .

95. Kindt (2021b, 136–37) also emphasizes Plutarch's even-handed critique of Greek and Egyptian ambiguity around essence versus medium.

96. *DIO* 73, 380e: ὁ γὰρ Ἆπις δοκεῖ μετ᾽ ὀλίγων ἄλλων ἱερὸς εἶναι τοῦ Ὀσίριδος.

Ἀφροδίτης ζῷον εἶναι). For Egyptians and Greeks alike, Plutarch takes pains to designate animals as sacred emblems rather than gods. Far from a one-off, a desire to clarify that Egyptian animal religion is zoomorphic rather than theriolatrous extends throughout Plutarch's discussion. With the proper contrast drawn, Plutarch's attitude becomes much more coherent.

Plutarch takes this idea of representation and uses it as a springboard for his discussion of philosophically rich representations of the divine. Plutarch endorses symbolic representations of the gods that are wonderfully batty. Thus, the sacred status of the ibis is clear because, when it drinks, its legs and beak form an equilateral triangle—a shape whose perfection was associated with divine order. Plutarch compares this to a statue of Zeus without ears, which he commends as a better representation of a god whose ubiquity in the universe makes the concept of "listening" vacuous. In short, once the idea of divine representation is put on a proper footing, Plutarch is remarkably catholic in his list of appropriate media. Pythagorean number theory, where different numbers are identified with different gods, also fits the bill.

In the end, Plutarch ends up preferring animals as a medium with which to identify the gods. This celebration of the animate as a medium for the divine caps what has been a step-by-step move away from a tidy barbarization or exoticization of Egypt, from the ready conclusion that Greeks and Romans found in sacred animals only a mirror for social change in Rome. When one compares the animate and the inanimate as media with which to envisage the divine, Plutarch chooses the animate:

> For it is not in colors nor in forms nor in a smooth finish that the divine is present, but whatever has had no share in life and cannot by nature share in it, is worse off than the dead. The nature, on the other hand, which lives and sees, which has its principle of movement from itself and knows what belongs to it and what does not, has imbibed an efflux of beauty and derives its lot from the intelligent being 'by whom the universe is guided' according to Heraclitus. *In view of this the divine is represented no less faithfully in these animals than in bronze and stone works of art, which equally take on gradations of color and tincture, but are by nature devoid of all perception and intelligence.* Concerning the animals honored, then, I approve especially of these views.[97]

To Plutarch, Egyptians' identification of the divine with the animate is philosophically preferable to the anthropomorphic statues central to Greek and Roman worship. This is a long way from Actium.

Plutarch repeats what has been a recurrent trend. An excerpted passage proves that Plutarch barbarized Egypt's animal worship. But when recontextualized, that

---

97. *DIO* 76, 382b–c: ὅθεν οὐ χεῖρον ἐν τούτοις εἰκάζεται τὸ θεῖον ἢ χαλκοῖς καὶ λιθίνοις δημιουργήμασιν, ἃ φθορὰς μὲν ὁμοίως δέχεται καὶ ἐπιχρώσεις, αἰσθήσεως δὲ πάσης φύσει καὶ συνέσεως ἐστέρηται. Translation from Griffiths (1970).

passage reveals Plutarch's comparative interest in the philosophical pros and cons of anthropomorphic versus zoomorphic, and animate versus inanimate, media for the divine. This was certainly true of Cicero and Pliny the Elder, both of whom gave a philosophical comparison of zoomorphic and anthropomorphic conceptions of the divine. These cross-cultural comparative discussions used different tools to forge meaningful connections between Greek, Roman, and Egyptian norms. In some cases, reverence for animals helps to underline superstition's universality; in others, an omnipotent, formless, universal god is failed equally by the adulterous emotional volubility of Greco-Roman anthropomorphism and by the monstrosity of Egyptian theriomorphism.

CONCLUSION: REDRESSING ANUBIS

By way of conclusion, I would like to return to the "barker" Anubis. He allowed Virgil to widen the distance that separated Roman and Egyptian norms around the divine. Egypt's lowly animal gods were irreparably divided from proper august (and Augustan) divinities. In the meantime, I have reemphasized the other literary, historical, and philosophical currents that shaped Greeks' and Romans' interest in Anubis. The emperor Hadrian and his Egyptophilia provide a final, striking representative strategy for Egypt's divine animals. Hadrian populated his palace at Tivoli with an assemblage of Egyptian and Egyptianizing material culture.[98] It is easy to get bogged down in Hadrian's biography and the motivations surrounding his enthusiasm for Egyptian religion. The death of his lover Antinous in Egypt definitely looms large. It became an inflection point for the presence of Egyptian material culture in Rome and, with the foundation of the metropolis Antinoöpolis, for Roman administration of Egypt. For present purposes, the statues today in the Vatican's Gregorian Egyptian Museum speak to the dynamic and changing relationship between Egyptian and Roman religious conventions, rather than to a single man's biography.

These statues are remarkable for their ability to capture the flexible connections between gods and sacred animals in Egyptian religion. Two statues reflect well the tenor of discussions around Egypt's animals in both Aegyptiaca and Greco-Roman literature. First, a statue of Anubis, found on the grounds of the Villa Pamphili in 1750, represents the Egyptian god in a hybrid anthro/zoomorphic form (fig. 3). The dress and accessories of Anubis promote his syncretic identification with Mercury and Hermes. This mixed Hermanubis's role as psychopomp bridged Greek, Roman, and Egyptian eschatology.[99] Plutarch's *DIO* notes Hermanubis's chthonic

---

98. Catalogued by Raeder (1983) and discussed by Mari and Sgalambro (2007) and Mari (2008).

99. This explains Hermes's identification with Anubis, rather than the much more common Hermes-Thoth syncretism reflected in the Hermetic tradition.

FIGURE 3. Statue of the god Anubis-Mercury. From the Villa Pamphili, Anzio, 1st–2nd century CE. Gregorian Egyptian Museum, Vatican Museums Cat. 22840, Rome. Photo courtesy of the author.

associations. Apuleius describes (*Met.* 11.11.1) Anubophores who looked a lot like Hermanubis when they marched in Isiac festivals.

The statue, and its engagement with Isiac iconography around Hermanubis, offer dramatic proof that Augustus's self-definition against Isis and her retinue of animal gods quickly gave way to imperial support for Isis. Thus, Domitian cemented the Flavians' close connection to Isis through the obelisk that he erected in Rome's Isis temple. As Laurent Bricault has noted, the *Historia Augusta* (*Vita Commodi* 9.4–6) claims that the emperor Commodus helped carry a statue of Anubis in an Isiac procession.[100] Domitian, Hadrian, and Commodus all cemented their own authority in a multicultural empire by aligning themselves with, rather than defining themselves against, Anubis.

But Egypt's animals did not simply weather Julio-Claudian antipathy before enjoying wide acceptance. Later Greek philosophers remained critical of the cultural mixedness of this Hermanubis figure. As the Neoplatonic philosopher Porphyry notes, Hermanubis is a "half-Greek."[101] This is an apt pejorative for mixed identity, one that aligns religious syncretism with the formulation of creole identities in Roman Egypt. Hermanubis, then, has a lot in common with Pancrates, whose culturally mixed self-presentation was also the target of Lucian's loaded criticism.[102]

The second statue (fig. 4) is a two-headed figure, rediscovered in 1736 on the grounds of Hadrian's palace at Tivoli. When viewed from one side, you see a fully anthropomorphic statue of Osiris in the visual language of the Ptolemaic period. But when you look from the opposite side, you see the head of the Apis bull juxtaposed, Janus-like, with Osiris's human head. This double-headed visual representation gives concrete form to a larger argument hinted at by Tibullus's alignment of Apis and Osiris. Like Tibullus and Ovid, the statue prioritizes association and interconnection, which Actian rhetoric of Egyptian religion's monstrosity doggedly refused.

Barbarizing reactions to Egypt's animals were certainly an important discourse in the early imperial period, one that continues to receive widespread scholarly attention.[103] There are good reasons for Virgil's, Lucan's, and Juvenal's tendentious representation of Egyptian zoomorphism, provided one appreciates that this mode of representation was neither an inevitable nor exclusive Roman attitude, in any dynastic period. Juvenal's fifteenth satire, with which I opened this chapter, barbarizes Egyptian practices as a riposte to Hadrianic visions of a coherent empire vividly embodied by these statues. In its two-headed form, the Apis/Osiris statue represents the opposite impulse of Juvenal's barbarizing non-translation. It is vividly symbolic, bringing together two halves of an otherwise sundered whole.[104] What is interesting is not so much a vivid accuracy in this alignment of Apis

---

100. Bricault (2000–2001, 30–31).

101. Porph. *De Imag.* F 8 (cf. Benaissa 2010): μιξέλλην.

102. From Lucian *Philops.* 34, as I discussed in chapter 2.

103. Per Gasparini (2017, 399), "animal worship in the Graeco-Roman world was perceived not just as inappropriate, but as outlandish, despicable, and monstrous." Eleni Manolaraki has noted authors who avoid Actian rhetorics of theriomorphism's monstrosity, *viz.* Pliny (Manolaraki 2018, 353–59) and Statius (Manolaraki 2013, 198–206).

104. To lean heavily on the original semantics of the verb συμβάλλειν, which denoted the two halves of a contract, discussed by Struck (2004, 79–80).

FIGURE 4. Statue of Osiris-Apis. From Hadrian's Villa, Tivoli, reign of Hadrian. Gregorian Egyptian Museum, Vatican Museums Cat. 22807, Rome. Photo courtesy of Marie-Lan Nguyen / Wikimedia Commons.

bull and Osiris. It is instead important to see how the statue creatively connects animal and god.

The statues, then, reflect the disparate processes through which Egypt's sacred animals were translated into forms legible to a Greek and Roman audience. They confirm, corporally and dramatically, that Egypt's animals contributed to cross-cultural conversations about the ties connecting animals and the divine. Some of those ancient discourses have received more scholarly attention than others. The cult of Isis framed Roman interest in Anubis and the Apis bull, not least because Anubis and Sarapis rounded out the Isiac triad.[105] It makes good sense that much work on Anubis broaches his animality through the exotic appeal—or danger—of Isiac religion across the empire. I have tried to show what is risked when barbarization and the cult of Isis monopolize scholarship on Rome's interest in Egypt's animals. The enduring importance of Typhon, Herodotean utilitarian explanations picked up by Plutarch, and Cicero's comparison of medium versus essence point toward other literary traditions that engaged with Egypt's animals from very different perspectives and with very different conclusions.

It is via these other literary traditions that authors of Aegyptiaca enter into Greek and Roman discussions of Egypt's animals. In the next chapter, I chart the path of cross-cultural translation that authors of Aegyptiaca undertook. By shifting conversation around Egypt's animals away from barbarizing projection and toward philosophical dialogue, it becomes clear that Greeks and Romans were open to the presentation of Egyptian practices offered by authors like Manetho, Apion, and Chaeremon.

---

105. Sfameni Gasparro (2018) notes how views of Anubis changed because of his role in the cult of Isis.

4

. . . To Translation

Aegyptiaca, Seth/Typhon, and Human/Animal/Divine Permeability

There is a lot to be gained by taking a synoptic view of Greeks' and Romans' heterogeneous interest in Egypt's animals. Overemphasis on barbarizing strands of Roman literature hides spaces where Egyptian religious practices were discussed in starkly different terms. Philosophical literatures used Egypt's religious animals as a point of departure for comparative discussions about how humans imagine gods. In this comparative framework, animal-shaped, zoomorphic gods are not inherently less opportune than anthropomorphic ones.[1] By juxtaposing different approaches to a fundamental human issue—giving shape and physical form to transcendent metaphysical entities—authors like Cicero, Pliny, and Plutarch brought Egyptian and Roman practices onto a par with each other.

It is not just that some strategies of cultural representation of Egypt's animals have been given more attention than others. It is also that the very framework of cultural representation falls short. The previous chapter made the first of these two interrelated arguments—that barbarism, exoticism, and the cult of Isis do not fully encompass Greek and Roman discussions of Egypt's sacred animals. This chapter sets out to make the second argument, to replace a model of cultural representation with a framework of translation that better captures the movement of the animal/ god nexus from Egyptian-language contexts, through Greek-language Aegyptiaca, to Greek and Roman authors.[2] It will follow this path in reverse, starting with

---

1. Kindt (2019) and Bremmer (2021) both trace the way that scholarship has broached (and often tried to minimize) zoomorphism in Greek religion. Buxton (2009, 32) summarizes earlier theories in which Greek anthropomorphism evolved from, and thus was superior to, more primitive zoomorphism.

2. Kindt (2021b) is illustrative; she reevaluates with nuance the motivations for Greeks' engagement with zoomorphism, but her exclusive focus on cultural representation fossilizes an association

Plutarch's *On Isis and Osiris*, the text that closed the previous chapter. Then I will trace the thread of translation back to authors of Aegyptiaca and the Egyptian-language evidence on which they drew, before ending with Apuleius's own debt to Aegyptiaca and its presentation of animal symbolisms.

Anthropomorphism, Animal Worship, and Other False Premises

There are several false premises that foreclose the possibility of cultural translation. In one, dynastic periodization dictates when and how authors barbarized (Julio-Claudians) or domesticated (Flavians) Egypt's animals. In another, the Apis cult and the Anubophores of Isis religion imply that "animal worship" encapsulates Romans' engagement with Egypt's sacred animals.[3] Both premises box out Egyptians' own presentation of sacred animals to a Greco-Roman audience. Ovid's etiology of Egypt's animal-gods via Typhon and fugitive Olympians (*Met.* 5.321–31) points to a key vein of inquiry hidden by both the Julio-Claudian/Flavian dichotomy and by the "animal worship" concept.[4] Through Ovid, one begins to see the processes of translation—from Egypt to Rome and between human, animal, and divine—that I will focus on in this chapter. This form of "translation" coordinates a shift between forms (human, animal) and a physical movement between Greece and Egypt. Both modes of translation create a bridge that connects across difference.

Typhon shows both that Greco-Roman narratives of the divine had long relied on zoomorphism and that "animal worship" has hidden Aegyptiaca's contributions to the sacred animal *topos*.[5] Hesiod, whose *Theogony* includes one of the first extant descriptions of Typhon, is a good starting point:

> When Zeus had driven the Titans from the sky, huge Earth, because of golden Aphrodite, made love with Tartarus and bore as her youngest son Typhon. His hands are holding deeds upon strength, and tireless the strong god's feet; *and from his shoulders there were a hundred heads of a snake, a terrible dragon's, licking with their dark tongues*; and on his prodigious heads fire sparkled from his eyes under the eyebrows, and from all of his heads fire burned as he glared. And there were voices in all his terrible heads, sending forth all kinds of sounds, inconceivable: for sometimes they would utter sounds as though for the gods to understand, and at other times the sound of a loud-bellowing, majestic bull, unstoppable in its strength, at other times

---

of Egyptian religion with zoomorphism that fails to capture an Egyptian-centered perspective on this issue.

3. To reiterate, this is not so much a criticism of Smelik and Hemelrijk (1984), who place "animal worship" in the title of their work, as it is a critique of the sense that animal worship circumscribes the issue of animals and the divine.

4. Bremmer (2021, 113n124), relying on Griffiths (1960b), shows how Ovid is the inheritor of an Egyptian tradition filtered through Alexandria. On this specific Typhonic myth, see also the brief synopsis of Griffiths (1960a).

5. Aston (2017, 21–23), for Egyptian influence on Greek mixanthropy, and Bremmer (2021, 108–11), for Poseidon and Dionysus, underline the centrality of zoomorphism in Greek religion.

118   EGYPT'S ANIMALS

that of a lion, with a ruthless spirit, at other times like young dogs, a wonder to hear, and at other times he hissed, and the high mountains echoed from below.[6]

Animals allow Hesiod to paint a vivid portrait of Typhon in all his monstrosity.[7] Typhon is the same kind of impossible, multiform figure—a collage of animal and human parts—that is so regularly associated with Egypt's animal-headed, human-bodied gods. Typhon's theriomorphism is even more obvious in his visual representation. Throughout his iconography—Corinthian vase production, reliefs, shield decorations—Typhon is winged and has a serpentiform tail.[8] This constellation of body parts underlines his fearsomeness and transcendent metaphysics. Typhon's different representations were flexible; they drew on zoomorphism and polyphony in various proportions according to media and context. That flexibility in representation reveals just how inbuilt zoomorphism, theriomorphism, and multiform bodies were to Greek imaginations of the divine world. The same holds true for Egypt, where Egyptian gods could occupy the full suite of corporal media, variously anthropomorphic, zoomorphic, or a mixture of the two.

Typhon also shows the limits of the phrase "animal worship." As a paradigmatically anti-order, anti-Olympian figure, Typhon is not the object of cult worship. Nor does he fit very well into a vision of the divine oriented around gods worshiped in temples. But he points to the essential role animals played in Greco-Roman cosmological thinking. When one pivots to the Egyptian side and to authors of Aegyptiaca, pushing past the animal worship template recenters central divine-animal pairs, like Seth and his animals. Egypt's relatively well-known animal cults are certainly important, but they threaten to drown out the core role of animals as a means of characterization and identification of the divine.[9]

This broad issue of identification is the critical one. The semantics of the relevant Egyptian terms *ba* and *wḥm* specify that animals were a medium with which to imagine and approach the divine, rather than independently divine in and of themselves.[10] Animals like the Apis bull or a Horus falcon were earthly impressions (*ba*) or incarnations (*wḥm*: lit. "repetition") of different gods. The basic idea is relatable across religions. Whether Catholic transubstantiation, Hindu avatars, or

6. Hes. *Th.* 820–35, text and (adapted) translation from Most (2006), who obelizes the phrase "deeds upon strength." The italicized passage reads ἐκ δέ οἱ ὤμων / ἦν ἑκατὸν κεφαλαὶ ὄφιος δεινοῖο δράκοντος, / γλώσσῃσι δνοφερῇσι λελιχμότες.

7. Per Strauss Clay (2020, 318), Typhon's serpentiform hybridity is inherited by the catalogue of monsters (Hes. *Th.* 306–33) he and Echidna beget.

8. For examples, see *LIMC* 8.1 148–52.

9. Kessler (1989) and Ikram (2005) remain the best sources on Egypt's animal cults. Te Velde (1980) does a fine job broaching this larger domain of animals in Egyptian religion.

10. For overview, see Kessler (1989, 12–15) and Hornung (1982, 136–38). As I discussed in the previous chapter and as Kindt (2021b, 135–37) makes clear in the case of Plutarch, Greek and Roman authors couched their authority in part on their ability to see animals and statues as media for rather than objects of worship.

Hawaiian kinolau, the embodiment and incarnation of the divine are fundamental issues. In both anthropomorphic and zoomorphic representations of the divine, medium can bleed into essence. I do not want to over-schematize the distinction between god and the incarnation of said god.[11] As with wooden statues, there was certainly fluidity between animals as a vehicle for the divine and animals as divine *per se* in Egyptian thinking.[12] But prioritizing the identification of animals with gods, rather than the divinity of animals *per se*, creates space for authors of Aegyptiaca, whose authority rested on philosophically inflected explanations of the connections made between animals like hippopotamuses and gods like Seth.

SETH/TYPHON AND THE PATH FROM REPRESENTATION TO TRANSLATION
Plutarch and the Philosophy of Animal Identification

Plutarch's *De Iside et Osiride* (*DIO*) creates a bridge from Greco-Roman interest in Egypt's animals back to authors of Aegyptiaca.[13] I do not want to rehash here the introduction I gave in the previous chapter for Plutarch's philosophical framing of the Osiris myth. There, I recentered Plutarch's surprisingly enthusiastic endorsement of animals as medium in which to imagine the divine. Plutarch was just one participant in a longer debate about the risks and benefits of anthropomorphism and zoomorphism. That comparative impulse and its importance to imperial philosophy is reflected in Plutarch's discussion of the Apis bull, criticism of Ovid's Typhon etiology, and preference for living animals over inorganic statues as divine media. But I have deferred until now the core role that animals play in Plutarch's presentation of the Osiris myth. Animals associated with Seth/Typhon justify Plutarch's philosophical presentation of Seth/Typhon's stupidity, passion, and volubility.

My use of the composite phrase Seth/Typhon, while conventional in discussing the *DIO*, speaks to a cross-cultural translation of this specific god that is worth pausing over.[14] I have freely discussed the Egyptian god Seth where Plutarch refers to the Greek monster Typhon. This is, in and of itself, not a major problem, and I

---

11. Plutarch had, in the section of the *DIO* (71, 379c–e) about looting gods' statues quoted in the previous chapter, made precisely this point about the separability of medium and the actual divinity accessed through that medium.

12. This is an issue shared by Egypt's statues and Egypt's animal cult. The complementarity of the incarnated divine and the inaccessibly distant divine is well theorized by Dunand and Zivie-Coche (2004, 71–104).

13. For text and commentary, see Griffiths (1970). For scholarship, see particularly Parmentier (1913), Griffiths (1960b, 1970), Hani (1979), and Richter (2001; 2011, 207–29).

14. Pfeiffer (2015) presents Egyptian examples of *interpretatio Graeca* (using a Greek god's name to identify an Egyptian god) as a form of "translation," largely by focusing on Greek-language inscriptions in Egypt.

am in good company when doing so.[15] Seth and Typhon had long been identified with each other.[16] Plutarch himself, in a discussion of the natural-philosophical resonances of the Osiris myth, clarifies that Typhon and Seth are alternative names for the same divinity: "That's why the Egyptians always call Typhon 'Seth.'"[17] Diodorus, Ovid, pseudo-Apollodorus, Antoninus Liberalis, and presumably Nicander all referred to Seth as Typhon. There is similar evidence for the Seth/Typhon pairing in both Greek and Demotic papyri from Ptolemaic and Roman Egypt.[18] The felicity of the mutual identification is obvious, at least for Seth as he came to be understood in the Late through Roman periods.[19] Seth and Typhon both represented principles of disorder and opposition to the divine rule of Osiris or Zeus. The unambiguously inimical view of Seth in the *DIO*, fossilized through an identification with the anti-Olympian Typhon, aligns well with the later role of Seth as a god connected with outsiders, the foreign, and the dangerous.[20] This departs from his earlier role in Egyptian accounts of the Osiris myth, where his claim to the throne is legitimized by his protection of Ra and defeat of the abominable snake Apepi during the sun's underworld journey.[21] For most of pharaonic history, Seth cult flourished in sites like Avaris.[22]

In other words, Seth and Typhon are uniquely suited to a cross-cultural translation that syncs fundamental Greek and Egyptian myths of divine conflict and underlines the role of animal identification in them both. Their pairing reflects a specific cultural context—Hellenistic and imperial Alexandrian intellectual culture—that incentivized a set of culturally mixed Egyptian authors of Aegyptiaca to make a strategic identification of kindred cultural symbols. The Hellenistic social dynamics that motivated this cross-cultural identification is often lost in the conventional use of the term "syncretism," which presents the divine pairing of

15. See von Lieven (2016, 71).

16. Griffiths (1970, 259).

17. *DIO* 41, 367d: διὸ τὸν Τυφῶνα Σὴθ [ἀεὶ] Αἰγύπτιοι καλοῦσιν.

18. See Dieleman (2005, 130–38) for Egyptian-language perspectives on the Seth/Typhon pairing. Similar is the presence of Seth/Typhon in magical papyri, as discussed by Pintaudi (1977). Antoninus Liberalis (§28) epitomizes Nicander (cf. Diod. Sic. 1.21–2, Ov. *Met.* 5.321–31, and pseudo-Apollodorus 1.6.3).

19. The nuances of Seth's role in Egyptian religion, especially his earlier role as a patron of Upper Egypt and protector of the sun during its nightly journey in the Duat, were leveled over time; by the Ptolemaic period he had become the chaos-sowing antagonist connected with foreignness (though cf. Moyer 2011, 178, for the continued popularity of the *Contendings* and the Horus/Seth trial in the Hellenistic period). See Kees (1924), Griffiths (1960a), te Velde (1977, 2002), DuQuesne (1998) for this evolution of Seth's divine role.

20. As discussed by Griffiths (1960b), te Velde (1977, 109–51), and Loprieno (1988, 72–83).

21. That claim is still present (4, 5) in the Ramesside *Contendings of Horus and Seth*, an important if problematic source for the Seth/Horus myth. This presentation of Seth as legitimate claimant to the throne is also important to the *Memphite Theology* (lines 7–47), a Twenty-Fifth Dynasty text that claims to copy an Old-Kingdom original (on which see Sethe 1928 and Junker 1940).

22. See the discussion of the Seth temple at Avaris in Bietak (1996, 36–48).

Seth/Typhon as a *fait accompli* rather than a continually renewed argument sustained by Egyptians and Greeks alike.[23]

As in Typhon's multiform theriomorphism, Seth came to be known through animals. This begins with the predynastic king Peribsen, who for reasons that are still opaque swapped out Horus for Seth in his titulature. For the remainder of Egyptian dynastic history, Seth was represented with the aptly if uncreatively named "Seth animal," a fictional creature that Greeks and Romans usually associated with asses.[24] The strength of the Seth/Typhon pairing resides, in part, on the importance of animal iconography for them both. Typhon's hybrid animal form and changing animal voices mirror the chaos and disorder that Typhon exemplifies; Seth too came to be associated with wild and fierce animals like the hippopotamus to cement his later, antagonistic role as combatant of Horus.

Plutarch's philosophical analysis of the Osiris myth spends a good deal of time discussing Seth/Typhon's animal resonances.[25] Early in the *DIO*, Plutarch (8, 354a) suggests that the pig is an animal connected to Seth/Typhon:[26] explicitly, because Seth/Typhon was hunting a pig when he came upon Osiris's coffin, and implicitly, because the pig's uncleanliness links it up with the essential qualities that Plutarch assigns to Seth/Typhon.[27] Soon thereafter, Plutarch introduces Seth/Typhon's identification with donkeys to underline a symbolic association between Seth/Typhon and everything that hinders philosophical inquiry: "That's why they allot Typhon the stupidest domesticated animal, the ass, and the most savage wild animals, the crocodile and the hippopotamus."[28] Once he enters into the Seth/Typhon section proper (72, 380c), Plutarch additionally mentions dogs and the Oxyrhynchus fish, though it is possible they are only an aside, rather than meant as Seth animals.[29] Plutarch's emphasis on the wide range of Seth animals is well encapsulated by his catch-all phrase "these animals" to refer back to all the animals he had designated as Sethian.[30] Different Seth animals help Plutarch make

---

23. To repeat the caution around (but ultimate validation of) the term syncretism in Frankfurter (2018, 15–20).

24. The predynastic king Peribsen replaced the typically falcon-topped serekh with one topped with the Seth animal, a choice (when seen through Khasekhemwy's shift to a dual falcon/Seth animal serekh) whose political and religious significance has been debated, as outlined by Wilkinson (1999, 75–79).

25. Smelik and Hemelrijk (1984, 1960–65) spend very little time on this aspect of Plutarch's discussion. Seth animals are mentioned only in passing (1963).

26. It is worth noting that this connection is included among Manetho's fragments: *DIO* 8, 353f–354a = *BNJ* 609 F 23b.

27. For this phase of the myth, see Assmann (2001a, 125–29).

28. *DIO* 50, 371c = *BNJ* 609 F 20: διὸ καὶ τῶν μὲν ἡμέρων ζῴων ἀπονέμουσιν αὐτῷ τὸ ἀμαθέστατον, ὄνον· τῶν δ' ἀγρίων τὰ θηριωδέστατα, κροκόδειλον καὶ τὸν ποτάμιον ἵππον. See also: 8, 353e–354a; 19, 358d; 30–1, 362f–363a; and 49–50, 371c–d.

29. Griffiths (1970, 549) prefers this reading.

30. *DIO* 73, 380c: ταῦτα τὰ ζῷα.

122   EGYPT'S ANIMALS

different arguments, a flexibility concordant with the various representations of Typhon one sees across Hesiod and material culture.

Plutarch's enthusiastic coordination of Typhon with Seth via their animal associations might be well precedented, but referring to Seth as Typhon remains a textbook example of *interpretatio Graeca*. In this view, Plutarch only narrates the Osiris myth because he thinks it fits Middle Platonism's dualistic cosmology so well. Platonic philosophy is a straightjacket that reduces the myth—in its variability and multiplicity when viewed within Egyptian-language evidence—into a schematic tale of good's triumph over evil.[31] To other scholars, the latent rivalry between Greek and Egyptian wisdom that runs throughout the text deserves the largest emphasis.[32] Plutarch regularly marks out the unseemliness of Egyptian interpretations of the myth. He offers pained reactions to various facets—the god Horus decapitating his mother Isis in a fit of rage, for example—that he suggests are inappropriate.[33] In both arguments, the fact of equivalence-drawing one sees in the *DIO* gives way to Plutarch's attempts to center and elevate Greek culture in a culturally mixed world.

By presenting Plutarch as a bridge to Aegyptiaca and by underlining the pedigree of the Seth/Typhon pairing, I have already played my interpretative hand. Both arguments fail to capture essential elements of the *DIO*. This is not to trivialize Plutarch's hellenocentric interpretation and elevation of Greek cultural sensibilities. Plutarch's defense of Hellenism against barbarism elsewhere shows how readily he perpetuates—if winkingly and perhaps subversively—a binary that separates out Greek self from non-Greek others.[34] But it is all too easy to miss out on the translation of specific Egyptian cultural traditions from Egyptian-language sources into Plutarch's text. It is striking, for instance, that Plutarch's description of Seth/Typhon's birth and eruption through his mother Nut's side seems to match evidence from the Old-Kingdom Pyramid Texts.[35]

I do not want to use slippery and dangerous words like "correct" or "accurate" to characterize this alignment of Plutarch with earlier pharaonic discussions of this same material. That risks essentializing culture into a singular form that flattens out heterogeneity across time—Egyptians discussed the Osiris myth for thousands of years—and across different groups. So, to borrow from the famous description of ethnographic fidelity offered by Clifford Geertz, it might be better to say that Plutarch's *On Isis and Osiris* is so striking because it recognizes the

---

31. That multiplicity is well demonstrated by Assmann (2001a, 123–47).

32. Richter (2011, 192–98); cf. Richter (2001, 195–97) for discussion of the Greek-language Isis etymology.

33. Plut. *DIO* 20, 358e.

34. *On the Malice of Herodotus*—discussing Herodotus's lenient view of the Egyptian Busiris at 12, 857a–b—is a good example of that hellenocentrism and the playful way that Plutarch delivers it.

35. *Spr.* 222, 205a–b, ed. Sethe (1908).

"winks" of Egyptian myths where other Greek and Roman authors see "blinks."[36] As a Greek-language author discussing Egyptian material, he offers a much thicker description of an Egyptian myth than all of the authors whom I discussed in the previous chapter.

This is not so much praise for Plutarch himself as it is for the authors of Aegyptiaca who were his informants. Plutarch's concordance with Egyptian-language discussions of the Osiris myth bespeaks the remarkable power and efficacy of Egyptian authors of Aegyptiaca. Only by juxtaposing source (Egyptian-language discussions of the Horus-Seth cycle) and destination (Plutarch's presentation of the quarrel of Isis and Osiris against their brother-turned-enemy Seth/Typhon) can one appreciate the deft cultural translations that authors of Aegyptiaca undertook. By the same token, the path of translation reveals the different ways that different authors in different cultural contexts used the same syncretism of Seth/Typhon.

Seth Animals in Manetho

Authors of Aegyptiaca are the ones providing Plutarch the means to identify Seth/Typhon with animals like hippopotamuses. This means of access to Aegyptiaca via Plutarch is as exciting as it is perilous. It opens up a can of worms of *Quellenkritik* that can be a bit tedious.[37] But even if source criticism is old-fashioned, it can reveal a path of translation for Seth/Typhon, one that begins in Egypt, travels through authors of Aegyptiaca, and continues to Greek and Roman authors like Apuleius and Plutarch.

The only author cited for information in Plutarch's section on Seth animals is, perhaps unsurprisingly, Manetho. The association is important in both directions. First, it makes clear that Manetho's authority derived in no small part from his explanation of Egyptian religion, in addition to his dynastic history.[38] Second, it shows how Plutarch skirts the intervening authors of Aegyptiaca on his way to Manetho, as a rubber-stamp of his presentation of Egyptian religion. Plutarch reaches back to the exalted archetype of Aegyptiaca even as he remains indebted to the larger sweep of Aegyptiaca and imperial-era authors like Apion and Chaeremon. But even if he is named explicitly, to some scholars Manetho remains less persuasive as the key source of Plutarch's information about Egypt's sacred animals. J. Gwyn Griffiths, whose work on the *DIO* is still authoritative, is the most important of these doubters: "Manetho is the only writer named, but the material

---

36. This, and the following "thick description," are from Geertz (1973, 3–30).

37. For the sources of the *DIO*, see Wellmann (1896, refuted by Griffiths 1970, 88–93), Frisch (1907), and Parmentier (1913, 28–30). For broader discussion of Plutarch as citing authority, see Theander (1951), Helmbold and O'Neil (1959), and Cornell (2013, 105–13).

38. This is often slotted to the background in work reconstructing Manetho's historical narrative (Dillery 2015, 301–47) or annalistic framework (Redford 1986, 203–30).

124 EGYPT'S ANIMALS

is factually not up to his standard."[39] It is not my goal here to critique Griffith's source criticism.[40] But it is still important to push back a bit against this slippery concept of "standards." It captures a common view of Manetho as unimpeachable cultural authority that is understandable, but often marginalizes the more problematic fragments.

Manetho's animal fragments have posed commentators the biggest problems, because they fail when judged by a "correct" versus "incorrect" rubric that is more often calibrated to pharaonic-Egyptian than to contemporary Ptolemaic-Egyptian evidence. But it is worth asking if this mode of evaluation is running in the wrong direction. In a tradition as fragmentary as Aegyptiaca, it is difficult to know with any certainty what really constitutes Manetho's own standards as arbitrator of Egyptian religious knowledge. It is a critical question for the *DIO*, where claims vouchsafed via Manetho are sometimes iffy. To make sense of these citations, we need an inductive process that replaces the overly disjunctive language of standards with more evidentiarily sound analysis of how cultural concepts change when they are translated between Egyptian, Greco-Egyptian, and Greek intellectual domains.

On two occasions Plutarch cites Manetho during a discussion of Seth animals. The first passage comes at the end of Plutarch's recapitulation of the cosmogonic implications of the Osiris myth generally, and Seth/Typhon's antagonism specifically. As a Platonist, Plutarch is keen to show that this macrocosmic quarrel is mirrored in each individual person, whose constituent parts mix Typhonic and Isiac elements. This discussion of a soul's Typhonic aspects segues naturally into the consequent animals associated with Seth/Typhon, which I quoted above:[41]

> Typhon is the impassioned, Titan-ic, illogical, impulsive part of the soul and the perishable, sickly part of the body, the one prone to the seasons and bad air and solar and lunar eclipses, which one might call the outbursts and rebellions of Typhon. The name Seth, by which they refer to Typhon, speaks volumes: it indicates the overpowering and constraining, and frequent reversal and transgression. *Some say Bebon was one of Typhon's companions, but Manetho says that Typhon himself was also called Bebon.* The name means restraint or prevention, as when Typhon's power disrupts well-conducted affairs heading in the right direction. *That's why they allot him the stupidest domesticated animal, the ass, and the most savage wild animals, the crocodile and the hippopotamus.*[42]

39. Griffiths (1970, 98).

40. Griffiths (1970, 75–100, with a helpful breakdown on 98–99). I find Plutarch's at-least-partial use of Apion (defended by Wellmann 1896, 249 and Lévy 1910, 177–96) more probable than Griffiths does.

41. This is the passage as excerpted in the relevant fragment of *BNJ* 609 F 20, written by Lang (2014).

42. *DIO* 49–50, 371b–c = *BNJ* 609 F 20: Βέβωνα δέ τινες μὲν ἕνα τῶν τοῦ Τυφῶνος ἑταίρων γεγονέναι λέγουσιν, Μάνεθος <δ'> αὐτὸν τὸν Τυφῶνα καὶ Βέβωνα καλεῖσθαι ... διὸ καὶ τῶν μὲν ἡμέρων ζῴων ἀπονέμουσιν αὐτῶι τὸ ἀμαθέστατον, ὄνον· τῶν δ' ἀγρίων τὰ θηριωδέστατα, κροκόδειλον καὶ τὸν ποτάμιον ἵππον.

One has to decide where Manetho's original information ends and Plutarch's extrapolation begins, which is why source criticism is so tricky. Plutarch cites Manetho only for a small piece of information—that Bebon is in fact a name for Seth/Typhon, rather than one of his companions. But that identification is the springboard for the causal chain that nests consecutive sentences in a logically interconnected sequence. Manetho's identification of Typhon with Bebon is a prerequisite for the subsequent etymology Plutarch applies to Typhon. That etymology then allows Plutarch to underline Seth/Typhon's disruptive role, which itself explains why stupid and savage animals are considered Typhonic. Through this logical sequence—Bebon, its Greek etymology, and the animal identifications—Plutarch implicates Manetho into the larger constellation of associations that radiate out from Seth/Typhon.

Through Bebon, Manetho helps Plutarch underwrite the natural-philosophical connections between Typhon and the natural world. I have already suggested that a model of co-authorship is the soundest way to deal with these embedded citations of fragmentary authors.[43] Co-authorship captures the collaborative constitution of this network of meaning around Seth/Typhon. Pragmatically, it avoids aporetic debates about where to bound these loose citations of fragmentary authors that so often bleed into their immediate narrative context. There are also, to my mind, good reasons why Manetho might reasonably be the source for the Seth/animal pairing. Plutarch assigns the actual identification of the donkey, hippopotamus, and crocodile as Seth animals to a vague "they" that seems to recast his specific informant Manetho into Egyptians writ large. Plutarch's debt to Manetho for this cultural datum is further supported, if admittedly circumstantially, by an argument *ex silentio*. The identification of hippopotamus and crocodile with Seth required a source with knowledge beyond that typically displayed in the Greco-Roman tradition. Diodorus Siculus and his own source Hecataeus of Abdera make no mention of the hippopotamus or crocodile as Seth animals.[44]

But even if one takes a narrow point of view and restricts oneself to the explicitly cited information, Manetho's clarification about Bebon's connections to Typhon is illustrative on two grounds. First, it provides a good example of Manetho's interest in Egypt's religious topography. In this instance, he spent time explaining the process of identification that linked together major (Seth) and regional (Bebon) Egyptian gods. That mutual identification of gods with overlapping roles was a critical part of the Egyptian religious landscape that Greeks and Romans encountered. The tripartite deity Ptah/Sokar/Osiris, well represented in Ptolemaic and Roman Egyptian grave goods, is the product of the same process through which

43. As I have discussed more fully in chapter 1, in Pliny the Elder's citation of Apion (Plin. *HN* 30.18 = *BNJ* 616 F 15).

44. The crocodile and hippopotamus are discussed at Diod. Sic. 1.35, with no mention of Seth/Typhon. For Hecataeus's fragments, see Lang (2012). For Diodorus's use of Hecataeus, see Murray (1970).

126   EGYPT'S ANIMALS

regional gods (in this case of the city Memphis) were "combined" with the major god Osiris.[45] Second, and more importantly for present purposes, the Bebon gloss refocuses attention on Seth's importance to Manetho and those who read Manetho. As a god who became, over the Late and Ptolemaic periods, associated exclusively with disorder and foreignness, Seth was a prime object of attention.[46] That should not be lost sight of just because it falls between the disciplinary cracks that separate those interested in Manetho's dynastic history and those interested in Greek representations of Egypt's sacred animals. Manetho's citation of the Bebon/ Seth pairing begins to reveal how Seth's cosmogonic role created systems of significance that looped together myth, the natural world, and animals in ways that have yet to be captured by a cultural representation model.

Plutarch's other reference to Manetho's discussion of Seth/Typhon implicates ritual into that web of significance. Manetho reappears after Plutarch has listed the various animals identified with Seth, a catalogue whose extensiveness helps Plutarch prove Typhon's symbolic representation of the bestial and irrational.[47] As a part of his focus on god-animal pairings, Plutarch makes clear that Egyptians' views of Seth/Typhon shape their behavior toward animals identified with him. To show appropriate deference to Seth/Typhon's power, they honor his animals. When in times of drought they need to use stick rather than carrot, they threaten Seth/Typhon by sacrificing his animals. In this instance, Plutarch's claim aligns well with representations (fig. 5) of ritual sacrifice of red-colored (and thus Sethian) asses and bulls in the first east Osiris chapel in the Temple of Hathor at Dendera.[48]

Plutarch cites Manetho for one of the more striking examples of this kind of apotropaic sacrifice: "Indeed in Eileithyiaspolis they used to burn men alive, as Manetho has recorded, calling them Typhonians."[49] Once more, there is striking evidence that Manetho took time to build out the set of ritual practices that were bound up in Egyptians' hatred of Seth/Typhon. Once more, it poses immediate difficulties when measured against a correct/incorrect dichotomy.[50] The specific designation of some people as Typhonian—perhaps because of their red complexion,

---

45. That impulse, called "combinatory" by Dunand and Zivie-Coche (2004, 40), is discussed by Hornung (1982, 91–99).

46. The exact chronology of Seth's demonization is tricky to pin down, as te Velde (1977, 138–51) makes clear.

47. This helps explain why he uses the vague "these animals," which tries to present as large a group of Seth animals as possible, per Griffiths (1960, 549–50).

48. For Plutarch's discussion of Egyptian sacrifice of red-colored cattle and hatred of red-colored asses, see *DIO* 30–1, 362e–363d. The east wall of the first east Osiris chapel at Dendera (published by Cauville 1997, 51–54; 1990, 68–71, for outline) narrates the Khoiak festivals, including the ritual sacrifice of asses and bulls identified with Seth.

49. *DIO* 73, 380c-d = *BNJ* 609 F 22 (translation from Griffiths 1970): καὶ γὰρ ἐν Εἰλειθυίας πόλει ζῶντας ἀνθρώπους κατεπίμπρασαν, ὡς Μανέθως ἱστόρηκε, Τυφωνείους καλοῦντες.

50. I take it as significant that such a troublesome fragment is not included in Moyer (2011) or Dillery (2015).

FIGURE 5. The goddesses Isis and Nephthys preparing a chained and bound donkey, identified with the god Seth, for sacrifice. From the east wall of the first east Osiris chapel of the Temple of Hathor, Dendera, late Ptolemaic to Roman period. Photo courtesy of the author.

128 EGYPT'S ANIMALS

if Diodorus is to be believed—suggests that some humans count toward the set of animals identified with Seth.[51] If it were not for the human sacrifice part, this coordination of animals and humans would be a representative—albeit ghastly—example of Egyptians' remarkable non-anthropocentrism and relative disinterest in human exceptionalism. But regardless, I would de-emphasize human sacrifice, which is attention-grabbing but difficult to corroborate with Egyptian evidence. Instead, it is worth reemphasizing that Manetho's specific discussions—Bebon, sacrifice at Eileithyiaspolis (Egyptian Nekheb, modern El-Kab)—spun around the figure of Seth/Typhon a network of significance that included divine syncretism, animal-god pairings, and a cult geography of Egyptian rituals.

Aelian, the author of a sprawling text on animals, provides corroborating evidence that Manetho took time to discuss Seth animals. In his Egyptian section, Aelian mentions Manetho's discussion of the Egyptian abhorrence for pigs.[52] Manetho, as Aelian hears it, says that the pig is "most hateful to the sun and moon," a claim that must depend upon the pig's Sethian associations and the common identification of sun and moon with Osiris and Isis.[53] Aelian's citation helps confirm that Manetho is the probable source behind Plutarch's own etiology of the Egyptian hatred for pigs. It is more likely than not that Aelian and Plutarch reflect the same path of transmission of Manetho's original passage, even if the exact contours of that path are impossible to reconstruct fully.[54] The end results might be distorted via textual transmission, but Manetho's original presentation of the association between Seth and pigs is well founded: as texts like the Edfu reliefs and the Book of Gates make clear, Seth was himself identified with and represented as a pig.[55] As a pair, Aelian and Plutarch call attention to Manetho's importance as a source for Seth/Typhon's association with animals and the rituals and festivals whose significance depends on those animals' Sethian connotations.

51. On the shared complexion, see Diod. Sic. 1.88.5. Cf. *DIO* 30, 362e, where Plutarch similarly mentions scorn directed at redheads. For ritual sacrifice of red-colored Seth animals, see Frankfurter (1998, 204–5).

52. For Aelian's Egyptian material, see Smith (2014, 149–65); for his mention of Manetho's interest in pigs, see *NA* 10.16 = *BNJ* 609 F 23a.

53. Osiris *qua* Ptah/Sokar/Osiris played a key role in, and was closely associated with, the solar deity's nightly travel through the Duat.

54. Lang (2014) agrees, including both Aelian's and Plutarch's pig passages as Manetho's Fragments 23a and 23b, respectively (*DIO* 8, 353f–354a = *BNJ* 609 F 23b). It is possible that Aelian is relying on Plutarch's own text, while claiming that Manetho is the original source for Plutarch's pig/Typhon pairing. I find it more probable that they each rely on the same tradition of Aegyptiaca, but integrate citations in different ways. Per Smith 2014 149–53, in his Egyptian section Aelian names Herodotus (8.24, 11.10) and Apion (10.29, 11.40) twice, and Manetho (10.16), Eudoxus (10.16), Aristagoras (11.10), Eudemus (5.7), Pammenes (16.42), Phylarchus (17.5), Ptolemy Philopator (7.40), and Theophrastus (15.26) once.

55. A resonance (sometimes explained by seeing the Seth-animal as a pig) discussed by Bonneau (1991) and te Velde (1992, 21–22).

Manetho's interest in Seth/Typhon and his animals is only coherent when integrated into a full picture of ritual, kingship, and myth that remains out of view when a *topos* like zoomorphism is cleaved off and repackaged as a stand-alone object of cultural representation. Even when Manetho's presentation of Seth and Seth animals appears indirectly in Plutarch, one can still see that different Seth animals looped Seth into different cultural contexts. Plutarch recognizes that the significance of Seth's connections to asses and his connections to hippopotamuses are distinct. To trace these different threads, I will follow Plutarch's lead, dividing out Seth's associations with wild animals from his identification with an ass.

SETH AND THE HIPPOPOTAMUS FROM EDFU TO PLUTARCH

To chase down those different webs of significance, one must individuate the paths of translation that Seth's hippopotamus and ass pairings took from Egypt, through Aegyptiaca, to Greek and Roman literature. For the Seth/hippo pairing, that web of significance includes the royal ideology that Manetho includes in his dynastic history. To be sure, Manetho's kings list is a very indirectly transmitted text, so one needs to be careful not to overstep the available evidence.[56] But that said, Manetho's kings list loops in Seth animals at interesting moments. This occurs twice: the first king of the First Dynasty, Menes, was seized by a hippopotamus; Akhthoes, the mad first king of the Ninth Dynasty, was killed by a crocodile.[57] The former has some corroborating evidence, most notably in the Palermo Stone, the royal annals composed sometime during the Fifth Dynasty. This records that a First-Dynasty king (likely Den) undertook a ritual called "the harpooning of the hippopotamus."[58] In other words, there is something interesting in Manetho's hippopotamus reference. Menes's death by hippopotamus points toward hippopotamus hunts, among the many pastimes that communicated Egyptian kings' fight against and control over the wild and savage. By killing these animals, kings participated in a symbolic assertion of order over chaos prefigured by the Osiris myth and Seth's role therein.

---

56. Here I leave aside the probable role of Seth in Manetho's Hyksos narrative, on which see Moyer (2011, 123–25) and Dillery (2015, 317). The succession in question is laid out explicitly in the Armenian redaction of Eusebius's *chronographia*, Euseb. Armen. (ed. Karst) 63.15–69.30 = *BNJ* 609 F3a. Menes's death by hippopotamus is also included in Syncellus's epitome of Eusebius, at p. 100 (ed. Dindorf) = *BNJ* 609 F 2.

57. Manetho's Menes is an alternate *nebty* name for the early-Dynastic king Narmer, of Narmer palette fame.

58. Dillery (2015, 176–77) cites the passage in the same vein and also mentions seals in which Den hunts hippos. I would add to Dillery's list of corroborating evidence the presence of wooden hippo models in the temple equipment listed in the Abusir papyri (translated in Strudwick 2005 no. 91.A; see 173n6 for explanation). For the relevant passage of the Palermo stone, see Wilkinson (2000, 112).

Manetho's interest in man-eating hippos and crocodiles recenters the heterogeneous significance underlying the nexus of animality, the Seth/Horus conflict, and royal ideology. Since the Pyramid Texts, Seth's murder of Osiris and subsequent struggle for rule with Horus had been a mythological reflection of the death of a king, the threat of disunity in the succession, and the consolidation of the "two lands" of Egypt into a unified state supportive of the new king's rule.[59] That literary motif is one of many Manetho relies on to explain royal ideology to a non-Egyptian audience.[60] It helps explain why his dynastic history begins with the rules of Osiris, Seth/Typhon, and then Horus.[61] An etiology of the royal succession is a core function of the whole Osiris myth, which created a drama that heightened and then resolved the tension that came with the transfer of power from father to son. Hippopotamuses' connections to Seth play one small part in this work. By killing hippopotamuses, as Den does in the Palermo Stone, kings play the part of Horus and reassert order by conquering the savage and chaotic. Menes's hippo death is certainly only the most indirect view onto these dynamics, but it offers a valuable insight into the threads connecting the Manetho that appears in the dynastic history and the Manetho that appears in the *DIO*.

By the time Manetho was writing in the early-Ptolemaic period, hunting hippos continued to be a display of pharaonic strength framed against the Horus/Seth struggle for power. The madness of the Ninth-Dynasty king Akhthoes and his death by crocodile might very well point to the same idea. It is significant that these folkloric tags—death by hippo and by crocodile—are attached to the consolidation and then disintegration of the Old Kingdom in the First and Ninth Dynasties, moments when a myth of royal succession was especially apposite.[62] References to hippos and crocodiles in Manetho's kings list hint at larger points of connection between animals, annalistic history, and the trial of Horus and Seth.

The Horus/Seth conflict dramatized at the Temple of Edfu provides an Egyptian-language *comparandum* for the Seth/hippo pairing in the *DIO* and Manetho's dynastic history.[63] The Edfu reliefs show how authors of Aegyptiaca translated Egyptian religious lore around animal identifications into a Greek mode that Plutarch and others then incorporated into their own texts. The Temple of Horus at Edfu also reemphasizes that authors of Aegyptiaca were translating an Egyptian culture specific to the times in which they lived. It is exciting to show how Manetho's text aligns with evidence, like the Palermo Royal Annals, that

---

59. On display in *Memphite Theology* 7–47 and argued by Assmann (2001a, 123–47).

60. Moyer (2011, 84–141, esp. 140–41).

61. Again, from the Armenian recension of Eusebius's *Chronographia* (*BNJ* 609 F 3a).

62. Per Moyer (2011, 128n144), crocodile death can indicate divine punishment, which fits well with the cruelty that Manetho assigns to Akhthoes.

63. Horus was displayed spearing Seth in the guise of hippopotamuses and crocodiles in his temple at Edfu, a Ptolemaic construction which Dillery (2015, 176–77) persuasively connects to the hippopotamus reference in Manetho.

predates him by some two thousand years. But the Temple of Edfu is reflective of Ptolemaic-Egyptian culture in ways that should not be glossed over.

To provide some of the basics: the Temple of Horus at Edfu (Apollinopolis Magna) was constructed in the late third century BCE, soon after Manetho was writing his *Aegyptiaca*.[64] The relief cycle contains a specifically Ptolemaic recapitulation of the Horus/Seth conflict, written in the typically arcane "Ptolemaic hieroglyphic" script.[65] The mythic cycle, like the script in which it is written, thus simultaneously builds on and departs from earlier, canonized pharaonic equivalents. The Horus myths that it relates rely heavily on animal metamorphosis and on a flatly inimical, rather than ambivalent, characterization of Seth.

The Tales narrate the victory of Horus of Beḥdet—a version of Horus specific to Edfu—over Seth and the latter's expulsion from Egypt. In the temple relief cycle, Horus of Beḥdet fights on behalf of Re-Herakhte, and Ptah provides running commentary. The explanation of the text's historical framework has been various. Some see it as an allusion back the expulsion of the Hyksos, the Second Intermediate Period kings of West Asian descent whose associations with and worship of Seth at Avaris were well-known in later periods. Others present the myth's etiologies of sites of cult worship as a politically inflected debate about the on-the-ground worship of Horus and Seth in the Late and Ptolemaic periods.[66] Regardless of motivation, the myth crystallizes a contrast between Horus of Beḥdet, pharaonic power, and the falcon on the one hand, and Seth, foreignness, and the hippopotamus and crocodile on the other. There is a nexus of signification—Egyptians and non-Egyptians, order and chaos—on which Horus's and Seth's different zoomorphisms depend.

In the Edfu text, Horus chases Seth northward and fights him after Seth had metamorphosed into male hippopotamuses and crocodiles (fig. 6).[67] These fights served as aetiologies of key entries in the Egyptian cult calendar, of cult locales (Edfu chief among them), and of the standards of each Egyptian nome, a long-standing administrative subdivision of Egypt.[68] Of even more importance for Manetho's allusions to hippopotamus and crocodile hunts in the deaths of Menes and Akhthoes, the Horus/Seth myth related at Edfu further underlines the mythological resonances of pharaonic beast hunts, through which the Egyptian king embodies Horus and his fight against Seth.

---

64. For an overview of the Edfu material, see Finnestad (1985) and Kurth (1994). For text, see Chassinat (1897–1934), Kurth (1994), and the Göttingen Edfu Project (https://adw-goe.de/la/forschung /abgeschlossene-forschungsprojekte/akademienprogramm/edfu-projekt/die-datenbanken-des-edfu -projekts/edfu-datenbank/, accessed January 2024), with Fairman (1935) and Budge (1994, 57–95) for the Seth cycle. For interpretation, see Alliot (1950), Griffiths (1958), and Fairman (1974).

65. It is *the* corpus of Ptolemaic hieroglyphic, as Wilson (1997) makes clear. For the role of the Horus/Seth myth in Edfu's wider cosmological program, see Finnestad (1985, 15, 87).

66. Griffiths (1958) provides an overview of the different interpretations of the myth's significance.

67. As opposed to the female hippopotamus, associated with Taweret (and by extension the affiliated goddesses Ipet, Reret, and Hedjet).

68. Fairman (1974, 27–33), from which the translation is taken.

FIGURE 6. The god Horus spearing a hippopotamus identified with the god Seth. From the internal east enclosure wall of the Temple of Horus, Edfu, Ptolemaic period. Photo courtesy of the author.

The story cycles through different animal metamorphoses. The sheer variety of animals into which both gods transform speaks to the centrality of animals as a mode of identification for gods, rather than as objects of worship per se. It also provides some legitimacy to Plutarch's open-ended list of Typhonic animals. At one point Horus, taking on the guise of a hawk, fights Seth, who had transformed into a serpent:

> ... From this day, the seventh day of the first month of the season *Pr-t* [= 7 Tybi] shall be called the 'Festival of the Sailing.' Then Seth took upon himself the form of a hissing serpent, and he entered into the earth at this place without being seen. Ra said, 'Seth hath taken upon himself the form of a hissing serpent. Let Horus, the son of Isis, in the form of a hawk-headed staff, set himself over the place where he is so that he may never be able to come forth again.'[69]

This presentation of animals and the divine, typical of Egyptian thinking of the Ptolemaic period, serves to tether animal metamorphoses of the type seen in Ovid to emic accounts of gods' fluidity of form. The actual hieroglyphs are worth looking at, if only to emphasize the natural scope of zoomorphism as a category. The second half of the second line, representing as it does the Seth animal, the *hmhm.tj* serpent ("roarer," an epithet of Apepi when identified with Seth), and (in the third line) the Horus falcon, helps reemphasize the primacy of zoomorphism as a key association of a Greco-Roman audience presented with Egyptian iconography and hieroglyphic signs.[70] This specific section of the larger Horus myth, and the image of Horus-as-falcon atop Seth animals, makes its way into Plutarch.[71] The presence of this same imagery in the *DIO* shows that Greco-Roman authors did have access to this Egyptian material via authors of Aegyptiaca. In this case, it is unclear just what path of translation the passage took from Edfu to Plutarch. Manetho would be a good guess, given his temporal proximity to the Edfu temple and general

---

69. Text from Chassinat (1931, 121, ll. 9–11) (digitized on the Göttingen Edfu Project, https://adw-goe.de/la/forschung/abgeschlossene-forschungsprojekte/akademienprogramm/the-inscriptions-of-the-ptolemaic-temple-of-edfu/the-database-of-the-edfu-project/, accessed January 2024). Translation from Budge (1994, 77), though for translation and commentary see also Fairman (1935, 1974).

70. This change in the Seth/Apepi relationship is a telling example of the flattening of Seth's later mythic significance. At Edfu, Seth is identified with Apepi. But texts like the *Memphite Theology* make clear that Seth claimed the throne because he *killed* Apepi. I address hieroglyphic signs as a mode of animal signification in chapter 5.

71. In his discussion, te Velde (1977, 59) notes a similar translation from Edfu to Plutarch of a different theme, of Seth's castration by Horus.

134   EGYPT'S ANIMALS

authority. Even if we might not know for certain the specific author of *Aegyptiaca* who translated this Seth/Horus animal imagery into Greek, clearly *somebody* did so. Placing the Edfu material beside Plutarch shows beyond any doubt the ability of Egyptian thinking about animals to move into Greek and Roman contexts:

> *In Hermopolis they display a statue of Typhon as hippopotamus, on whom stands a hawk fighting with a serpent.* By the hippopotamus they indicate Typhon, and by the hawk power and rule. When Typhon gains power by force, he is often stirred again, simultaneously confused by his own evil and causing confusion himself. That's why, when sacrificing on the seventh day of Tybi, which they call "Isis's arrival from Phoenicia," they stamp a bound hippopotamus on their sacred cakes. In Apollinopolis it is a custom for absolutely everyone to eat crocodile.[72]

There is certainly a mishmash of elements, but core components of the Edfu imagery reappear in due order here in Plutarch.[73] Plutarch clearly has in mind the same festival, providing the same exact date (7th Tybi) as the one given in the Egyptian-language Edfu text. The scene of hawk fighting serpent, and the explanation provided for it, matches the Edfu passage quoted above. Even more definitively, Plutarch locates crocodile-eating specifically at Edfu (Apollinopolis in Greek). This all speaks to a remarkable translation of the Edfu narrative for a Greek audience, one that paves the way for the wider cosmological significance that Plutarch attaches to the Seth/Horus myth and its animal symbolisms. To be sure, Manetho is not named by Plutarch as his source for this specific Edfu-adjacent narrative. If my goal were the reconstruction of Manetho's work specifically, rather than of *Aegyptiaca* generally, this evidence would be a bridge too far.[74] But the alignment of the two passages draws an *Aegyptiaca*-sized outline that sits between the original Edfu material and Plutarch's representation of it.[75] Even if it is debatable which author of *Aegyptiaca* is the source for this specific bit of information, it had to be one of them—not least because whoever is presenting Edfu material in Greek for a Greek and Roman audience is, by that very fact, an author of *Aegyptiaca* in the way I am defining that term.

A model of cultural translation creates space for this incorporation of Edfu material into Plutarch's text in ways that cultural representation cannot. Important dynamics of divine transformation into animals canonized in Ptolemaic-Egyptian cult sites were available to Greek and Roman authors. That fact speaks to the authors

---

72. *DIO* 50, 371c–d: ἐν Ἑρμοῦ πόλει δὲ Τυφῶνος ἄγαλμα δεικνύουσιν ἵππον ποτάμιον, ἐφ' οὗ βέβηκεν ἱέραξ ὄφει μαχόμενος. . . .

73. Kindt (2021b, 135) touches on this passage of the *DIO*, but does not position it against the Edfu material or the Seth-Horus cycle.

74. Griffiths (1970, 490–91) notes the Edfu material and its relevance for this passage in Plutarch, but underlines the incongruities separating the specific imagery in Edfu and in Plutarch.

75. Despite Plutarch's own travel to Egypt, I find it more likely (with Griffiths 1970, 98) that Plutarch depended on literary sources (rather than autopsy) for the *DIO*'s animal and hieroglyphic material.

of Aegyptiaca who not only laid out the transformations between god and animal, but also underlined the ideological significance which those transformations— especially Seth's metamorphosis into wild and threatening animals—facilitated. Plutarch reads into a falcon/hippopotamus fight a philosophical narrative of order's victory over disorder. It is only because of authors of Aegyptiaca that he was able to do so. There are certainly limits to source criticism; there is more we do not know than there is that we do know. The specific animal imagery on display in Edfu does not find a perfect match in Plutarch's rendition. But that ambiguity notwithstanding, it is clear that the Egyptian source Plutarch drew on for this Edfu anecdote translated this material. So too is it clear that Edfu and its Egyptian exegete, no less than Plutarch, were the authors of the deeper systems of significance which are often taken as Plutarch's Platonist projections. Long before Plutarch, Seth/ Typhon's identification with pigs, crocodiles, and hippopotamuses already was symbolically significant. Put another way, it is not just important to see that Manetho and other Egyptians presented animals that were not objects of worship. It is also essential to appreciate that they talked about those animals as part of a larger mythic-cum-historical narrative through which the animal/divine pairing became meaningful. Scholarly discussions of Rome's interest in Egypt's animals that abstract said animals from these original webs of significance cannot but conclude that animal identifications were either meaningless or an entirely Greek projection.

APULEIUS AND THE EXODUS: MAKING AN ASS OF SETH

The translation of the Seth/hippo pairing is appealing largely because of its relatively direct path from Edfu, through Aegyptiaca, to Plutarch. The paths of translation around the Seth/ass pairing are more wending, but no less productive. Like the hippo's royal-ideological significance, Seth's asinine associations also show how animals and the divine were bound up in other essential areas that defined Aegyptiaca—in the ass's case the Exodus story and imperial philosophy. As in the Temple of Horus at Edfu and its representation of Seth's metamorphoses into hippopotamuses and crocodiles, depictions of sacrificed asses in the Temple of Dendera (fig. 5) provide a point of origin for the Seth/ass pair's translation from Egyptian-language evidence, through Aegyptiaca, to Greek and Roman literature.[76] The Seth animal builds on one of this chapter's themes while introducing a new one. Apuleius's *Metamorphoses* is a text that, like Plutarch's *DIO*, seeks to underline the felicity of the Seth/Typhon-ass pairing for a philosophical reading of the Osiris myth. But unlike the hippopotamus imagery, the pairing of Seth and

---

76. The first and second registers of the east wall of the first east Osiris chapel (published by Cauville 1997, 51–54) shows ritual sacrifice of a Seth-identified ass and bull, an event known to Plutarch (see n48, above) through authors of Aegyptiaca (likely Manetho).

ass shows how animals became an important part of the intellectual antagonism between Jewish and Egyptian authors.

Seth's asinine pairing returns to a foundation of Aegyptiaca, a genre defined in large part by the vociferous criticism it receives in Josephus.[77] Seth, as a ritually hated god eventually associated with foreigners, was particularly important within debates between Egyptian and Jewish authors. Both groups tried to disparage the other's religious practices and assimilate themselves to Greek and Roman norms. Seth was one among many ropes through which the Jewish/Egyptian historiographic tug-of-war was contested. Since Manetho, Egyptians forged a connection between the Exodus story and the Hyksos kings of the Fifteenth Dynasty.[78] The Hyksos, Levantine "rulers of the mountains" who controlled the Delta during the Second Intermediate Period, were retroactively identified as Jews who migrated into and were then expelled from Egypt. Seth was worshipped by the Hyksos at his cult site (and their capital) Avaris due to his easy identification with the Canaanite god Baal.[79] As a result, Seth entered into the debates about the Exodus that form such an important thread in Aegyptiaca. Apion's discussion of Jewish history and religion, at least as it is presented in the thoroughgoing takedown offered by Josephus in the *Against Apion*, leveraged Seth's asinine associations to disparage Judaism. According to Apion, the Temple of Jerusalem included a gilded ass's head: "For Apion presumed to publish that Jews had placed the head of an ass in this shrine, and that they cherished it and deemed it worthy of great religious devotion; and he maintains that this had been disclosed when Antiochus Epiphanes pillaged the temple and the head was discovered, fashioned from gold and worth a lot of money."[80] The specific interest in the ass has clear resonances with Seth, as Bezalel Bar-Kochva has explained.[81] As far as one can reasonably surmise, Apion concatenated Seth, the Seth-animal-turned-ass, the Hyksos, and Jews. Apion bends this chain of association to his own purposes. Hyksos support of Seth turns into Jewish worship of an ass-headed god.

Plutarch offers another vantage on the connection between Seth and the Exodus debates. In a passage on Seth/Typhon's flight from his battle with Horus, Plutarch mentions a version of the myth in which Seth/Typhon "begat Hierosolymus and Judaeus," but concludes that the Egyptian propagators of this version of the

---

77. I use "foundation" only in reference to the central role of Josephus in Jacoby's consolidation of authors of Aegyptiaca, as I discuss in the Introduction.

78. For Manetho's interest in and development of the Hyksos narrative, see Moyer (2011, 118–25) and Dillery (2015, 315–42).

79. For the identification of Seth with Baal, see the material remains discussed by Bietak (1996, 36–48) and the historical overview provided by te Velde (1977, 120–29).

80. Joseph. *Ap.* 2.79 = *BNJ* 616 F 4h: in hoc enim sacrario Apion praesumpsit edicere asini caput collocasse Judaeos, et eum colere ac dignum facere tanta religione, et hoc affirmat fuisse depalatum, dum Antiochus Epiphanes expoliasset templum et illud caput inventum ex auro compositum multis pecuniis dignum.

81. Bar-Kochva (2010, 244).

myth "are manifestly, as the very names show, attempting to drag Jewish traditions into the legend."[82] When viewed alongside the condemnation of Jewish donkey-icons, this anecdote from Plutarch points to a sustained tradition that triangulated Judaism, the Seth/Horus conflict, and religious animals. Seth animals thus played an important role in debates about Judaism's and Egyptian religion's proximity to or distance from Greco-Roman norms.

This donkey head is certainly a looser translation of Seth's animal connections than Plutarch's rendition of the Edfu myth. Apion's reference to ass icons in the Temple of Jerusalem continues the same dynamics of looseness and creativity that have distinguished his from Manetho's cultural authority. This ass icon datum does not have as exalted a pharaonic pedigree as royal hippopotamus hunts. But it does similar work, showing how *topoi* that are analyzed independently in their Roman reception were interconnected in the original texts in which they appeared.

Any discussion of the philosophical significance of donkeys demands mention of Apuleius. His *Metamorphoses* hinges on the transformation of the bon vivant Lucius into an ass. What is otherwise a picaresque adventure story that catalogues Lucius's asinine travails is, famously, reframed by its conclusion. Early in Book 11, Lucius learns in a dream that the Egyptian goddess Isis, an object of cult worship across the Mediterranean, will be the instrument of his salvation. She instructs him to meet one of her priests, who will offer Lucius the roses he needs to change back to a human. After his transformation back to human form, Lucius becomes an Isis devotee in a succession of initiations whose repetitiveness has become fodder in the debate about the tone of Book 11.[83] It is not my purpose here to wade into that debate.[84] No matter the tone, Lucius's turn to the cult of Isis injects an Egyptian mythological framing that complements the overarching philosophical resonances of Lucius's journey.[85]

---

82. *DIO* 31, 363c–d: οἱ δὲ λέγοντες ἐκ τῆς μάχης ἐπ' ὄνου τῷ Τυφῶνι τὴν φυγὴν ἑπτὰ ἡμέρας γενέσθαι καὶ σωθέντα γεννῆσαι παῖδας Ἱεροσόλυμον καὶ Ἰουδαῖον, αὐτόθεν εἰσὶ κατάδηλοι τὰ Ἰουδαϊκὰ παρέλκοντες εἰς τὸν μῦθον.

83. Winkler (1985, 215–47), van Mal-Maeder (1997, 105–10), and Harrison (2000, 238–52) all point to some kind of comic note in these initiations, even as they differ over the serious message that might exist together with that comedy. Shumate (1996) emphasizes the "conversion" motif, and Finkelpearl (2004) sees the later initiations as an "epilogue." Mazurek (2022, 41–45) teases out the history of Isiac initiation from *Met.* 11 and epigraphic evidence.

84. The tone of Book 11 has long been the subject of disagreement (Tilg 2014, ch. 5, provides valuable background). Winkler (1985) first championed a serio-comic reading; Schlam (1992) and Egelhaaf-Gaiser (2012) have followed in this vein. Harrison (2000, 2012) underlines Book 11's tonal similarity to the more comic Books 1–10; Sandy (1978) and Graverini (2012a, 2012b) argue for a shift toward philosophical sincerity. More recently, an "aporetic" approach has been defended by myself (Kelting 2021, 129) and others (Benson 2019, 226–33).

85. O'Brien (2002), Graverini (2012a), and Fletcher (2014) offer Platonic readings of the *Metamorphoses* that show how the turn to Isis continues the themes which they ("discourse," the high/low genre dynamics, and impersonation respectively) suggest connect the *Met.* to Apuleius's own Platonism.

138   EGYPT'S ANIMALS

Instead, I want to build on those like Jack Winkler who have emphasized the importance of the Seth/ass pairing to the themes developed in Book 11 of the *Metamorphoses*.[86] The turn to Isis in Book 11 reorients the significance that readers are meant to attach to Lucius's metamorphosis into a donkey. Scholars too have had to decide how to balance the Egyptian mythological framing of Lucius's time as an ass with the Platonic resonances that animate the earlier books.[87] That Egyptian turn is already hinted at in the prologue's mention of an Egyptian reed pen.[88] As a result, an audience familiar with Lucius's eventual initiation into the cult of Isis reads Lucius's time as an ass through the prism of the Osiris myth and the role of donkeys therein.

Apuleius very intentionally clues readers into the connection between Lucius's donkey exterior and the Seth/ass pairing. Isis's instructions to Lucius during his dream reference the mythological background that connects his current asinine form with her inveterate enemy Seth: "Immediately divest yourself of the hide of that most terrible beast, long loathsome to me."[89] It is unsurprising, but still important, that a North African author like Apuleius is aware of the Seth/ass pairing. Apuleius shows the potential for the metamorphosis narratives one sees in the Temple of Horus at Edfu to enter into and enrich Greco-Roman metamorphosis literature.[90] It is typical of Apuleius that this critical evidence for the Roman reception of the Seth/ass pair is plunked into a brief, one-sentence allusion that does not actually mention the name Seth. Book 11 is challenging and enriching in equal measure precisely because Apuleius winkingly buries essential mythological framing in character speech that is all too easy to miss. As a final tag, the specific way that Apuleius has Isis refer to the Seth/ass pairing emphasizes the importance of ritual hatred as an object of cultural translation, a point that I have tried to underline throughout this chapter. Lucius's Sethian associations are put into the mouth of Isis precisely because, in her eyes, Lucius's asinine form makes him loathsome and in need of redemption.

CONCLUSION: ANIMALS AS A DIVINE SYMBOLISM

The Seth animal's entrance into Apuleius's *Metamorphoses* was one among several paths of translation that Egypt's animals took. I have chosen to prioritize Seth

86. Winkler (1985, 292–321), who cites the Seth/ass pairing as part of an argument about the "golden ass" title.

87. DeFilippo (1990) does a good job presenting those connections.

88. This circularity has long been an object of scholarly attention, not least in Kahane and Laird (2001).

89. *Met.* 11.6.2: pessimae mihique detestabilis iam dudum beluae istius corio te protinus exue. Text from Zimmerman (2012). See Griffiths (1975, 162) for the Seth reference.

90. In addition to Seth's hippopotamus transformations, the Edfu inscription also narrates Seth's transformation into a donkey in Section E, per the division of Fairman (1935, 26–27) (Chassinat 1931, 222 l. 4 in the overall Edfu text).

animals in this chapter, but one could tell a similar story about animals connected with solar deities. In key cosmological texts like the Book of Gates and the Book of Hours, the nascent sun was identified with and represented as the scarab-god Khepri.[91] Apion, the author of Aegyptiaca with whom I opened this book, had promoted the connection. To Pliny the Elder, Apion's explanation is as well-intentioned as it is unimpressive: " . . . the scarab beetle that rolls balls of dung. For this reason most of Egypt worships scarab-beetles among the gods, in Apion's elaborate interpretation, in which he gathers that the labor of the sun is similar to this animal's, to make excuses for the rites of his own people."[92] Apion touts the direct connection of natural philosophy and animal to ward off the charges of misdirected worship that the lowly scarab beetle invited. Apion is briefly, but obviously, attempting to redirect attention to the network of significance that explained why a scarab beetle was a felicitous way to represent the sun. It is a different application of the same impulse that led Manetho to translate the network of meanings that clustered around Seth's animals.

While Pliny appreciates the excusatory intent of Apion's *curiosa interpretatio* of scarabs, he ultimately dismisses it as a coerced defense of his countrymen's behavior. Apion's explanation of the scarab points to a larger backdrop against which Roman criticisms of Egypt's sacred animals should be read. This holds particularly true for the biting criticism of imperial authors like Lucan and Juvenal, whose denunciation of Egyptian animal worship is so pronounced.[93] Barbarizing Egypt's animals was, in an interconnected imperial world, reactionary rather than unmarked. That is as true under Hadrian as it is under Nero or Domitian or Augustus. The popularity of Aegyptiaca is what makes Lucan's epic and Juvenal's satires so productively unrepresentative of, and deliberately inimical to, the times in which they were written. Lucan and Juvenal are a nice contrast to Plutarch's and Apuleius's enthusiastic reception of these explanations. Even when translations of sacred animals' significance were rejected (as in Pliny) rather than endorsed (in Plutarch and Apuleius), the fact of translation remains.

I have prioritized the networks of meaning where the significance of Seth's connections to hippos or asses or crocodiles resided in Egyptian culture. Those webs of significance were the focus of authors of Aegyptiaca, who translated the cultural practices, cult geography, and annalistic history that surrounded Seth's animal associations. That concept of "network of meaning" or "web of significance" brings one onto the doorstep of "symbol," "enigma," "allegory," and other hermeneutics of the Greek philosophical and literary-critical tradition, whose

91. *LdÄ* 1.934–40 and Dunand and Zivie-Coche (2004, 189).

92. Plin. *HN* 30.99 = *BNJ* 616 F 19: scarabaeum, qui pilas volvit. propter hunc Aegypti magna pars scarabaeos inter numina colit, curiosa Apionis interpretatione, qua colligat solis operum similitudinem huic animali esse, ad excusandos gentis suae ritus.

93. I discuss both authors in chapter 3. As an example, Geue (2017, 263) suggests that Juvenal's tale about Egypt's barbarism is "the type of thing on every Hadrianic subject's lips."

140   EGYPT'S ANIMALS

presence in Aegyptiaca is the focus of the next section.[94] That contiguity matters. It is not entirely surprising that when Egypt's animal-shaped gods were mentioned in Greek and Roman philosophical literature, they were discussed in a language of symbol or enigma that had long been used to push past the superficially strange to access underlying meaning.

The Seth animal did not just connote Seth. It also, literally, denoted him in the hieroglyphic script. As the Edfu text quoted above suggests, the Egyptian language is far and away the most obvious piece in the network of association that constituted Egypt's animal symbolisms. Animals were multifaceted, troubling the line that divides language and image. Khepri, as a scarab beetle connected to the sun, was a mechanic of solar iconography reflected in widespread solar-scarab imagery.[95] But the thread connecting sun and scarab runs through language. To see a scarab is to read the Egyptian verb 𓆣 *kheper*, meaning "to come into existence" or "to be born." The scarab, as hieroglyphic sign, signified a core cosmological concept, the "birth" (*kheper*) of the sun each morning. That is the necessary framework through which Apion's identification of the scarab with the sun makes sense. The denotative function of hieroglyphic characters spun the thread connecting animals with the divine. Animal-shaped gods will thus give way to animal-shaped words for animal-shaped gods, to which I turn in the next chapter. It is through this symbolic function of hieroglyphic characters that I will respond to the questions of cultural legitimacy that have hounded latter-day authors of Aegyptiaca.

94. See the intellectual history of the symbol provided by Struck (2004).
95. For example, the winged scarab amulets through which the deceased identified herself with the sun's rebirth, per Andrews (1994, 58).

PART THREE

What's Egyptian for "Philosopher"?

5

Not Dead Yet!

Legitimizing Imperial-Period Hieroglyphic Symbolisms

Lucius's transformation into an ass in Apuleius's *Metamorphoses* integrates the Egyptian god Seth into metamorphosis literature. By linking Lucius and Seth, Apuleius aligns the *Metamorphoses'* Platonic themes with systems of significance that surrounded the Seth/ass pairing in Egyptian religion. This puts Apuleius in close company with Plutarch. Both authors broached Seth's associations with disorder, chaos, and all that hinders philosophical contemplation through the animals—like the ass, hippopotamus, and crocodile—with which he was identified. This is a web of meaning that surrounded Seth's animals as they were translated from Egyptian-language sources, through Aegyptiaca, to Plutarch and Apuleius.

The nexus of Seth, his animals, and the cosmological concepts that he signified is not just a Platonic projection. In a very basic way, the Seth animal means "chaos"; the connection is direct and semantic. Looking at the Egyptian-language words tagged with the Seth animal as a classifier bears this out. A range of disorder verbs were lumped together into one coherent semantic field by means of a Seth-animal written at their end as a so-called determinative sign.[1] Key vocabulary like 𓊃𓏤𓃩 *shꜣ* (to be in confusion), 𓊃𓏤𓃩 *khb* (to be violent, to roar), 𓊃𓏤𓃩 *hꜣhꜣtj* (storm), 𓊃𓏤𓃩 *nšnj* (rage/disaster/storm), and 𓊃𓏤𓃩 *hnn* (to disturb/tumult) all use the Seth animal as a determinative.[2] The Seth animal was semantically tied to chaos vocabulary like *hnnw* and *nšnj*, both antonyms to important words of universal order (*mꜣ't* and *htp* respectively). Animals are

---

1. Te Velde (1977, 25). For the world-organizational role of determinatives, see Goldwasser (2002); for the lexical semantics of determinatives, Grossman and Polis (2012). Goldwasser (2006) prefers "classifier," which I also use.

2. *shꜣ*: Wb. 3.206; *khb*: Wb. 5.137; *hꜣhꜣtj*: Wb. 3.363, where this spelling is a New Kingdom variant; *nšnj*: 2.340; *hnn*: Wb. 3.383.

143

embedded in the language of disorder, in the same way that a scarab is embedded in the semantics of autogenesis. To talk about animals and the divine is to discuss the animal-shaped characters through which the Egyptian language bound together gods and cosmological concepts.

The Animal/Hieroglyph Nexus

This interconnection of animal, iconography, and script is not limited to Egyptian-language evidence. Apuleius leverages the contiguity of animals and the hieroglyphic script to coordinate Lucius's asinine metamorphosis with his initiation into Isiac religion. When Lucius finally transforms back into a human and then undergoes his promised initiation into the cult of Isis, he glimpses the sacred texts on which Isiac lore is written:

> From a hidden and inner part of the temple the priest produces some rolls written in unknown letters. Some of those rolls suggest, through all kinds of animal characters, concise versions of solemn formulae; others have their meaning protected from the curiosity of the uninitiated by letters that are intricate, twisted into themselves like a wheel, and thickly knotted like vine-tendrils.[3]

The Isis cult's liturgical texts reinject animal symbolism into a narrative of initiations.[4] After Lucius's metamorphosis back into human form, Apuleius exploits hieroglyphs' evocation of symbolically laden, gated-off knowledge.[5] Through these hieroglyphic animal characters, the ability to "read" animal figures becomes a precondition for initiation and salvation. Apuleius deliberately shifts from "letters" (*litteris*) to "characters" (*figuris*) to underline the figurative quality of hieroglyphs. Greeks and Romans generally thought that hieroglyphic was an ideogrammatic script comprised of animal "figures."[6] Apuleius builds on this association of animal and script to bind together linguistically encoded wisdom and recognition of animal characters. Animal characters present the cult of Isis's exclusivity in the same terms as the long-postponed recognition of Lucius's inner humanity, which was also hidden behind an otherwise inscrutable and illegible asinine exterior. Apuleius's final book relies on this bivalence of the "figure" to stitch together Lucius's metamorphosis and initiation.

Animal-shaped gods and animal-shaped characters circularly reinforced each other's significance. The hieroglyphic script adds a semiotic underpinning to the

---

3. Apul. *Met.* 11.22.8: de opertis adyti profert quosdam libros litteris ignorabilibus praenotatos, partim figuris cuiusce modi animalium concepti sermonis compendiosa verba suggerentes, partim nodosis et in modum rotae tortuosis capreolatimque condensis apicibus a curiositate profanorum lectione munita.

4. For more on this continuity of hieroglyphic and animal metamorphosis, see Kelting (2021), from which this paragraph and part of the next are taken.

5. Burkert 1972 (176) and Struck (2004, 80–88) trace the symbol back to its roots as a passcode. Benson (2019, 212–13) frames *Met.* 11.23.6–7 through the passwords used in mystery cults.

6. Exemplary is Tac. *Ann.* 11.14.

discussions of the philosophical and literary receptions of Egypt's animal-shaped gods highlighted in the previous part of this book. The basic mechanics of the Egyptian language and its tripartite structure of phonograms that communicate sound values, ideograms that communicate images, and determinatives that classify lexemes into semantic fields go a long way in explaining the overlap between zoomorphism and hieroglyphic.[7] The two were mutually dependent cultural forms. That is clear no matter where in the chain of cultural translation you look. On the close and semantic level of the hieroglyphic script, the Seth animal literally determined cosmological concepts of chaos and disorder. When discussed by Apuleius, Egypt's animal hieroglyphs and Lucius's asinine exterior both hide an inner truth that is knotty, opaque, and difficult to access.

Authors of Aegyptiaca were the mediators who presented the Egyptian language to a Greek and Roman audience. The interconnection between iconography and script allowed authors of Aegyptiaca to triangulate language, animal, and cosmological principle. That holds particularly true for the ideograms and determinatives on which these authors focused. For both types of signs, the linguistic identification of the divine through animal characters is inextricable from the iconographic identification of gods with either fully or partially zoomorphic figures. This inextricability of language and divine zoomorphism is poorly served in a "cultural representation" model. Different scholars write different books on different *topoi* surrounding Egypt in Greco-Roman literature. As a result, isolated scholarship on hieroglyphs and on animals in the Roman imagination fail to account for the explanatory systems that arise when these two categories are juxtaposed.[8] This has been exacerbated by a general ambiguity in reception scholarship about whether the object of focus is purely the hieroglyphic script—and thus grammatically conservative "Traditional Egyptian"—or the Egyptian language as it was actually spoken in the Ptolemaic and imperial periods.[9] Greek and Roman interest in the Egyptian language is not wholly circumscribed by hieroglyphic characters, just like animal worship does not encapsulate fully the connection between animals and the divine.

How did authors of Aegyptiaca present the Egyptian language? The question reasserts the basic task of the translator, which has skirted around the margins of the model of cultural translation I have been promoting. Drilling down on

7. For a basic introduction to the principles of the Egyptian language, see Allen (2000, 1–14). For more information on Egyptian linguistics, see Loprieno (1995).

8. The standard work on hieroglyphic's reception is Iversen (1961; see also 1971). As an example of this silo effect, hieroglyphic animal signs are unmentioned by Rosati (2009) and Kindt (2021b) (cf. the passing analogization offered by Smelik and Hemelrijk 1984, 1861).

9. Roman-Egyptian interest in and adaptation of the hieroglyphic script is well discussed by Iversen (1961, 1971) and Love (2021, see 339–44 for overview). "Traditional Egyptian" (only really studied by corpus, rather than synoptically—as the bibliography of Engsheden 2016 makes clear) is a term for the grammar of Persian-, Ptolemaic-, and Roman-Egyptian hieroglyphic inscriptions, a term complementary to "Ptolemaic Egyptian" (Kurth 2008), which is primarily used to distinguish Ptolemaic (versus pharaonic) hieroglyphic orthography.

discreet acts of translation dramatizes the precarious authority that defines latter-day authors of Aegyptiaca. They were writing at a time when the hieroglyphic script was falling out of use. That is an essential framework that hangs over their presentation of the Egyptian language. So far, I have avoided a restrictive dichotomy of correct/incorrect to evaluate the cultural translation in Aegyptiaca. But how can that latitude withstand moments when an author like Chaeremon seems to fake his way through the Egyptian language?[10] Just how much leeway should we give to authors of Aegyptiaca who promote symbolic and philosophical readings of the hieroglyphic script that run roughshod over the actual semantics of the Egyptian language?

All of which is to say, the Egyptian language itself can provide an acid test of the agency and flexibility I am trying to assign to authors of Aegyptiaca. Language puts in stark relief the gap between equally valuable frames for Aegyptiaca: Glissant's creolizing web of relation, which promotes ongoing, dynamic, and non-teleological mixture, and the fact of the hieroglyphic script's "death." I will be pushing back against the utility of the "death of hieroglyphic" narrative in this chapter, but the hieroglyphic script did in fact fall out of use—if well after the end point of this book.[11] This fact can enrich, rather than erode, the way we approach Aegyptiaca. Glissant's effusive defense of the translator is a helpful point of departure:

> What does this mean if not that, just as the poet invents a *langage* in his own language, the translator has to invent a *langage* going between one language and the other? A necessary *langage* going from one language to the other, a *langage* common to both of them, but in some sense unforeseeable with regard to each of them. The translator's *langage* works like creolization and Relation in the world, that is, it produces the unforeseeable. An art of the imaginary, in this sense translation is a true operation of creolization.[12]

Authors of Aegyptiaca are translators in this vein. They provide a view onto a unique cultural formation that derives from, but is independent of, the Greek and Egyptian languages between which it is suspended. Glissant is so dogged in individuating the translator's *langage* because he wants to emphasize its particularity, dynamism, and informality. Assaying the authenticity of language in a culturally mixed environment, whether in antiquity or in the twentieth century, is to misconstrue that language's creativity and undervalue its imaginativeness. Both are essential qualities of the translations of the Egyptian language one sees in Aegyptiaca. They lack the formality and unambiguity of bilingual stelae and papyri, but they are no less important as artifacts of the intellectual horizons of creolization

---

10. For the status of hieroglyphic as an object of scribal education, the widely copied Book of the Temple (e.g., P. Jumilhac) is a key source, summarized by Love (2021, 28–33) and analyzed by Iversen (1958) and Quack (among others, 2000, 2005, and 2021).

11. Conventionally dated to 394 CE, with an inscription at Philae. For the end of hieroglyphic, see Stadler (2008).

12. Glissant (2020, 27). For a fuller analysis of Glissant's use of *langage*, see Britton (1999, 30–31).

NOT DEAD YET!   147

in the ancient Mediterranean.[13] Chaeremon has often been taken as proof that the hieroglyphic script was in the process of dying.[14] But as I move through the different stakeholders—authors of Aegyptiaca, philosophers, and emperors—who made hay of Egyptian's rich symbolism, I will argue that we must appreciate on its own terms the messy and imperfect but still legitimate expertise one sees in imperial-era discussions of the Egyptian language. The fact of the matter is that authors of Aegyptiaca were translators. What remains to be seen, in this chapter and the next, is just what kinds of translations they provided.

MANETHO THE TRANSLATOR AND ETYMOLOGIZER

Manetho, as the representative of Aegyptiaca in its tidiest and most authoritative guise, is a good starting point. First, it requires little argument that Manetho was fluent in spoken Egyptian (*viz.* Demotic) and drew on inscribed Egyptian written in the grammatically conservative hieroglyphic script. Second, that authority over the Egyptian language is a primary point of reference for the Greek and Roman authors who discussed him. Third, attention to Manetho as translator furthers an argument I have been making across this book: that his expertise ranged much more widely than the annalistic history for which he is best known today.

Translating "Translation"

Ancient authors who discuss Manetho regularly highlight his access to Egyptian-language evidence. Josephus is no fan of Manetho, as any reader of the *Against Apion* will soon learn. But Josephus establishes a set pattern that repeatedly flags Manetho's access to hieroglyphic inscriptions to divide up Manetho's narrative into proper history based on written records and spurious mythological interpolation.[15]

The first mention of Manetho in the *Against Apion* is representative: "Manetho was an Egyptian by birth and had a Greek education, as is obvious; for he wrote a history of his home country in Greek, having made a translation from the hieroglyphic, as he himself says."[16] Ironically, it is not easy to translate the phrase

---

13. Discussed by Fewster (2002), Dieleman (2005), Kidd (2011), and Vierros (2012) (bilingualism and translation in specific dream, magical, and documentary papyrological archives); Papaconstantinou (2010) and Evans and Obbink (2010) (wide-ranging volumes on Greek/Traditional Egyptian/ Demotic interaction); Daumas (1952) (bilingualism in the Canopus and Memphis decrees); and Hoffmann, Minas-Nerpel, and Pfeiffer (2009) (the trilingual Gallus stele).

14. Fowden (1986, 65) and Burstein (1996, 602–3).

15. Dillery (2015, 204–6) quotes this passage at greater length. He emphasizes Josephus's insistence that the "textual" component of Manetho's history (the material I quote) exculpates Jews where Manetho's much weaker oral and mythological source material (not included in my excerpt) casts Jews as leprous Egyptians.

16. Joseph. *Ap.* 1.73 = *BNJ* 609 T 7a: Μανεθὼν δ᾽ ἦν τὸ γένος Αἰγύπτιος, ἀνὴρ τῆς Ἑλληνικῆς μετεσχηκὼς παιδείας, ὡς δῆλός ἐστιν· γέγραφεν γὰρ Ἑλλάδι φωνῆι τὴν πάτριον ἱστορίαν ἔκ τε τῶν ἱερῶν <γραμμάτων>, ὥς φησιν αὐτός μεταφράσας.

148   WHAT'S EGYPTIAN FOR "PHILOSOPHER"?

"having made a translation from the hieroglyphic (ἱερῶν γραμμάτων)." First, my translation of "hieroglyphic" is anodyne, but surprisingly heterodox. Most published translations suggest that here *hierôn grammatôn* denotes Egyptian inscribed chronologies. Lang's translation of "sacred records" in her *Jacoby* entry points in that direction.[17] But a simpler translation is the better one. To jump directly from hieroglyphic to evidentiary records like kings lists is an overreach. The more generic term "hieroglyphic" fits with the standard use of *hieroi grammatoi* since Herodotus: to indicate the Egyptian language in its hieroglyphic script.[18] It also better renders a boilerplate formula that Josephus uses to describe translations from a native language.[19] This is more than just nit-picking. Stripping *hieroi grammatoi* to its basic meaning relocates the discussion away from Manetho's bona fides as an annalistic history-writer toward Manetho's importance as a translator of the Egyptian language and the range of generic traditions that it contained.[20]

The translation of the very word "translate" is also worth pausing over. Josephus twice uses variations of the phrase "translated from the Egyptian language" to situate Manetho's authority. But both variations of the verb "translate" emphasize the deliberation and circumspection that come with moving Egyptian-language generic traditions into Greek. The first example: "For this same Manetho, who endeavored to translate (μεθερμηνεύειν) Egyptian historiography from hieroglyphs. . . ."[21] The root verb, *hermêneuô*, foregrounds ideas of explanation. In the process, it becomes clear that this translation is a rearticulation of a tradition that must undergo reframing in its new cultural context. Of course, this is true of all translations, so there is nothing exceptional in that. But the "hermeneutic" core of *hermêneuô* does highlight the creativity of interpretation that characterizes Glissant's translator. The verb's attested usages cluster around cross-cultural translations of gods' names and etymologies.[22] These divine etymologies emphasize a bi-cultural equivalence-seeking that sets this particular form of translation apart.

---

17. Lang (2014). Waddell (1940, 77) chooses "sacred tablets" (cf. Dillery 2015, 204, "sacred writings," and Verbrugghe and Wickersham (1996, 129), "priestly writings"). Waddell's justification—"Manetho would naturally base his History upon temple-archives on stone as well as on papyrus"—speaks to a circularity against which I am pushing back.

18. As suggested by its first attested use, Hdt. 2.106. See also Pl. *Ti.* 23e and 27b.

19. Compare Joseph. *AJ* 8.144.

20. Some supporting evidence for this focus on pure access to inscribed Egyptian, on script rather than on genre, comes from Eusebius. He cites (*BNJ* 609 T 9) an apparent Manethonian text called the "Sacred Book," a title (see Verbrugghe and Wickersham 1996, 101) that seems to reemphasize the religious, rather than annalistic, connotations of Egypt's "sacred letters."

21. Joseph. *Ap.* 1.228 = *BNJ* 609 F 10a: ὁ γὰρ Μανεθὼς οὗτος ὁ τὴν Αἰγυπτιακὴν ἱστορίαν ἐκ τῶν ἱερῶν γραμμάτων μεθερμηνεύειν ὑπεσχημένος. . . .

22. It is used repeatedly in that sense of cultural translators, in Eudoxus (F 374 ed. Lasserre), Hecataeus of Abdera (Diod. Sic. 1.11.2–4, 12.2–3, 12.5 = *BNJ* 264 F 25), and Alexander Polyhistor (*BNJ* 273 F 131). In the string of Diodorus/Hecataeus examples, it describes Egyptian-language etymologies of gods' names translated into Greek.

In other words, *methermêneuein* is a felicitous anchor for my wider use of the phrase "cultural translation" across this book. Josephus chooses this interpretatively laden term for translation because it suits his purpose, which is to push back against Manetho's representation of Jews. Through the specific choice of reinterpretation-qua-translation, Josephus suggests that even as Manetho draws from hieroglyphic evidence, his reinterpretation (*methermêneuein*) of said evidence is far from automatic or assured.

Even Josephus's above-quoted "by the numbers" denotation of "translation" ("Manetho was an Egyptian by birth. . . .") points toward the mediation of cultural traditions. The operative term (μεταφράσας) is relatively rare. At its core, it denotes concepts of consideration and elaboration that are at the heart of the root verb (φράζω). Early uses in Homer and Dionysius (the earliest extant authors to use the verb) point toward "consider" and "elaborate on," respectively.[23] Even when used in a sense of "translation," the valences of interpretation and reconsideration are still prominent. Already in antiquity, there remains an emphasis on the creative qualities of the translator that, at least according to Josephus, indicates Manetho's dynamic, unforeseeable, and ultimately controvertible cultural production.

Etymologizing: Fake It Til You Make It

The specific acts of translation assigned to Manetho—especially the verb *methermêneuein*—prioritize "reinterpretation." As a result, Manetho's access to hieroglyphic texts broadens into a larger task of repositioning Egyptian historiographic traditions in a new Greek-language context. Josephus's set phrase "ancestral history" positions literary genre as a literal object of translation.[24] This translation of genre required Manetho to move Egyptian annalistic memorialization into a Greek historiographic framework over which Herodotus loomed particularly large. Ian Moyer and John Dillery have debated how and in what ways Manetho translates history-writing between Egyptian and Greek conventions.[25] That is an essential conversation, one that locates Manetho's intellectual production in a culturally mixed environment while emphasizing the endurance of inherited historiographic traditions. I would emphasize that Manetho is a valuable point of departure not just for generic translation of historiography, but also for the acts of reinterpretation that cluster around the "sacred" half of Egypt's "sacred letters." Manetho's translations of Egyptian religious names bear out the interpretative creativity toward which *methermêneuein* points.

---

23. Representative are Dion. Hal. *Ant. Rom.* 3.32 and Phil. *De vit. Mos.* 2.38, which emphasize the different intentions that yield different translations of the same term.

24. In Greek, τὴν πάτριον ἱστορίαν, which is the direct object of the participle μεταφράσας.

25. Dillery (1999, 97–98) positions Manetho primarily against Herodotus; Moyer (2011, 84–141) responds by reemphasizing Manetho's debt to Egyptian annalistic conventions; and Dillery (2015, 32, 341–42) attempts to balance both perspectives.

150   WHAT'S EGYPTIAN FOR "PHILOSOPHER"?

Through these creative etymologies, one can do two things, both of which are salutary. First, and most importantly, it is possible to demonstrate concretely a path of translation that begins with Egyptian-language etymologies of gods' names, travels through Manetho, and then reaches Plutarch. In a tradition as lacunose as Aegyptiaca, the verifiability of one of Manetho's etymological translations is striking:

> Also, though most people think that Amoun is the name for Zeus among the Egyptians (which we pronounce 'Ammon'), Manetho of Sebennytus believes that 'being hidden' or 'concealment' is signified by this phrase. . . . That's why, when invoking the first god, whom they consider an embodiment of the universe, as invisible and hidden, and asking him to be visible and clear to them, they call him 'Amun.' That, in sum, is why Egyptians' reverence for wisdom in divine matters was so great.[26]

It would be overly positivist to say that Manetho provides for Plutarch a correct Egyptian-language etymology. But, it is in fact correct—at least in the social context of elite scribes and priests who practiced this kind of etymologizing. Manetho really does give Plutarch an etymology of Amun that offers essential background on Amun's semantics of removal and primacy. As Manetho clearly knew, in Egyptian Amun's name was the past participle of the verb *jmn*, "to conceal."[27] Beyond the slippery slope of accuracy, the passage reconfigures the site where a mixed etymological and symbolic presentation of the divine is taking place. It is worth appreciating that Plutarch, for one, assigns philosophically inclined etymologies to Manetho and, through Manetho, to Egyptians writ large. By referencing Manetho's etymologies, Plutarch can persuasively align his own Platonic metaphysics with similar discussions taking place in Egyptian-language sources. Amun and concealment help Manetho (and, by extension, Plutarch) define what it means to be divine. That assignation of philosophically rich interpretation to Aegyptiaca is something I will return to in chapter 6, but it is worth proleptically gesturing to here.

Egyptian-language texts reveal the body of evidence from which Manetho draws this Amun-as-hiddenness gloss. No specific text can be singled out as *the* source—wordplay around Amun's name is widespread. But the famous New Kingdom hymns to Amun, contained in P. Leiden I 350, provide a good example.[28] The hymns, which assert the centrality of Amun in the Egyptian cosmogony, are rife with *figurae etymologicae* that help establish his primacy and unknowability. To provide one example among many:

---

26. *DIO* 9, 354c–d = *BNJ* 609 F 19: ἔτι δὲ τῶν πολλῶν νομιζόντων ἴδιον παρ' Αἰγυπτίοις ὄνομα τοῦ Διὸς εἶναι τὸν Ἀμοῦν (ὃ παράγοντες ἡμεῖς Ἄμμωνα λέγομεν) Μανεθὼς μὲν ὁ Σεβεννύτης τὸ κεκρυμμένον οἴεται καὶ τὴν κρύψιν ὑπὸ ταύτης δηλοῦσθαι τῆς φωνῆς. . . .

27. *Wb.* 1.83. For the larger function of Manetho's etymologies within his historical narrative, see Dillery (2015, 324–28).

28. Published by Zandee (1948).

One is Amun, concealing (*jmn*) himself from them [𓇋𓏠𓈖𓄿𓀢𓏤𓂋𓂝𓋴𓏏𓏏𓏏]:
He is hidden from the gods, and his nature is unknown. He is farther from the sky,
he is deeper than the Duat. No god knows his true appearance, no image of his is
revealed through inscriptions, no one testifies to him accurately. He is too secret to
uncover his awesomeness, he is great to investigate, too powerful to know.[29]

The etymological wordplay forms the passage's opening salvo. One can see
clearly the repetition of *Jmn* / Amun [𓇋𓏠𓈖𓄿/𓇋𓏠𓈖𓀢] in the Egyptian text. The
Amun described here works well with Plutarch's Amun. When Plutarch says that
"the Egyptians believe Amun to be the universe" this is not just Greek philosophical grandstanding. It fits in smoothly with Amun's role as proto-creator in the Theban cosmogony.[30] That proto-creator role explains the general emphasis on his
primacy and distance in the many prayers made to him from the New Kingdom
onward.[31] At least in the case of Amun, one cannot claim that Plutarch smears
Egyptian etymologies with Greek philosophical conceptions of the divine. Plutarch's basic goal in the *DIO*, the search for a hidden god, is explicitly linked to
Egyptian beliefs in Amun—articulated through phrases like "he is great to investigate"—that gesture in the same direction. One only gets a shadow of the discussion Manetho would have undertaken via this Amun etymology. But even
if its details remain out of reach, Manetho's text clearly translates Amun's long-
standing semantics of hiddenness into Greek. In the process, Manetho enables
readers like Plutarch to emphasize the concordance between Egyptian and Greek
philosophizing etymologies of gods' names.

Manetho's other divine etymology is similar to, if a good deal messier than, his
explanation of Amun. As I mentioned in chapter 4, Plutarch cites Manetho for the
association of Seth with the red-faced baboon god Bebon: "*Some say Bebon was
one of Typhon's companions, but Manetho says that Typhon himself was also called
Bebon. The name means restraint or prevention, as when Typhon's power disrupts
well-conducted affairs heading in the right direction.*"[32]

There are a couple of difficulties. I need not rehash here the question of where
to bracket Manetho's original information. Whereas in the Amun etymology
Plutarch unambiguously attributed authority to Manetho, things are less cut and
dried here. It is unclear just who is associating Bebon with hindrance. I take it as
probable that Plutarch is representing some kernel of an etymology that Manetho

---

29. From the Hymns to Amun (P. Leiden I 350 4, 17–19). Text taken from Gardiner (1905, 33–34);
translation from Allen (2000, 182); see also the discussion by Dunand and Zivie-Coche (2004, 33).

30. Klotz (2017, 132–33) notes Plutarch's awareness of the Amun etymology in his general argument
about Plutarch's engagement with Theban religion.

31. The continued importance of these Amun hymns is reflected in the Persian-period examples
assembled by Klotz (2006).

32. *DIO* 49, 371c = *BNJ* 609 F 20: Βέβωνα δὲ τινὲς μὲν ἕνα τῶν τοῦ Τυφῶνος ἑταίρων γεγονέναι
λέγουσιν, Μανεθὼς <δ'> αὐτὸν τὸν Τυφῶνα καὶ Βέβωνα καλεῖσθαι.

152   WHAT'S EGYPTIAN FOR "PHILOSOPHER"?

provided.[33] But no matter the author, the etymology is idiosyncratic. There is no clear way to corroborate the etymology with either Greek or Egyptian semantics of "hindrance." To complicate matters, Manetho is not the only author to discuss the Seth/Bebon pairing. Another fragmentary Greek historian, Hellanicus of Lesbos, refers to Seth/Typhon as *Babys*.[34]

Even the claim directly attributed to Manetho, that Bebon was an alternate name for Seth, brings one into a gray area. There is some clear support from Egyptian evidence. The baboon-shaped god Baba or Babawy had a broad set of connections to darkness, evil, and chaos. In those guises, he came to be closely aligned with, and sometimes identified as, Seth. Any survey of Egyptian-language mentions of Babawy leads immediately to the slipperiness of this distinction between Babawy as "Sethian" and Babawy as "Seth." Babawy's role in the *Contendings of Horus and Seth* and his Sethian epithet Nebed in the Papyrus Jumilhac underline a close relationship between Seth and Baba that often verges into syncretistic identification of the two.[35] This is nothing new. Minor divinities in Egypt often followed a process in which they first were identified with major deities who shared a quality or cult site with them, and then were entirely subsumed into them.[36] Manetho is, then, trying to capture an on-the-ground reality in Egypt, where local and national gods were aligned with each other. That is important to stress, even if the dichotomy (comrade versus syncretistic pair) that Plutarch is structuring this Manetho citation around is ultimately wrongheaded. But no matter what, there is still a clear and identifiable path of translation that moves from Egyptian language sources connecting a baboon god to Seth, through Manetho, to Plutarch. Even if some specifics are lost, the Baba material is still making its way into Plutarch.

Casting a wider net for Manetho's etymologies makes things even less tidy. There is plenty of evidence that even an exegete of Egyptian culture as exalted as Manetho provides etymologies whose Egyptian-language credentials are sketchy. That ambivalence of accuracy is also a salutary lesson to take away from Manetho's etymologizing. The main non-Plutarch source for Manetho's etymologies comes from Josephus and the debate about the Exodus. Frustratingly, it occurs in a much-disputed passage.[37] In Josephus's larger recapitulation of Manetho's

33. This is a problem that comes inevitably with fragmentary authors. For my use of "co-authorship," see chapter 1.

34. Ath. *Deipn.* 15, 679f–680a = *BNJ* 4 F 54.

35. As explained by Griffiths (1970, 487–89). For texts, *Contendings* 3, 9–10 (Broze 1996), P. Jumilhac 16, 22 (Vandier 1962).

36. Well discussed by Hornung (1982, 91–99).

37. As Barclay (2000 56–57n316) makes clear, Joseph. *Ap.* 1.83 is a textually suspect passage. He summarizes well the various proposed solutions and tentatively concludes that this is an interpolation. I find the more commonly endorsed alternative "2" the most attractive, in which the passage reflects an edited version of Manetho. The presence of the "shepherds" gloss in Manetho's annalistic history offers enough support that the etymology is Manetho's, even if Barclay is right and this passage is an interpolation. Moyer (2011, 122–25) and (especially) Dillery (2015, 206–10) defend the passage's utility for reconstructing Manetho's narrative.

version of the Exodus, Manetho turns to the common tradition associating the Jews of the Exodus with the Hyksos migration. The Hyksos were a set of Delta-based dynasties of the Second Intermediate Period. They ruled an area that had undergone demographic changes during the Middle Kingdom, when mass resettlement of West Asians in the Delta led to a mixed Levantine-Egyptian cultural milieu. But after the Thebans of the Seventeenth Dynasty defeated the Hyksos kings, a far-reaching *damnatio memoriae* consigned the Hyksos to the ranks of chaotic, foreign-born, non-Egyptian foes whose expulsion helped restore Maat and universal harmony. It was in that spirit that subsequent annalists, like Manetho, began to connect the Hyksos period and its roots in West Asian immigration with the debate about the historicity of the Exodus.

On to the etymology itself. Josephus mentions that Manetho gave two etymologies for the Hyksos: "shepherds" and "captives."[38] Fortunately, there is corroborating evidence that the etymology is well and truly Manetho's. In his annalistic history, Manetho labels the Fifteenth Dynasty the "shepherd-kings."[39] "Shepherds" is not an ideal gloss for the Hyksos, a Greek transliteration of *ḥḳꜣw ḫꜣswt*, "rulers of the foreign lands."[40] It seems clear that this gloss is both a misrepresentation of Egyptian etymologies of the Hyksos and safely attributable to Manetho. The combination of those two facts is of course troubling, as it seems to erode the foundations of Manetho's inimitable authority over the Egyptian language.

When taken as a group, the Amun, Bebon, and Hyksos glosses demand an approach to Manetho's use of language that avoids the pitfalls of a correct/incorrect rubric. In some cases, this is recuperative. Manetho's representation of the Hyksos kings is, *de facto*, an Egyptian explanation because Manetho was himself an Egyptian. To call it incorrect is a misguided approach to how and in what ways language and etymologies depend on the particular person giving it voice. I am far from the first to suggest that folk etymologies are correct in the eyes of the people who relied on them.[41] Manetho's "shepherd-kings" has its own kind of authority that can be appreciated on its own terms.

That also enriches the Amun etymology, which is underserved if it is only cited as correct. Amun-qua-hidden is a clear example of how systems of significance could travel between cultural and linguistic communities. Its value lies not in rubberstamping Manetho as a correct etymologizer; it lies instead in the way that Plutarch assigns to Manetho an exegetical role that places philosophically rich modes of interpretation unproblematically in an Egyptian's mouth. That assignation is the essential lesson to be taken away from Manetho as etymologizer and exegete

---

38. The alternative depends, per Joseph. *Ap.* 1.82, on the first syllable, *hyk*.

39. For shepherd-kings in the Fifteenth Dynasty, see Syncellos 113.7 (ed. Dindorf) = *BNJ* 609 F 2 (cf. Moyer 2011, 121). For Josephus's citation of the two etymologies, see F 8 (with Lang 2014 *ad loc.* for discussion).

40. Discussed most authoritatively by Ryholt (1997).

41. Filos (2019, 162, and see 160n2 for the origin of *Volksetymologie*) defines folk etymologies and emphasizes their independence from a correct/incorrect dichotomy.

154   WHAT'S EGYPTIAN FOR "PHILOSOPHER"?

of Egypt's gods. Manetho's flexible cultural translation maintains its emphasis on the structures that make Egyptian etymological data coherent and meaningful, no matter how precisely the etymologies in question succeed or fail when weighed against Egyptian-language sources from the distant Egyptian past. A collective impulse to celebrate Manetho's accuracy and bemoan his failure misses the picture that should be drawn with Manetho's use of language. Etymologies were a dynamic and malleable tool through which Manetho developed his exegetical authority.

HIEROGLYPHIC SYMBOLISM AND OTHER PRECARIOUS TRANSLATIONS

Chaeremon the Close-But-Not-Quite-Right Translator

Chaeremon amplifies the issues that Manetho has introduced. The mixed bag that we see in Manetho, where etymological explanations sometimes track and sometimes fail to track with Egyptian-language evidence, becomes decidedly more mixed in Chaeremon. This is not a rebuke of Chaeremon and later authors of Aegyptiaca, who have long been compared unfavorably with Manetho. It is instead a sign of how an authoritative explanation of the Egyptian language changes when the Ptolemaic gives way to the imperial period. As with sacred animals, imperial-era Egyptians' discussions of the hieroglyphic script frustrate any neat division between explanations vouchsafed by pharaonic evidence and tendentious, Greek "philosophications" of the Egyptian language. This builds on the general ambivalence in the other facet of Chaeremon's intellectual profile, which aligned philosophical and priestly practice into a composite form over which he could claim joint mastery.[42]

That ambiguity of authority extends to the main text that Chaeremon wrote, the *Hieroglyphica*. His explanation of hieroglyphic for a Roman audience was, as the title spells out, a defining feature of his intellectual profile. His is one of the two *Hieroglyphica* known from the ancient world. These two *Hieroglyphica*, of Chaeremon and the much later, difficult-to-date Egyptian priest Horapollo, offer symbolically and religio-philosophically laden explanations of hieroglyphic signs.[43] Chaeremon's specific presentation of Egyptian heightens the questions of authority over hieroglyphic introduced by Manetho. It is clear, by the very fact of his annalistic history, that Manetho had some demonstrable expertise with inscribed Egyptian texts. When one moves onward in Aegyptiaca to Chaeremon, that sort of authentication is harder to come by.

42. For the biography of Chaeremon, see Frede (1989), Frankfurter (1998, 224–25), and chapter 2 in this book. I analyze the mixed semantics of Chaeremon's philosopher-priest role in chapter 6.

43. While outside the chronological frame of this book, Horapollo's presentation of hieroglyphs (see Boas 1993, 15–18 for difficulties of dating) complements Chaeremon's, where heavy-handed philosophical glosses of hieroglyphs (discussed by Wildish 2017, 107–27 for symbolic explanations, 34–71 for natural-philosophical context) still show clear connections to the mechanics of Ptolemaic- and Roman-Egyptian hieroglyphic.

The very indirect preservation of Chaeremon's *Hieroglyphica* exacerbates the general questions of authority that arise alongside the shift from Manetho to Chaeremon. Put simply, the two main sources for Chaeremon's presentation of the Egyptian language are late and leave something to be desired.[44] The main citing authority, who offers the meatiest extant fragment of the *Hieroglyphica*, is Ioannes Tzetzes.[45] He lived in the twelfth century CE. The gap that separates him from the first century CE and Chaeremon is more than wide. Tzetzes's entry in the *Oxford Classical Dictionary* just about sums it up: "A copious, careless, quarrelsome Byzantine polymath."[46] An absolutely prolific author whose *History* canonized the Greek cultural tradition, Tzetzes's early exegetical work on the *Iliad* veered into the very type of allegorical interpretation for which hieroglyphic was such a frequent point of reference. His freewheeling style of quotation is not very encouraging—per the *OCD*, "he is extremely inaccurate." Besides Tzetzes, it remains possible that Chaeremon formed the source of Ammianus Marcellinus's discussion of the hieroglyphic script, though Chaeremon is never explicitly cited by Ammianus.[47]

So, the evidence is not exactly watertight. But even with this sorry state of affairs, it is worthwhile to see how a line of interpretation that emphasizes "symbolism" coexists with glosses of hieroglyphic signs that felicitously match the semantics of those signs in Egyptian. Even granting Tzetzes's shortcomings and distortions, there is some core value to the information that is assigned to Chaeremon. One certainly cannot take it as a verbatim quote, but I find it more probable than not that some of the discrete hieroglyph-plus-translation pairs were present in Chaeremon's original text.[48] The fragment is worth quoting in full:

> For Ethiopians do not have phonological letters, but instead all kinds of animals, their limbs, and other pieces.[49] *For the more ancient sacred-scribes, wanting to hide the natural philosophy of the gods, handed these things down to their children through allegories and symbols of this kind, as the sacred-scribe Chaeremon says.* And in place

---

44. Ioannes Tzetzes, who provides the longest fragments (T 6 and F 12, cf. T 12, F 13, 26D, 27D), though Ammianus Marcellinus is another potential source (F 28D), as Foster (2020, 889) argues, picking up the discussion of Schwyzer (1932, 98). Clement too (F 19D) might be a valuable (if never explicit) source for Chaeremon fragments, as van der Horst (1984, 68) argues.

45. F 12, discussed by Wendel (1940) and van der Horst (1984, 62–63).

46. Forbes, Browning, and Wilson (2016).

47. On which, Foster (2020, 889).

48. The general style of interpretation one sees in the Tzetzes fragment fits squarely with the alignment of Egyptian/religious and Greek/philosophical thinking on display in Chaeremon's other fragments from more chronologically proximate sources, e.g. Origen and Porphyry in F 3 and 4. For a fact-checking approach to the fragment's glosses and for a defense of Chaeremon's knowledge of hieroglyphic, see van der Horst (1984, 62–63).

49. Tzetzes presents the hieroglyphic script as Ethiopian in no small part due to the rise of the Kingdom of Axum, through which the distinction between Meroitic (on which Rilly and de Voogt 2012, 3) and Egyptian was lost on later Byzantine authors.

of 'joy' they wrote a woman beating a drum; in place of 'grief' a man holding up his chin with his hand and bowing to the earth; in place of 'misfortune' an eye crying; of 'not having' two empty, outstretched hands; of 'sunrise' a serpent coming out of a hole, of 'sunset' one entering it; in place of 'rebirth' a frog; of 'soul' hawk, as well as of 'sun' and 'god;' in place of 'daughter-bearing woman,' 'mother,' 'time,' and 'heaven' a vulture; of 'king' a bee; instead of 'birth' and 'autogenesis' and 'men' a beetle; instead of 'earth' a bull. The front of a lion indicates 'total sovereignty' and 'protection;' the back of a lion 'necessity'; a deer the 'year'; ditto the palm tree. A child indicates 'growing'; an old man 'decaying'; a bow 'keen power'; and thousands of others, from which Homer says these things.

If you choose, elsewhere I will also give the Ethiopic pronunciations of these characters, drawing on Chaeremon.[50]

Chaeremon no longer includes spoken Egyptian as a meaningful etymological source. As the end of the fragment makes clear, a discussion of Egyptian phonetics is a promise postponed. The straightforward pairs of signifier and signified suggest that Chaeremon is engaging exclusively with determinatives and ideograms. This fits generally with the changes that occurred to the hieroglyphic script during the Ptolemaic period, when hieroglyphic orthography increasingly relied on iconographic characters at the expense of the traditional grouping of phonograms plus a determinative.[51]

Even with this oversimplification, there remains in the quotation a stubborn grip on information that aligns with Egyptian-language sources. That is what makes the Tzetzes material worth the trouble. I certainly cannot say that everything Tzetzes includes here belongs to Chaeremon, nor that Tzetzes is accessing Chaeremon directly, rather than through an intermediary author or epitome. But caveats notwithstanding, the fragment makes clear that Chaeremon had some knowledge of the hieroglyphic script, all the more so because the hieroglyphic script had fallen out of use in 394 CE, some seven hundred years before Tzetzes was born.

The most impressive gloss, the one that comes closest to a real syntactic knowledge of Egyptian, is his explanation of "not having" as two empty, outstretched hands. Chaeremon clearly has in mind the ideogram and determinative for negation, *n/nn* ⌣. Second, Chaeremon makes the grade with bee as kingship; the bee was an identifier of kingship through the pharaonic *nswt-bjty* title, by which the king came to be associated with Upper and Lower Egypt.[52] Finally, the association of frog with resurrection has a clear Egyptian precedent. Heket, the goddess

50. F 12: βουλόμενοι γὰρ οἱ ἀρχαιότεροι τῶν ἱερογραμματέων τὸν περὶ θεῶν φυσικὸν λόγον κρύπτειν, δι' ἀλληγορικῶν [καὶ] συμβόλων τοιούτων καὶ γραμμάτων τοῖς ἰδίοις τέκνοις αὐτὰ παρεδίδουν, ὡς ὁ ἱερογραμματεὺς Χαιρήμων φησί.

51. Kurth (2007–2008) (cf. Wilson 1997) discusses the specific orthography of Ptolemaic hieroglyphic.

52. Von Beckerath (1984, 13–21). This specific gloss is also included in Ammianus, as discussed by Foster (2020, 884–85, 888–89).

NOT DEAD YET! 157

of childbirth, was zoomorphically represented as a frog. The frog determinative sometimes used in the phrase 𓆓𓆟𓋹𓈖𓆏 "repeating life" (*wḥm ʿnḫ*), which occurs after names of the deceased, speaks directly to a nexus of frogs, Heket, childbirth, and life after death. The widespread presence of frog lamps in Roman-Egyptian tombs, as a means of hinting at "repeating life" and resurrection of life after death, proves the ubiquity of the association that underlies Chaeremon's connection of frog hieroglyph with a return to life.[53]

Chaeremon has the verb 𓆣 *ḫpr* in mind when he glosses the beetle hieroglyph as "birth," "natural-grown," and "men." *ḫpr*, which variously denoted "to be born" and "to become," underlay Egyptian conceptions of autogenesis and emergence, whether of the individual person, of the world writ large, or of the sun each day. The last of these bears directly on the zoomorphic god Khepri, who tied together the semantics of the verb *ḫpr* with the tripartite solar ideology of Khepri the rising sun, Re the noonday sun, and Atum the evening sun. It is no surprise that authors of Aegyptiaca were quick to explain the semantics of birth that helped contextualize the otherwise odd ubiquity of scarab iconography. In this regard, it is worth recalling Apion's explanation of the scarab beetle (via Pliny).[54] Apion too spent some time underlining the solar connections of the scarab beetle. The mirroring between Apion and Chaeremon is striking. The two authors' scarab passages prove that discussions of zoomorphic gods and of hieroglyphic only gain coherence when connected to each other. Especially in the imperial period, that join is part of what makes it worthwhile to see Aegyptiaca as a coherent tradition, rather than a set of disparate authors discussed briefly and in isolation.

Chaeremon's glosses continue to doggedly resist a binary of emic authority and etic hucksterism. His philosophical bent continues with the hawk sign, which he associates jointly with "soul," "sun," and "god." This is all a bit hodgepodge, but there is still some meaningful connection to Egyptian zoomorphic iconography. Through the "soul" gloss, Chaeremon seems to refer to the *ba* bird. I could spend a good deal of time clarifying just how "soul" mistranslates the core concept of the *ba*, which instead indicated one's individuality and the impression one made on other people.[55] But since Herodotus, Greeks had identified *ba* and its iconography of a human-headed bird with the Greek soul.[56] So, Chaeremon's soul reading is not exactly original or authoritative, but it is still a well-established site of cross-cultural translation between Greek philosophies of the soul and Egyptian concepts of the *ba*.

53. For the use of Gardiner I7 in the phrase *wḥm ʿnḫ*, see Iacoby and Spiegelberg (1903). For frogs and rebirth, *LdÄ* 2.334–6.

54. Plin. *HN* 30.99 = *BNJ* 616 F 19, discussed in chapter 1. For Khepri's solar associations, see Hornung (1982, 97–98).

55. For an introduction to the role of the *ba* in the afterlife, see most systematically Zabkar (1968), but also Dunand and Zivie-Coche (2004, 168–69) and Allen (2011, 3–11).

56. Hdt. 2.123 connects the *ba* bird to animal metempsychosis, a trend continued by Diod. Sic. 1.98.

158 WHAT'S EGYPTIAN FOR "PHILOSOPHER"?

The hodgepodge quality comes mainly from the shift from the *ba* bird—a type of stork—to the glosses ("sun," "god") that seem to refer to the Horus falcon. The Horus falcon could meaningfully be tied into solar religion via Re-Horakhty, whose iconography included Horus's falcon zoomorphism. It is in that domain that Chaeremon's general "god" gloss could gain some sense, even if that is a bit of a stretch. While the Horus falcon was an ideogram for various divine words—all connected in some way to Horus—the blanket term "god" was reliably denoted by the flag-pole sign *netjer*. Put simply, there is something to this threefold explanation of the hawk; it creatively sews together the avian imagery of the *ba* with the related avian imagery of the winged sun. This synthesis is certainly novel and easily labeled incorrect. But to rush to that conclusion misses out on an associative impulse that synthesizes otherwise separate domains of Egyptian culture—language, animals, metaphysics—into a coherent whole. Chaeremon's hawk gloss requires as joint framing Glissant's defense of the translator's creativity and the obsolescence of hieroglyphic tied to changes in priestly training.[57]

Chaeremon paints a philosophical portrait of hieroglyphic, focusing exclusively on religious and cosmogonic vocabulary. His discussion of language thus fits into his larger project, which bound together Egyptian religious and Greek philosophical expertise.[58] If the selection is not purely the whim of Tzetzes, the hieroglyphs' collective emphasis on metaphysics and the emotions would fit in well with Chaeremon's Stoicism. Chaeremon's apparent connection to Cornutus, the Stoic allegorizer, is relevant context for Chaeremon's specific mode of glossing. Porphyry mentions Chaeremon in the same breath as Cornutus, as they were the two authorities for Stoic allegoresis of Greek gods: "Origen also made use of the books of Chaeremon the Stoic and of Cornutus, from which he came to know the substitutive (*metalêptic*) approach to the Greek mysteries. . . ."[59] Hieroglyphic, and particularly its use of ideograms and determinatives, fits in perfectly in this push and pull between the Stoic physics of which Chaeremon had some mastery and his presentation of Egyptian cosmogonic thinking.[60]

An Enigmatical Sort of Wisdom: From Aegyptiaca to Plutarch

It was Manetho and Chaeremon who developed the creative explanations of Egyptian one sees in Plutarch. Authors of Aegyptiaca etymologized divine names, coordinated animal, god, and nature, and generally prioritized the

---

57. Quack (2021) gives a fine overview of this latter-day priestly training.

58. On display in FF 5–9.

59. Euseb. *Hist. eccl.* 6.19.8 = T 9: ἐχρῆτο δὲ καὶ Χαιρήμονος τοῦ Στωϊκοῦ Κορνούτου τε ταῖς βίβλοις παρ' ὧν τὸν μεταληπτικὸν τῶν παρ' Ἕλλησιν μυστηρίων γνοὺς. . . .

60. Particularly if one keeps in mind the explicit role of allegory in the division of the Egyptian language offered by Clement of Alexandria (*Strom.* 5.4.20 = Chaeremon F 20D), which van der Horst (1984, 69) (following Vergote 1941) suggests is indebted to Chaeremon's presentation of hieroglyphic.

significance of language. In some moments, like the glosses of Amun (from Manetho) and linguistic negation (from Chaeremon), these symbolic explanations align with Egyptian-language evidence. But at other times, they decidedly do not. I have been suggesting that this does not so much threaten the accuracy of authors of Aegyptiaca as it does demand a theoretical approach to translation that prioritizes creativity and inventiveness between languages. Aegyptiaca's "Greegyptian" argot of religio-philosophical vocabulary contains its own imaginative logic, responsive to the times and sociocultural contexts that defined it. It was a sociocultural context that aligned Chaeremon with Plutarch, since both turned to etymology as a mixed Greek and Egyptian tradition essential to philosophical and religious expertise.[61]

Plutarch uses an etymology to bolster the very premise of the *On Isis and Osiris* (*DIO*): he moves from a paean of truth-searching to the Osiris myth through an etymology of Isis from "to know" (οἶδα), which coordinates Isis-worship with philosophy through the love of knowledge shared by both. As a part of this etymology, Plutarch clarifies: "Isis is a Greek word."[62] This has been a contentious etymology, one whose coordination of an Egyptian god with a Greek verb invites readings that emphasize cultural priority.[63] As I will discuss more fully in the next chapter, racing to cultural priority misses the forest for the trees. The etymology is a point of departure for Plutarch's attempts to align priests and philosophers as kindred truth-seekers. For now, I want to emphasize the foundational role of the etymology in the narrative. It is the crux of the *DIO*'s goals.

Pragmatically, the Isis etymology is given pride of place, but the *DIO* repeatedly turns to Egyptian- rather than Greek-language etymologies.[64] The etymologies that Plutarch assigns to Manetho are just two instances. There are also several examples that cannot be directly tethered to a named Egyptian author. While the path of translation from Egypt to Plutarch cannot be directly charted for these cases, they still speak to a literary milieu in which Egyptian-language material was brought over into Greek. By prioritizing the tradition of Aegyptiaca rather than an individual author, these "orphaned" passages can be brought into the fold of Aegyptiaca's reception among Greek and Roman authors.

---

61. Griffiths (1970, 100–1) traces Plutarch's Stoic etymologizing back to Cornutus. Given the testimonium (T 8) presenting Chaeremon and Cornutus as the two canonical Stoic etymologizers, it is tempting to insinuate Chaeremon into this intellectual lineage.

62. *DIO* 2, 351f: Ἑλληνικὸν γὰρ ἡ Ἰσίς ἐστι.

63. It is critical to the eristic reading of Richter (2001; 2011, 192–98) and to the argument for Plutarch's universalizing view of Greek philosophy offered by Görgemanns (2017, 11–12). See too Brenk (1999).

64. By this I mean etymologies which, though delivered in Greek, are oriented toward an originally Egyptian word or phrase. Griffiths (1970, 106–10) helpfully lists these etymologies and "linguistic elements," notably avoiding the Isis-as-"to know" etymology.

Plutarch's linguistic connection of the fish hieroglyph to hatred is a good place to start.[65] Fish are a recurrent presence in the *DIO*: first, as a bridge between the old Homeric chestnut about fish (Homeric heroes never eat fish) and Egyptians' hatred for the fish that ate Osiris's dismembered penis.[66] The fish returns when Plutarch underlines the associations between the sea and Seth/Typhon, which spirals out into a discussion of Egyptians' suspicion of salt and maritime traders: "And not least on these grounds [the sea's Typhonic associations] they find fish guilty, and write out 'hatred' with a fish."[67] In a strict and positivist sense, the gloss holds water. Since the Old-Kingdom Pyramid Texts, Egyptians had written *bwt* ("hatred") as 𓃀𓏏𓂋.[68] By the New Kingdom, the fish determinative in the previous spelling was used by itself as an abbreviation for the same idea of hatred. This is not so much a celebration of a victory in a correct/incorrect template I have been avoiding. The gloss's cultural fidelity to Ptolemaic hieroglyphic spelling is, instead, valuable as a shadow that delineates the outline of an author of Aegyptiaca who remains out of view.

Besides the *DIO*, the fish/hatred concept is reflected indirectly elsewhere in Plutarch and in Apuleius. In Book 1 (1.25) of Apuleius's *Metamorphoses*, Lucius's magistrate friend takes vengeance on a huckster fishmonger by stomping on all his fish. The scene is odd enough, and Apuleius generally invested enough in esoterica, that Nicolas Lévi has suggested a play on the coordination of feet and fish in the above hieroglyphic spelling.[69] But one cannot be certain. No matter Apuleius's potential continuation of this tradition, Plutarch's interest in hieroglyphs is clear enough. In addition to the fish, he coordinates a falcon with "god," a pair similar to that offered by Chaeremon. The specific source for Plutarch is hard to pin down. Plutarch claims that the inscription that included these fish and falcon hieroglyphs was from Sais. Any reconstruction of a source purely on that basis is necessarily tentative.[70] Regardless, one sees in Plutarch a discussion of hieroglyphic signs that matches animal and concept in much the same way that Chaeremon had done. That is certainly a reconfiguration of the hieroglyphic script, but the fact remains that "hatred" is spelled with a fish glyph in inscribed Egyptian texts.

---

65. *DIO* 32, 363f.

66. Fish abstention and Homer: *DIO* 7, 353c–e (cf. the discussion of Pythagoras's abstention from fish and its Egyptian origins in Plut. *Quaest. Conv.* 8.8.3, 729d–e, with Meeusen 2017, 222–23); for fish's consumption of Osiris's penis, see *DIO* 18, 358a–b.

67. Plut. *DIO* 32, 363f: οὐχ ἥκιστα δὲ καὶ τὸν ἰχθὺν ἀπὸ ταύτης προβάλλονται τῆς αἰτίας καὶ τὸ μισεῖν ἰχθύι γράφουσιν. The association of fish with hatred occurs also in Clement of Alexandria *Strom.* 5.7.41.3–42.3, included as a dubious fragment of Chaeremon in van der Horst (1984, F 19D).

68. *Wb.* 1.453, s.v. *bwt*.

69. Lévi (2014, 433–34).

70. Griffiths (1970, 105–6, 422–23) hazards a reconstruction based on the signs mentioned and concludes: "Enough is right to show that he [Plutarch] was in contact with a source to which the hieroglyphs were not unfamiliar" (423).

As in Chaeremon, hieroglyphic spelling offers Plutarch fodder for symbolic etymologies of gods' names. The best example is Osiris, whose name Plutarch unpacks both hieroglyphically and phonetically. In the former case, Plutarch cites the spelling of Osiris with scepter and eye to suggest that Egyptian iconography is symbolically rich in the same ways as Pythagoreanism, which correlates a numerological concept (cube) with a god (Poseidon).[71] Plutarch extrapolates from this spelling a wider symbolic significance, in which the eye-sign's connotations of vision and "many-eyed" suitably underline the omnipresence and omniscience of the king of the gods. Strictly as a reflection of contemporary hieroglyphic spelling, Plutarch finds corroboration in Ptolemaic monuments, which also spell Osiris (*Wsr*) with an eye and scepter ⸢⸣.[72] Once again, there is enough of a toehold in contemporary orthographic practices to gesture hazily toward an Egyptian source whose authority depends on contemporary practices rather than much earlier pharaonic norms.

Plutarch does not just emphasize hieroglyphic signs and their symbolic significance. He takes a phonetic tack too. Plutarch, keen to identify Osiris with the principle of moisture, cites the Greek mythographer Hellanicus for the pronunciation "Hysiris."[73] While totally unconnected to the Greek hydrological vocabulary to which Plutarch tries to yoke Hysiris, this spelling does represent a better transliteration of the Egyptian pronunciation.[74] Even more importantly, this interest in pronunciation clarifies that hieroglyphs and determinatives do not circumscribe the Egyptian language and its reception among Greek and Roman authors.

This push beyond hieroglyphs introduces new types of cultural translation rooted in language. So, for example, Plutarch identifies *Arouêris* as either Apollo or the elder Horus. One can see quite clearly the move from elder Horus, *Ḥr-Wr* in Egyptian, to the phonetically similar *Arouêris*. There is also a broader form of cultural translation at play. In the overarching passage in which the transliteration occurs, Plutarch depends on an author of Aegyptiaca to translate into Greek a common narrative of the birth of Nut's children (Isis, Osiris, the elder Horus, Seth/Typhon, and Nephthys) on the succession of five epagomenal days that ended the Egyptian year.[75]

---

71. *DIO* 9, 354f. For the wider use of this Pythagoreanism-Egypt symbolism, see chapter 6 in this book.

72. *DIO* 10, 354f–355a. For spelling of *wsr*, see Wb. 1.359.

73. *DIO* 34, 364d–e: Ὕσιριν.

74. This association with moisture is, in and of itself, an *interpretatio Graeca*, though it does have some basis in later Egyptian belief, given Osiris's role in fertility and the consequent identification of Osiris with Nun. This Hellanicus is the same as the famous chronographer.

75. *DIO* 12, 355e and 356a. Plutarch here (cf. Eudoxus F 290 ed. Lasserre) reflects the standard Ptolemaic translation of *Ḥr-Wr*, the "great/elder" Horus (discussed by Junker 1917, 42) specific to a prominent Heliopolitan cosmogony (reflected in inscriptions at the Hathor temple at Dendera, per Cauville 1991, 93–94).

162   WHAT'S EGYPTIAN FOR "PHILOSOPHER"?

There are other religious translations similar to this *Aroûeris* example. One can add, for good measure, Plutarch's translation of the text in an amulet purportedly worn by Isis. Plutarch renders it "true of voice."[76] While its relevance to the amulet in particular is unclear, the phrase must represent a translation of the Egyptian *mꜣꜥ ḥrw* ("true of voice/justified"), a ubiquitous expression for the dead who have "spoken truly" by making the negative confession, a key stage in Egyptian eschatology.[77] The hodgepodge quality of these orphaned fragments hints at a heterogeneous corpus of religious and eschatological topics that authors of Aegyptiaca sought to translate. Plutarch certainly projects a good deal onto the Egyptian language, as a cipher for the divine truth that is the *DIO's* idealized object of philosophical investigation. But that does not mean that authors like Manetho or Chaeremon were not presenting the Egyptian language in the same way, in ways more (Amun, fish, hawk/Horus) or less (deer for year) proximate to pharaonic evidence, but consistently creative and imaginative.

DOMITIAN'S OBELISK, OR, "NOT DEAD YET!"

The hieroglyphic script was a material reality across the Mediterranean. That is an absolutely critical frame for the discussions of the Egyptian language one sees in Plutarch and imperial Aegyptiaca. The presence of Egyptian inscriptions in Italy anchors Chaeremon's *Hieroglyphica* in the pragmatic questions of how hieroglyphic was composed in Rome in the imperial period. Disciplinarily, hieroglyphic monuments help bring Chaeremon into conversation with the work of Stephanie Pearson, Molly Swetnam-Burland, Miguel John Versluys, and all those who have surveyed Italy's material, rather than literary, Aegyptiaca.[78] Both Chaeremon and hieroglyphic-inscribed obelisks traveled from Egypt to Rome on roads paved by the exigencies of empire.

While there are many recycled hieroglyphic inscriptions in Rome, the list of Rome's new hieroglyphic compositions is, unsurprisingly, pretty short. But one example suffices.[79] The obelisk now found in the Piazza Navona was originally commissioned with a new inscription by the emperor Domitian. It was placed in

76. *DIO* 68, 378b: φωνὴ ἀληθής.

77. *BD* Spell 125, translated in Allen 1974 97–101 and discussed by Assmann (1990, 130, 136–40, as a component of Maat, and 2001b, 137, as a part of Egyptian approaches to death).

78. The list of work on Egyptian material culture in Italy is too long to list. Apposite is Versluys (2002, 23, 421); Swetnam-Burland (2015), who discusses hieroglyphic inscriptions, Chaeremon, and Domitian's obelisk (41–53); Barrett (2019); Pearson (2021); and the series of conference volumes on Isis cult (Bricault 2004; Bricault, Versluys, and Meyboom 2007; Bricault and Versluys 2010, 2014).

79. Note also the so-called Antinous obelisk (on which Meyer 1994 for edition, Grimm 1994, 27–88, for text and translation, and Sorek 2010, 89–100, for discussion), another case in which a new hieroglyphic inscription was added to an obelisk, in its case to consolidate the cult to Antinous. See too the small obelisk erected in the *horti sallustiani*, discussed by Pearson (2021, 170).

Rome's Isis temple when the latter was rebuilt by Domitian as a part of his building program in the Campus Martius.[80] The obelisk's inscription, and particularly its celebration of the Roman emperor, tethers the symbolic expositions of the Egyptian language I have traced across this chapter to the social and political contours that surrounded Egyptian-looking stuff in Rome. Through the obelisk, Domitian celebrates the successes of his, his brother Titus's, and his father Vespasian's military and civic achievements. In doing so, Domitian both consolidates the Flavians into an identifiable dynasty and casts Roman power in the language and imagery of pharaonic rule.[81]

Domitian's obelisk has been productively studied. Several have highlighted the exoticizing function of hieroglyphic writ large, the obelisk form as a projection of power, and imperial obelisks as index of the principate's evolving self-definition against Egyptian religion.[82] These are all extrinsically significant. The obelisk's original location, in the so-called *Iseum Campense*, integrates a monument trumpeting the Flavians' power into the practice of Isis religion in Rome. That emperor/Isis pairing shows just how much things had changed since the Augustan and then Tiberian rejection of Isis cult. Under Domitian, Egypt was back in favor. Egyptians like Crispinus prospered, much to the ire of Romans like Juvenal who explained all that was wrong with Rome via the prominence, wealth, and prestige that Crispinus, the "Nile's trash," gained under Domitian's patronage.[83] But part of the value of Domitian's obelisk requires one to push past the bare signification of an Egyptian-looking monument that is often the stopping point in discussions of Egyptian material culture in Rome. Domitian's obelisk is not purely a tabula rasa of broad and cultural, rather than narrow and linguistic, import.

It is not just that obelisks are a frame for Aegyptiaca. It is also that Aegyptiaca is a frame for the presence of hieroglyphic inscriptions in Rome, one that can move beyond exoticism as the inevitable meaning attached to such objects.[84] Reducing hieroglyphs' significance solely to their exotic appeal leaves the contents of these inscriptions out of reach. Certainly, the readership of the obelisk was slim. But the significance that Egyptians attached to inscribed hieroglyphic, as a powerful speech act, holds true regardless of potential readership. What's more,

---

80. The text of the obelisk is published by Erman (1917) and Grenier (1987) (cf. Lembke 1994, 210–12, for translation; D'Onofrio 1965, 222–29, for its relocation to the Piazza Navona). For discussion, see too Parker (2003).

81. Vittozzi (2014, 243–46) discusses the dynasticism motif with reference to the obelisk; that dynasticism is also broadcast through the *Templum gentis Flaviae* (cf. Jones 1992, 87–88).

82. Iversen (1968, 76–92) and Sorek (2010, 79–84) catalogue the Roman obelisks. For Domitian and Isis see Lembke (1994, 69–70), and for obelisks as objects in motion see Parker (2003; 2007, 212–13).

83. To quote Juvenal's programmatic first satire (1.26). For Juvenal's treatment of Crispinus, see the historicizing approach of Baldwin (1979); Vassileiou (1984); and for Crispinus as a programmatic satiric target, Keane (2015, 49).

84. To build on a point made by Swetnam-Burland (2015, 43).

a differentiation between viewership and readership depends on an image/text binary that is a poor fit for Egyptians' understanding of hieroglyphic.[85] No matter who read (or viewed) it, the text still communicated a culturally mixed message of imperial power. It was a message that sought to fuse together Egypt's monumental royal ideology and the new needs of a Roman emperor wishing to consolidate his family's achievements. On the level of syntax and genre alike, the obelisk is a document in creolization. It is another text that emphasizes the intersecting layers of discreet, linguistic translation and broader generic translation, in this case of dynastic power between Egypt and Rome.

On a more basic level, the obelisk offers a point of reference for the presentation of hieroglyphic in Aegyptiaca. It provides an ideal *comparandum*, one that shows how Chaeremon's discussion of the hieroglyphic script squares with the syntax of hieroglyphic written at the beginning of the end of its history.[86] It can offer a corrective for a collective impulse to unfairly evaluate the Egyptian authority of post-Manetho authors of Aegyptiaca against a pharaonic yardstick. Like the messy Egyptian identity of authors of Aegyptiaca, imperial-era hieroglyphic suffers from a black mark of posteriority that singles it out as lesser than its Ptolemaic predecessor, to say nothing of pharaonic hieroglyphic monuments. That has long been the reason why the intra-textual, rather than extra-textual, significance of the obelisk's inscription has withered. From the perspective of Egyptologists equipped to read the text, Domitian's obelisk is boring and derivative. Most write off Domitian's text as a rehash of the basic formulae of obelisk inscriptions. Adolf Erman, a pioneer in the study of Rome's Egyptian obelisks, is far from enthusiastic. He concludes that the obelisk's inscription is "virtually devoid of content."[87]

The basic mechanics of the inscription shed light on the status of hieroglyphic. For Chaeremon, the evidence available suggests he focused exclusively on determinatives and ideograms and did not have complete mastery of the phonetic value of hieroglyphs. Domitian's obelisk and its transliteration of the Flavian emperors serve as proof that Egyptians still knew how to transliterate Latin names into Egyptian via alphabetic transcription.[88] So Domitian is rendered *dmtyᵢns*, Titus *ḏyds*, and Vespasian *wsᵢpʿns*.[89] This was but the continuation of transliteration that had been occurring in Egypt since the Ptolemies came to town and that was critical

---

85. The idea of writing as a speech act is essential to the efficacy and power of hieroglyphic spelling, as discussed by Dunand and Zivie-Coche (2004, 176) and Hornung (1992, 17–36, esp. 30–34).

86. Chronologically, the obelisk was erected during the reign of Domitian (81–96 CE), not long after Chaeremon's *floruit* in the 30s–60s CE.

87. Erman (1917, 9): eigentlich ohne jeden Inhalt.

88. The transliteration of Greek and Latin names into Egyptian was instrumental to the modern decipherment of Egyptian, proving as it does the phonetic value of hieroglyphs, on which see Pope (1999, 11–84).

89. There is some ambiguity in the reading of Vespasian, in particular, the reading of the egg sign (Gardiner H8).

NOT DEAD YET!   165

to the decipherment of hieroglyphic in the nineteenth century. Transliteration is a demonstration of competence that is certainly ho-hum; but the literal incorporation of Roman dynasts into an Egyptian and hieroglyphic narrative is still significant. This alphabetic transliteration tweaks the hieroglyphic script, one among many ways that contact between Egypt and Rome produced new cultural forms. But purely as an evaluation of the state of hieroglyphic, the ability to transliterate Roman names into Egyptian points to the continued phonetic importance of the hieroglyphic script. That should caution one from authoritatively writing off Chaeremon's ability to engage with Egyptian as a language, or with hieroglyphic as a phonological script with which to write that language.[90] All the more so because Tzetzes is such a tenuous source. Hieroglyphic was certainly changing, but it was not dead yet.

The inscription's recycling of pharaonic formulae, far from dispiriting proof of imperial-era Egyptians' inability to produce anything new, emphasizes Romans' adoption of tropes of pharaonic kingship, the translation of dynasticism from Egypt to Rome, and the continuation of the divinely-nursed-king motif in a new Roman context of Isiac religion. As an example of the former, the *topos* of Domitian as unapproachable and fear-inducing continues a motif repeated throughout famous pharaonic inscriptions like Ramesses II's Qadesh Inscription and Thutmose III's Poetical Stele from Karnak.[91] In the case of the king's divine support, the text adds a specific path of cultural translation around Isis that is missed when the obelisk is discussed only contextually and extrinsically, as an imperial monument located in Rome's Isis temple. The inscription reiterates the typical claim that the king was suckled at the breast of Isis and Nephthys.[92] To Erman, this is rote and boring—all kings were nursed by Isis. But the trope provides a model of translation of divine support that both completely contradicts Virgil's Actian rhetoric—where Octavian battles with Isis—and reveals the often-underappreciated points of connection between pharaonic religion and Rome's Isis cult.

One particular *topos* best exemplifies the changes that define imperial-era hieroglyphic and its presentation by authors of Aegyptiaca. Domitian, in the obelisk, "is strong of arm, who acts with his arm."[93] The phrase recurs throughout royal monuments and literature, to underline kings' effectiveness. In a typical pharaonic example from the Tale of Sinuhe, Sinuhe praises Senusret I in similar terms: "He is also a forceful one who acts with his forearm."[94] The spelling that each text uses is telling. To write "forearm," Domitian's obelisk uses the ideogram ⏤ꟷ (ʿ) where

---

90. Daumas (1988–1995) remains the authority on the phonetics of imperial-era hieroglyphic.

91. For translation, see Lichtheim (1976, 57–72 for the Qadesh Inscription and 35–39 for the Thutmose III stele).

92. Erman (1917, 9, 27) (= Obelisk IVc).

93. Erman (1917, 21) (= Obelisk IIa): *nḫt ʿjr m ʿ.f.*

94. Sinuhe R 77: *nḫt pw grt jr m ḫpš.f.* For the text of Sinuhe, see Koch (1990) for *editio princeps*, or Allen (2015, 55–154). For translation, see Lichtheim (1975, 222–35) or Simpson (2003, 54–66).

Sinuhe uses the full phonetic group *ḫpš*. This tracks a larger trend in imperial-era hieroglyphic spelling, which was increasingly pictorial and cryptographic.[95] Domitian's spelling of forceful (*nḫt*) is also slightly garbled. The verb *jr* lacks a determinative in the Domitianic version.[96] This is one among many examples of the cryptic, determinative- and ideogram-laden form of hieroglyphic complementary to the alphabetization one sees in the Flavians' hieroglyphic names.

This close-but-not-quite-right quality of the obelisk inscription encapsulates in a nutshell the type of engagement with the Egyptian language I have been prioritizing. To catalogue Plutarch's hazy Egyptian sources, or Manetho, or Chaeremon according to whether they got hieroglyphic right or wrong is doomed to failure. For one, it assumes that hieroglyphic, as a script, was a static thing. Chaeremon's explanation of hieroglyphic is more or less concordant with contemporary sources, both in Rome and in Egypt. For another thing, it unduly sunders a script (hieroglyphic) from a language (Egyptian). If it is divorced from the actual language that it spelled out, hieroglyphs will inevitably be an empty signifier of exotic wisdom, rather than one part of a wider conversation around language and the pursuit of religious and philosophical meaning. And for a third thing, it leaves no space for creativity and agency in the ways that Egyptians attached symbolic weight to a script that had always been marked out for its sacrality. The shift from Manetho to Chaeremon need not be a sign of hieroglyphic's slow death. The two authors can instead help trace the rise of a new and increasingly enigmatic approach to hieroglyphs' "visual poetics."[97]

CONCLUSION: HIEROGLYPHS AND RELIGIO-PHILOSOPHICAL WISDOM

Domitian's obelisk, its use of the hieroglyphic script, and its location in Rome's Isis temple show, concretely, that the translation of hieroglyphic texts was bound up in larger systems of cultural translation between Egypt and Rome. The connection between animal and the divine on display in Isis temples enriched, and was itself enriched by, the discussions of animals, gods, and the hieroglyphic script one sees in Aegyptiaca. Apuleius's "Isis Book" makes that much clear. The semantic overlap of hieroglyphic and metamorphic "characters" allowed Apuleius to underline the dynamics of form versus essence shared by Lucius, animal-shaped gods, and hieroglyphic inscriptions alike. Romans—and not just Apuleius—were quick to connect animal-shaped signs and their semiotic significance with animal-shaped

---

95. On the rise of cryptographic hieroglyphic spelling in the imperial period, see Darnell (2020, 7) (cf. Stadler 2008, 163–66). This is on clear display in the purely cryptographic Hymns at Esna, discussed by Morenz (2002).

96. Erman (1917, 7–8) for orthography and spelling peculiarities.

97. This is the term Morenz (2008) uses to describe scribes' playful manipulation of hieroglyphs' intersecting phonetic and visual meanings.

gods and their own webs of meaning. I opened with the god Seth and the Seth animal, which both connoted and denoted disorder. If nothing else, it is important to recognize that isolating the Roman reception of these various threads—Isis cult, zoomorphism, and hieroglyphic—robs them of the web of significance on which authors of Aegyptiaca relied. That web of significance is on display throughout Egyptians' presentation of the Egyptian language, whether etymologies of gods' names, glosses of hieroglyphic signs, or translations of Egyptian-language texts.

That current of Aegyptiaca should not be lost in a rush to grade Egyptians' knowledge of the hieroglyphic script. To be sure, the move from Manetho to Chaeremon, like the move from pharaonic, to Ptolemaic, to Roman-Egyptian inscriptions, shows how the hieroglyphic script was increasingly distant from vernacular Egyptian. There is a process of fossilization at work here, and I do not want to pretend that that is not the case. Be that as it may, it is still wrongheaded to claim that a comparison of Manetho and Chaeremon serves only to prove that the former knew hieroglyphic and the latter did not. Both authors sought to foreground the systems of meaning that lay underneath language. As his Hyksos and Bebon glosses reveal, Manetho's etymologizing is also fuzzy and sometimes hard to pin down, just like Chaeremon's. Aegyptiaca is such a rich tradition because it troubles the water of authoritative cultural exposition. It is all too easy to fixate on an elusive rubric of accuracy so doggedly that one loses sight of the larger goals that lead these authors to orient their texts around language exposition.

Those goals were, in a nutshell, to prioritize the symbolic significance of the hieroglyphic script. Plutarch, Apuleius, Manetho, and Chaeremon alike set out to present the Egyptian language as a symbolically rich object of investigation. The mechanics of symbolism—of the move from script and signifier to underlying signified—was an essential component of how authors of Aegyptiaca brought their own presentation of Egyptian traditions into alignment with a philosophical lingua franca of enigma, allegory, and symbol. All three were tools with which to unpack language, in Egyptian, Greek, and Roman traditions alike.

It remains to be seen how authors of Aegyptiaca positioned their own expertise through this philosophical lingua franca. These authors' expertise in symbol and allegory lay in between areas denoted by religion and philosophy. The philosophy-religion nexus has been hovering around the margins of this book, but now needs to move center stage. The different occupations assigned to authors of Aegyptiaca can facilitate a final reevaluation of how to best frame the expertise that authors of Aegyptiaca claimed. Within and without the confines of language, authors of Aegyptiaca advertised their authority in a tradition of symbolic exegesis that hovers between priestly and philosophical traditions. I have been using periphrases like "web of meaning" and "systems of significance," but I cannot fully avoid the disciplinary quicksand of drawing geographic and cultural boundaries around symbol, allegory, and enigma. "Symbolism" as a term has been a battleground for competing visions of how Greek and Roman intellectual traditions fit in with, or

168 WHAT'S EGYPTIAN FOR "PHILOSOPHER"?

stood apart from, other cultures of the Mediterranean world. I have postponed the questions of cultural rivalry and priority that define the different work that different scholars want Plutarch's *On Isis and Osiris* to do. Symbolism has long been a dirty word, one that smacks of Greco-Roman exceptionalism and cultural projection. Its recuperation will help center a process of dialogue in which authors of Aegyptiaca had a central role.

6

Recuperating the Philosopher-Priest

Embracing a Mixed Intellectual Authority

Depending on whom you ask, Egyptian priests are either the font of all philosophical wisdom or complete hucksters. As soon as Greeks began to reconstruct the origins of something called "philosophy," a set biography emerged that connected Greek philosophers with trips to Egypt. Thales, the first Milesian philosopher, traveled to Egypt and borrowed from its priests the cosmogonic primacy of water. Ditto Anaximander. Scanning Herodotus, or Plutarch, or Diogenes Laertius, there is a path of intellectual transmission from Egypt to Greece time and time and time again.[1] It is an origin story that lasted well into the Hellenistic and imperial periods.

But as time went on, a very different narrative around Egyptian priests emerged. To many Romans living in the early-imperial period, Isis priests scammed people out of their money and got paid to help adulterers cheat on their spouses. Juvenal at least thinks so. In his sprawling diatribe against women, the cult of Isis is the regular site of trysts and bribery.[2] Meanwhile, Josephus blames Isis priests for enabling Decius Mundus's sexual assault of the Isis devotee Paulina. The episode segues directly to Tiberius's destruction of Rome's Isis temple to underline the social danger posed by Isiac religion.[3]

---

1. Froidefond (1971, 192–96) traces Egyptian influence on early philosophy. For the thorny issue of early Greek philosophy's origins, see the important, if controversial, work of Frankfort and Groenewegen-Frankfort (1949), West (1971), and Burkert (1995). Thales's intellectual debt to Egypt is outlined by Kirk, Raven, and Schofield (1983, 92–93).

2. Juv. 6.533–41, where this sex and bribery criticism intersects with the "barker Anubis" (see chapter 3).

3. Joseph. *AJ* 18.65–80 and Gasparini (2017), with Malaise (1972b, 389–95) on the historical aftermath.

170 WHAT'S EGYPTIAN FOR "PHILOSOPHER"?

These two narratives of priestly wisdom and moral degeneracy take divergent perspectives on the same issue. Movement around the Mediterranean brought Egyptian, Greek, and Roman traditions into contact. No matter what view one takes about Greece's cultural debt to Egypt, an interconnected Mediterranean requires us to position different knowledge traditions against each other.[4] It is easy to populate ancient texts with contemporary concerns about how Greek and Roman intellectual practices fit into the wider Mediterranean. To some, Greeks and Romans of the imperial period were animated by a desire to reestablish the priority of philosophy over Egyptian or Babylonian or Indian religious traditions.[5] To others, it is important to clarify the cultural hegemony inbuilt to *interpretatio Graeca*, Greeks' projection of their own religious and philosophical apparatus onto others' traditions.[6] To yet others, there is a need to define the patterns of thought—symbol, enigma, allegoresis—that individuate Greco-Roman intellectual history from other wisdom traditions of the ancient Mediterranean world.[7] That need to individuate Greco-Roman philosophy can itself be animated by very different motivations. It might help push back against a false sense that Greek and Roman intellectual history is the only Mediterranean knowledge tradition worth talking about. But it might also work to opposite effect, touting Greeks' and Romans' exclusive control of rationalist inquiry as the preamble of a Greek miracle narrative.[8]

Much of this disciplinary baggage hinges on the ambiguity around the labels philosopher and priest.[9] Mixed philosopher-priests trouble all these issues. They make clear that the Egyptian priest and Greek philosopher were interconnected and co-constituted in the imperial world; that labeling a priest a philosopher is sometimes, to quote David Frankfurter, Egyptians' own "stereotype appropriation" rather than Greeks' cultural projection;[10] and that the broad tradition of the

4. This has been argued most famously, albeit controversially, by Bernal (1987–2006) (with the response of Lefkowitz and Rogers 1996 and the re-response of Bernal 2001). I am deliberately postponing a fuller discussion to the Conclusion.

5. Richter (2011, 183, 205) proposes this argument and emphasizes Plutarch's self-conscious contraposition against the longstanding narrative of the reverse, Greek philosophy's non-Greek origins.

6. Görgemanns (2017, 11–13) reads the opening of the *DIO* in this way, as a projection of philosophical inquiry onto indigenous religious traditions. This becomes a mainstay in later imperial Greek literature. For example, visits to Brahmans and Naked Sages in Philostratus's *Life of Apollonius of Tyana* offer a teleological narrative of Greek philosophy's origins steeped in *interpretatio Graeca*, as Flinterman (1995, 101–6) and Swain (1996, 386–87) make clear.

7. This is more a corollary to than a central premise of Struck (2004), who notes (182, 203) moments of equivalence-drawing between Greek and non-Greek symbolic traditions.

8. Laks (2018, particularly 53–67, on rationality) and Burkert (2008, 60–62) summarize this nineteenth-century narrative.

9. Laks (2018, 35–36) has called attention to this ambiguity.

10. Frankfurter (1998, 225) for the term "stereotype appropriation." He cites Chaeremon as a chief example. Besides philosophical wisdom (223–24), Frankfurter also notes priests' self-positioning as magicians (cf. Dickie 2001, 205).

symbol has meaningful antecedents in both priestly and philosophical expertise in both Egypt and Greece.

To be sure, this requires a broader view of just what work a word like "symbolism" is meant to accomplish. But the core semantics of symbol-qua-"casting together," where the two halves of a token are reunited, justify this broader view.[11] As a result, symbolism can meaningfully span its Greek-philosophical and literary-critical applications, Egyptian traditions of figurative language, and the authors of Aegyptiaca who "symbolically" juxtaposed these two different traditions.[12] The philosopher-priest poses essential questions of how to square two different knowledge traditions that were, in the eyes of Egyptians, Greeks, and Romans alike, interconnected.

Partly, this is to recuperate the label "philosophy" as a frame for Egyptian religious traditions; to insist that Egyptians who position Egyptian culture in the conceptual language of philosophy can still call themselves scribal priests. But it is also to reemphasize the points of connection that Greeks and Romans promoted between imperial philosophy and the cult of Isis. The cultic and religious aspect of philosophy is particularly well exemplified by Pythagoras, a figure whose importance and popularity in the imperial world is hard to understate.[13] As I will go on to discuss, Pythagoras and his very-cultic-leaning followers occupied a paradigmatic position in the Greek philosophical tradition. That position is as well attested in ancient texts as it is tiptoed around by some scholars of ancient philosophy.

I have already hinted at this muddying of priestly and philosophical labels. Chaeremon was called both a Stoic philosopher and an Egyptian scribal priest. As I discussed in chapter 2, Pancrates was a Pythagorean philosopher or a magician or a panegyrist. This chapter takes up and fleshes out that theme. With the philosopher-priest as a frame, it becomes clear that authors of Aegyptiaca were constantly navigating a bifurcated vision of how to label their own authority. They wrote at a time of canon formation. Imperial biographers like Diogenes Laertius and Iamblichus fossilized a narrative of cultural transmission from Egyptian priests to Greek philosophers whose antecedents appear already in Herodotus.[14] This narrative of

---

11. Struck (2004, 78–80). Struck 2004 well notes the development of a broader semantics of symbolism that I will be further underlining in this chapter—particularly the role of symbol as shibboleth and symbolic interpretation as a religio-philosophical mainstay.

12. For symbolism's utility and limitations when applied to Egyptian religion, see Finnestad (1985, 127); for cryptographic hieroglyphic as a form of "symbolic writing," Morenz (2002, 83). Wilkinson (1994) uses a much wider, more loosely defined, sense of "symbolism." See too Derchain (1976), defending "symbolism" as a designation of Egyptian-language play, and Baines (1976), for architectural symbolism. For Egyptian figurative language, see Griffiths (1967, 1969) and Pries (2016, 2017).

13. Kahn (2001) gives an historical overview of Pythagoras. Cornelli et al. (2013) and Huffman (2014) provide a good coverage of core Pythagorean themes and authors. On the distance between Pythagoreans and Pythagoras, see Zhmud (2012, 169–205).

14. I use "fossilization" and "harden" to make clear that, while these narratives were well-developed much earlier—as Herodotus's (2.123) anecdote on Empedocles's and Pythagoras's debts to Egypt make

cultural influence, as it came to be told via post hoc biographies, provides essential background for the decisions that authors of Aegyptiaca made about navigating these different labels. But this also runs in the other direction. Authors of Aegyptiaca synthesized philosophical and priestly roles in ways that helped the imperial narrative of philosophy's priestly origins harden, particularly as it pertained to the world-traveling philosopher Pythagoras.

Authors of Aegyptiaca and their fluid use of Greek and Egyptian traditions of indirect signification puts paid to any narrative of Greeks' and Romans' exclusive ownership of symbolism and enigma. Manetho and later authors of Aegyptiaca played a major role in the story of philosophy's origins as it came to be told in the Hellenistic and imperial periods. Aegyptiaca sits between imperial Greeks like Plutarch and Diogenes and the no-longer-extant early philosophers who became the archetypes of Greek philosophy's debt to Egypt.[15] In what follows, I underline the equivalence-drawing between philosophical and priestly wisdom one sees across imperial Greek literature, Aegyptiaca, and Egyptian-language literature.

PYTHAGORAS AND THE ORIGINS OF PHILOSOPHY

Plutarch's Philosophers and Priests: Replacing Priority with Parallelism

As both a Platonist and priest of Apollo, Plutarch sought to draw parallels between philosophical and religious inquiry.[16] This runs to the core of the *On Isis and Osiris* (*DIO*), a text that seeks to align the Osiris myth with Platonic philosophy. The reasons why Plutarch does so have been contentious.[17] The *DIO* has been a Rorschach test in which different visions of multicultural intellectual history of the Mediterranean world take shape. I have frequently alluded to these different visions, but have deferred offering my own until now, when I can use it as a springboard to a broader discussion about culturally mixed intellectual authority.

One popular reading of the *DIO*, promoted by Daniel Richter, emphasizes Plutarch's arguments for Greek philosophy's temporal priority and ecumenical ubiquity.[18] Philosophy was prior to, and suffused into, non-Greek wisdom traditions. In another reading, the philosopher-priest provides a way for Plutarch

---

clear—they took on a more central role in the Hellenistic and imperial periods, when a biographical canonization (in Pythagoras's case, those offered by Diogenes Laertius, Porphyry, and Iamblichus) of philosophers' intellectual development intensified.

15. I use "early philosophers" in place of "presocratic," a term whose modern origins are laid out by Laks (2018, 1–18).

16. For Plutarch's priesthood, see Casanova (2012). For Plutarch's Platonism, see Dillon (1997, 184–230). For his pursuit of religio-philosophical truth, Brenk (1987, 294–303).

17. Brenk (2017, 59–60) reviews different scholars' arguments around Plutarch's interest in Egyptian religion.

18. Richter (2001) focuses exclusively on the *DIO* and its argument for Greek philosophy's priority. This is incorporated into Richter (2011, 207–29), which continues this argument for Greece's philosophical priority (and thus superiority) in the *DIO*.

RECUPERATING THE PHILOSOPHER-PRIEST   173

to layer onto the Osiris myth a thick impasto of Platonic metaphysics. Egyptologists have often tried to scrape away the layers of Middle Platonism to recover an Osiris/Isis narrative that is only available in snatches in Egyptian-language evidence.[19] To scholars like Ellen Finkelpearl and Joseph DeFilippo, Plutarch's philosopher-priest is yet another example of the contiguity between Isis religion and Platonic philosophy on display in the final book of Apuleius's *Metamorphoses*.[20] In a similar vein, C. Urs Wohlthat has emphasized that Plutarch's attempts to integrate cult worship of Isis with Middle Platonic philosophy is only legible against the background of the Second Sophistic and its system of values.[21]

It is not my place to wrestle a multifaceted text into one exclusive shape. But I still take it as significant that Plutarch sets up the *DIO* with an introduction that binds together divine and philosophical inquiry into one indissociable form. It is the opening salvo on which the rest of the *DIO* depends. In other words, I would like to prioritize a more intuitive reading of the *DIO*, one that takes the programmatic opening as actually programmatic. To reemphasize this equivalence-drawing impulse is a first step in the larger argument of this chapter: that what matters is that Greek, Egyptian, and Greco-Egyptian authors sought above all to underline the parallelism of Egyptian and Greek, priestly and philosophical, knowledge traditions.

Before diving into the Osiris myth, Plutarch first articulates a vision of the contemplative life that is shot through with language of religious initiation. Cult initiation, as a step toward divine *theoria*, helps Plutarch connect the *DIO*'s presentation of the Osiris myth with his overarching philosophical worldview, in which the pursuit of the divine looms large.[22] The coordination of religious and philosophical contemplation animates the *DIO* from its first sentence: "Men of good sense must seek all good things from the gods, and especially we pray to acquire from them knowledge of them—insofar as it is humanly possible."[23] To Plutarch, philosophical inquiry is necessarily a consideration of sacred subjects. The proof of the overlap of sacred and philosophical inquiry, and the key pivot to the Isis/

19. For example, see Parmentier (1913) and Hani (1979). This archaeological approach is certainly worthwhile, even as I am suggesting it promotes a false dichotomy.

20. DeFilippo (1990, 483–89), Finkelpearl (2012), and Van der Stockt (2012, 175–79) underline the Platonic themes of *Met.* Book 11 through reference to the *DIO*.

21. Wohlthat (2021, 111–49), who notes especially that the wide-ranging social backgrounds of Isiac initiates help explain Plutarch's pains to individuate circumspect striving for divine truth—that practiced by initiates with elite habitus—from the mechanistic and unconsidered worship (so-called habitude) of other adherents.

22. Plutarch's conceptualization of the search for the divine is presented by Alt (1993. 185–204) and Roskam (2017). For this pursuit as a mixture of philosophical and religious contemplation, see Opsomer (1998, 171–86).

23. *DIO* 1, 351d: Πάντα μέν, ὦ Κλέα, δεῖ τἀγαθὰ τοὺς νοῦν ἔχοντας αἰτεῖσθαι παρὰ τῶν θεῶν, μάλιστα δὲ τῆς περὶ αὐτῶν ἐπιστήμης ὅσον ἐφικτόν ἐστιν ἀνθρώποις μετιόντες εὐχόμεθα τυγχάνειν παρ᾽ αὐτῶν ἐκείνων.

174   WHAT'S EGYPTIAN FOR "PHILOSOPHER"?

Osiris myth, is Plutarch's description of a philosophical Isis. Plutarch exploits his addressee Clea's worship of Isis to link together cult and philosophy into one coherent form: "Above all else, [the consideration of sacred matters] is pleasing to this goddess whom you worship, *a goddess singularly wise and a philosopher*. As her name Isis seems to suggest, knowledge and understanding belong to her above all. For Isis is a Greek word."[24] The Greek etymology—which Daniel Richter and Herwig Görgemanns read as a bid for Greece's priority and universality—is certainly significant; imperial Greek authors like Philostratus try to position Greek wisdom as the *lingua franca* of all religious traditions.[25] But I think it is also important not to lose the forest for the trees. Plutarch sets up the text and addresses it to an Isis devotee because he wants to paint philosophical inquiry in the colors of mystery cult, and to paint Isis cult in the colors of philosophical inquiry.

Readings that emphasize cultural priority miss the way that Plutarch leverages a term for "initiation," *epopteia*, to solidify this mixture of cult and philosophy. *Epopteia* is a term rooted in the semantics of religious initiation that Plutarch repurposes to describe privileged philosophical wisdom.[26] In essence, it denotes a "vision" or "contemplation" reserved for a select few. First used to describe a particularly high rank in the Eleusinian Mysteries, it became a wider term for religious initiation in the imperial world. Plutarch still uses it in this vein to describe the tyrant Demetrius's desire to be initiated into the inner ranks of the Eleusinian Mysteries. Plutarch's philosophical repackaging is noteworthy, both as a heuristic for the *DIO* and as a sign of the cultic turn philosophy takes in the imperial period. Plutarch is the first extant author to use *epopteia* to denote philosophical initiation into a privileged vision of the world as it really is.[27] He does so retrospectively, to characterize Aristotle's and Plato's ability to enter into the rarefied domain of unmediated philosophical vision. Plutarch reads that philosophical initiation into

---

24. *DIO* 2, 351e–f: οὐχ ἥκιστα δὲ τῇ θεῷ ταύτῃ κεχαρισμένον, ἣν σὺ θεραπεύεις ἐξαιρέτως σοφὴν καὶ φιλόσοφον οὖσαν, ὡς τοὔνομά γε φράζειν ἔοικε παντὸς μᾶλλον αὐτῇ τὸ εἰδέναι καὶ τὴν ἐπιστήμην προσήκουσαν. Ἑλληνικὸν γὰρ ἡ Ἶσίς ἐστι.

25. Flinterman (1995, 101–6) and Swain (1996, 386–87) note Philostratus's world-wide vision of Greek culture. See Richter (2011, 207–29) and Görgemanns (2017, 11–12) (cf. Brenk 1999) for the etymology's role in rivalrous and universalizing readings of the *DIO*.

26. The term is a felicitous analog to the more widely used *theoria*, which also denotes philosophical contemplation, but has a much longer pedigree, going back to Aristotle (as summarized by Adkins 1978). Plutarch uses *epopteia* in the sense of initiation (a technical term, per Mylonas 1961, 274–78) at *Dem.* 26, 900.3. Clement (*Strom.* 1.28.176.2, 4.1.3.2) picks up on this mixed initiatory and philosophical usage.

27. Though *epopteia* does not occur before Plutarch, Plato (unlike Aristotle) does use the related adjective ἐποπτικός (*Symp.* 210a) and verb ἐποπτεύω (*Phdr.* 250c, cf. *Leg.* 951d for a different usage) to liken philosophical contemplation to religious initiation. Note too the related agentive variant *epoptês*, "overseer/watcher/witness," a term used more widely and by earlier authors, through which Plutarch (Plut. *Alc.* 22, 202.3) denotes an Eleusinian initiate.

the care that Isis-devotees take with Osiris's cloak, whose inaccessibility and stylistic simplicity Plutarch associates with the world of the Forms:

> For this reason they put on the robe of Osiris only once and then take it off, preserving it unseen and untouched, whereas they use the Isiac robes many times. For the things that are perceptible and near at hand are in use and afford many revelations and glimpses of themselves as they are variously interchanged at various times. But the understanding of what is spiritually intelligible and pure and holy, having shone through the soul like lightning, affords only one chance to touch and to behold it. *For this reason both Plato and Aristotle call this branch of philosophy the 'epoptic part,' since those who have passed beyond these conjectural, confused, and widely varied matters spring up by force of reason to that primal, simple, and immaterial element;* and having directly grasped the pure truth attached to it, they believe that they hold the ultimate end of philosophy in the manner of a mystic revelation.[28]

This interconnection of Egyptian priestly knowledge and philosophical inquiry into the world's true form is fundamental to Plutarch's philosophical program, both within and without the *DIO*.[29] There are certainly dynamics of cultural priority that one can read into the text; but one should not minimize the value that Plutarch attaches to the mixed religio-philosophical path to wisdom connoted by *epopteia*.

Pythagoras on Vacation

A comparison of Osiris's cloak and Plato's initiation helps Plutarch align Platonic philosophy and Egyptian religion. That impulse is also on display in imperial biographies that suggested that Plato had traveled to Egypt.[30] Apuleius's lesser-read biography of Plato, *On Plato and His Doctrine*, repeats just that datum: "And, because Plato felt that the Pythagorean way of thinking was aided by other schools, . . . he went all the way to Egypt to pursue astrology, and also in order to learn the rites of the soothsayers from that same source."[31] Plato's visit to Egypt is itself dependent, at least according to Apuleius, on Plato's mentor Pythagoras. Already

---

28. *DIO* 77–8, 382d–e: διὸ καὶ Πλάτων καὶ Ἀριστοτέλης ἐποπτικὸν τοῦτο τὸ μέρος τῆς φιλοσοφίας καλοῦσιν, ὡς οἱ τὰ δοξαστὰ καὶ μεικτὰ καὶ παντοδαπὰ ταῦτα παραμειψάμενοι τῷ λόγῳ πρὸς τὸ πρῶτον ἐκεῖνο καὶ ἁπλοῦν καὶ ἄϋλον ἐξάλλονται. . . . Translation adapted from Griffiths (1970).

29. The same term reappears in the *On the Failure of Oracles* (22, 422c), where a philosophical "initiation" (τῆς ἐποπτείας) into seeing the world "as it is" is explicitly compared to cultic initiation—"as if in a mystic initiation" (καθάπερ ἐν τελετῇ καὶ μυήσει). For this robe metaphor and its role in Plutarch's conceptualization of philosophical "searching," see Roskam (2017, 211–14).

30. I take this visit as a datum of heuristic value for imperial Platonists, while leaving aside its historicity.

31. *De Plat.* 1.3: et, quod Pythagoreorum ingenium adiutum disciplinis aliis sentiebat, . . . astrologiam adusque Aegyptum ivit petitum, ut inde prophetarum etiam ritus addisceret. Text from Beaujeu (1973).

176 WHAT'S EGYPTIAN FOR "PHILOSOPHER"?

in Cicero, Plato's purported trip to Egypt was motivated by Pythagoras's.[32] These authors—Cicero, Apuleius, and Plutarch—wrote at a time when authors saw a good deal of overlap between Middle Platonism and Neo-Pythagoreanism.[33] They inherited a narrative of Plato's debt to Pythagoras that was already taking hold in the fourth century BCE.[34] As a result, an interest in Egyptian wisdom cements the links between Platonism and Pythagoreanism that imperial Platonists like Plutarch and Apuleius were keen to strengthen.

There were many philosophers who reputedly visited Egypt, but few loomed larger than Pythagoras. Plutarch invokes these philosophers' visits as proof of the widely accepted value of Egyptian religious wisdom:

> Egyptians' reverence for wisdom in divine matters was so great. Proof to this are also the wisest of the Greeks, Solon, Thales, Plato, Eudoxus, and Pythagoras, and, according to some, Lycurgus too, all of whom came to Egypt and consulted with priests . . . Pythagoras especially, it appears, marveling at and a marvel to Egyptian priests. . . .[35]

The who's-who list of philosophers serves to underline the thoroughgoing impact of Egyptian religious wisdom on Greek political, natural, and ethical philosophy. Plutarch pivots from this general list, through the specific priests with whom each philosopher studies (omitted above), to the particular importance ("especially this person") of Pythagoras in this model of philosophical debt to Egypt.[36]

Pythagoras's place of honor at the end of Plutarch's list of philosophical visitors to Egypt speaks to his vaunted role as the semi-mythologized inventor of philosophy.[37] The issue is not just Pythagoras's influence on Plato and the way it was reflected in successive visits to Egypt. It is also a matter of Pythagoras's influence on philosophy, plain and simple. The canonization of philosophy's debt to Egypt

---

32. Cic. *De Rep.* 1.16 (cf. Beaujeu 1973, 251) says that Plato follows in Pythagoras's footsteps by visiting Egypt.

33. The Neopythagorean Numenius (F 24, l. 57, ed. de Places) uses "Pythagorize" (Πυθαγορίζω) to evoke Plato's debt to Pythagoreanism. For an overview of Pythagoras's impact on Middle Platonism in particular, see Dillon (1988, 111–13; 1997, 341–83).

34. Plato's intellectual debt to Pythagoras was apparently widespread; Pythagorean influence was detectable in the forms, the cosmos, and the mathematization of dialectic. For an overview, see Palmer (2014), and for "mathematical" Pythagoreanism see Horky (2013). This influence was prosopographically reconstructed through Plato's connections to the Pythagoreans Archytas (Schofield 2014) and Philolaus (Graham 2014, *pace* Brisson 2007). Plato's successors (especially Speusippus and Xenocrates, but see Zhmud 2013, 331–42 for Aristotle) canonized Plato's Pythagoreanism. This became further entrenched in Eudorus of Alexandria (on which Dillon 2019, 2, 53; Chiaradonna 2009, 89–93; Moreschini 2015, 22) and the anonymous Pythagorean texts of the Hellenistic period (collected by Thesleff 1961, 1965).

35. Plut. *DIO* 9–10, 354d–e: ἡ μὲν οὖν εὐλάβεια τῆς περὶ τὰ θεῖα σοφίας Αἰγυπτίων τοσαύτη ἦν. μαρτυροῦσι δὲ καὶ τῶν Ἑλλήνων οἱ σοφώτατοι, Σόλων Θαλῆς Πλάτων Εὔδοξος Πυθαγόρας, ὡς δ᾽ ἔνιοί φασι, καὶ Λυκοῦργος, εἰς Αἴγυπτον ἀφικόμενοι καὶ συγγενόμενοι τοῖς ἱερεῦσιν. I pick up the quote below.

36. Plut. *DIO* 10, 354f: μάλιστα δ᾽ οὗτος.

37. For Pythagoras's foundational role see Laks (2018, 10–11, 43–44).

passes through Pythagoras. It is for that reason that, by the fourth century BCE, he comes to be the very inventor of the category philosophy. This claim to fame is already on display in the rhetorician Isocrates. In his playful rhetorical exercise on the cruel Egyptian king Busiris, Isocrates stitches together Pythagoras's visit to Egypt and invention of philosophy. Among the general admirers of Egyptian piety, Pythagoras is notable: "Pythagoras came to Egypt and became a student of the Egyptians, and besides he was the first person to bring philosophy to Greece. . . ."[38] Isocrates imagines philosophy as an object of movement. Through parataxis, Isocrates implies that Pythagoras's trip to Egypt and introduction of philosophy to Greece are logically connected.[39] The soundbite—Pythagoras visited Egypt and introduced philosophy to Greece—was a durative one. It was also productively malleable.[40] Isocrates molds it to his purposes, using Pythagoras's adoption of Egyptian vows of silence to make a droll joke that stacks Isocrates's own eloquence unfavorably with Pythagoreans who keep their mouths shut.[41] But even in a ludic rhetorical exercise, Pythagoras's biographical data are well established.

Even more importantly than Isocrates, Diogenes Laertius also calls Pythagoras the first person to invent philosophy. That is significant. Diogenes Laertius's *Lives of the Eminent Philosophers* is *the* canon of a Greek philosophical tradition. It is as essential as it is badmouthed by scholars for its all-too-credulous acceptance of doxography.[42] Even if it is to many a necessary evil for the history of philosophy, its importance still stands. Both ideologically and practically, it fossilized the narrative of Greek philosophy's birth and remains the key citing authority for now-lost early Greek philosophers.

Diogenes's prologue is so rich because it approaches the same narrative of philosophical debt to non-Greek traditions from the opposite direction. The opening of the text uses a broadly constructed, anonymized and pluralized straw man to reject arguments for the non-Greek origins of philosophy: "Some say that the work of philosophy began with barbarians."[43] Diogenes then sets out to reject this

---

38. Isoc. *Bus.* 11.28: . . . ὧν καὶ Πυθαγόρας ὁ Σάμιός ἐστιν· ὃς ἀφικόμενος εἰς Αἴγυπτον καὶ μαθητὴς ἐκείνων γενόμενος τήν τ᾽ ἄλλην φιλοσοφίαν πρῶτος εἰς τοὺς Ἕλληνας ἐκόμισεν. . . . Text from Brémond and Mathieu (1963). On Pythagoras and the *Busiris*, see Livingstone (2001, 155–62).

39. This plays into the much larger (and still debated) question of Greek philosophy's non-Greek precursors. For overview of early Greek accounts of philosophy's origins, see most recently Cantor (2022, 730–31 on Pythagoras and Egypt), and also West (1971).

40. Horky (2013, 90–94) emphasizes this section's particular interest in political philosophy as an object of translation from Egypt to Pythagoras's Southern-Italian political communities.

41. Apuleius's *Florida* (15.26) makes a similar joke. Pythagoreans' forced silence is laid out in Diog. Laert. 8.10 and Iambl. *VPyth.* 17.72.

42. Graham (2010, 9) is representative. He calls Diogenes Laertius "more a cut-and-paste hack than a scholar," but then admits that "he preserves priceless information." For ad hoc criticisms of Diogenes's treatment of a given philosopher see, among others, Moraux (1955) and Janda (1969).

43. Diog. Laert. 1.1: Τὸ τῆς φιλοσοφίας ἔργον ἔνιοί φασιν ἀπὸ βαρβάρων ἄρξαι. Text from Dorandi (2013). For this tradition of philosophy's non-Greek origins, see the synopsis provided by Burkert (2008, 60–62).

178   WHAT'S EGYPTIAN FOR "PHILOSOPHER"?

argument and elevate Greek philosophy as an autochthonous tradition. The only problem is that, as the prologue continues to describe non-Greek religious traditions, Diogenes makes these anonymous others' case a bit too forcefully. By the time the prologue's catalogue of foreign religious traditions reaches its last stop, Egypt, it is all too easy for readers to lose track of its stated goal: to prove that humankind and philosophy alike arose with Greeks. This is all the more apparent when Diogenes segues immediately from Egyptians' invention of geometry, astronomy, and arithmetic to Pythagoras, who is given pride of place in the birth of philosophy: "Pythagoras was the first person to come up with the name 'philosophy' and to call himself a philosopher."[44]

In other words, Diogenes might try to disprove the path of transmission from Egyptian religion to Greek philosophy, but the actual narrative flow of the prologue goes a long way in making the opposite case. His direct transition from Egyptian wisdom to Pythagoras's invention of the term philosophy is deeply ambivalent. On the surface, it makes a case for Greeks' invention of the term philosophy. But the specific emphasis on arithmetic, geometry, and astronomy as Egyptian wisdom traditions echoes the standard catalogue of knowledge traditions that Pythagoras learned in Egypt.[45] When Diogenes credits Egypt with the creation of geometry, he signals the common datum repeated by Cicero and Apuleius, among others: that Pythagorean number theory developed out of Egyptian geometry.[46] Diogenes's own biography of Pythagoras in the *Lives* repeats these same claims. His opening of Pythagoras's biography emphasizes Egypt's constitutive role in Pythagoreanism, so much so that Pythagoras even learned hieroglyphic! Later in the biography, Diogenes doubles back to geometry and makes explicit what was only implicit in the prologue—that Pythagoras learned geometry in Egypt.[47] It is as if the biography finally splices the two threads that had already lined up in the prologue: the mythological Egyptian king Moeris invented geometry; Pythagoras brought it to Greece and then invented the idea of a philosopher.

Riddle Me This: Translating Symbolism

There are good reasons why Pythagoras was the liminal figure bridging Egyptian religious wisdom and Greek philosophy. Pythagoreanism was hard for many Greeks and Romans to get their heads around, which is precisely why it was aetiologized through Egypt. This is particularly true for the so-called "acousmatic" branch of Pythagoreanism, whose emphasis on oral teachings and secret knowledge makes

---

44. Diog. Laert. 1.12: φιλοσοφίαν δὲ πρῶτος ὠνόμασε Πυθαγόρας καὶ ἑαυτὸν φιλόσοφον.

45. This is developed most fully in Iamblichus's biography (*VPyth.* 158), and arises already in Hecataeus of Abdera (*BNJ* 264 F 25 = Diod. Sic. 1.69.4), on which see Riedweg (2005, 26).

46. Cic. *Fin.* 5.87, Apul. *Fl.* 15.15. On this Pythagorean lineage, see Lévi (2014, 300).

47. Diog. Laert. 8.11 (see 8.3 for the hieroglyphic anecdote) casts Pythagoras as the perfector of geometry, and the Egyptian Moeris as its inventor. For Diogenes's particular portrait of Pythagoras—which emphasizes the Pythagorean way of life and the cultic—see Laks (2014).

its practitioners outré figures in the history of philosophy. Scholars of ancient philosophy often strive to separate out the cult practices of "acousmatic" Pythagoreans—where the contiguity with Egypt is particularly prevalent—to recuperate the historical, Capital-P philosopher Pythagoras lionized by the "mathematic" tradition.[48] But for present purposes, I would like to broach a typical division between Pythagoras and Pythagoreans from the opposite direction. Where the division normally allows ancient and modern philosophers alike to recuperate the original Pythagoras from the wacky cult practices associated with later Pythagoreans, I would like to put imperial Pythagoreanism, with all its cultic and mystic baggage, center stage without the burden of recovering an original, pure Pythagoras that can justify his role as first founder of philosophy.[49]

Plutarch and other imperial Platonists saw in Pythagoras two fundamental dynamics of philosophical inquiry. First, knowledge of Pythagoras's oral teachings functioned as a password that cordoned off the initiated and in-the-know from the uninformed. Symbols, of which Pythagoras's oral teachings were a prime example, were important as a tool for community formation. The coherence of the Pythagorean community depended on the privileged knowledge to which they—and they alone—had access. Second, and interrelated, was a belief that the path from the superficial world of perception to a profound and divine truth was necessarily wending. Only an adept knowledge of symbol and enigma could help a person traverse this gap between superficial and profound. Pythagoras's famous sayings bound together symbol as a form of gatekeeping and as an index of philosophical authority. Pythagoras's role as first philosopher was built, in large part, on his successful translation of these two facets of symbolism from Egypt to Greece.

As the symbol par excellence, hieroglyphic signs had a major role in the larger narrative of the Egyptian origins of Greek philosophy.[50] Plutarch's above-quoted list of philosophers who visited Egypt gives way to a path of cultural translation that begins with hieroglyphs and ends with Pythagoras's enigmatic sayings:

> It seems Pythagoras especially, marveling at and a marvel to Egyptian priests, copied their symbolism and mysterious rites, mingling his doctrines in with enigmas. Most of the Pythagorean sayings do not at all fall short of the so-called hieroglyphic letters, such

---

48. Barnes (1982, 78–79) (cf. the more neutrally wisdom-oriented approach of Burkert 1972, 2008) broaches the same dynamic from the opposite direction, claiming that the "Newtonian Pythagoras" masks a real Pythagoras "more reminiscent of Joseph Smith." He underlines the centrality of the acousmatic branch and deduces from that fact Pythagoras's relative unimportance to Greek philosophy.

49. In this regard, Dickie (2001, 200–12) notes well a contiguity I too am trying to underline: imperial Pythagoreans and their interest in occult wisdom were closely connected to the religio-magical expertise of authors of Aegyptiaca, most notably Pancrates.

50. Chaeremon's philosophical exposition of the hieroglyphic script had already pointed in this direction. The same goes for the description of hieroglyphs in Apuleius's *Metamorphoses*, as I discussed in chapter 5.

180   WHAT'S EGYPTIAN FOR "PHILOSOPHER"?

as: 'do not eat upon a stool,' 'do not sit upon a bag of grain,' 'do not trim a palm tree's shoots,' 'Do not stir a fire with a dagger within the house.'[51]

The reciprocity embedded in the phrase "marveling at and a marvel to" (θαυμασθεὶς καὶ θαυμάσας) is easy to miss, but encapsulates this chapter's overarching argument. The active and passive participles promise a mutual intelligibility and respect that enriches the story of cultural transmission from Egyptian priests to Greek philosophers. The passage also shows how Plutarch's occasional penchant for cultural rivalry can coexist with a general narrative of parallel wisdoms. Plutarch is proud to note that the Pythagorean "sayings"—the ancient corpus collected under the title *Acousmata* or *Symbola*—do not "fall short" of the hieroglyphic script.[52] The distance traveled from superficial meaning to underlying significance is as great in the *Acousmata* as in hieroglyphic. There is a hometown pride that can trumpet Greek patterns of enigma even as the *DIO* is set up to mark the parallel paths that Isis cult and imperial philosophy follow. These rivalrous moments do not dislodge the centrality of parallelism.

To Plutarch, symbolism itself is an object of cultural translation from Egypt to Greece. Pythagoras's intellectual admiration for Egypt leads him to imitate Egyptians priests' "symbolic logic" and "mysteriousness."[53] The dual roles of the symbol—as path to the profound and as a form of gatekeeping—help show that a mixed cult/philosophy applies not only to its destination in Greece, but also its origins in Egypt. Symbolism's combination of community formation and exclusionary initiation was already on display in Plato's and Aristotle's mystery-cult-adjacent form of philosophical contemplation. But Plutarch's—and Apuleius's—insistence on the symbolic function of hieroglyphic makes clear that the symbol's translation from Egypt to Greece relies on the mixture of cult and philosophy in both Pythagoreanism and Isis cult.[54]

This tale of Pythagoras's general debt to Egyptian symbolism soon gives way to a comparison of hieroglyphic signs and Pythagorean *Acousmata*. Plutarch's pivot to language is telling. It introduces hieroglyphic as an object of translation through which a core technique of encoding wisdom enters the Greek world via Pythagoreanism. This offers a different perspective on the same phenomenon at play in Chaeremon's *Hieroglyphica*, which also set out to position hieroglyphic as a set of philosophically rich signs whose exegesis guaranteed Chaeremon his religio-philosophical authority. The Pythagorean *Acousmata* operated in the same way.

---

51. Plut. *DIO* 10, 354e–f: μάλιστα δ᾽ οὗτος, ὡς ἔοικε, θαυμασθεὶς καὶ θαυμάσας τοὺς ἄνδρας ἀπεμιμήσατο τὸ συμβολικὸν αὐτῶν καὶ μυστηριῶδες, ἀναμίξας αἰνίγμασι τὰ δόγματα. τῶν γὰρ καλουμένων ἱερογλυφικῶν γραμμάτων οὐθὲν ἀπολείπει τὰ πολλὰ τῶν Πυθαγορικῶν παραγγελμάτων. . . .

52. Plut. *DIO* 10, 354f: ἀπολείπει. For an overview of the *Acousmata* see Thom (2013).

53. Plut. *DIO* 10, 354f: τὸ συμβολικὸν and μυστηριῶδες, respectively.

54. At *Met.* 11.22.7–8.

As Plutarch puts it, the *Acousmata* are a way "to encode doctrines in enigmas."[55] Before the *Acousmata* are even introduced, their general function and contiguity with hieroglyphic are clear. Hieroglyphs and the *Acousmata* are both an object of expertise whose general inscrutability defines priests' and Pythagoreans' community and substantiates their authority.

Pythagoras's *Acousmata* were a tool of community formation that were as important as they were divisive. The *Acousmata* were short quotations that ranged from precepts and prohibitions ("One should not use the public baths") to cosmological and numerological tenets ("what is wisest?—Number"). The *Acousmata* were a foundation of the Pythagorean tradition. They were collected, published, and commented on by Aristotle, Alexander Polyhistor, Iamblichus, and many others. While the original function of the *Acousmata* has been debated, these short sayings cemented a later association between Pythagoreanism and symbolism.[56] The hiddenness inbuilt into the *Acousmata* both added an air of exclusivity to Pythagorean initiation and elevated the metaphysical truths that such sayings contained. What is to others laughable incomprehensibility ("Do not poke a fire with a sword inside the house") is to Plutarch proof of their efficacy as enigmas. Plutarch's enthusiasm for Pythagoreanism's deliberately arcane sayings—"don't sit on a stool"—is a double-edged sword. Plutarch sees the latent profundity of sayings that are to others patently absurd.[57] That double-edged sword is in many ways constitutive of the divisions that ran through the Pythagorean tradition, where the "acousmatic" and "mathematic" branches took divergent approaches to this corpus of *Acousmata*. The same goes for modernity, where debates about the function of the *Acousmata* reflect a much larger question—whether Pythagoreanism belongs within or without the normative definition of philosophy.[58] For now, it is worth following Plutarch's lead. He presents the *Acousmata*'s cultic and symbolic associations as definitive of, rather than a later accretion onto, Pythagoras's original philosophical mission.

---

55. *DIO* 10, 354f: ἀναμείξας αἰνίγμασι τὰ δόγματα. As Struck (2004, 96–107) makes clear, the *Acousmata* (as riddling speech) are similar in kind to the enigma, which also tethers a password function to a technique of interpretation honed through philosophical inquiry.

56. The origins of the *Acousmata* remain the object of debate. Burkert (1972, 166–92) traces an evolution from literal to symbolic interpretation; Zhmud (1997, 169–205) positions the cosmological and numerological question-and-answer type as the kernel of the collection; Thom (2013) offers a middle position.

57. This mixed reaction applies particularly to the "Sayings" that pertained to diet, which were a regular object of derisive humor, in Juv. 15.171–4 (McKim 1986, 69–70) and the Greek comic fragments (Battezzato 2008).

58. This partially maps onto the division between those who endorse and those who reject the shamanistic Pythagoras presented by Burkert (1972, 121–65). Barnes (1982, 79) sees the proscriptive and cultic quality of the "Sayings" as proof of the real Pythagoreanism's religious rather than philosophical character.

182   WHAT'S EGYPTIAN FOR "PHILOSOPHER"?

Plutarch is similarly enthusiastic about Pythagorean number theory, which he compares favorably to Egyptian representations of the divine: "For my part I believe that people calling the monad Apollo, the dyad Artemis, the hebdomad Athena, and the first cube Poseidon is similar to the dedications, sacrifices, and inscriptions of [Egyptians'] sacred rites."[59] Pythagorean numerology and Egyptian religious practices are mirror images. Statues, inscriptions, and numerology are similar strategies of appropriately representing the divine. The ambiguity of antecedents in the above quote (which people? whose sacred rites?) partially elides the distinction between Egyptians and Pythagoreans to further underline their parallelism. This reemphasizes the inextricability of cross-cultural conversations around language and image. How to denote the divine in language and how to represent the divine iconographically are interconnected. Once again, this runs to the heart of Plutarch's enthusiasm for esoteric symbolisms that divide the religio-philosophically initiated from the broader public.[60] To see in the number "two" the goddess Artemis is kindred to seeing a falcon—whether as hieroglyphic sign or as sacred animal—and imagining Horus.

To Plutarch, it is a matter of common sense to align Egyptian priests' and Greek philosophers' entrance into privileged knowledge. But in our collective quest to recover an original Pythagoras, Plutarch's common sense is no longer common. During the wrangling over the historicity of early philosophers' visits with Egyptian priests, the archetypal (versus historical) import of these visits has exited the conversation. But by the imperial period, Pythagoras was the image of a mixed religious and philosophical expertise. To recenter the place of a Pythagorean version of imperial philosophy—with all its messy cultic and enigmatic associations—is to help naturalize the path of cultural translation through which the philosopher-priest gained social prestige both in Egypt and in Rome. It is to create a web of divine symbolism implicating numbers, shapes, riddles, language, and animals. That symbolism, in the interconnected world of the imperial period, constructed an overarching suite of indirect signification that bridged Egypt, Greece, and Rome. The philosophers-visits *topos* is at its most productive when viewed as an etiology for precisely this kind of symbolically rich, mixed religio-philosophical contemplation endorsed by Plutarch and associated with Pythagoras.

AEGYPTIACA AND THE PHILOSOPHER-PRIEST

Hieroglyphic signs and the *Acousmata* are kindred objects of symbolic interpretation, with the former discussed in Aegyptiaca, the latter by Pythagoreans. That

---

59. *DIO* 10, 354f: δοκῶ δ᾽ ἔγωγε καὶ τὸ τὴν μονάδα τοὺς ἄνδρας ὀνομάζειν Ἀπόλλωνα καὶ τὴν δυάδα Ἄρτεμιν, Ἀθηνᾶν δὲ τὴν ἑβδομάδα, Ποσειδῶνα δὲ τὸν πρῶτον κύβον ἐοικέναι τοῖς ἐπὶ τῶν ἱερῶν ἱδρυμένοις καὶ δρωμένοις νὴ Δία καὶ γραφομένοις.

60. This is a facet of the *Acousmata* well discussed by Struck (2004, 96–107), who notes the role of the "Sayings" in the development of an "ideology of exclusiveness" essential to the gestation of symbol and enigma alike.

alignment of Aegyptiaca and Pythagoreanism is the structure around which the passages of Plutarch (*DIO* 9–10, 354c–e) and Diogenes (1.10–12) discussed above take shape. The two authors approach Greek philosophy's antecedents from different angles. But they both take time to underline Pythagoras' essential contributions to the philosophical tradition. Even as both doff their caps at the Milesian school and Thales's purported debt to Egyptian wisdom, Pythagoras becomes a point of origin for philosophy precisely because of his reputation as a traveler and the points of alignment between Pythagorean and Egyptian arcana.[61]

Manetho and Pythagoras as Binary Stars

Both Plutarch and Diogenes only pivot to Pythagoras after they have introduced a version of Egyptian wisdom indebted explicitly to Aegyptiaca. Concretely, both authors cite Manetho before transitioning to Pythagoras. That is a shared join between Aegyptiaca and Pythagoras of real significance. In both Diogenes and Plutarch, Manetho exemplifies a symbolic explanation of Egyptian religion that paves the way for Pythagoras's own importance as a philosopher. Immediately before describing Egyptian geometry and naming Pythagoras as philosophy's founder, Diogenes presents Manetho as a representative authority on, to use his term, "the philosophy of the Egyptians:"

> The philosophy of the Egyptians concerning the gods and justice is as follows: they state that matter was the first principle, then the four elements were separated out from it, and thus all living things were made; that the sun and moon are gods, called Osiris and Isis respectively. *They enigmatically represent these through the scarab and snake and hawk and others, as Manetho says in the epitome of* On Natural Things *and Hecataeus in his first book* On the Philosophy of the Egyptians.[62]

Diogenes's portrait of Egyptian wisdom relies on Manetho to emphasize the systems of enigma that connect animals like the hawk and gods like Horus. The assignation of enigma to Egyptian zoomorphism bolsters the phrases "Egyptian philosophy," "matter," "elements," and "separation," which themselves underline the contiguity of Greek and Egyptian physics. That contiguity is only visible when animals are seen as indirect signs of a coherent underlying cosmogony. Diogenes comfortably uses the concept of enigmatic representation to describe the way that Manetho and Hecataeus connect animal and god. In the process, he is a surprising source of support for the argument that sustained the previous section—that authors of Aegyptiaca sought to translate the systems of significance that surrounded Egyptian zoomorphism, in ways hidden by a cultural

---

61. This is a mainstay of the Middle Platonic Pythagoras, one visible in the Greek historians (Schorn 2014) and in his biography in Diogenes (Laks 2014) and Porphyry (Macris 2014). For the historical development of these themes, see Riedweg (2005, 7–8, 55–60).

62. Diog. Laert. 1.10 = *BNJ* 264 F 1 = *BNJ* 609 F 17: αἰνίττεσθαί τε αὐτοὺς διά τε κανθάρου καὶ δράκοντος καὶ ἱέρακος καὶ ἄλλων, ὥς φησι Μανέθως ἐν τῆι Τῶν Φυσικῶν ἐπιτομῆι καὶ Ἑκαταῖος ἐν τῆι πρώτηι Περὶ τῆς τῶν Αἰγυπτίων φιλοσοφίας.

184   WHAT'S EGYPTIAN FOR "PHILOSOPHER"?

representation template.[63] Diogenes might stump for the Greek exclusivity of the term philosophy, but in the Egypt section he claims that authors of Aegyptiaca use the specific concept of enigma to frame Egyptian zoomorphic iconography.

Plutarch too uses philosophy as a hinge that connects Egyptian and Greek modes of signification around the divine. The flow of Plutarch's line of thinking begins with the etymological significance of the god Amun discussed in the previous chapter, continues with a claim that that significance proves Egyptians' philosophical profundity, and bolsters that profundity by citing Greek philosophers'—and Pythagoras's particular—intellectual debt to Egyptian priests. A key fragment of Manetho I discussed in chapter 5 contains Pythagoras at its margins. Plutarch seeks to underline the philosophical significance of the name Amun by citing Manetho, who claims that the name Amun means "concealed" or "concealment." This attribution to Manetho of theological etymologizing—one concordant with earlier Egyptian-language texts—paves the way for the conclusion that Plutarch deduces from Amun's etymological connections to concealment: "Egyptians' reverence for wisdom in divine matters was so great. Proof to this are also the wisest of the Greeks. . . ."[64]

Both passages make clear that one needs to see Aegyptiaca as a key frame for Pythagoras, and Pythagoras as a key frame for Aegyptiaca. Chapter 2's discussion of Pancrates, a latter-day author of Aegyptiaca associated with Pythagoreanism by the author Lucian, made that much clear. But the Aegyptiaca/Pythagoras pairing was also applied to Manetho, around whose extant fragments Pythagoras hovers just outside of frame.[65] There are benign reasons why Pythagoras has been cropped out of Aegyptiaca's picture. It is unwieldy to quote huge gobs of text. This is an honest but admittedly lame apology—both for my own and my predecessors' discussion of these two Manetho fragments.[66] But word counts notwithstanding, the interconnection of Manetho and Pythagoras is important. The train of thought of Diogenes and Plutarch stitches together threads I have been laying out across this book. Plutarch and Diogenes cite Manetho's engagement with Egypt's language (Plutarch) and its sacred animals (Diogenes) to describe an Egyptian wisdom on whose basis philosophy was then founded.

---

63. Kindt (2019, 2021b) do not mention the passage. Smelik and Hemelrijk (1984, 189n270) only allude to the passage in passing to justify their exclusion of indirectly transmitted texts. Where the dual citation of Manetho and Hecataeus poses problems for those trying to reconstruct each individual author's work, it supports rather than undermines this chapter's argument: that Aegyptiaca was a multi-author tradition central to Diogenes's narrative of Pythagoras's debt to Egypt and invention of philosophy.

64. Plut. *DIO* 9, 354d: ἡ μὲν οὖν εὐλάβεια τῆς περὶ τὰ θεῖα σοφίας Αἰγυπτίων τοσαύτη ἦν. The quote is picked up by the passage quoted above.

65. In addition to these two fragments, Pythagoras also appears in Syncellus's quotation of Manetho's annalistic history (*BNJ* 609 F 28, p. 170).

66. As an example, Lang (2014) makes no mention of Pythagoras in her discussion of these two fragments.

Both Plutarch and Diogenes introduce a temporal circularity in which the culturally mixed explanations of Egyptian religion one sees in Aegyptiaca exemplify the Egyptian religious symbolism that retroactively forms the origin story for Greek philosophy. An already-underway cultural mixture inbuilt into Aegyptiaca forms the Egyptian wisdom that Pythagoras brings to Greece and founds philosophy around. Within the progression of the Plutarch passage, Manetho's is the Egyptian symbolism that Pythagoras translates from Egypt to Greece. Authors of Aegyptiaca (here collapsed into the genre's paradigmatic founder) thus help crystallize the larger issue of aligning philosophical and priestly authority. A Hellenistic and imperial literary tradition of Aegyptiaca and its mixed philosopher-priest define the Egyptian religious symbolism that priests teach philosophers. That circularity is an essential part of the narrative of philosophy's origins that took root in the imperial period.

Chaeremon and the Semantics of the Philosopher-Priest

To many, Aegyptiaca's mixed "philosopher-priest" is one among many projections of Greek concepts onto Egyptian religious traditions. Diogenes's use of the term "Egyptian philosophy" has come into precisely this kind of criticism. When viewed in this light, Diogenes's representation of Manetho changes hue. His assignation of "enigmatically represent" to Manetho's coordination of animal and god is an act of cultural projection, not cross-cultural alignment. The language of enigma forces Manetho's text into a constrictive and inappropriate Greek-philosophical guise that was not of its own choosing. This charge of cultural projection is even more frequently applied to Chaeremon, who more than any other author of Aegyptiaca worked to synthesize the expertise of philosopher and priest.

Chaeremon is so valuable because he shows that, while sometimes useful, this anxiety around the presence of "philosophy" in the extant fragments of Aegyptiaca can be counterproductive. In the case of Chaeremon, it is clear that "philosopher" is a perfectly felicitous label for his culturally mixed authority. Restricting oneself to professional labels (should we call Chaeremon a priest, scribe, or philosopher?) better facilitates a cross-cultural conversation around professional wisdom-seeking.[67] By presenting the issue in these terms, I hope to recuperate imperial authors of Aegyptiaca, whose authority over and contact with a nebulously defined real or unmixed or pharaonic-looking Egyptian culture is on a much shakier foundation than Manetho's.

So, what was Chaeremon called? It is a basic question, but an important one. It returns to the "where the rubber hits the road" aspect of identity labels with which I opened. As with Apion, the answers are revealing. In addition to the label "Stoic"

---

67. Derchain (2000, 22–24) notes the mixed Greek and Egyptian cultural milieu in which many scribal priests operated.

186 WHAT'S EGYPTIAN FOR "PHILOSOPHER"?

or "philosopher," Chaeremon is twice called a "sacred scribe" (*hierogrammateus*).[68] As bilingual inscriptions make clear, *hierogrammateus* is a Greek translation of the Egyptian "scribe of the House of Life" (*sḫ pr-ʿnḫ*), an upper-level position in Ptolemaic and then Roman Egyptian temple administration.[69]

It is worth pausing to call attention to the cultural framework that surrounds Chaeremon's two different professional identities, philosopher and sacred scribe. When called a *hierogrammateus*, Chaeremon is connected to the constellation of literary and religious training that is inbuilt into the Egyptian scribal tradition generally, and the institution of the House of Life specifically. These paired Greek (*hierogrammateus*) and Egyptian (*sḫ pr-ʿnḫ*) terms for upper-level scribal priests gesture toward a much larger process of cultural translation, one that illustrates for a non-Egyptian audience just how important Houses of Life were as libraries, repositories of knowledge, and mechanisms for cultural transmission. Houses of Life were located in the broad confines of Egypt's temples and as such were tied to religious practice generally, and Osiris cult specifically.[70] But they housed a wide range of textual traditions and connoted knowledge writ large, not just magical arcana.[71] The *hierogrammateus*- "scribe of the House of Life" pairing is only one node in a larger web of translations for mixed priestly and scribal expertise. This includes the "feather-bearer" (*pteropheros*), which translates the Egyptian "scribe of the sacred book" (*sḫ md-nṯr*), a position associated with magic, wisdom, and esoteric priestly knowledge.[72] Even more broadly, scribal priests fell into the overarching category of Egyptian "sage" (*rḫ-ḫt*, literally "the one who knows things").

It is, then, important to see the *hierogrammateus* as a translation both of a specific scribal position and of the wider Egyptian semantics of learnedness. Bilingual texts like the Rosetta Stone can make this coordination of Greek and Egyptian terms seem automatic or assured, a match game between two identical categories denoted in two different languages. But there is much more variability and fluidity

---

68. He is called a sacred scribe in T 6, F 4, F 12, F 13, on which see van der Horst (1984, x, 61), Legras (2019, 145), and Escolano-Poveda (2020, 105–6). Note that in Josephus's recapitulation of Chaeremon's Exodus account, Joseph and Moses are called *hierogrammateis*, which is meant to connote magical and prophetic expertise, on which see Catastini (2010).

69. For Greek and Egyptian terms for Egyptian priestly positions, see the helpful chart offered by Vandorpe and Clarysse (2019, 417).

70. Gardiner (1938) remains an authoritative overview of Egyptian mentions of the House of Life, though see more recently Ryholt (2019, 444–48) and Hagen (2019, 252–62).

71. Hagen (2019, 254–55) (cf. Ryholt 2019, who emphasizes their more narrowly cultic function) presents the House of Life as a "culturally prestigious institution" associated with a broad, encyclopedic kind of wisdom and learning.

72. For example, *pterophoros* and *hierogrammateus* are close pairs in the Canopus and Rosetta decrees. Ryholt (1998, 168–69) argues persuasively that the two terms, both in Demotic and in Greek, were overlapping, as Diodorus's (1.87) mention of a feather-wearing *hierogrammateus* attests. As Ryholt (168n128) points out, the variation of order in a Demotic variant of the Canopus Decree even more closely aligns the *hierogrammateus* with the magical associations of the scribe of the sacred book.

at play. To provide one example of the inextricability of the narrow and broad semantics of the *hierogrammateus*: the Canopus and Rosetta Decrees coordinate the Greek *hierogrammateus* alternatively with the more generic Egyptian term "wise one" (*rḫ-ḫt*, Canopus l. 3) and with the more technical "staff of the House of Life" (*ty.(t) pr-ʿnḫ*, Rosetta l. 7).[73]

When we keep in view the cultural associations made with the scribe of the House of Life, Chaeremon's different identities gain some coherence. It is far from surprising that authors citing Chaeremon, in his authority as culturally mixed scribal priest, reach both for a technical equivalent (*hierogrammateus*) and the less technical, but no less accurate, label philosopher. The Egyptian *rḫ-ḫt* ("one who knows things") and Greek *philosophos* ("lover of knowledge") both define a person through their pursuit of knowledge, providing a broad frame of reference that complements, rather than undercuts, stricter professional terms in Greek (*hierogrammateus*) and Egyptian (*sḫ pr-ʿnḫ*).

The strategies of translation at play in Chaeremon's professional identities reveal the wide-ranging labels for learned elite in both Egyptian and Greek.[74] The centrality of wisdom in the different scribal positions which collectively constitute "those who know things" is best preserved when translated into a Greek frame of reference similarly focused on knowledge. It is wrong-headed to claim that philosopher is an unwarranted Greek projection that disqualifies Chaeremon (or Pancrates, another *hierogrammateus*-cum-philosopher) from an Egyptian identity label. Chaeremon's mixture of philosophical, scribal, and priestly labels translates knowledge, as a fundament of learned elite, between Egyptian, Greek, and Roman idioms.[75] For Chaeremon, one needs a theoretical lens that does not assume, a priori, that Greek cultural frames of interpretation (such as Stoicism) prove that Chaeremon can no longer be an Egyptian scribal priest. The label philosopher is just as reasonable a translation for Egyptian conceptions of priestly wisdom as more technical labels like sacred scribe.

This specific pairing of identity labels distills issues that run to the heart of Chaeremon's intellectual program. Chaeremon blended Egyptian-religious and Greek-philosophical life into a mixture on which his authority resided. An example shows this process at work:

73. For texts, see Sharpe (1870, plate 1) and Budge (1904, 189), with Gardiner (1938, 170) for the observation. See also Daumas (1952), who compares the Egyptian and Greek passages of the decrees, and Jasnow (2016, 244–45), who notes the strategies of translation around "scribes of the house of life."

74. Ryholt (1998, 169) makes a similar argument about the denotation of Egyptian wisdom figures in the Inaros cycle.

75. Jasnow and Zauzich (2021, 18) note the way that wisdom-seeking in the *Book of Thoth* entails a desire for social respectability. It is important to realize that this translation between labels is necessarily filtered through the citing authorities who choose them. I assume, based on variety of citing authorities, that Chaeremon actively arrogated the label philosopher. I also find it likely that, in Alexandria, he claimed the label sacred scribe (*hierogrammateus*), in the tradition of Hellenized Egyptians, as Frede (1989, 2068) lays out.

Chaeremon the Stoic, a most eloquent man, says about the life of the ancient Egyptian priests that, laying aside all the business and cares of the world, they were always in the temple and they surveyed the nature and causes of things, and also the calculations of the stars.[76]

Chaeremon's portrait of Egyptian religion draws readers' attention to the common ground between Egyptian and Greek accounts of nature. In this regard, Chaeremon's description of Egyptian religion is similar to that which Diogenes attributed to Manetho and Hecataeus. The natural-philosophical buzzwords *rerum naturas causasque* redirect Greek and Roman associations with Egyptian priests away from the world of cult and toward philosophical inquiry into the world's origins and constitution. This is certainly a rosy-hued portrait of priestly life. But it is not exactly, as is sometimes claimed, "philosophizing" Egyptian religion. That would suggest that emphasis on knowledge of the world's origins is an external layer that is easily peeled off to reveal an authentic, non-philosophical Egyptian substrate. The very existence of the label sage in Egyptian should caution against viewing Chaeremon's philosophical persona as a superficiality entirely indebted to his Greek education.

These general superficial metaphors have undergirded the phrase *interpretatio Graeca*. The concept certainly has heuristic value: Plutarch refers to the Egyptian god Seth by the Greek name Typhon, a way of translating one culture's gods into a Greek frame of reference.[77] But often *interpretatio Graeca* balloons in size into all acts of aligning Greek and non-Greek wisdom traditions.[78] This approach espouses a zero-sum game, where Chaeremon's embrace of Greek philosophical vocabulary proves either his divestment of or ignorance about Egyptian knowledge traditions. As soon as one sees philosophical language like *rerum naturas*, there is a red flag that proves that Chaeremon has entered the world of Greek philosophy and left behind authoritative views of Egyptian religion on display in Houses of Life.[79] That approach ends up cutting Egypt out of the picture. It denies

---

76. Jerome *Jov.* 2.13 = F 11: Chaeremon stoicus, vir eloquentissimus, narrat de vita antiquorum Aegypti sacerdotum, quod omnibus mundi negotiis curisque postpositis semper in templo fuerint et rerum naturas causasque ac rationes siderum contemplati sint.

77. On the creativity of Egypt-originating *interpretationes Graecae*, see Henri (2017). Note that many use the term in a more limited sense, to refer to the practice of using a Greek name for Egyptian gods—for example, von Lieven (2016). Conversely, Dillery (1998) understands *interpretatio Graeca* broadly.

78. This reliance on an *interpretatio Graeca* heuristic extends to Egypt in visual culture. Per Mazurek (2022, 119), Isis devotees in Greece preferred a Greek visual paradigm because they "wanted to portray a version of the Egyptian gods that had always been part of the Greek pantheon." As with Richter (see n5, above), I find that this unnecessarily bakes a framework of priority (cf. Mazurek 2022, 87) into processes of cultural equivalence-drawing.

79. Both Fowden (1986, 65) and Burstein (1996, 603) have characterized Chaeremon's presentation of Egyptian priests in this way, seeing in Chaeremon a canary-in-the-coal-mine signal of the transition toward Hermeticism and the exoticization of Egyptian priests' secret lore.

any possibility that Egyptian religious life includes a pursuit of knowledge that can be reasonably denoted in Greek philosophical terms. To return to an anthropological lens, as soon as one turns to Greek, the perspective has turned from insider and emic to outsider and etic. It is much more productive to see in Chaeremon and his alignment of priest and philosopher larger processes of creolization through which these two knowledge traditions have become interconnected.

WHAT'S EGYPTIAN FOR "PHILOSOPHER"?

The Book of Thoth: *Translating the Philosopher*

Turning to Egyptian-language evidence makes it absolutely clear that Chaeremon's mixture of priest and philosopher reflects wider Egyptian priestly practice. It is easy to write off Chaeremon as a Greek projectionist out of touch with Egyptian religion. It is harder, but more important, to see how Chaeremon mirrors the changes that were occurring in scribal texts of the Ptolemaic and Roman periods. The Egyptian priestly culture over which Chaeremon—and even the unimpeachably Egyptian Manetho!—claimed authority is indebted to, but not consubstantial with, its pharaonic antecedents.

The Demotic and Hieratic manuscripts that the Demotists Richard Jasnow and Karl-Theodor Zauzich have called the *Book of Thoth* provide an Egyptian-language perspective on the philosopher/priest.[80] The *Book of Thoth* has only entered into scholarly discussion (relatively) recently, thanks to the herculean activity of Jasnow, Zauzich, and Joachim Quack.[81] There have long been hints of the potential for a *Book of Thoth*. Clement of Alexandria tantalizingly describes a procession of priests who carried "all the necessary books" written by Thoth. In addition to Clement's list of titles, the walls of the House of Life at the Temple of Horus at Edfu also include a catalog of texts for scribes that were ranged under the title *Books of Thoth*, in acknowledgment of Thoth's role as patron of scribal learning.[82]

But until 2005, the actual contents of a text associated specifically with the imperial-era House of Life were out of view.[83] The outline of the narrative runs

---

80. For a larger review of priests in Demotic literature, see Escolano-Poveda (2020, 13–83; see too 108–9, connecting the philosopher/priest in Chaeremon to the *Book of Thoth*).

81. Jasnow and Zauzich (2005), the slimmer retranslation Jasnow and Zauzich (2014), the edits suggested by Quack (2007a, 2007b), and the reedition of Jasnow and Zauzich (2021).

82. Fowden (1986, 58–59), Clem. *Strom.* 6.4.35–7. Titles cited by Clement include one book of hymns, four books on astrology, ten books on hieroglyphic, ten books on education and sacrifice, and several others. Aufrère and Marganne (2019, 514) argue that Chaeremon was likely the source of Clement's information. The House of Life inscription mentions two texts on the rising stars (which must resemble the discussion of deacon stars in Chaeremon) and a book "on the threatening," a text typically taken as "on the threatening of Seth," which would connect it with the Seth-animal-hunting texts in the rest of the temple, which I discussed in chapter 4.

83. Fowden (1986) certainly made good use of the material he had, but the new textual evidence makes clear that it is not the obvious precursor to Hermeticism he would have wanted.

something like this: in format, the *Book of Thoth* is a question-and-answer conversation between master and disciple. The latter ("the-one-who-loves-knowledge") is a scribal initiate; the former (referred to alternatively as "He-of-Heseret" and "He-who-praises-knowledge") is either the god Thoth, a mortal ritually arrogating the role of Thoth, or an anonymous mentor.[84] The text describes priestly and scribal information that the disciple must learn to be initiated into privileged knowledge that Thoth made available for the scribes of the House of Life.[85] Different versions of the text contained different elements, depending on the local needs of a temple. But a mainstay of the text is the symbolic association of the House of Life, as a setting to which the scribe hopes to gain access, and the underworld.

The *Book of Thoth* recurrently presents linguistic training in symbolic terms. Thus, the "sacred words" (hieroglyphs in Greek, *mdw nṯr* in Egyptian) that the initiate is to learn metamorphose into the animals through which said words are denoted.[86] Often, this occurs on the level of individual signs. When the text catalogues a list of animals—"these dogs, these jackals, these bulls"—it is in fact self-consciously individuating the signs that constitute the hieroglyphic script.[87] In addition to an iconographic substitution of animal for animal-shaped hieroglyph, the text also plays with hieroglyphic signs through homophony. The author repeatedly uses sound play to (literally) recharacterize the way that linguistic expertise is framed: "The-one-who-loves-knowledge, he says: 'I desire to be a bird-catcher of the hieroglyphic signs of Thoth.'"[88] This reflects a thoroughgoing identification of scribal books as the bas of Re, and, by extension, birds. In this metaphorical framework, bird-catching stands in for learning sacred texts, based in no small part on the homophony of "document" (⟨glyph⟩, *sš*) and "nest" (⟨glyph⟩, *sš*). Animals and hieroglyphic signs are interconnected systems of significance. They jointly constitute the web of meaning which the scribal initiate must traverse on his way to the sacred teachings safeguarded by Thoth, the patron of scribes.

This elevation of hieroglyphic as a self-conscious object of symbolic significance is a critical point of reference for the discussions of hieroglyphic and sacred animals one sees in Aegyptiaca. The *Book of Thoth*'s sign-by-sign glossing of hieroglyphic's animals is consonant with the approach of Chaeremon and the sources that Plutarch drew on, who also made a match-pair of animal and concept. With the *Book of Thoth* in view, Chaeremon's hieroglyphic catalogue seems a good deal less out of touch. Chaeremon's animal-heavy approach to sacred characters is

---

84. Jasnow and Zauzich (2021, 11–14) review the issue, both by hedging their own initial identification of the master with Thoth and by rejecting Quack's preference for an anonymous mentor.

85. For the importance of initiation as a theme of the *Book of Thoth*, see Quack (2007a).

86. I am indebted here to the discussion of the *Book of Thoth*'s metaphoric language in Jasnow (2011).

87. 613 = L01 (V.T.), x+4/15: *nꜣy jwjw.w nꜣy wnš.w nꜣy kꜣ.w*. For this passage in particular, see Quack (2007b).

88. 245 = V01, 2/16–17: *Mr-rḫ ḏ≤f tw≤y wḫꜣ jr wḥy r nꜣ twꜣ.w n jstn mtw≤y grg [nꜣy≤f] bꜣ.w*.

kindred with the *Book of Thoth*'s unimpeachably authoritative presentation of the hieroglyphic script's significance to Egyptian scribal priests (*hierogrammateis*) of the imperial period.[89]

The *Book of Thoth* is so helpful because it reemphasizes that authors of Aegyptiaca were cultural ambassadors of Egyptian religious traditions that were themselves operating in a creolizing world. Authors of Aegyptiaca leveraged language of symbolism and underlined the interconnection of philosophical and priestly knowledge because the same was occurring in Egyptian-language scribal literature. The very features—the philosopher/priest and the use of enigma/symbol—that many have seen as proof of the illegitimacy of Chaeremon's Egyptian bona fides in fact reflect his success, and not failure, in presenting the systems of significance laced throughout scribal and priestly literature of the early-imperial period.[90]

The title of the *Book of Thoth*'s protagonist, like Chaeremon's professional labels, grounds broad processes of cultural translation in discrete formulations for wisdom-seeking in Greek and Egyptian. The main character is the initiate who hopes to be inducted by Thoth into the knowledge to which a scribal priest has access. It makes sense, then, that he is called "he-who-loves-knowledge" (*mr-rḫ*). It is a title that provides an Egyptian correlative to the portrait of philosophical inquiry that Plutarch had offered in the opening of the *On Isis and Osiris*. As in that text, the pursuit of knowledge is bound up in the pursuit of the divine and is located in a temple setting. This returns to the constitutive importance of knowledge, on a lexical level, for the social position of these scribal priests. That was already on display in the *hierogrammateus* title leveraged by Chaeremon. It was a Greek title that translated both technical ("scribe of the House of Life") and generic ("one who knows things") identity labels for Egyptian scribal priests. The broad learnedness denoted by "one who knows things" (*rḫ-ḫt*) is essential to the self-fashioning seen in Aegyptiaca and Egyptian-language texts alike. The intersection of wisdom-seeking labels speaks to a creolizing mixture of expertise that is ill-served by a dichotomous view of philosophical and Greek, versus Egyptian and priestly, authority.

The interconnection of the philosopher's and scribe's pursuit of knowledge helps explain why the *Book of Thoth*'s protagonist matches the word philosopher so closely. While there is some overlap with the Ptolemaic title *rḫ-ḫt*, the precise wording of the disciple's name, "he-who-loves-knowledge" (*mr-rḫ*), is a neologism. Jasnow and Zauzich tentatively connect the *mr-rḫ* to the Greek term

---

89. For the religious and symbolic power of the hieroglyphic script, see Derchain (1976) and te Velde (1986); on the interplay between phonology and iconography in hieroglyphic, see Vernus (1986) and Morenz (2008).

90. Jasnow and Zauzich (2005, 13n36; cf. Jasnow and Zauzich 2021, 19) cite Chaeremon as an example of the alignment of priest and philosopher one sees in the *mr-rḫ*/φιλόσοφος pairing.

"philosopher," another "knowledge-lover."[91] The connection between *mr-rḫ* and *philosophos* is both wholly commonsense and a striking proof of cultural mixture. The dramatic equivalence of these two languages' "knowledge-lover" speaks to the synthesis of Greek and Egyptian ideas of scribal learning and philosophical training. It points, with real clarity, to the faulty definition of cultural authority that so often ignores a world in creolization. To present the priest as a wisdom-loving and wisdom-seeking figure *is* authoritatively Egyptian. It is tempting to write off Diogenes's use of the phrase "Egyptian philosophy" and separate it out from Manetho's original presentation of this material. But to unilaterally chalk up the presence of philosophical language in Manetho to Diogenes's or Plutarch's *interpretatio Graeca* is to sidestep essential conversations about how Egyptian culture remained Egyptian even as it incorporated Greek concepts.[92] The connections drawn between Egyptian- and Greek-language wisdom-seeking are better taken as a sign of Egyptian culture's vibrancy in the imperial period than as proof that Egyptian traditions were slowly dying.

The *Book of Thoth*'s protagonist, like Chaeremon's different titles, show that large processes of cultural translation of knowledge traditions hinge on minute translations of Greek and Egyptian terms. These processes of translation run in both directions simultaneously: Pythagoras first coined "philosopher" because of his visits with Egyptian priests. The scribal priest of the imperial period was defined in terms consonant with the concept "philosophy." Chaeremon's position was the product of multiple modalities of translation between knowledge-expertise in Greek and Egyptian idioms, whether the *hierogrammateus*, the sage, or the philosopher.

Juxtaposing Greek and Egyptian Wisdoms: Recuperating Lower-Case-S Symbolism

Symbolism can be similarly multimodal. It is a term of tripartite heuristic value. To be sure, its roots in a Greek literary-critical and philosophical tradition are important to put boundaries around. But as many scholars of Egyptology have

---

91. Jasnow and Zauzich (2005, 13n36) offer potential *comparanda* for the *mr-rḫ*/φιλόσοφος pairing. Their enthusiasm for the potential derivation of "he who loves knowledge" from *philosophos* in Jasnow and Zauzich (2005, 13) (cf. the elliptical reference to the derivation in Jasnow 2016, 325) is tempered in the retranslation (Jasnow and Zauzich 2014, 31), and dropped in the final edition (Jasnow and Zauzich 2021). But my own interest here, as in the larger chapter, is in emphasizing an equivalence-drawing impulse amply demonstrated by the parallelism of *mr-rḫ* and φιλόσοφος around themes of "love" (of wisdom), of the wisdom-seeking path, and of social respectability of the wisdom-seeker that are noted by Jasnow and Zauzich (2021, 17–20).

92. My own recuperative argument for Aegyptiaca's Greek translations of Egyptian concepts—and pushback against the overextension of the *interpretatio Graeca* dynamic—builds on Henri (2017), who also underlines the value of creative translations of Egyptian gods' names into Greek in inscriptions and papyri.

made clear, the animal-for-hieroglyph substitution one sees in the *Book of Thoth* speaks to a symbolic impulse in Egyptian literary and material culture that is equally vibrant and equally worthy of attention.[93] Aegyptiaca represents a third, no less important but much less frequently discussed, mode of lower-case-s symbolism. This is a symbolism in which Greek and Egyptian symbolic traditions are juxtaposed to show the points of connection that they shared. In making space for this third kind of symbolism, I am trying to return symbol to its etymological roots, as a technique of "association" and "juxtaposition." This is a more diffuse symbolism to be sure, but one fundamental to the creolization of wisdom-seeking one sees across Plutarch's *DIO*, Chaeremon's *Aegyptiaca*, and scribal texts like the *Book of Thoth*.

The very materiality of the *Book of Thoth* exemplifies this cross-cultural symbolism of wisdom traditions. Several witnesses of the *Book of Thoth* are on papyri that also contain Greek texts, either as a palimpsest or on their reverse. One such manuscript, the "Vienna Papyrus," contains the *Book of Thoth* on one side and a Greek-language astronomical text on the other.[94] That text, written during the reigns of Caligula and Nero, is in the wheelhouse of Aegyptiaca, whose authors so regularly used astronomy to bolster their Egyptian intellectual bona fides. That is particularly true for Chaeremon, Thrasyllus, and Tiberius Claudius Balbillus, authors of Aegyptiaca writing in that period on that subject. To many Egyptologists and papyrologists, this kind of pairing is ho-hum. But I want to recentralize the theoretical potential of these interconnected knowledge traditions. It is a concrete, material product of a world in creolization.

The two-sided papyrus is an ideal apologetic for the cultural authority of post-Manetho authors of Aegyptiaca. On one side, the *Book of Thoth*: its translation of the "knowledge-lover" between Greek and Egyptian, its figurative presentation of language via animals, its initiatory approach to the sacred knowledge contained within the House of Life. On the other, astronomy: a text that demonstrates another join where philosophical and priestly expertise coalesced. All of this, in one way or another, seeps into Chaeremon's extant fragments, which range between the language-animal pairing, the astronomical expertise of Egyptian priests, and the natural-philosophical inquiry practiced in Egypt's temples.[95] That papyrological background is what makes Aegyptiaca as a creolizing intellectual tradition so valuable. Authors of Aegyptiaca were the media through which the cultural mixture happening on the ground in the Houses of Life was broadcast outward to authors like Plutarch and Diogenes. They help explain why knowledge-seekers of

93. For symbolism in Egyptian religious thinking, see n12.

94. For the status of the papyri, see Jasnow and Zauzich (2005, 77–88, with orthographic and grammatical observations at 88–109).

95. Jasnow (2011, 315) cites Chaeremon when discussing the *Book of Thoth*'s representation of scribes' way of life.

194   WHAT'S EGYPTIAN FOR "PHILOSOPHER"?

different backgrounds remade their own knowledge traditions in ways that made space for those practiced by others.

CONCLUSION: AEGYPTIACA, AUTHORIAL AGENCY, AND THE BENEFIT OF THE DOUBT

Through the *Book of Thoth*, I am asking to give authors of Aegyptiaca the benefit of the doubt. There are good reasons why they used the mixed philosopher-priest as a springboard into a conversation about the joins between Egyptian and Greek modes of inquiry. Those joins are legitimated on a material level: astronomy, as a culturally mixed, Greek-language, natural-philosophical tradition is the very literal flipside of Egyptian-language scribal initiation. The imperial period saw a movement toward a mixed philosopher-priest detectable in Egyptian-language texts, etiologies of Pythagoreanism's debt to Egypt, and authors of Aegyptiaca who integrated philosophical and religious wisdom. To underline unduly one direction of cultural influence, to focus unilaterally on the cultural hegemony of Diogenes's and Plutarch's philosophication of Egyptian religion, is to mischaracterize the processes of cultural contact and mixture that encouraged imperial authors to see the philosopher and priest as interconnected categories. It is also to wholly erase the historical context that paved the way for authors of Aegyptiaca to arrogate authority as experts in this increasingly blurry picture of the philosopher-priest. Apion and his mixed authority in scarabs and Homer encompass three different types of symbolic exegesis: Greek literary criticism, scarab ideology, and the coordination of Egyptian and Greek symbolic traditions into a newly mixed form.

The messiness of the philosopher/priest is what makes an intellectual history of the imperial period so worthwhile. It is a time when Pythagoras's world-traveling took on new proportions. The cultic, fringe-y, and rampantly symbolized philosophy of imperial Pythagoreans, their interest in animals, arithmetic, and enigmatic *Acousmata*, were retroactively aetiologized through Egypt-visits.[96] This is one among many imperial narratives in which Greek philosophers were meant to visit Egypt. Often, that fact has led to conversations about whether early Greek thought was or was not indebted to Egypt.[97] I have suggested here that, regardless of historicity, these narratives have a different value. They reflect their imperial context, a time when a widely practiced mixture of philosophical and religious traditions was projected back into, and thus circularly naturalized through, a story of Greek philosophy's non-Greek origins.

---

96. Kahn (2001, 94–138) well notes the general inability of the term "Neopythagorean" to capture this rise of a semi-religious Pythagoras (discussed on 139–72), rather than to denote imperial philosophers (like Eudorus, Nichomachus, and Numenius) who stressed Plato's debt to Pythagoras.

97. Lefkowitz (2012) surveys these visits generally, and de Vogel (1966) those of Pythagoras specifically. Most recently, Riedweg (2005, 42–97) has tried to recover from these later accretions a historical Pythagoras.

The coordination of Manetho and Pythagoras one sees in Plutarch and Diogenes is a commonplace of the imperial period that has fallen out of view. We need Pythagoras to make sense of Aegyptiaca and the popularity of its authors, and we need Aegyptiaca to make sense of Pythagoras's popularity in the imperial period. There are several reasons why this association has yet to be fully recognized. To some extent, it is because of the realities of publishing fragmentary texts, where Pythagoras lurks on the margins of Manetho, and Aegyptiaca lurks on the margins of Pythagoras. But that cannot wholly explain things. The Manetho/Pythagoras pairing and its creative rearticulation of the "origins of philosophy" narrative depend on a logic that is necessarily "mythological" and retrospective. That logic remakes a classical past into a myth-time that prefigures and thus makes meaningful what was happening, on the ground, in the imperial period. In the domains of both Roman-Egyptian scribal wisdom and imperial Platonism-cum-Pythagoreanism, new interconnections abounded. Philosophical and religious authority blurred into a new form over which authors of Aegyptiaca, scribal priests, and Pythagoras himself could all claim authority. As I head toward the Conclusion, I want to individuate this imperial-era mythologization of Egypt's influence on Greece and underline Aegyptiaca's central role in it. In doing so, I hope to push back against models of cultural influence (like Martin Bernal's) that by vaunting Egypt's place out ahead of, and prior to, Greece and Rome end up erasing the vibrancy of Aegyptiaca specifically, and Ptolemaic- and Roman-Egyptian cultural mixture more broadly.

Conclusion

Acoreus, Aegyptiaca, and the Question
of Cultural Influence

Aegyptiaca enabled its authors to display a mixed expertise that was couched simultaneously in philosophical, scribal, and priestly traditions. The mixed philosopher-priest—an author of Aegyptiaca based in Alexandria but with broadly defined pharaonic bona fides—gave shape to narratives of philosophy's Egyptian origins. When tracing philosophy's roots, Plutarch and Diogenes Laertius imagined a form of wisdom that was at once authentically Egyptian and a tailor-made precursor of Greek natural philosophy. In large part because of Manetho and his successors, Greek authors retrojected a Hellenistic and culturally mixed presentation of Egyptian religion back to a distant Egyptian past that Plato and Pythagoras supposedly encountered. But as I discussed in chapter 6, the connection between philosophical and priestly self-fashioning was far from an external Greek projection that bastardized Egyptian religious sensibility. Both Egyptian- and Greek-language texts produced in Egypt show how imperial Egyptians increasingly blended scribal and philosophical initiations into privileged knowledge. By advertising their mixed initiation into religio-philosophical wisdom, authors of Aegyptiaca sought to bolster their expertise and social clout before a Greek and Roman audience.

To conclude, I want to continue in this vein of the philosophically framed scribal priest while returning to a central premise of this book: that Aegyptiaca meaningfully shaped the way Romans talked about Egypt. Aegyptiaca was such an impactful genre because of its authors' effective use of the philosopher-priest persona. It allowed Chaeremon to present to his pupil Nero a description of Egyptian priestly life in which contemplation of the stars took center stage. This combination of traditions did not happen in a vacuum, but because of the

198   CONCLUSION

opportunities outside of Egypt that made this combination socially advantageous. The reception of the philosopher-priest in Rome will thus tie together the two key frames I have been using for Aegyptiaca, root and road: the heterogeneous web of traditions to which the mixed philosopher/priest points, and the socially and politically circumscribed paths that dictated how authors of Aegyptiaca and their work moved between Egypt, Greece, and Rome.

ACOREUS AND AEGYPTIACA

Lucan's historical epic poem, the *Bellum Civile*, combines these twin facets of Aegyptiaca. The *Bellum Civile's* cast of characters includes the Egyptian sage Acoreus, a lightly fictionalized author of Aegyptiaca whose discourse on Egypt ranges across the poem's final book. Acoreus and his conversation with Caesar provide ample opportunity to reflect on Aegyptiaca, its social context, its strategic presentation of Egyptian culture, and its alternatively warm (by figures like Apuleius and Plutarch) or cold (in the case of authors like Pliny the Elder, Seneca, Josephus, and Aulus Gellius) reception outside of Egypt. Lucan's approach to Egypt is productively ambivalent—he underlines both Egypt's philosophical profitability and its political culpability. In the latter vein, Lucan recurrently criticizes Ptolemaic rule. Egypt is the site of Pompey's (and by extension the Republic's) death, a fact which Lucan bemoans in no uncertain terms.[1] The civil war allows Lucan to proleptically anticipate Rome's adoption of the Ptolemies' luxury and tyranny.[2] Egypt slots tidily into Lucan's general critique of Rome's slide into dictatorship, a critique inevitably colored by the poem's unfinished ending and Lucan's own death at Nero's hands.[3] Through Lucan, one can see how Roman reactions to Aegyptiaca and its popularity outside of Egypt are shot through with anxiety about the principate and social changes in Rome.

Egyptians and Alexandrians were regularly the foils through which Romans complained about obsequious advisers. Per Suetonius (*Nero* 20.3), Nero considered Alexandrians the ideal sycophantic audience because they clapped so well. Juvenal is singularly frustrated with the "Nile's trash" (*verna Canopi*, 1.26) Crispinus because he is an exogenous, enabling adviser in the court of Domitian, another Egyptophile emperor demonized by senatorial elite.[4] Within the *Bellum Civile*, it

1. Tracy (2014) analyzes Egypt's ideological significance in the *Bellum Civile* (part 1 discusses Pompey, part 2 Caesar).

2. McCloskey and Phinney Jr. (1968) argue that Lucan critiques Nero via Ptolemy XIII.

3. Fantham (2011) lays out a biography of Lucan and the sources on which that biography is based. Lucan's attitude to Nero is an object of debate (cf. Kimmerle 2015, 110–16), one that clusters around the paradoxical criticism of Caesar and praise of Nero (on which see Holmes 1999).

4. It is hard to translate, but important to note, the mixed semantics of *verna*, which binds together a pejorative for "natives" with a term for a house slave. For the historical Crispinus, see Vassileiou (1984) and Jones (1992, 70). See also the prosopographical approach of White (1974, 377–78) and Baldwin (1979, 110–11), the former of whom sees Crispinus not as an official but as a mere gourmand.

is Pothinus who poisons the ear of Ptolemy XIII. In a council scene, Ptolemy XIII weighs whether to welcome Pompey or kill him after the latter flees to Egypt in the wake of his defeat at Pharsalia. A palace eunuch of humble birth, Pothinus is best able to deliver morally bankrupt but self-serving advice to a tyrant all too ready to take the easy path: "But Pothinus, better able to counsel evil and know tyrants, dared to condemn Pompey to death."[5] This image of the corrupt and non-Roman adviser, here located around the Ptolemies, is both an etiology for and retroactively produced by the dangerous amount of power unscrupulous confidants had with "bad" emperors like Nero and Domitian.[6] Lucan and Juvenal thus offer a contrastive view on the paths taken by authors of Aegyptiaca who made the move from Alexandria to Rome and the emperor. One such author, Tiberius Claudius Balbillus, leveraged his astrological knowledge to justify Nero's summary execution of Roman elite.[7] In the eyes of Roman authors navigating the dangerous reigns of Nero and Domitian, Egyptians and their presentation of Egyptian history help translate tyrannical rule to Rome.

Into this general picture of Egypt as site and etiology of Rome's turn to tyranny enters Acoreus, an Egyptian priest who also serves as adviser to Ptolemy XIII. Through Acoreus's mixed position as learned figure and imperial adviser, Lucan reflects on the structures that surround and enable tyrannical rule, in Egypt and—by implication—in Rome. As an epic poet writing in the paranoia-ridden court of Nero, Lucan at once sees himself in the figure of Acoreus—who must also navigate the dangerous curiosity of a Caesar—and defines himself and all Romans against the Egyptian adviser's cozy relationship with tempestuous Ptolemaic dynasts.[8] That tension is what makes Acoreus, as a figure who reflects doubly the history of Egyptian authors of Aegyptiaca and the new realities facing Lucan, Chaeremon, Seneca, Petronius, and others writing under Nero's shadow, so interesting.

As a mixed adviser and exegete of Egyptian culture, Acoreus is a more complex figure than the flatly demonized Pothinus. Unlike Pothinus, Acoreus urges Ptolemy to remain loyal to Pompey. When Acoreus enters the *Bellum Civile* during this council scene, Lucan highlights both Acoreus's good advice to Ptolemy and his general wisdom in Aegyptiaca. Acoreus thus coordinates two poles around which I have been positioning authors of Aegyptiaca—a direct connection to the emperor and a broad expertise in Egyptian culture:

> Among the council Acoreus's speech came first, Acoreus serene in his old age and made mild by his broken years. Memphis, ostentatious in its sacred rights, the

---

Demougin (1994, 293) discusses Domitian's elevation of equestrian freedmen. For Domitian's connections to Egypt, see Klotz (2008).

5. Luc. *Bell. Civ.* 8.482–3: sed melior suadere malis et nosse tyrannos / ausus Pompeium leto damnare Pothinus.

6. Flamerie de Lachapelle (2010) emphasizes the Roman-imperial resonances of Pothinus's speech.

7. Per Suet. *Ner.* 36.1, which I discuss in chapter 2.

8. Feldherr (2021, 139) notes the deliberate blurring of Cleopatra/past into Nero/present in Book 10.

protector of the Nile inundation, gave him birth. As he tended the gods many Apises had lived out the spans imposed by their Diana.[9]

Acoreus embodies the *longue durée* of Egyptian history. His old age metonymically represents Egypt's age-old wisdom and explains his (attempted) moderating influence on a young king. The Stoic catchwords "placid" (*placidus*) and "moderate" (*modestior*) make clear that Acoreus embodies the philosophical peace that Lucan and his uncle Seneca both associated with Egypt. His mixed adviser-philosopher role recalls the Stoic and sacred scribe Chaeremon. Jonathan Tracy and Eleni Manolaraki have unsurprisingly looked both to Chaeremon and to the other adviser of Nero, Lucan's uncle Seneca, for Acoreus's historical model.[10] Both were older tutors attempting to temper Nero's rash tempestuousness.

Acoreus's association with Memphis strengthens his embodiment of Egypt's cultural patrimony. Memphis is, after all, the site of Egypt's antiquity par excellence. It was the Old Kingdom capital and pharaonic counterpart to the paradigmatically Ptolemaic Alexandria. Lucan makes Memphis and its signification of all things pharaonic an immediate frame through which to make sense of Acoreus. Lucan's introduction of Acoreus drills down on three specific examples (Nilometers, the Apis bull, and lunar cult) of the mixed religious and natural-philosophical bona fides associated with Memphis and constitutive of Acoreus's priestly authority. Acoreus's old age and position as priest are the source of his expertise over the otherwise quite heterogeneous traditions of hydrometry, animal cult, and astronomy. In this way Acoreus exemplifies the same pattern I have been underlining for authors of Aegyptiaca. The Nile, the Apis bull, and the moon tidily delineate a wide field of cultural authority for the fictional Acoreus and the historical authors of Aegyptiaca after whom he is patterned.

Acoreus makes only a brief appearance in the council scene (his advice cannot stack up with Pothinus's), but he is the central figure of the *Bellum Civile's* final book. It is there, in a banquet that shifts from feasting to natural-philosophical conversation, that the systems of Roman imperial power that gave shape to Aegyptiaca take center stage. Justifiably, most attention turns to the speech that Acoreus gives about the origins of the Nile. It runs for some 137 lines (10.194–331).[11] The speech rewards the critical attention paid to it: Acoreus deftly coordinates superficially neutral natural-philosophical curiosity with the latent ideologies of southern conquest animating the historical Nubian expeditions of Senwosret, Cambyses, Augustus, and Nero; a penchant for natural philosophy present across Lucan's epic

---

9. Luc. *Bell. Civ.* 8.475–80: . . . quos inter Acoreus / iam placidus senio fractisque modestior annis / (hunc genuit custos Nili crescentis in arva / Memphis vana sacris; illo cultore deorum / lustra suae Phoebes non unus vixerat Apis) / consilii vox prima fuit.

10. For the identification with Seneca (partially based on Seneca's tract on the Nile in *Nat. Quaest.* 4a), see Williams (2008, 231–34), Manolaraki (2013, 64), and Tracy (2014, 153–69). For the identification with Chaeremon, see Manolaraki (2013, 108–10) and Tracy (2014, 10n31, 174).

11. In particular, the readings of Manolaraki (2013, 80–117) and Tracy (2014, 181–224).

and consonant with his uncle Seneca's *Natural Questions* takes center stage as the work reaches its (unfinished) conclusion; the détente between the philosophically valorous Acoreus and the politically destructive Caesar allows Lucan to work through his own relationship to Nero.[12]

But it is Caesar's introductory speech that sets out a Roman perspective on Aegyptiaca. When Caesar asks Acoreus about Egypt, he does so in a way that reflects well Aegyptiaca's broad cultural ambit. Caesar's concluding promise to abandon imperial conquest and the civil war makes explicit that the knowledge offered by Acoreus and constitutive of Aegyptiaca was bound up in the processes of imperial ambition and institutional collapse that Lucan's Neronian audience was facing:

> O you aged devotee of sacred matters, and—as your age attests—not neglected by the gods, explain the origins of the Egyptian *gens*, the lay of the land, the customs of its people, and the gods' rites and shape. Bring forth whatever is inscribed on the ancient inner sancta and reveal gods who want to be known. If your ancestors taught Athenian Plato their sacred learning, what guest was ever more worthy of hearing this, more able to contain the world. . . . But although such virtuousness, such love of the truth lives in me, there is nothing I'd rather know than the causes and the unknown source of the Nile inundation—hidden over so many centuries. Let there be a definite hope of seeing the source of the Nile, I'll abandon civil war.[13]

Caesar's speech homes in on the areas of Aegyptiaca I have centered in this book. He echoes a heterogeneity of subjects absolutely crucial for the social function of Aegyptiaca. Ethnography, geography, etiology, and religious exegesis all swirl together. That range of intellectual traditions is too easily lost when Aegyptiaca is collapsed into history-writing and the model provided by Manetho's dynastic history. Within the logic of the narrative, Caesar can reasonably ask somebody like Acoreus to cover all these different areas. Rome's appetite for knowledge was expansive. Responding to the kinds of requests for auto-ethnographic exposition made by Caesar is what created the opportunities on which Apion, Chaeremon, Pancrates, Julia Balbilla, and other authors of Aegyptiaca capitalized.

The last in Caesar's laundry list of subjects, "the gods' rites and shapes," reflects a crux of the argument I have tried to make via Aegyptiaca. The specific phrasing (*ritus formasque deum*) matters. Caesar displays a curiosity about the divine that deprioritizes animal worship—to which he tangentially refers via "rites"—and instead emphasizes the different forms that gods take. That question of form, of

---

12. For the shadow cast by Nero's (failed) expedition on this exchange, see Tracy (2014, 186).

13. Luc. *Bell. Civ.* 10.176–83: "o sacris devote senex, quodque arguit aetas, / non neglecte deis, Phariae primordia gentis / terrarumque situs vulgique edissere mores / et ritus formasque deum; quodcumque vetustis / insculptum est adytis profer, noscique volentes / prode deos. si Cecropium sua sacra Platona / maiores docuere tui, quis dignior umquam / hoc fuit auditu mundique capacior hospes? . . . sed, cum tanta meo vivat sub pectore virtus, / tantus amor veri, nihil est quod noscere malim / quam fluvii causas per saecula tanta latentis / ignotumque caput: spes sit mihi certa videndi / Niliacos fontes, bellum civile relinquam."

202   CONCLUSION

human- versus animal-shaped gods, was a critical avenue for cross-cultural conversations in which Greek and Roman philosophers and authors of Aegyptiaca all took part. It is interesting that where a few lines earlier (10.158–9) Lucan's authorial voice takes pot shots at the Egyptian animal and vegetable gods on that evening's dinner menu, Caesar asks about Egyptian religious practices much more evenhandedly. Even in a poem whose barbarization of Egyptian religion I discussed in chapter 3, there are clear signs that Lucan knows well the terms of the zoomorphic debate occurring in Cicero, Ovid, Diodorus, Plutarch, and Aegyptiaca. In other words, Lucan's rejection of animal worship earlier in the poem is not an unconsidered cultural chauvinism.[14] It is an instrumental, passage-specific rhetorical effect through which to concatenate luxury and barbarity.

Acoreus has authority over this list of "Egyptian things" because he can publish hieroglyphic texts hidden in temples. After asking about a range of traditions, Caesar changes tacks and asks Acoreus to disclose everything written in hieroglyphic. Both spatially and metaphorically, hieroglyphic's appeal depends on its inaccessibility. It resides in "sancta" (*adytis*) that can only be brought out into the light (*profer*) by somebody with Acoreus's skillset. Acoreus's authority over a linguistic tradition associated specifically with inscribed temple texts is consonant with the expertise advertised by authors of Aegyptiaca. Starting already with Manetho, auto-ethnographic authority was expressed as a translation into Greek of hieroglyphic source material.[15]

That translation occurred on multiple levels. It was, of course, lexical. Authors of Aegyptiaca presented in Greek concepts and traditions that had been linguistically Egyptian in origin—whether that "Egyptian" is a hieroglyphic temple inscription or a Demotic text. So, scribal labels like "the scribe of the house of life" (*sḫ pr-ʿnḫ*) or the more general "sage" (*rḫ-ḫt*) were translated flexibly into either "sacred scribe" (*hierogrammateus*) or "philosopher." Manetho offers a gloss of Amun's name that foregrounds the philosophical importance of removal and hiddenness. Apion's presentation of Egyptian pharmacology uses two different translations of a specific herb (*osiritis* and *cynocephalia*) to underline the interconnection of technical botanical knowledge and Osiris mythology.[16] But beyond discrete acts of translating between languages, Aegyptiaca itself was a broader form of cultural translation. Its authors sought to rearticulate the contextual meaning of gods, animals, royal power, and cosmology in terms compatible with philosophy and legible to an external Greek and Roman audience.

Caesar makes a provocative comparison to legitimize his own request of Acoreus. His conversation with Acoreus naturally succeeds Plato's earlier lessons from pharaonic priests. This is another important example of the mythologization of philosophers' visits to Egypt, whose importance to imperial-era Aegyptiaca I

---

14. As I discuss in chapter 3, Lucan criticizes Isis cult's popularity in Rome at Luc. *Bell. Civ.* 8.831–2.
15. As is made clear in Joseph. *Ap.* 1.73 = *BNJ* 609 T 7a, which I discuss in chapter 5.
16. Plin. *HN* 30.18 = *BNJ* 616 F 15, discussed in chapter 1.

unpacked in chapter 6. Platonism is but one of the proliferation of philosophical traditions that Greek and Roman authors traced back to Egypt and its priests. As the logic goes, Caesar is only asking for a set of answers that had already been freely given to earlier visitors. The banquet in Alexandria, at the liminal moment of transition from Ptolemaic to Roman rule, self-consciously adapts itself to the transfer of wisdom and wisdom-seeking from Egyptian priests to Greek philosophers.

The tenor of Acoreus's discourse on the Nile helps prove natural philosophy's Egyptian origins. His speech naturally touches on doxography of the Nile's sources. But it is no accident that Acoreus opens with a precis of astronomy and its role in Egypt's seasonal cycle, a kind of Greco-Egyptian knowledge tradition central to Aegyptiaca. That is both a good fit for the astronomical bent of the *Bellum Civile* and a reflection of imperial Aegyptiaca's interest in the stars, on display in authors like Chaeremon, Thrasyllus, and Tiberius Claudius Balbillus. By performing a priestly knowledge steeped in natural-philosophical traditions practiced in Alexandria, Acoreus continues the same circular feedback loop that I called attention to in the case of Manetho, in chapter 6. Aegyptiaca, as a mixed Greco-Egyptian intellectual tradition situated at the intersection of religious and philosophical expertise, provides the substance of an original Egyptian wisdom that priests taught to Plato and Pythagoras and that then metamorphosed into "philosophy." Acoreus's culturally mixed presentation on the Nile and the stars is, to Caesar, the authentically pharaonic material that Plato molded into philosophy.

Caesar's self-comparison to Plato draws attention to the political stakes of religio-philosophical knowledge-seeking. The otherwise innocent claims to curiosity touted by Caesar are entirely unconvincing. His disingenuity is betrayed by the phrasing he uses to underline his suitability as Acoreus's pupil. He arrogates for himself a capacity for knowledge—"more able to contain the world" (*mundique capacior*)—that slips into a language of imperial conquest. That culminates in the overbold promise that caps Caesar's opening speech: he would happily quit the civil war if he could set eyes on the Nile's sources. Of course, the phrase *mundi capacior* deliberately blurs seeing the Nile and conquering Egypt. To see the Nile's sources, to know the Nile, would be an act of expansion grander than any of Caesar's predecessors.

Acoreus is entirely aware of this. He draws out a lineage of knowledge-seeking dynasts who have tried to conquer the Nile: "The desire you have to know the Nile was shared by Egyptian, Persian, and Macedonian kings."[17] The lineage of power-hungry and expansionist kings—Senwosret/Sesostris, Cambyses, and Alexander—complement Plato as a no less important aetiological prelude to Caesar's thirst for imperial knowledge. It also broadens the scale in which Acoreus's auto-ethnography gains coherence. There is a long list of dynasts who have attempted to leverage the kind of knowledge safeguarded by Acoreus and typical

---

17. Luc. *Bell. Civ.* 10.268–9: quae tibi noscendi Nilum, Romane, cupido est, / et Phariis Persisque fuit Macetumque tyrannis. . . .

of Aegyptiaca. For as long as there have been power-hungry conquerors, there have been folks like Acoreus, or Manetho, or Chaeremon, or Pancrates who have been forced to figure out how to shape their expertise around the dangerous curiosity of their powerful interlocutors.

In other words, Rome is but one, latter-day entrant in this history of politically fraught external interest in Egyptian traditions. In a narrow sense, Manetho begot Aegyptiaca as the same kind of Ptolemaic adviser as the fictional Acoreus. His cultural translation of Egyptian dynastic history was born under the same set of circumstances: navigating how best to present Egyptian sensibilities around kingship to Ptolemaic dynasts keen both to adopt Egyptian trappings of rule and to elevate Greekness as a proxy for citizenship and socioeconomic mobility. That dual framework constantly overhangs imperial-era Egyptians' approach to Aegyptiaca. Their attempts to naturalize the joins between things Greek and things Egyptian, Homer and the Nile, or Stoicism and hieroglyphic, reflect well the way that auto-ethnographers ancient and modern must carefully navigate the uneven terrain on which they and their audience stand.

Authors of Aegyptiaca thus sought simultaneously to remain faithful to inherited Egyptian sensibilities, reflect ongoing cultural mixture within Egypt, and advance along the paths to Rome and the emperor carved by the layered histories of Kushite, Persian, Ptolemaic, and Roman control of Egypt. To assess Aegyptiaca exclusively through a yes-no evaluation of cultural fidelity misses out on the interconnected motivations that animate cultural translation under colonial rule. But by the same token, authors of Aegyptiaca wrote what they wrote with set social and economic motivations in mind. Chaeremon, one popular choice for Acoreus's inspiration, leveraged his expertise in priestly wisdom and the hieroglyphic script to become Nero's tutor. Apion gained Alexandrian citizenship because of his intellectual production. Pancrates's interview with Hadrian secured him membership in the Museum. Presentation of the Exodus story, one through-line for Aegyptiaca, responded to the zero-sum game for Roman support that pitted Alexandrian Greeks, Jews, and Egyptians against each other. Acoreus is such a productive figure for a retrospective on Aegyptiaca because his interview with Caesar collapses the broad social hierarchies surrounding auto-ethnography into a one-on-one interview between thinker and tyrant, Egyptian and Roman, speaker and audience.

AEGYPTIACA, BERNAL, AND THE IMPORTANCE OF POSTERIORITY

Acoreus's meeting with Caesar, like Aegyptiaca's presentation of Egyptian traditions to Greeks and Romans, is self-consciously posterior. Caesar and Acoreus both position themselves against a mythologized set of encounters through which the former's imperial ambition and the latter's elucidation of long-guarded Egyptian wisdom gain shape. That mythologization is so potent because it imagines an original moment of cultural contact that precedes those latter-day meetings—like Acoreus with Caesar or Apion with Caligula or Chaeremon with Nero—on which the *ur*-meeting is patterned. I have tried to reapproach the self-conscious posteriority undergirding Aegyptiaca. Imperial Egyptians' engagement with and presentation of cultural commonplaces like animal cult, hieroglyphic inscriptions, and scribal learning displayed the same inventiveness, playfulness, and strategic rearrangement as that found in imperial Greeks' self-positioning against the classical past.[18]

The Egyptian culture on display in Aegyptiaca gains its authority through a rhetoric of access and of cultural purity that was plastic. It was something constantly molded, shaped, and reformed by imperial Egyptians who were not at all naïve about the reality of cultural mixture that had always been underway in Egypt, from the early-dynastic period onwards. The threads these authors used to splice their own culturally mixed, but still doggedly Egyptian wisdom traditions into a grand narrative of changeless pharaonic culture form a picture of cultural creativity worth viewing on its own terms. The narratives of cultural degradation that have been used to unfavorably compare mixed authors like Apion and Chaeremon with the true-blue Egyptian Manetho speak not to any truth about pharaonic versus Ptolemaic versus Roman Egypt.[19] They instead reflect scholarly anxieties around policing disciplinary boundaries conventionally tethered to ethnic (Greek, Egyptian) and temporal (pharaonic, Ptolemaic, Roman) ones. A need for temporal-cum-disciplinary boundaries makes it so appealing to reach back for a historical moment of cultural contact between the purely Egyptian and Egyptological and the purely Greek and classical.

Martin Bernal's *Black Athena* remains a powerful example of the promise and peril of chasing down a prototypical original meeting, in whose shadow the Acoreus-Caesar encounter operates.[20] The trope of the philosopher's visit to Egypt has become the crux of arguments for Egypt's influence on Greece and, by extension, for Africa's intellectual history and its marginalization in the modern university. Scholars like Bernal and Cheikh Anta Diop zoom in on Pythagoras's and Plato's visits to Egypt when underlining the transmission of canonized bodies of knowledge from Egypt to Greece.[21] There is a long shadow cast by this archetypal narrative. In antiquity, Caesar tendentiously imagines himself as an intellectually curious tutee to add philosophical legitimacy to his Roman cooption of Egyptian ideologies of Nile conquest. In the twentieth century, figures like Pythagoras and

---

18. Whitmarsh (2001, 32) captures well imperial Greeks' creative rather than slavish imitation of the classical past.

19. Fowden (1986, 65) and Burstein (1996, 603).

20. Bernal (1987–2006) broadly covers Egypt's (and Phoenicia's) influence on the formation of Greek culture and the European (Aryan Model, in his terms) tradition that has sought to erase that influence. Part of the lingering controversy is in Bernal's insistence on the historicity of narratives of Egyptian colonization of Greece and of philosophers' visits to Egypt. For a measured response, see the archaeological perspective offered by Morris (1989).

21. Bernal (1987–2006, I.71–2, 103–18) and Diop (1974, xiv).

206   CONCLUSION

Plato proved that Egypt, and Africa more broadly, attained significant cultural achievements in which Africans and Africans in the diaspora should take pride.[22]

I have tried to show, in the specific *topos* of philosophy's Egyptian origins, how frequently that narrative was shaped and bent. It underwent constant rearticulation, simultaneously indebted to and making meaningful the translation of Egyptian wisdom that took hold in the social conditions of Ptolemaic and Roman Egypt. This is not to erase any possibility for tracing back moments of contact and influence into the past. Already in Herodotus, Pythagoreanism's, Empedocleanism's, and Orphism's Egyptian roots were being postulated. Certainly, the narrative of origins—of Egypt's place out and ahead of the formation of Greek culture—is an important one whose place in Afrocentrist thought I do not want to discount or minimize. But to confidently stake claims for the genesis of that contact hits up against the ongoing and expansive process of cultural mixture that I have been underlining through Glissant's creolization.

In other words, there is something to be said for a making and remaking and remaking again of the "Greek" that abandons origins in favor of an ongoing formation of cultural canons. After all, the Greek past only became classical under Rome, with Aulus Gellius's retrospective view.[23] That has inaugurated a raft of important work on the social conditions that gave rise to imperial Greeks' creative reimagination of the classical past in their own moment. What has yet to be appreciated is how Aegyptiaca (and beyond it the mixture of Greek and indigenous traditions broadly characteristic of the Hellenistic world) is an equally important mode of reforming and reimagining the classical past. Thrasyllus, a Greco-Egyptian author, canonized Plato and his corpus. A philosophy of the soul became the object of a set path of movement from India and Egypt to Greece and then Rome. As Apion makes clear, the consolidation of Homeric scholarship in Alexandria was not immune to that city's mix of Greek and Egyptian intellectual milieux. Seeing this work of cultural mixture in process better shows how the plural identities of the imperial world—onto which Aegyptiaca provides a view—is not just relevant to, but is in fact constitutive of the gestation of a canon of traditions that then became classical. Authors who were simultaneously African and Greek and Roman occupied an inarguably central role in this post hoc making of the classical, whether that "classical" is the Greek or pharaonic past.

MULTICULTURALISM BEYOND RECEPTION

Aegyptiaca can be a productive place where core, unresolved questions posed by Bernal can continue to be discussed without the strain that historical origins tend

---

22. Pythagoras's visit to Egypt is the opening gambit of James (1954, 9), a key if controversial text representing US Afrocentrist engagement with this issue.

23. For the passage, see Aul. Gell. 19.8.15, and discussion by Citroni (2007), who notes the analogization between canonized authors and Rome's social structure.

CONCLUSION   207

to place on the available linguistic or archaeological or literary evidence. There is an eighteenth- and nineteenth-century history that explains the division of mixed Greek and Egyptian intellectual expertise into separable parts slotted into disparate disciplinary fiefdoms.[24] Apion the Homerist lives apart, in a distinct repository of knowledge, from Apion the chronicler of Egyptian history. Pancrates the magician only approaches Pancrates the Alexandrian poet tangentially, in the margins of commentaries that are themselves deeply marginal to disciplinary centers. Tiberius Claudius Balbillus the capable Roman administrator and Tiberius Claudius Balbillus the Greco-Egyptian astrologer become two entirely different people.

The list goes on. But part of what makes this division of the Greco-Roman from the Egyptian so troublingly durative is that it is often much less ideologically malicious than Bernal's history would have it. German Romanticism and the rise of the modern university, whose formation of an isolated Greece Bernal and others have analyzed, cannot explain entirely the acts of erasure that have plagued Aegyptiaca and other literatures that mixed indigenous and canonically "classical" bodies of knowledge. I have tried to show that much of the problem is mundane— it runs into the nitty-gritty of prosopography and fragments and alienatingly technical knowledge traditions. Put simply, much of the ancient world's vibrant cross-cultural mixture has resided in disciplinary nooks and crannies. These sites of entanglement between Greco-Roman and other Mediterranean intellectual histories have not so much been erased as they have gathered dust.

I find that surprisingly reassuring. There is nothing inevitable or necessary in the glue binding Classics's subject and method. One can move away from a singular focus on Greece and Rome while maintaining the methodological values— doing a lot with little evidence; close reading and incisive lexicography; working between historical and archaeological and literary-critical sensibilities—that have come to define the discipline. In fact, I hope to have suggested in this book that we *need* those methodological tools to push back against Greece and Rome's outsized place in the study of the ancient Mediterranean.

A rich engagement with those values is a point of departure for a more significant reevaluation of where to locate the boundaries of the classical. When thinking through those boundaries, I hope to have shown that Classics should not only be broadened by reception studies, by widening the communities who engaged with a canon of Greek and Roman traditions. We must also begin to widen the peoples and traditions that are considered central to the study of the ancient Mediterranean world. The integration and then reinvention of the Greek and Roman within a local context—the dynamics that make reception studies so vibrant—have been

---

24. This history obviously intersects with that treated by the first volume of Bernal (1987–2006), but has its own points of departure. Dionisotti (1997) discusses the much longer history of collecting fragments, which has materially contributed to the continued marginalization of Aegyptiaca as a tradition.

208   CONCLUSION

there from the beginning, if on the disciplinary sidelines. Already in the ancient world, culturally mixed authors blended their own traditions with a socially, politically, and economically valorized canon of Greek knowledge remade under the shadow of a Roman imperial regime. If the reception of *that* ancient Mediterranean world has not been written, it might yet be.

WORKS CITED

Acosta-Hughes, Benjamin, and Susan A. Stephens. 2012. *Callimachus in Context: From Plato to the Augustan Poets*. Cambridge, UK: Cambridge University Press.

Adkins, A. W. H. 1978. "*Theoria* versus *Praxis* in the *Nicomachean Ethics* and the *Republic*." *Classical Philology* 73, no. 4: 297–313.

Adler, Ada. 1928–1938. *Suidae Lexicon*. 5 vols. Leipzig: Teubner.

Aicher, Peter. 1989. "Ennius' Dream of Homer." *American Journal of Philology* 110, no. 2: 227–32.

Allen, James P. 2000. *Middle Egyptian: An Introduction to the Language and Culture of Hieroglyphs*. Cambridge, UK: Cambridge University Press.

———. 2011. *The Debate between a Man and His Soul: A Masterpiece of Ancient Egyptian Literature*. Leiden: Brill.

———. 2015. *Middle Egyptian Literature: Eight Literary Works of the Middle Kingdom*. Cambridge, UK: Cambridge University Press.

Allen, Thomas George. 1974. *The Book of the Dead or Going Forth by Day: Ideas of the Ancient Egyptians Concerning the Hereafter as Expressed in Their Own Terms*. Chicago: University of Chicago Press.

Alliot, Maurice. 1950. "Le culte d'Horus à Edfou au temps des Ptolémées." *Revue de l'histoire des religions* 137, no. 1: 59–104.

Alston, Richard. 1997. "Philo's *In Flaccum*: Ethnicity and Social Space in Roman Alexandria." *Greece & Rome* 44, no. 2: 165–75.

Alt, Karin. 1993. *Weltflucht und Weltbejahung: zur Frage des Dualismus bei Plutarch, Numenios, Plotin*. Mainz: Akademie der Wissenschaften und der Literatur.

Althusser, Louis. 2001. *Lenin and Philosophy, and Other Essays*. Translated by Ben Brewster. New York: Monthly Review Press.

Anagnostou-Canas, Barbara. 1989–1990. "Rapports de dépendance coloniale dans l'Egypte ptolemaique: I. L'appareil militaire." *Bullettino dell'Istituto di Diritto Romano "Vittorio Scialoja"* 31–32: 151–236.

———. 1992. "Rapports de dépendance coloniale dans l'Égypte ptolémaïque: II. Les rebelles de la chôra." In *Proceedings of the XIXth Congress of Papyrology, Cairo, 2–9 September 1989*, edited by A. A. S. El-Mosalamy, 323–72. Cairo: Ain Shams University, Center of Papyrological Studies.

Anderson, Benedict. 1991. *Imagined Communities: Reflections on the Origin and Spread of Nationalism*. New York: Verso.

Andrews, Carol. 1994. *Amulets of Ancient Egypt*. London: British Museum Press.

Arnold, Dieter. 1999. *Temples of the Last Pharaohs*. Oxford: Oxford University Press.

Assmann, Jan. 1990. *Ma'at: Gerechtigkeit und Unsterblichkeit im alten Ägypten*. Munich: Beck.

———. 2001a. *The Search for God in Ancient Egypt*. Translated by David Lorton. Ithaca: Cornell University Press.

———. 2001b. *Tod und Jenseits im alten Ägypten*. Munich: Beck.

———. 2002. "Pythagoras und Lucius: zwei Formen 'ägyptischer Mysterien.'" In *Ägyptische Mysterien?*, edited by Jan Assmann and Martin Bommas, 59–75. Munich: Wilhelm Fink.

Aston, Emma. 2017. *Mixanthrôpoi: Animal-Human Hybrid Deities in Greek Religion*. Liège: Presses universitaires de Liège.

Aufrère, Sydney. 2014. "Manéthon et la médiation du *Livre Sacré*." In *Alexandrie la divine*, edited by Charles Méla, et al., 538–43. Genève: Éditions de la Baconnière.

Aufrère, Sydney, and Marie-Hélène Marganne. 2019. "Encounters Between Greek and Egyptian Science." In *A Companion to Greco-Roman and Late Antique Egypt*, edited by Katelijn Vandorpe, 501–18. Medford, MA: Wiley-Blackwell.

Ax, Wilhelm, ed. 1980. *M. Tulli Ciceronis scripta quae manserunt omnia. Fasc. 45: De natura deorum*. Berlin: De Gruyter.

Bagnall, Roger S. 1997. "Decolonizing Ptolemaic Egypt." In *Hellenistic Constructs: Essays in Culture, History, and Historiography*, edited by Paul Cartledge, Peter Garnsey, and Erich S. Gruen, 225–41. Berkeley: University of California Press.

Bailey, David R. Shackleton, ed. 1997. *Marcus Annaeus Lucanus. De bello civili libri X*. 2nd ed. Berlin: De Gruyter.

———. 2015. *Statius: Silvae*. Cambridge, MA: Harvard University Press.

Baines, John. 1976. "Temple Symbolism." *RAIN* 15: 10–15.

Baker, Philip, and Peter Mühlhäusler. 2007. "Creole Linguistics from Its Beginnings, through Schuchardt to the Present Day." In *Creolization: History, Ethnography, Theory*, edited by Charles Stewart, 84–107. Walnut Creek, CA: Left Coast Press.

Baldwin, Barry. 1979. "Juvenal's Crispinus." *Acta Classica* 22: 109–14.

Barclay, John M. G. 1998. "Josephus v. Apion: Analysis of an Argument." In *Understanding Josephus: Seven Perspectives*, edited by Steve Mason, 194–221. Sheffield: Sheffield Academic Press.

———. 2007. *Flavius Josephus: Translation and Commentary. Vol. 10: Against Apion*. Leiden: Brill.

Bar-Kochva, Bezalel. 2010. *The Image of the Jews in Greek Literature: The Hellenistic Period*. Berkeley: University of California Press.

Barnes, Jonathan. 1982. *The Presocratic Philosophers*. London: Routledge.

Barrett, Caitlín Eilis. 2019. *Domesticating Empire: Egyptian Landscapes in Pompeian Gardens*. Oxford: Oxford University Press.

Barzanò, Alberto. 1985. "Cheremone di Alessandri." *Aufstieg und Niedergang der römischen Welt* 2.32.3: 1981–2001.

Battezzato, Luigi. 2008. "Pythagorean Comedies from Epicharmus to Alexis." *Aevum Antiquum* N.S. 8: 139–64.

Beagon, Mary. 2009. "Ordering Wonderland: Ovid's Pythagoras and the Augustan Vision." In *Paradox and the Marvellous in Augustan Literature and Culture*, edited by Philip Hardie, 288–309. Oxford: Oxford University Press.

Beaujeu, Jean. 1973. *Apulée. Opuscules philosophiques (Du dieu de Socrate, Platon et sa doctrine, Du monde) et Fragments*. Paris: Les Belles Lettres.

Benaissa, Amin. 2010. "The Onomastic Evidence for the God Hermanubis." In *Proceedings of the 25th International Congress of Papyrology: Ann Arbor, July 29-August 4, 2007*, edited by Traianos Gagos, 67–68. Ann Arbor: University of Michigan Library.

Benson, Geoffrey C. 2019. *Apuleius' Invisible Ass: Encounters with the Unseen in the Metamorphoses*. Cambridge, UK: Cambridge University Press.

Berardi, Roberta. 2021. "Collecting Fragments for a Fragmentary Literary Genre: The Case of Greek Hellenistic Oratory." In *The Continuity of Classical Literature through Fragmentary Traditions*, edited by Francesco Ginelli and Francesco Lupi, 79–102. Berlin: De Gruyter.

Bernal, Martin. 1987–2006. *Black Athena: The Afroasiatic Roots of Classical Civilization*. 3 vols. New Brunswick, NJ: Rutgers University Press.

———. 2001. *Black Athena Writes Back: Martin Bernal Responds to His Critics*. Edited by David Chioni Moore. Durham: Duke University Press.

Bernand, André, and Étienne Bernand. 1960. *Les inscriptions grecques et latines du Colosse de Memnon*. Paris: Imprimerie de l'institut français d'archéologie orientale.

Betz, Hans Dieter, ed. 1986. *The Greek Magical Papyri in Translation, Including the Demotic Spells*. 2nd ed. Chicago: University of Chicago Press.

Bhabha, Homi. 1990. "The Third Space." In *Identity: Community, Culture, Difference*, edited by Jonathan Rutherford, 207–21. London: Lawrence and Wishart.

———. 1994. *The Location of Culture*. London: Routledge.

Bietak, Manfred. 1996. *Avaris, the Capital of the Hyksos: Recent Excavations at Tell El-Dab'a*. London: British Museum Press.

Bilde, Per. 2006. "The Jews in Alexandria in 38–41 CE." *Hephaistos* 24: 257–67.

Blackman, Aylward M., and W. Vivian Davies. 1988. *The Story of King Kheops and the Magicians Transcribed from Papyrus Westcar (Berlin Papyrus 3033)*. Reading, UK: J. V. Books.

Blackman, Aylward M., and H. W. Fairman. 1942. "The Myth of Horus at Edfu—II. C. The Triumph of Horus over His Enemies: A Sacred Drama." *Journal of Egyptian Archaeology* 28: 32–38.

———. 1946. "The Consecration of an Egyptian Temple According to the Use of Edfu." *Journal of Egyptian Archaeology* 32: 75–91.

Boas, George. 1993. *The Hieroglyphics of Horapollo*. Princeton: Princeton University Press.

Boissevain, Ursul Philip, ed. 1895–1901. *Cassii Dionis Cocceiani historiarum Romanarum quae supersunt*. 3 vols. Berlin: Weidmannos.

WORKS CITED

Bonneau, Danielle. 1991. "Le sacrifice du porc et Liloïtion en Pactiôn." *Chronique d'Egypte* 66, no. 131–132: 330–40.

Bowditch, P. Lowell. 2011. "Tibullus and Egypt: A Postcolonial Reading of Elegy 1.7." *Arethusa* 44, no. 1: 89–122.

Bowersock, G. W. 1997. "Jacoby's Fragments and Two Greek Historians of Pre-Islamic Arabia." In *Collecting Fragments [Fragmente sammeln]*, edited by Glenn W. Most, 173–85. Göttingen: Vandenhoeck und Ruprecht.

Bowie, Ewen L. 1990. "Greek Poetry in the Antonine Age." In *Antonine Literature*, edited by D. A. Russell, 53–90. Oxford: Clarendon Press.

Bowman, Alan K., and Dominic Rathbone. 1992. "Cities and Administration in Roman Egypt." *Journal of Roman Studies* 82: 107–27.

Bremmer, Jan M. 2021. "The Theriomorphism of the Major Greek Gods." In *Animals in Ancient Greek Religion*, edited by Julia Kindt, 102–25. London: Routledge.

Brenk, Frederick E. 1987. "An Imperial Heritage. The Religious Spirit of Plutarch of Chaironeia." *Aufsteig und Niedergang der römischen Welt* 2.36.1: 248–349.

———. 1999. "'Isis Is a Greek Word': Plutarch's Allegorization of Egyptian Religion." In *Plutarco, Platón y Aristóteles: Actas Del V Congreso Internacional de La I.P.S. (Madrid-Cuenca, 4–7 de Mayo de 1999)*, edited by Aurelio Pérez Jiménez, José García López, and Rosa María Aguilar, 227–38. Madrid: Edition Clásicas.

———. 2017. "'Searching for Truth?': Plutarch's *On Isis and Osiris*." In *Platonismus und spätägyptische Religion: Plutarch und die Ägyptenrezeption in der römischen Kaiserzeit*, edited by Michael Erler and Martin Andreas Stadler, 55–77. Berlin: De Gruyter.

Brennan, T. Corey. 1998. "The Poets Julia Balbilla and Damo at the Colossus of Memnon." *Classical World* 91, no. 4: 215–34.

Bricault, Laurent. 2000–2001. "Les Anubophores." *Bulletin de la Société égyptologique de Genève* 24: 29–42.

———, ed. 2004. *Isis en occident: actes du IIème Colloque international sur les études isiaques, Lyon III 16–17 mai 2002*. Leiden: Brill.

Bricault, Laurent, Miguel John Versluys, and Paul G. P. Meyboom, eds. 2007. *Nile into Tiber: Egypt in the Roman World: Proceedings of the IIIrd International Conference of Isis Studies, Faculty of Archaeology, Leiden University, May 11–14, 2005*. Leiden: Brill.

Bricault, Laurent, and Miguel John Versluys, eds. 2010. *Isis on the Nile: Proceedings of the IVth International Conference of Isis Studies, Liege, November 27–29, 2008*. Leiden: Brill.

———, eds. 2014. *Power, Politics, and the Cults of Isis: Proceedings of the Vth International Conference of Isis Studies, Boulogne-Sur-Mer, October 13–15, 2011*. Leiden: Brill.

Brisson, Luc. 2007. "Aristoxenus: His Evidence on Pythagoras and the Pythagoreans. The Case of Philolaus." In *Die griechische Biographie in hellenistischer Zeit: Akten des internationalen Kongresses vom 26–29. Juli 2006 in Würzburg*, edited by Michael Erler and Stefan Schorn, 269–84. Berlin: De Gruyter.

Britton, Celia. 1999. *Edouard Glissant and Postcolonial Theory: Strategies of Language and Resistance*. Charlottesville: University of Virginia Press.

Broze, Michèle. 1996. *Les aventures d'Horus et Seth dans le Papyrus Chester Beatty I: mythe et roman en Egypte ancienne*. Leuven: Peeters.

Budge, E. A. Wallis. 1904. *The Decrees of Memphis and Canopus*. London: K. Paul.

———. 1994. *Legends of the Egyptian Gods: Hieroglyphic Texts and Translations*. London: Dover.

Bull, Christian H. 2018. *The Tradition of Hermes Trismegistus the Egyptian Priestly Figure as a Teacher of Hellenized Wisdom*. Leiden: Brill.

Burkert, Walter. 1972. *Lore and Science in Ancient Pythagoreanism*. Translated by Edwin L. Minar Jr. Cambridge, MA: Harvard University Press.

———. 1995. *The Orientalizing Revolution: Near Eastern Influence on Greek Culture in the Early Archaic Age*. Translated by Margaret E. Pinder. Cambridge, MA: Harvard University Press.

———. 2008. "Prehistory of Presocratic Philosophy in an Orientalizing Context." In *The Oxford Handbook of Presocratic Philosophy*, edited by Daniel W. Graham and Patricia Curd, 55–87. Oxford: Oxford University Press.

Burstein, Stanley M. 1996. "Images of Egypt in Greek Historiography." In *Ancient Egyptian Literature: History and Forms*, edited by Antonio Loprieno, 591–604. Leiden: Brill.

———. 2015. "Thrasyllos of Mendes (622)." In *Brill's New Jacoby*, edited by Ian Worthington. Leiden: Brill.

———. 2016. "Pankrates the Egyptian (625)." In *Brill's New Jacoby*, edited by Ian Worthington. Leiden: Brill.

Buxton, Richard. 2009. *Forms of Astonishment: Greek Myths of Metamorphosis*. Oxford: Oxford University Press.

Cameron, Alan. 2004. *Greek Mythography in the Roman World*. Oxford: Oxford University Press.

Cantor, Lea. 2022. "Thales—the 'First Philosopher'? A Troubled Chapter in the Historiography of Philosophy." *British Journal for the History of Philosophy* 30, no. 5: 727–50.

Casanova, Angelo. 2012. "Plutarch as Apollo's Priest at Delphi." In *Plutarch in the Religious and Philosophical Discourse of Late Antiquity*, edited by Lautaro Roig Lanzillotta and Israel Muñoz Gallarte, 151–57. Leiden: Brill.

Catastini, Alessandro. 2010. "*Hieogrammateus* in Flavius Josephus, *Contra Apionem* I, 290." *Rivista di cultura classica e medioevale* 52, no. 1: 133–37.

Cauville, Sylvie. 1990. *Le temple de Dendera: guide archéologique*. Cairo: Institut français d'archéologie orientale.

———. 1991. "Les inscriptions dédicatoires du temple d'Hathor à Dendera." *Bulletin de l'institut français d'archéologie orientale* 90: 83–114.

———. 1997. *Le temple de Dendara: les chapelles osirienne*. 3 vols. Cairo: Institut français d'archéologique orientale.

Chakrabarty, Dipesh. 2008. *Provincializing Europe: Postcolonial Thought and Historical Difference*. Princeton: Princeton University Press.

Chassinat, Émile. 1897–1934. *Le Temple d'Edfou*. 14 vols. Cairo: Imprimerie de l'institut français d'archéologie orientale.

———. 1931. *Le Temple d'Edfou. Vol. 6*. Cairo: Imprimerie de l'institut français d'archéologie orientale.

Chauveau, Michel. 2017. "L'Agneau revisité ou la révélation d'un crime de guerre ignoré." In *Illuminating Osiris: Egyptological Studies in Honor of Mark Smith*, edited by Richard Jasnow and Ghislaine Widmer, 37–69. Atlanta: Lockwood Press.

214   WORKS CITED

Chiaradonna, Riccardo. 2009. "Autour d'Eudore: les débuts de l'exégèse des Catégories dans le Moyen Platonisme." In *The Origins of the Platonic System: Platonisms of the Early Empire and Their Philosophical Contexts*, edited by Mauro Bonazzi and Jan Opsomer, 89–111. Leuven: Peeters.

Chrubasik, Boris, and Daniel King, eds. 2017. *Hellenism and the Local Communities of the Eastern Mediterranean: 400 BCE–250 CE*. Oxford: Oxford University Press.

Cichorius, Conrad. 1927. "Der Astrologe Ti. Claudius Balbillus, Sohn des Thrasyllus." *Rheinisches Museum für Philologie* 76, no. 1: 102–5.

Citroni, Mario. 2007. "Gellio, 19, 8, 15 e la storia di classicus." *Materiali e discussioni per l'analisi dei testi classici* 58: 181–205.

Clarysse, Willy. 2009. "The Real Name of Dionysios Petosarapis." In *Elkab and Beyond: Studies in Honour of Luc Limme*, edited by Wouter Claes, Herman de Meulenaere, and Stan Hendrickx, 213–22. Leuven: Peeters.

Clarysse, Willy, and Dorothy J. Thompson. 2006. *Counting the People in Hellenistic Egypt*. Cambridge, UK: Cambridge University Press.

Clausen, Wendell, ed. 1992. *A. Persi Flacci et D. Juni Juvenalis saturae*. Oxford: Clarendon Press.

Cohen, Getzel M. 1983. "Colonization and Population Transfer in the Hellenistic World." In *Egypt and the Hellenistic World. Proceedings of the International Colloquium, Leuven, 24–26 May 1982*, edited by Edmond Van't Dack, P. van Dessel, and Wilfried van Gucht, 63–74. Leuven: Orientaliste.

Collins, John Joseph. 2005. "Anti-Semitism in Antiquity? The Case of Alexandria." *Archiv für Religionsgeschichte* 7: 86–101.

Cornell, Tim J., ed. 2013. *The Fragments of the Roman Historians. Vol. I: Introduction*. Oxford: Oxford University Press.

Cornelli, Gabriele, Richard D. McKirahan, Constantinos Macris, and Beatriz Bossi, eds. 2013. *On Pythagoreanism*. Berlin: De Gruyter.

Coussement, Sandra. 2016. *"Because I Am Greek": Polyonymy as an Expression of Ethnicity in Ptolemaic Egypt*. Leuven: Peeters.

Cramer, Frederick Henry. 1954. *Astrology in Roman Law and Politics*. Philadelphia: American Philosophical Society.

Cumont, Franz Valéry Marie. 1937. *L'Égypte des astrologues*. Brussels: Fondation égyptologique reine Élisabeth.

Damon, Cynthia. 2008. "'The Mind of an Ass and the Impudence of a Dog': A Scholar Gone Bad." In *KAKOS, Badness and Anti-Value in Classical Antiquity*, edited by Ineke Sluiter and Ralph M. Rosen, 335–64. Leiden: Brill.

———. 2011. "Pliny on Apion." In *Pliny the Elder: Themes and Contexts*, edited by Roy Gibson and Ruth Morello, 131–46. Leiden: Brill.

Darnell, John Coleman. 2020. "Ancient Egyptian Cryptography: Graphic Hermeneutics." In *Enigmatic Writing in the Egyptian New Kingdom. Vol. I: Revealing, Transforming, and Display in Egyptian Hieroglyphs*, edited by David Klotz and Andréas Stauder, 7–48. Berlin: De Gruyter.

Daumas, François. 1952. *Les moyens d'expression du Grec et de l'Egyptien comparés dans les décrets de Canope et de Memphis*. Cairo: Imprimerie de l'institut français d'archéologie orientale.

———. 1988–1995. *Valeurs phonétiques des signes hiéroglyphiques d'époque gréco-romaine.* 4 vols. Montpellier: Université de Montpellier.

de Plinval, Georges, ed. 1968. *Cicéron: traité des lois.* Paris: Les Belles Lettres.

DeFilippo, Joseph G. 1990. "*Curiositas* and the Platonism of Apuleius' *Golden Ass.*" *American Journal of Philology* 111, no. 4: 471–92.

Delatte, Armand. 1915. *Études sur la littérature pythagoricienne.* Paris: Champion.

Deleuze, Gilles, and Félix Guattari. 1980. *Mille plateaux: capitalisme et schizophrénie.* Paris: Les Éditions de Minuit.

Delia, Diana. 1988. "The Population of Roman Alexandria." *Transactions of the American Philological Association* 118: 275–92.

———. 1991. *Alexandrian Citizenship during the Roman Principate.* Atlanta: Scholars Press.

Demougin, Ségolène. 1994. "L'ordre équestre sous Domitien." In *Les années Domitien: colloque organisé à l'Université de Toulouse-Le Mirail,* edited by J.-M. Pailler and R. Sablayrolles, 289–99. Toulouse: Presses universitaires du Mirail.

Dench, Emma. 2013. "The Scope of Ancient Ethnography." In *Ancient Ethnography: New Approaches,* edited by Eran Almagor and Joseph Skinner, 257–67. London: Bloomsbury.

Depuydt, Leo. 1995. "Murder in Memphis: The Story of Cambyses's Mortal Wounding of the Apis Bull (ca. 523 B.C.E.)." *Journal of Near Eastern Studies* 54, no. 2: 119–26.

Derchain, Philippe. 1976. "Symbols and Metaphors in Literature and Representations of Private Life." *RAIN,* no. 15: 7–10.

———. 2000. *Les impondérables de l'hellénisation: littérature d'hiérogrammates.* Turnhout: Brepols.

Dickie, Matthew. 2001. *Magic and Magicians in the Greco-Roman World.* London: Routledge.

Dieleman, Jacco. 2005. *Priests, Tongues, and Rites: The London-Leiden Magical Manuscripts and Translation in Egyptian Ritual (100–300 CE).* Leiden: Brill.

Dijkstra, Jitse H. F. 2008. *Philae and the End of Ancient Egyptian Religion: A Regional Study of Religious Transformation (298–642 CE).* Leuven: Peeters.

Dillery, John. 1998. "Hecataeus of Abdera: Hyperboreans, Egypt, and the *Interpretatio Graeca.*" *Historia* 47, no. 3: 255–75.

———. 1999. "The First Egyptian Narrative History: Manetho and Greek Historiography." *Zeitschrift für Papyrologie und Epigraphik* 127: 93–116.

———. 2002. "Quintus Fabius Pictor and Greco-Roman Historiography at Rome." In *"Vertis in Usum": Studies in Honor of Edward Courtney,* edited by John F. Miller, Cynthia Damon, and K. Sara Myers, 1–23. Leipzig: Teubner.

———. 2003. "Putting Him Back Together Again: Apion Historian, Apion *Grammatikos.*" *Classical Philology* 98, no. 4: 383–90.

———. 2015. *Clio's Other Sons: Berossus and Manetho, with an Afterword on Demetrius.* Ann Arbor: University of Michigan Press.

———. 2016. "Literary Interaction between Greece and Egypt: Manetho and Synchronism." In *Greco-Egyptian Interactions: Literature, Translation, and Culture, 500 BCE–300 CE,* edited by Ian Rutherford, 107–37. Oxford: Oxford University Press.

Dillon, John M. 1988. "'Orthodoxy' and 'Eclectism': Middle Platonists and Neo-Pythagoreans." In *The Question of "Eclecticism:" Studies in Later Greek Philosophy,* edited by A. A. Long and John M. Dillon, 103–25. Berkeley: University of California Press.

———. 1997. *The Middle Platonists, 80 B.C. to A.D. 220.* Ithaca: Cornell University Press.

216 WORKS CITED

———. 2019. *The Roots of Platonism: The Origins and Chief Features of a Philosophical Tradition*. Cambridge, UK: Cambridge University Press.

Dionisotti, Anna Carlotta. 1997. "On Fragments in Classical Scholarship." In *Collecting Fragments [Fragmente sammeln]*, edited by Glenn W. Most, 1–33. Göttingen: Vandenhoeck und Ruprecht.

Diop, Cheikh Anta. 1974. *The African Origin of Civilization: Myth or Reality*. Translated by Mercer Cook. New York: L. Hill.

D'Onofrio, Cesare. 1965. *Gli obelischi di Roma*. Rome: Bulzoni.

Dorandi, Tiziano. 2013. *Diogenes Laertius: Lives of Eminent Philosophers*. Cambridge, UK: Cambridge University Press.

Drabinski, John E. 2019. *Glissant and the Middle Passage: Philosophy, Beginning, Abyss*. Minneapolis: University of Minnesota Press.

Droge, A. J. 2001. "Retrofitting/Retiring 'Syncretism.'" *Historical Reflections* 27, no. 3: 375–87.

Droysen, Johann Gustav. 1836–43. *Geschichte des Hellenismus*. 3 vols. Hamburg: Perthes.

Dunand, Françoise. 1973. *Le culte d'Isis dans le bassin oriental de la Méditerranée*. 3 vols. Leiden: Brill.

Dunand, Françoise, and Christiane Zivie-Coche. 2004. *Gods and Men in Egypt: 3000 BCE to 395 CE*. Translated by David Lorton. Ithaca: Cornell University Press.

DuQuesne, Terence. 1998. "Seth and the Jackals." In *Egyptian Religion: The Last Thousand Years: Studies Dedicated to the Memory of Jan Quaegebeur*, edited by Willy Clarysse, Anton Schoors, and Harco Willems, 613–28. Leuven: Peeters.

Edmonds, J. M. 1925. "The Epigrams of Balbilla." *Classical Review* 39, no. 5/6: 107–10.

Egelhaaf-Gaiser, Ulrike. 2000. *Kulträume im römischen Alltag: das Isisbuch des Apuleius und der Ort von Religion im kaiserzeitlichen Rom*. Stuttgart: Franz Steiner.

———. 2012. "The Gleaming Pate of the *Pastophorus*: Masquerade or Embodied Lifestyle?" In *Aspects of Apuleius' Golden Ass. Vol. III: The Isis Book*, edited by Wytse Hette Keulen and Ulrike Egelhaaf-Gaiser, 42–70. Leiden: Brill.

Engsheden, Åke. 2016. "Traditional Egyptian II." In *UCLA Encyclopedia of Egyptology*, edited by Julie Stauder-Porchet, Andréas Stauder, and Willeke Wendrich. https://escholarship.org/uc/item/8g73w3gp.

Erler, Michael, and Martin Andreas Stadler, eds. 2017. *Platonismus und spätägyptische Religion: Plutarch und die Ägyptenrezeption in der römischen Kaiserzeit*. Berlin: De Gruyter.

Erman, Adolf. 1917. *Römische Obelisken*. Berlin: Verlag der königlichen Akademie der Wissenschaften zu Berlin.

Escolano-Poveda, Marina. 2020. *The Egyptian Priests of the Graeco-Roman Period: An Analysis on the Basis of the Egyptian and Graeco-Roman Literary and Paraliterary Sources*. Wiesbaden: Harrassowitz.

Evans, James. 1998. *The History and Practice of Ancient Astronomy*. Oxford: Oxford University Press.

Evans, T. V., and Dirk Obbink, eds. 2010. *The Language of the Papyri*. Oxford: Oxford University Press.

Fairman, H. W. 1935. "The Myth of Horus at Edfu: I." *Journal of Egyptian Archaeology* 21, no. 1: 26–36.

———, ed. 1974. *The Triumph of Horus: An Ancient Egyptian Sacred Drama*. London: Batsford.

Fantham, Elaine. 2011. "A Controversial Life." In *Brill's Companion to Lucan*, edited by Paolo Asso, 3–20. Leiden: Brill.

Farrell, Joseph. 1998. Review of *Vergil's Aeneid: Augustan Epic and Political Context*, by Hans-Peter Stahl. *Vergilius* 44: 115–25.

Feldherr, Andrew. 2021. "Caesar or Cleopatra? Lucan's Tragic Queen." In *Identities, Ethnicities and Gender in Antiquity*, edited by Jacqueline Fabre-Serris, Alison Keith, and Florence Klein, 135–52. Berlin: De Gruyter.

Fentress, Elizabeth. 2013. "Strangers in the City: Élite Communication in the Hellenistic Central Mediterranean." In *The Hellenistic West: Rethinking the Ancient Mediterranean*, edited by Jonathan R. W. Prag and Josephine Crawley Quinn, 157–78. Cambridge: Cambridge University Press.

Fewster, Penelope. 2002. "Bilingualism in Roman Egypt." In *Bilingualism in Ancient Society: Language Contact and the Written Text*, edited by J. N. Adams, Mark Janse, and Simon Swain, 220–45. Oxford: Oxford University Press.

Filos, Panagiotis. 2019. "Aspects of Folk Etymology in Ancient Greek: Insights from Common Nouns." In *Studies in Greek Lexicography*, edited by Georgios K. Giannakis and Christophoros Charalambakis, 159–81. Berlin: De Gruyter.

Finkelpearl, Ellen. 2004. "The Ends of the Metamorphoses, Apuleius *Met.* 11.26.4–11.30." In *Metamorphic Reflections: Essays Presented to Ben Hijmans at His 75th Birthday*, edited by Maaike Zimmerman and R. Th. van der Paardt, 319–42. Leuven: Peeters.

———. 2012. "Egyptian Religion in *Met.* 11 and Plutarch's *DIO*: Culture, Philosophy, and the Ineffable." In *Aspects of Apuleius' Golden Ass. Vol. III: The Isis Book*, edited by Wytse Hette Keulen and Ulrike Egelhaaf-Gaiser, 183–201. Leiden: Brill.

Finnestad, Ragnhild Bjerre. 1985. *Image of the World and Symbol of the Creator: On the Cosmological and Iconological Values of the Temple of Edfu*. Wiesbaden: Harrassowitz.

Flamerie de Lachapelle, Guillaume. 2010. "Nature et rôle du début du discours de Pothin dans le *Bellum ciuile* de Lucain (8.484–495)." In *Lucain en débat: rhétorique, poétique et histoire: actes du colloque international, Institut Ausonius (Pessac, 12–14 juin 2008)*, edited by Olivier Devillers and Sylvie Franchet d'Espèrey, 313–25. Paris: Éditions de Boccard.

Fletcher, Richard. 2014. *Apuleius' Platonism: The Impersonation of Philosophy*. Cambridge, UK: Cambridge University Press.

Flinterman, Jaap-Jan. 1995. *Power, Paideia & Pythagoreanism: Greek Identity, Conceptions of the Relationship Between Philosophers and Monarchs, and Political Ideas in Philostratus' Life of Apollonius*. Amsterdam: J. C. Gieben.

Forbes, Peter Barr Reid, Robert Browning, and Nigel Wilson. 2016. "Tzetzes, Johannes." In *Oxford Classical Dictionary*, edited by Tim Whitmarsh, 4th ed., 1523–24. Oxford: Oxford University Press.

Foster, Frances. 2020. "Bees and Vultures: Egyptian Hieroglyphs in Ammianus Marcellinus." *Classical Quarterly* 70, no. 2: 884–90.

Fowden, Garth. 1986. *The Egyptian Hermes: A Historical Approach to the Late Pagan Mind*. Cambridge, UK: Cambridge University Press.

Frankfort, Henri, and Henriette A. Groenewegen-Frankfort. 1949. *Before Philosophy: The Intellectual Adventure of Ancient Man*. Harmondsworth: Penguin Books.

Frankfurter, David. 1998. *Religion in Roman Egypt: Assimilation and Resistance*. Princeton: Princeton University Press.

―――. 2018. *Christianizing Egypt: Syncretism and Local Worlds in Late Antiquity*. Princeton: Princeton University Press.

Fraser, P. M. 1972. *Ptolemaic Alexandria*. 3 vols. Oxford: Clarendon Press.

Frede, Michael. 1989. "Chaeremon der Stoiker." *Aufsteig und Niedergang der römischen Welt* 2.36.3: 2067–2103.

Frisch, Paulus. 1907. "De compositione libri Plutarchei qui inscribitur *Peri Isidos kai Osiridos*." Burgiae: Academia Georgia Augusta.

Froidefond, Christian. 1971. *Le mirage égyptien dans la littérature grecque d'Homère à Aristote*. Aix-en-Provence: Publications universitaires des Lettres et Sciences humaines d'Aix-en-Provence.

Gabba, Emilio. 1984. "The Historians and Augustus." In *Caesar Augustus: Seven Aspects*, edited by Fergus Millar and Erich Segal, 61–88. Oxford: Clarendon Press.

Gaisser, Julia H. 1971. "Tibullus 1. 7: A Tribute to Messalla." *Classical Philology* 66, no. 4: 221–29.

Galán, José M. 1995. *Victory and Border Terminology Related to Egyptian Imperialism in the XVIIIth Dynasty*. Hildesheim: Gerstenberg.

Galinsky, Karl. 1996. *Augustan Culture: An Interpretive Introduction*. Princeton: Princeton University Press.

Gambetti, Sandra. 2009. *The Alexandrian Riots of 38 C.E. and the Persecution of the Jews: A Historical Reconstruction*. Leiden: Brill.

Gardiner, Alan H. 1905. "Hymns to Amon from a Leiden Papyrus." *Zeitschrift für Ägyptische Sprache und Altertumskunde* 42: 12–42.

―――. 1938. "The House of Life." *Journal of Egyptian Archaeology* 24, no. 2: 157–79.

Gasparini, Valentino. 2017. "Negotiating the Body: Between Religious Investment and Narratological Strategies. Paulina, Decius Mundus and the Priests of Anubis." In *Beyond Priesthood: Religious Entrepreneurs and Innovators in the Roman Empire*, edited by Richard L. Gordon, Georgia Petridou, and Jörg Rüpke, 385–416. Berlin: De Gruyter.

―――. 2018. "Les acteurs sur scène. Théâtre et théâtralisation dans les cultes isiaques." In *Individuals and Materials in the Greco-Roman Cults of Isis: Agents, Images, and Practices*, edited by Valentino Gasparini and Richard Veymiers, 714–46. Leiden: Brill.

Gasparini, Valentino, and Richard Veymiers, eds. 2018. *Individuals and Materials in the Greco-Roman Cults of Isis: Agents, Images, and Practices*. 2 vols. Leiden: Brill.

Geertz, Clifford. 1973. "Thick Description: Toward an Interpretive Theory of Culture." In *The Interpretation of Cultures: Selected Essays*, 1–30. New York: Basic Books.

Geue, Tom. 2017. *Juvenal and the Poetics of Anonymity*. Cambridge, UK: Cambridge University Press.

Ginelli, Francesco, and Francesco Lupi. 2021a. "Introduction." In *The Continuity of Classical Literature through Fragmentary Traditions*, edited by Francesco Ginelli and Francesco Lupi, 1–17. Berlin: De Gruyter.

―――, eds. 2021b. *The Continuity of Classical Literature through Fragmentary Traditions*. Berlin: De Gruyter.

Glissant, Édouard. 1996. *Introduction à une poétique du divers*. Paris: Gallimard.

―――. 1997. *Traité du tout-monde*. Paris: Gallimard.

―――. 2009. *Philosophie de la relation: poésie en étendue*. Paris: Gallimard.

―――. 2020. *Introduction to a Poetics of Diversity*. Translated by Celia Britton. Liverpool: Liverpool University Press.

Goldwasser, Orly. 2002. *Prophets, Lovers and Giraffes: Wor(l)d Classification in Ancient Egypt*. Wiesbaden: Harrassowitz.

———. 2006. "On the New Definition of Classifier Languages and Scripts." *Lingua Aegyptia* 14: 473–84.

Goodman, Martin. 1999. "Josephus' Treatise Against Apion." In *Apologetics in the Roman Empire: Pagans, Jews, and Christians*, edited by M. J. Edwards, Martin Goodman, S. R. F. Price, and Christopher Rowland, 45–58. Oxford: Oxford University Press.

Görgemanns, Herwig. 2017. "Plutarchs Isis-Buch: Hellenisches und Ägyptisches." In *Platonismus und spätägyptische Religion: Plutarch und die Ägyptenrezeption in der römischen Kaiserzeit*, edited by Michael Erler and Martin Andreas Stadler, 7–20. Berlin: De Gruyter.

Graham, Daniel W., ed. 2010. *The Texts of Early Greek Philosophy: The Complete Fragments and Selected Testimonies of the Major Presocratics*. 2 vols. Cambridge, UK: Cambridge University Press.

———. 2014. "Philolaus." In *A History of Pythagoreanism*, edited by Carl A. Huffman, 46–68. Cambridge, UK: Cambridge University Press.

Graverini, Luca. 2012a. *Literature and Identity in the Golden Ass of Apuleius*. Translated by Benjamin Todd Lee. Columbus: Ohio State University Press.

———. 2012b. "*Prudentia* and *Prouidentia*: Book XI in Context." In *Aspects of Apuleius' Golden Ass. Vol. III: The Isis Book*, edited by Wytse Hette Keulen and Ulrike Egelhaaf-Gaiser, 86–106. Leiden: Brill.

Grenier, Jean-Claude. 1987. "Les inscriptions hiérogliphiques de l'obélisque Pamphili." *Mélanges de l'école française de Rome* 99, no. 2: 937–61.

Griffith, F. Ll., and Herbert Thompson. 1921. *The Demotic Magical Papyrus of London and Leiden*. Oxford: Clarendon Press.

Griffiths, J. Gwyn. 1958. "The Interpretation of the Horus-Myth of Edfu." *Journal of Egyptian Archaeology* 44: 75–85.

———. 1960a. *The Conflict of Horus and Seth from Egyptian and Classical Sources: A Study in Ancient Mythology*. Liverpool: Liverpool University Press.

———. 1960b. "The Flight of the Gods Before Typhon, an Unrecognized Myth." *Hermes* 88, no. 3: 374–76.

———. 1967. "Allegory in Greece and Egypt." *Journal of Egyptian Archaeology* 53: 79–102.

———. 1969. "The Tradition of Allegory in Egypt." In *Religions en Égypte hellénistique et romaine: Colloque de Strasbourg, 16–18 Mai, 1967*, edited by P. Derchain, 45–57. Paris: Presses universitaires de France.

———. 1970. *Plutarch's de Iside et Osiride*. Cardiff: University of Wales Press.

———. 1975. *Apuleius of Madauros: The Isis-Book (Metamorphoses, Book XI)*. Leiden: Brill.

———. 2012. "Isis in the *Metamorphoses* of Apuleius." In *Aspects of Apuleius' Golden Ass. Vol. III: The Isis Book*, edited by Wytse Hette Keulen and Ulrike Egelhaaf-Gaiser, 141–61. Leiden: Brill.

Grimm, Alfred. 1994. "Die Inschriften des Antinoosobelisken: Übersetzung und Kommentar." In *Der Obelisk des Antinoos: eine kommentierte Edition*, edited by Hugo Meyer, 27–88. Munich: Wilhelm Fink.

Grossman, Eitan, and Stéphane Polis. 2012. "Navigating Polyfunctionality in the Lexicon: Semantic Maps and Ancient Egyptian Lexical Semantics." In *Lexical Semantics in Ancient Egyptian*, edited by Eitan Grossman, 175–225. Hamburg: Widmaier.

Gruen, Erich S. 2002. *Diaspora: Jews amidst Greeks and Romans*. Cambridge, MA: Harvard University Press.

———. 2017. "Hellenistic Patronage and the Non-Greek World." In *The Hellenistic Court: Monarchic Power and Elite Society from Alexander to Cleopatra*, edited by Andrew Erskine, Lloyd Llewellyn-Jones, and Shane Wallace, 295–318. Swansea: Classical Press of Wales.

Guldin, Rainer. 2018. *Translation as Metaphor*. London: Routledge.

Gumbrecht, Hans Ulrich. 1997. "Eat Your Fragment! About Imagination and the Restitution of Texts." In *Collecting Fragments [Fragmente sammeln]*, edited by Glenn W. Most, 315–27. Göttingen: Vandenhoeck und Ruprecht.

Gundel, Wilhelm. 1966. *Astrologumena. Die astrologische Literatur in der Antike und ihre Geschichte*. Wiesbaden: Franz Steiner.

Haas, Christopher. 2007. *Alexandria in Late Antiquity: Topography and Social Conflict*. Baltimore: Johns Hopkins University Press.

Habinek, Thomas. 1997. Review of *Augustan Culture: An Interpretive Introduction*, by Karl Galinsky. *Vergilius* 43: 156–60.

Hagen, Fredrik. 2019. "Libraries in Ancient Egypt, c.1600–800 BCE." In *Libraries before Alexandria: Ancient Near Eastern Traditions*, edited by Kim Ryholt and Gojko Barjamovic, 244–318. Oxford: Oxford University Press.

Hall, Jonathan M. 2003. "'Culture' or 'Cultures'? Hellenism in the Late Sixth Century." In *The Cultures within Ancient Greek Culture: Contact, Conflict, Collaboration*, edited by Carol Dougherty and Leslie Kurke, 23–34. Cambridge, UK: Cambridge University Press.

Hani, Jean. 1976. *La religion égyptienne dans la pensée de Plutarque*. Paris: Les Belles Lettres.

Hannerz, Ulf. 1987. "The World in Creolisation." *Africa* 57, no. 4: 546–59.

Hardie, Philip. 1995. "The Speech of Pythagoras in Ovid *Metamorphoses* 15: Empedoclean Epos." *Classical Quarterly* 45, no. 1: 204–14.

Harman, Graham. 2018. *Object-Oriented Ontology: A New Theory of Everything*. London: Pelican.

Harrison, Stephen J. 2000. *Apuleius: A Latin Sophist*. Oxford: Oxford University Press.

———. 2012. "Narrative Subversion and Religious Satire in *Metamorphoses* 11." In *Aspects of Apuleius' Golden Ass. Vol. III: The Isis Book*, edited by Wytse Hette Keulen and Ulrike Egelhaaf-Gaiser, 73–85. Leiden: Brill.

Hayano, David M. 1979. "Auto-Ethnography: Paradigms, Problems, and Prospects." *Human Organization* 38, no. 1: 99–104.

Headland, Thomas N., Kenneth L. Pike, and Marvin Harris, eds. 1990. *Emics and Etics: The Insider/Outsider Debate*. Newbury Park, CA: Sage Publications.

Helck, Wolfgang. 1956. *Untersuchungen zu Manetho und den ägyptischen Königslisten*. Berlin: Akademie-Verlag.

Helmbold, W. C., and Edward N. O'Neil. 1959. *Plutarch's Quotations*. Baltimore: American Philological Association.

Hemelrijk, Emily Ann. 1999. *Matrona Docta: Educated Women in the Roman Élite from Cornelia to Julia Domna*. London: Routledge.

Henri, Océane. 2017. "A General Approach to *Interpretatio Graeca* in the Light of Papyrological Evidence." In *Platonismus und spätägyptische Religion: Plutarch und die Ägyptenrezeption in der römischen Kaiserzeit*, edited by Michael Erler and Martin Andreas Stadler, 43–54. Berlin: De Gruyter.

WORKS CITED   221

Heubner, Heinz, ed. 1994. *P. Cornelii Taciti libri qui supersunt. Tom 1: Ab excessu Divi Augusti*. 2nd ed. Stuttgart: Teubner.

Heyworth, Stephen J., ed. 2007. *Sexti Properti elegos*. Oxford: Clarendon Press.

Hine, Harry M., ed. 1996. *L. Annaei Senecae naturalium quaestionum libros*. Stuttgart: Teubner.

Hirst, Anthony, and M. S. Silk, eds. 2004. *Alexandria, Real and Imagined*. Burlington, VT: Ashgate.

Hoffmann, Friedhelm, Martina Minas-Nerpel, and Stefan Pfeiffer. 2009. *Die dreisprachige Stele des C. Cornelius Gallus: Übersetzung und Kommentar*. Berlin: De Gruyter.

Hofmann, Beate. 2004. *Die Königsnovelle: "Strukturanalyse am Einzelwerk."* Wiesbaden: Harrassowitz.

Holmes, Nigel. 1999. "Nero and Caesar: Lucan 1.33–66." *Classical Philology* 94, no. 1: 75–81.

Horky, Philip Sidney. 2013. *Plato and Pythagoreanism*. Oxford: Oxford University Press.

Hornung, Erik. 1982. *Conceptions of God in Ancient Egypt: The One and the Many*. Translated by John Baines. Ithaca: Cornell University Press.

———. 1992. *Idea into Image: Essays on Ancient Egyptian Thought*. Translated by Elizabeth Bredeck. New York: Timken.

Howley, Joseph A. 2018. *Aulus Gellius and Roman Reading Culture: Text, Presence, and Imperial Knowledge in the Noctes Atticae*. Cambridge, UK: Cambridge University Press.

Huffman, Carl A., ed. 2014. *A History of Pythagoreanism*. Cambridge, UK: Cambridge University Press.

Huss, Werner. 1994. *Der makedonische König und die ägyptischen Priester: Studien zur geschichte des ptolemaiischen Ägypten*. Stuttgart: Franz Steiner.

Iacoby, Adolf, and Wilhem Spiegelberg. 1903. "Der Frosch als Symbol der Auferstehung bei den Aegyptern." *Sphinx* 7, no. 1: 215–28.

Ikram, Salima, ed. 2005. *Divine Creatures: Animal Mummies in Ancient Egypt*. Cairo: American University in Cairo Press.

Ippolito, Antonella. 1996. "Tecnica compositiva e modelli letterari degli epigrammi di Giulia Balbilla." *Sileno* 22, no. 1–2: 119–36.

Iversen, Erik. 1958. *Papyrus Carlsberg Nr. VII: Fragments of a Hieroglyphic Dictionary*. Copenhagen: E. Munksgaard.

———. 1961. *The Myth of Egypt and Its Hieroglyphs in European Tradition*. Copenhagen: Gad.

———. 1968. *Obelisks in Exile. Vol 1.: The Obelisks of Rome*. Copenhagen: Gad.

———. 1971. "The Hieroglyphic Tradition." In *The Legacy of Egypt*, edited by J. R. Harris, 2nd ed., 170–96. Oxford: Clarendon Press.

Jacobson, Howard. 1977. "Apion's Nickname." *American Journal of Philology* 98, no. 4: 413–15.

Jacoby, Felix. 1923–1958. *Die Fragmente der griechischen Historiker*. Berlin: Wiedmann.

James, George G. M. 1954. *Stolen Legacy*. Nashville: James C. Winston.

Jan, Ludwig von, and Karl Friedrich Theodor Mayhoff, eds. 1967. *C. Plini Secundi Naturalis historiae libri XXXVII*. 6 vols. Stuttgart: Teubner.

Janda, Jan. 1969. "Die Berichte über Heraklits Lehre bei Diogenes Laertios." *Listy Filologické* 92, no. 2: 97–115.

Jasnow, Richard. 2011. "'Caught in the Web of Words'—Remarks on the Imagery of Writing and Hieroglyphs in the Book of Thoth." *Journal of the American Research Center in Egypt* 47: 297–317.

———. 2016. "Between Two Waters: The *Book of Thoth* and the Problem of Greco-Egyptian Interaction." In *Graeco-Egyptian Interactions: Literature, Translation, and Culture, 500 BC-AD 300*, edited by Ian Rutherford, 317–56. Oxford: Oxford University Press.

Jasnow, Richard, and Karl-Theodor Zauzich. 2005. *The Ancient Egyptian Book of Thoth: A Demotic Discourse on Knowledge and Pendant to the Classical Hermetica*. 2 vols. Wiesbaden: Harrassowitz.

———. 2014. *Conversations in the House of Life: A New Translation of the Ancient Egyptian Book of Thoth*. Wiesbaden: Harrassowitz.

———. 2021. *The Ancient Egyptian Book of Thoth II: Revised Transliteration and Translation, New Fragments, and Material for Future Study*. 2 vols. Wiesbaden: Harrassowitz.

Jones, Brian W. 1992. *The Emperor Domitian*. London: Routledge.

Jones, Kenneth R. 2005. "The Figure of Apion in Josephus' *Contra Apionem*." *Journal for the Study of Judaism* 36, no. 3: 278–315.

Jones, W. H. S. 1963. *Pliny: Natural History, Volume VIII: Books 28–32*. Cambridge, MA: Harvard University Press.

Jördens, Andrea. 2012. "Status and Citizenship." In *The Oxford Handbook of Roman Egypt*, edited by Christina Riggs, 247–59. Oxford: Oxford University Press.

Junker, Hermann. 1917. *Die Onurislegende*. Vienna: Adolf Holzhausen.

———. 1940. *Die Götterlehre von Memphis (Schabaka-Inschrift)*. Berlin: Verlag der Akademie der Wissenschaften.

Kahane, Ahuvia, and Andrew Laird, eds. 2001. *A Companion to the Prologue of Apuleius' Metamorphoses*. Oxford: Oxford University Press.

Kahn, Charles H. 2001. *Pythagoras and the Pythagoreans: A Brief History*. Indianapolis: Hackett.

Kákosy, Láslo. 1977. "Heliopolis." In *Lexikon der Ägyptologie*, edited by Wolfgang Helck, Eberhard Otto, and Wolfhart Westendorf, 2:1111–13. Wiesbaden: Harrassowitz.

Kamen, Deborah. 2012. "Naturalized Desires and the Metamorphosis of Iphis." *Helios* 39, no. 1: 21–36.

Kaster, Robert A., ed. 2016. *C. Suetoni Tranquilli De Vita Caesarum Libros VIII et De Grammaticis et Rhetoribus Librum*. Oxford: Clarendon Press.

Katzoff, Ranon. 1980. "Sources of Law in Roman Egypt: The Role of the Prefect." *Aufstieg und Niedergang der römischen Welt* 2.13: 807–44.

Keane, Catherine. 2015. *Juvenal and the Satiric Emotions*. Oxford: Oxford University Press.

Kees, Hermann Alexander. 1924. *Horus und Seth als Götterpaar*. Leipzig: J. C. Hinrichs.

Kelting, Edward. 2019. "Am I the Ibis or the Snake? Totemism, Satire, and Community in Juvenal Satire 15." *TAPA* 149, no. 2: 419–53.

———. 2021. "'Characterizing' Lucius: Pythagoreanism and the *Figura* in Apuleius' *Metamorphoses*." *American Journal of Philology* 142, no. 1: 103–36.

Kemezis, Adam. 2019. "Beyond City Limits: Citizenship and Authorship in Imperial Greek Literature." In *In the Crucible of Empire: The Impact of Roman Citizenship upon Greeks, Jews and Christians*, edited by Katell Berthelot and Jonathan Price, 73–103. Leuven: Peeters.

Kessler, Dieter. 1989. *Die heiligen Tiere und der König*. Wiesbaden: Harrassowitz.

———. 2005. "Tierische Missverständniss: Grundsätzliches zu Fragen des Tierkultes." In *Tierkulte im pharaonischen Ägypten und im Kulturvergleich: Beiträge eines Workshops am 7.6. und 8.6. 2002*, edited by Martin Fitzenreiter, 33–67. London: Golden House Publications.

Keyser, Paul T. 1994. "On Cometary Theory and Typology from Nechepso-Petosiris through Apuleius to Servius." *Mnemosyne* 47, no. 5: 625–51.

———. 2014. "Chairemon (618)." In *Brill's New Jacoby*, edited by Ian Worthington. Leiden: Brill.

———. 2015. "Apion of Alexandria (616)." In *Brill's New Jacoby*, edited by Ian Worthington. Leiden: Brill.

———. 2016. "Mineral Medicine in Apion of Oasis According to Pliny and Galen." *Mnemosyne* 69, no. 3: 453–72.

Kidd, Stephen. 2011. "Dreams in Bilingual Papyri from the Ptolemaic Period." *Bulletin of the American Society of Papyrologists* 48: 113–30.

Kimmerle, Nadja. 2015. *Lucan und der Prinzipat: Inkonsistenz und unzuverlässiges Erzählen im "Bellum Civile."* De Gruyter.

Kindt, Julia. 2019. "Animals in Ancient Greek Religion: Divine Zoomorphism and the Anthromorphic Body." In *Natur—Mythos—Religion im antiken Griechenland [Nature—Myth—Religion in Ancient Greece]*, edited by Tanja Susanne Scheer, 155–70. Stuttgart: Franz Steiner.

———, ed. 2021a. *Animals in Ancient Greek Religion*. London: Routledge.

———. 2021b. "Greek Anthropomorphism versus Egyptian Zoomorphism: Conceptual Considerations in Greek Thought and Literature." In *Animals in Ancient Greek Religion*, edited by Julia Kindt, 126–49. London: Routledge.

King, Daniel. 2017. "Medicine between Cultures in the Hellenistic Fayum." In *Hellenism and the Local Communities of the Eastern Mediterranean: 400 BCE–250 CE*, edited by Boris Chrubasik and Daniel King, 177–94. Oxford: Oxford University Press.

Kirk, G. S., J. E. Raven, and M. Schofield. 1983. *The Presocratic Philosophers: A Critical History with a Selection of Texts*. 2nd ed. Cambridge, UK: Cambridge University Press.

Klotz, David. 2006. *Adoration of the Ram: Five Hymns to Amun-Re from Hibis Temple*. New Haven, CT: Yale Egyptological Seminar.

———. 2008. "Domitian at the Contra-Temple of Karnak." *Zeitschrift für Ägyptische Sprache und Altertumskunde* 135, no. 1: 63–77.

———. 2012. *Caesar in the City of Amun: Egyptian Temple Construction and Theology in Roman Thebes*. Turnhout: Brepols.

———. 2017. "Elements of Theban Theology in Plutarch and his Contemporaries." In *Platonismus und spätägyptische Religion: Plutarch und die Ägyptenrezeption in der römischen Kaiserzeit*, edited by Michael Erler and Martin Andreas Stadler, 127–48. Berlin: De Gruyter.

Koch, Roland. 1990. *Die Erzählung des Sinuhe*. Brussels: Fondation égyptologique Reine Elisabeth.

Koenen, Ludwig. 1976. "Egyptian Influence in Tibullus." *Illinois Classical Studies* 1: 127–59.

Konstan, David. 1978. "The Politics of Tibullus 1.7." *Rivista di studi classici* 26: 173–85.

Kosmin, Paul J., and Ian S. Moyer, eds. 2022a. *Cultures of Resistance in the Hellenistic East*. Oxford: Oxford University Press.

———. 2022b. "Introduction." In *Cultures of Resistance in the Hellenistic East*, edited by Paul J. Kosmin and Ian S. Moyer, 1–30. Oxford: Oxford University Press.

Krappe, Alexander Haggerty. 1927. "Tiberius and Thrasyllus." *American Journal of Philology* 48, no. 4: 359–66.

Kuhrt, Amélie. 1987. "Berossus' *Babyloniaka* and Seleucid Rule in Babylon." In *Hellenism in the East: The Interaction of Greek and Non-Greek Civilizations from Syria to Central Asia after Alexander*, edited by Amélie Kuhrt and Susan Sherwin-White, 32–56. London: Duckworth.

Kurth, Dieter. 1994. *Treffpunkt der Götter: Inschriften aus dem Tempel des Horus von Edfu.* Munich: Artemis.

———. 2008. *Einführung ins Ptolemäische: Eine Grammatik mit Zeichenliste und Übungsstücken.* 2 vols. Hützel: Backe.

Kuster, Bruno. 1911. "De tribus carminibus papyri Parisinae magicae." Regimonti: Ex officina Hartungiana.

Laird, Andrew. 2010. "The Cosmic Race and a Heap of Broken Images: Mexico's Classical Past and the Modern Creole Imagination." In *Classics and National Cultures*, edited by Susan A. Stephens and Phiroze Vasunia, 163–81. Oxford: Oxford University Press.

Laks, André. 2014. "Diogenes Laertius' *Life of Pythagoras*." In *A History of Pythagoreanism*, edited by Carl A. Huffman, 360–80. Cambridge, UK: Cambridge University Press.

———. 2018. *The Concept of Presocratic Philosophy: Its Origin, Development, and Significance.* Translated by Glenn W. Most. Princeton: Princeton University Press.

Lang, Phillipa. 2012. "Hekataios (264)." In *Brill's New Jacoby*, edited by Ian Worthington. Leiden: Brill.

———. 2014. "Manetho (609)." In *Brill's New Jacoby*, edited by Ian Worthington. Leiden: Brill.

Leemreize, M. E. C. 2016. "Framing Egypt: Roman Literary Perceptions of Egypt from Cicero to Juvenal." PhD diss., Leiden University.

Lefkowitz, Mary R. 2012. "Visits to Egypt in the Biographical Tradition." In *Die griechische Biographie in hellenistischer Zeit: Akten des internationalen Kongresses vom 26.–29. Juli 2006 in Würzburg*, edited by Michael Erler and Stefan Schorn, 101–13. Berlin: De Gruyter.

Lefkowitz, Mary R., and Guy MacLean Rogers, eds. 1996. *Black Athena Revisited.* Chapel Hill: University of North Carolina Press.

Legras, Bernard. 2019. "Policymakers in a Changing World." In *A Companion to Greco-Roman and Late Antique Egypt*, edited by Katelijn Vandorpe, 139–46. Medford, MA: Wiley-Blackwell.

Lembke, Katja. 1994. *Das Iseum Campense in Rom: Studie über den Isiskult unter Domitian.* Heidelberg: Verlag Archäologie und Geschichte.

Lembke, Katja, Martina Minas-Nerpel, and Stefan Pfeiffer, eds. 2010. *Tradition and Transformation. Egypt under Roman Rule: Proceedings of the International Conference, Hildesheim, Roemer- and Pelizaeus-Museum, 3–6 July 2008.* Leiden: Brill.

Leventhal, Max. 2015. "Counting on Epic: Mathematical Poetry and Homeric Epic in Archimedes' Cattle Problem." *Ramus* 44, no. 1–2: 200–21.

Lévi, Nicolas. 2014. *La révélation finale à Rome: Cicéron, Ovide, Apulée.* Paris: Presses de l'université Paris-Sorbonne.

Levick, Barbara, and Howard Hayes Scullard. 2012. "Claudius Balbillus, Tiberius." In *The Oxford Classical Dictionary*, edited by Simon Hornblower, Antony Spawforth, and Esther Edinow, 4th ed., 325–26. Oxford: Oxford University Press.

Lévi-Strauss, Claude. 1987. *Introduction to the Work of Marcel Mauss.* Translated by Felicity Baker. London: Routledge.

Lévy, Isidore. 1900a. "Apion état-il Alexandrin?" *Revue des Études Juives* 41: 188–95.

———. 1900b. "Notes d'histoire et d'épigraphie." *Revue des Études Juives* 41: 174–95.

———. 1910. "Sarapis: IV.—La légende sinopique." *Revue de l'histoire des religions* 61: 162–96.

Lichtheim, Miriam. 1975. *Ancient Egyptian Literature: Volume I: The Old and Middle Kingdoms*. Berkeley: University of California Press.

———. 1976. *Ancient Egyptian Literature: Volume II: The New Kingdom*. Berkeley: University of California Press.

LiDonnici, Lynn R. 2003. "Compositional Patterns in *PGM* IV (= *P.Bibl.Nat.Suppl.* gr. no. 574)." *Bulletin of the American Society of Papyrologists* 40, no. 1/4: 141–78.

Little, D. A. 1974. "Non-Parody in *Metamorphoses* 15." *Prudentia* 6, no. 1: 17–22.

Livingstone, Niall. 2001. *A Commentary on Isocrates' Busiris*. Leiden: Brill.

Loprieno, Antonio. 1988. *Topos und Mimesis: zum Ausländer in der ägyptischen Literatur*. Wiesbaden: Harrassowitz.

———. 1995. *Ancient Egyptian: A Linguistic Introduction*. Cambridge: Cambridge University Press.

———. 1996. "The 'King's novel.'" In *Ancient Egyptian Literature: History and Forms*, edited by Antonio Loprieno, 277–95. Leiden: Brill.

Love, Edward O. D. 2021. *Script Switching in Roman Egypt: Case Studies in Script Conventions, Domains, Shift, and Obsolescence from Hieroglyphic, Hieratic, Demotic, and Old Coptic Manuscripts*. Berlin: De Gruyter.

Luck, Georg, ed. 1998. *Albii Tibulli aliorumque carmina*. 2nd ed. Stuttgart: Teubner.

Lüddeckens, Erich, ed. 1983. *Demotisches Namenbuch*. Bd. I, Lfg. 3. Wiesbaden: Reichert.

———, ed. 1986. *Demotisches Namenbuch*. Bd. I, Lfg. 6. Wiesbaden: Reichert.

Łukaszewicz, Adam. 1998. "Claudius to His Own City of Alexandria (*P. Lond.* VI 1912, 103–104)." *Journal of Juristic Papyrology* 28: 72–77.

Luke, Trevor S. 2016. "Pliny the Elder on Pythagoras." In *Papers of the Langford Latin Seminar. 16: Greek and Roman Poetry; The Elder Pliny*, edited by Francis Cairns and Roy Gibson, 285–313. Prenton: Cairns.

Macleod, M. D., ed. 1972–1987. *Luciani opera*. Oxford: Clarendon Press.

Macris, Constantinos. 2014. "Porphyry's Life of Pythagoras." In *A History of Pythagoreanism*, edited by Carl A. Huffman, 381–98. Cambridge, UK: Cambridge University Press.

Maehler, H. 2003. "Roman Poets on Egypt." In *Ancient Perspectives on Egypt*, edited by Roger Matthews and Cornelia Roemer, 203–15. London: University College London Press.

Malaise, Michel. 1972a. *Inventaire préliminaire des documents égyptiens découverts en Italie*. Leiden: Brill.

———. 1972b. *Les conditions de pénétration et de diffusion des cultes égyptiens en Italie*. Leiden: Brill.

———. 2005. *Pour une terminologie et une analyse des cultes isiaques*. Brussels: Académie royale de Belgique.

Manolaraki, Eleni. 2013. *Noscendi Nilum Cupido: Imagining Egypt from Lucan to Philostratus*. Berlin: De Gruyter.

———. 2018. "Domesticating Egypt in Pliny's Natural History." In *After 69 CE: Writing Civil War in Flavian Rome*, edited by Lauren Donovan Ginsberg and Darcy A. Krasne, 341–61. Berlin: De Gruyter.

Marganne, Marie-Hélène, and Sydney Aufrère. 2014. "La question de l'interface entre les sciences égyptiennes et grecques." In *Alexandrie la divine*, edited by Charles Méla,

Frédéric Möri, Sydney Aufrère, Gilles Dorival, and Alain le Boulluec, 395–401. Geneva: Éditions de la Baconnière.

Mari, Zaccaria. 2008. "The 'Egyptian Places' of Hadrian's Villa." In *The She-Wolf and the Sphinx: Rome and Egypt from History to Myth*, edited by Eugenio Lo Sardo, 122–31. Milan: Electa.

Mari, Zaccaria, and Sergio Sgalambro. 2007. "The Antinoeion of Hadrian's Villa: Interpretation and Architectural Reconstruction." *American Journal of Archaeology* 111, no. 1: 83–104.

Markiewicz, Tomasz. 2008. "Bocchoris the Lawgiver—or Was He Really?" *Journal of Egyptian History* 1, no. 2: 309–30.

Marotta, Valerio. 2017. "Egyptians and Citizenship from the First Century AD to the *Constitutio Antoniniana*." In *Citizens in the Graeco-Roman World: Aspects of Citizenship from the Archaic Period to AD 212*, edited by Lucia Cecchet and Anna Busetto, 172–98. Leiden: Brill.

Mathieu, Georges, and Émile Brémond, eds. 1963. *Isocrate. Discours*. Vol. 1. Paris: Les Belles Lettres.

Mazurek, Lindsey A. 2022. *Isis in a Global Empire: Greek Identity through Egyptian Religion in Roman Greece*. Cambridge, UK: Cambridge University Press.

McCloskey, Patrick, and Edward Phinney Jr. 1968. "Ptolemaeus Tyrannus: The Typification of Nero in the Pharsalia." *Hermes* 96, no. 1: 80–87.

McKay, Alexander G. 1998. "*Non Enarrabile Textum?* The Shield of Aeneas and the Triple Triumph of 29 BC: *Aeneid* 8.630–728." In *Vergil's Aeneid: Augustan Epic and Political Context*, edited by Hans-Peter Stahl, 199–222. London: Duckworth.

McKim, Richard. 1986. "Philosophers and Cannibals: Juvenal's Fifteenth Satire." *Phoenix* 40, no. 1: 58–71.

Meeusen, Michiel. 2017. "Egyptian Knowledge at Plutarch's Table: Out of the Question?" In *Space, Time and Language in Plutarch*, edited by Aristoula Georgiadou and Katerina Oikonomopoulou, 215–26. Berlin: De Gruyter.

Méla, Charles, Frédéric Möri, Sydney Aufrère, Gilles Dorival, and Alain le Boulluec, eds. 2014. *Alexandrie la divine*. 2 vols. Geneva: Éditions de la Baconnière.

Mélèze-Modrzejewski, Joseph. 1985. "Entre la cité et le fisc: le statut grec dans l'Égypte romaine." In *Symposion 1982: Actas de la Sociedad del Derecho Griego y Helenístico, Santander, 1–4 septiembre 1982*, edited by Francisco Javier Fernández Nieto, 5: 241–80. Valencia: Universidad de Valencia.

———. 1990. *Droit impérial et traditions locales dans l'Egypte romaine*. Aldershot: Variorum.

———. 1991. *Les Juifs d'Égypte: de Ramsès II à Hadrien*. Paris: Errance.

Merrills, Andy. 2017. *Roman Geographies of the Nile: From the Late Republic to the Early Empire*. Cambridge, UK: Cambridge University Press.

Meyer, Hugo, ed. 1994. *Der Obelisk des Antinoos: eine kommentierte Edition*. Munich: Wilhelm Fink.

Meyer, Ruth. 1961. "Die Bedeutung Aegyptens in der lateinischen Literatur der vorchristlichen Zeit." PhD diss., University of Zürich.

Miles, Graeme. 2016. "Incarnating Proteus in Philostratus' *Life of Apollonius of Tyana*." *Ancient Narrative* 13: 139–57.

Miller, John F. 1981. "Propertius' Tirade against Isis (2.33a)." *Classical Journal* 77, no. 2: 104–11.

Momigliano, Arnaldo. 1994. *Studies on Modern Scholarship*. Edited by Glen W. Bowersock and Tim J. Cornell. Berkeley: University of California Press.

Monaco Caterine, Mallory. 2019. "Entangled Imperial Identities: Citizen, Subject and Mentor in Plutarch's *Aratus*." In *Intellectual and Empire in Greco-Roman Antiquity*, edited by Philip R. Bosman, 89–101. London: Routledge.

Moore, Timothy J. 1989. "Tibullus 1.7: Reconciliation through Conflict." *Classical World* 82, no. 6: 423–30.

Moraux, Paul. 1955. "La composition de la *Vie d'Aristote* chez Diogène Laërce." *Revue des Études Grecques* 68, no. 319–323: 124–63.

Morenz, Ludwig D. 2002. "Schrift-Mysterium. Gottes-Schau in der visuellen Poesie von Esna—Insbesondere zu den omnipotenten Widder-Zeichen zwischen Symbolik und Lesbarkeit." In *Ägyptische Mysterien?*, edited by Jan Assmann and Martin Bommas, 77–94. Munich: Wilhelm Fink.

———. 2008. *Sinn und Spiel der Zeichen: visuelle Poesie im Alten Ägypten*. Cologne: Böhlau.

Moreschini, Claudio. 2015. *Apuleius and the Metamorphoses of Platonism*. Turnhout: Brepols.

Morris, Sarah P. 1989. "Daidalos and Kadmos: Classicism and 'Orientalism.'" *Arethusa* 22: 39–54.

Most, Glenn W., ed. 1997. *Collecting Fragments [Fragmente sammeln]*. Göttingen: Vandenhoeck & Ruprecht.

Moyer, Ian S. 2011. *Egypt and the Limits of Hellenism*. Cambridge, UK: Cambridge University Press.

———. 2022. "Revolts, Resistance, and the Materiality of the Moral Order in Ptolemaic Egypt." In *Cultures of Resistance in the Hellenistic East*, edited by Paul J. Kosmin and Ian S. Moyer, 148–74. Oxford: Oxford University Press.

Muntz, Charles Edward. 2008. "Diodorus Siculus, Egypt, and Rome." PhD diss., Duke University.

Murray, Oswyn. 1970. "Hecataeus of Abdera and Pharaonic Kingship." *Journal of Egyptian Archaeology* 56: 141–71.

———. 1972. "Herodotus and Hellenistic Culture." *Classical Quarterly* 22, no. 2: 200–13.

Myers, K. Sara. 1994. *Ovid's Causes: Cosmogony and Aetiology in the Metamorphoses*. Ann Arbor: University of Michigan Press.

Mylonas, George E. 1961. *Eleusis and the Eleusinian Mysteries*. Princeton: Princeton University Press.

Mynors, Roger Aubrey Baskerville, ed. 1969. *P. Vergili Maronis opera*. Oxford: Clarendon Press.

Neitzel, Susanne. 1977. "Ἀπίων Γλῶσσαι Ὁμηρικαί." In *Die Fragmente des Grammatikers Dionysios Thrax. Die Fragmente der Grammatiker Tyrannion und Diokles. Apions Glossai Homerikai*, edited by Konstanze Linke, Walter Haas, and Susanne Neitzel, 185–328. Berlin: De Gruyter.

Niehoff, Maren R. 2011. *Jewish Exegesis and Homeric Scholarship in Alexandria*. Cambridge, UK: Cambridge University Press.

———. 2018. *Philo of Alexandria: An Intellectual Biography*. New Haven: Yale University Press.

Neugebauer, Otto. 1975. *A History of Ancient Mathematical Astronomy*. Berlin: Springer.

228 WORKS CITED

Oberrauch, Lukas. 2005. "Metempsychose, Universalgeschichte und Autopsie: die Rede des Pythagoras in Ovid, *Met.* XV als Kernstück epischer Legitimation." *Gymnasium* 112, no. 2: 107–21.

O'Brien, Maeve C. 2002. *Apuleius' Debt to Plato in the Metamorphoses.* Lewiston, NY: E. Mellen Press.

Ogden, Daniel. 2004. "The Apprentice's Sorcerer: Pankrates and His Powers in Context (Lucian, *Philopseudes* 33–36)." *Acta Classica* 47: 101–26.

———. 2007. *In Search of the Sorcerer's Apprentice: The Traditional Tales of Lucian's Lover of Lies.* Swansea: Classical Press of Wales.

Oliver, Revilo P. 1980. "Thrasyllus in Tacitus (*Ann,* 6.21)." *Illinois Classical Studies* 5: 130–48.

Oltramare, Paul, ed. 1961. *Questions naturelles: livres I à VII.* 2e éd. Paris: Les Belles Lettres.

Opsomer, Jan. 1998. *In Search of the Truth: Academic Tendencies in Middle Platonism.* Brussels: Paleis der Academiën Hertogsstraat I.

Orlin, Eric M. 2008. "Octavian and Egyptian Cults: Redrawing the Boundaries of Romanness." *American Journal of Philology* 129, no. 2: 231–53.

———. 2010. *Foreign Cults in Rome: Creating a Roman Empire.* Oxford: Oxford University Press.

Osgood, Josiah. 2011. *Claudius Caesar: Image and Power in the Early Roman Empire.* Cambridge, UK: Cambridge University Press.

Paganini, Mario C. D. 2017. "Greek and Egyptian Associations in Egypt: Fact or Fiction?" In *Hellenism and the Local Communities of the Eastern Mediterranean: 400 BCE–250 CE,* edited by Boris Chrubasik and Daniel King, 131–54. Oxford: Oxford University Press.

Palmer, John. 2014. "The Pythagoreans and Plato." In *A History of Pythagoreanism,* edited by Carl A. Huffman, 204–26. Cambridge, UK: Cambridge University Press.

Palmié, Stephan. 2007. "The 'C-Word' Again: From Colonial to Post-Colonial Semantics." In *Creolization: History, Ethnography, Theory,* edited by Charles Stewart, 66–83. Walnut Creek, CA: Left Coast Press.

Pandey, Nandini B. 2018. *The Poetics of Power in Augustan Rome: Latin Poetic Responses to Early Imperial Iconography.* Cambridge, UK: Cambridge University Press.

Papaconstantinou, Arietta, ed. 2010. *The Multilingual Experience in Egypt, from the Ptolemies to the Abbasids.* Burlington, VT: Ashgate.

Parker, Grant. 2003. "Narrating Monumentality: The Piazza Navona Obelisk." *Journal of Mediterranean Archaeology* 16, no. 2: 193–215.

———. 2007. "Obelisks Still in Exile: Monuments Made to Measure?" In *Nile into Tiber: Egypt in the Roman World. Proceedings of the IIIrd International Conference of Isis Studies, Leiden, May 11–14 2005,* edited by Laurent Bricault, Miguel John Versluys, and Paul. G. P. Meyboom, 209–22. Leiden: Brill.

———. 2011. "India, Egypt and Parthia in Augustan Verse: The Post-Orientalist Turn." *Dictynna,* no. 8.

———. 2018. "Monolithic Appropriation? The Lateran Obelisk Compared." In *Rome, Empire of Plunder: The Dynamics of Cultural Appropriation,* edited by Matthew Loar, Carolyn MacDonald, and Dan-el Padilla Peralta, 137–59. Cambridge, UK: Cambridge University Press.

Parmentier, Léon. 1913. *Recherches sur le Traité d'Isis et d'Osiris de Plutarque.* Brussels: H. Lamertin.

Patch, Diana Craig. 2018. "A Monumental Gift to The Met." The Metropolitan Museum of Art. September 28, 2018. https://www.metmuseum.org/about-the-met/curatorial-departments/egyptian-art/temple-of-dendur-50/gift-to-the-met.

Pearson, Stephanie. 2021. *The Triumph and Trade of Egyptian Objects in Rome: Collecting Art in the Ancient Mediterranean*. Berlin: De Gruyter.

Pfeiffer, Rudolf. 1968. *History and Classical Scholarship from the Beginnings to the End of the Hellenistic Age*. Oxford: Clarendon Press.

Pfeiffer, Stefan. 2013. "Egypt and Greece Before Alexander." In *UCLA Encyclopedia of Egyptology*, edited by Wolfram Grajetzki and Willeke Wendrich. https://escholarship.org/uc/item/833528zm

———. 2015. "Interpretatio Graeca: Der 'übersetze Gott' in der multikulturellen Gesellschaft des hellenistischen Ägypten." In *Der übersetzte Gott*, edited by Melanie Lange and Martin Rösel, 37–53. Leipzig: Evangelische Verlagsanstalt.

Pflaum, Hans-Georg. 1960–1961. *Les carrières procuratoriennes équestres sous le Haut-Empire romain*. Paris: Librairie orientaliste P. Geuthner.

Pike, Kenneth L. 1967. *Language in Relation to a Unified Theory of the Structure of Human Behavior*. The Hague: Mouton.

Pintabone, Diane T. 2002. "Ovid's Iphis and Ianthe: When Girls Won't Be Girls." In *Among Women: From the Homosocial to the Homoerotic in the Ancient World*, edited by Nancy Sorkin Rabinowitz and Lisa Ann Auanger, 256–85. Austin: University of Texas Press.

Pintaudi, Rosario. 1977. "Invocazione a Seth-Typhon." *Zeitschrift für Papyrologie und Epigraphik* 26: 245–48.

Pohlenz, Max, ed. 1982. *M. Tulli Ciceronis scripta quae manserunt omnia. Fasc. 44: Tusculanae Disputationes*. Berlin: De Gruyter.

Pope, Maurice. 1999. *The Story of Decipherment: From Egyptian Hieroglyphs to Maya Script*. Rev. ed. New York: Thames and Hudson.

Popko, Lutz, and Michaela Rücker. 2011. "P.Lips. Inv. 1228 und 590: eine neue ägyptische Königsliste in griechischer Sprache." *Zeitschrift für ägyptische Sprache und Altertumskunde* 138: 43–62.

Preisendanz, Karl. 1942. "Pachrates." In *Realencyclopädie der classischen Altertumswissenschaft*, edited by August Pauly, et al., Bd. 18.2, Hbd. 36.1:2071–74. Stuttgart: Metzler.

Preisendanz, Karl, and Albert Henrichs. 1973–1974. *Papyri Graecae Magicae / Die griechischen Zauberpapyri*. 2nd ed. 2 vols. Stuttgart: Teubner.

Pries, Andreas H. 2016. "ἔμψυχα ἱερογλυφικά I: Eine Annäherung an Wesen und Wirkmacht ägyptischer Hieroglyphen nach dem indigenen Zeugnis." In *Sapientia Felicitas: Festschrift für Günter Vittmann zum 29. Februar 2016*, edited by Sandra Luisa Lippert, Maren Schentuleit, and Martin Andreas Stadler, 449–88. Montpellier: Université Paul-Valéry.

———. 2017. "ἔμψυχα ἱερογλυφικά II: Aspekte von Wesen und Wirkmacht ägyptischer Hieroglyphen im Spiegel der platonischen Anschauung." In *Platonismus und spätägyptische Religion: Plutarch und die Ägyptenrezeption in der römischen Kaiserzeit*, edited by Michael Erler and Martin Andreas Stadler, 293–304. Berlin: De Gruyter.

Putnam, Michael C. J. 2017. "Statius *Siluae* 3.2: Reading Travel." *Illinois Classical Studies* 42, no. 1: 83–139.

WORKS CITED

Quack, Joachim Friedrich. 2000. "Das Buch vom Tempel und verwandte Texte. Ein Vorbericht." *Archiv für Religionsgeschichte* 2, no. 1: 1–20.

———. 2004. "Organiser le culte idéal: Le Manuel du temple." *Bulletin de la Société Française d'Égyptologie* 160: 9–25.

———. 2005. "Die Überlieferungsstruktur des Buches vom Tempel." In *Tebtynis und Soknopaiu Nesos: Leben im römerzeitlichen Fajum: Akten des Internationalen Symposions vom 11. bis 13. Dezember 2003 in Sommerhausen bei Würzburg*, edited by Sandra Luisa Lippert and Maren Schentuleit, 105–15. Wiesbaden: Harrasowitz.

———. 2007a. "Die Initiation zum Schreiberberuf im Alten Ägypten." *Studien zur Altägyptischen Kultur* 36: 249–95.

———. 2007b. "Ein ägyptischer Dialog über die Schreibkunst und das arkane Wissen." *Archiv für Religionsgeschichte* 9: 259–96.

———. 2009. *Einführung in die altägyptische Literaturgeschichte III: Die demotische und gräko-ägyptische Literatur*. 2nd ed. Münster: LIT.

———. 2021. "Priestly Scholars in Late Egypt: The Theoretical Side." *Journal of Ancient Near Eastern History* 8, no. 1–2: 73–90.

Quinn, Josephine Crawley. 2013. "Monumental Power: 'Numidian Royal Architecture' in Context." In *The Hellenistic West: Rethinking the Ancient Mediterranean*, edited by Jonathan R. W. Prag and Josephine Crawley Quinn, 179–215. Cambridge, UK: Cambridge University Press.

Quinn, Josephine Crawley, and Jonathan R. W. Prag, eds. 2013. *The Hellenistic West: Rethinking the Ancient Mediterranean*. Cambridge, UK: Cambridge University Press.

Raeder, Joachim. 1983. *Die statuarische Ausstattung der Villa Hadriana bei Tivoli*. Berne: P. Lang.

Redford, Donald B. 1984. "The Meaning and Use of the Term *gnwt*, 'Annals.'" In *Studien zu Sprache und Religion Ägyptens*, edited by Friedrich Junge, 327–42. Göttingen.

———. 1986. *Pharaonic King-Lists, Annals, and Day-Books: A Contribution to the Study of the Egyptian Sense of History*. Mississauga: Benben Publications.

Reed, Joseph D. 1998. "The Death of Osiris in *Aeneid* 12.458." *American Journal of Philology* 119, no. 3: 399–418.

Reinhold, Meyer, and P. M. Swan. 1990. "Cassius Dio's Assessment of Augustus." In *Between Republic and Empire: Interpretations of Augustus and His Principate*, edited by Kurt A. Raaflaub and Mark Toher, 155–73. Berkeley: University of California Press.

Reiß, Katharina, and Hans J. Vermeer. 1984. *Grundlegung einer allgemeinen Translationstheorie*. Tübingen: Niemeyer.

Reymond, E. A. E. 1976. *From the Contents of the Libraries of the Suchos Temples in the Fayyum. Part 1. A Medical Book from Crocodilopolis: P. Vindob. D. 6257*. Vienna: Brüder Hollinek.

Rich, John William. 1990. "Dio on Augustus." In *History as Text: The Writing of Ancient History*, edited by Averil Cameron, 86–110. Chapel Hill: University of North Carolina Press.

Richter, Daniel S. 2001. "Plutarch on Isis and Osiris: Text, Cult, and Cultural Appropriation." *Transactions of the American Philological Association* 131: 191–216.

———. 2011. *Cosmopolis: Imagining Community in Late Classical Athens and the Early Roman Empire*. Oxford: Oxford University Press.

Richter, Daniel S., and William A. Johnson, eds. 2017. *The Oxford Handbook of the Second Sophistic.* Oxford: Oxford University Press.

Riedweg, Christoph. 2005. *Pythagoras: His Life, Teaching, and Influence.* Ithaca: Cornell University Press.

Riess, Ernst. 1892. "Nechepsonis et Petosiridis fragmenta magica." *Philologus. Supplementband* 6, no. 1: 325–94.

Rilly, Claude, and Alex de Voogt. 2012. *The Meroitic Language and Writing System.* Cambridge, UK: Cambridge University Press.

Ripat, Pauline. 2011. "Expelling Misconceptions: Astrologers at Rome." *Classical Philology* 106, no. 2: 115–54.

Robertson, Roland. 1995. "Glocalization: Time-Space and Homogeneity-Heterogeneity." In *Global Modernities,* edited by Mike Featherstone, Scott Lash, and Roland Robertson, 25–44. London: Sage.

Robinson, Douglas. 2014. *Translation and Empire.* London: Routledge.

Rodríguez, P. 2007. "Chérémon, Néron et l' Égypte hellenistique." In *Neronia VII: Rome, l'Italie et la Grèce: hellénisme et philhellénisme au premier siècle après J.-C.: actes du VIIe Colloque international de la SIEN (Athènes, 21–23 octobre 2004),* edited by Yves Perrin, 50–73. Brussels: Éditions Latomus.

Rosati, Gianpiero. 2009. "*Latrator Anubis*: Alien Divinities in Augustan Rome, and How to Tame Monsters through Aetiology." In *Paradox and the Marvellous in Augustan Literature and Culture,* edited by Philip Hardie, 268–87. Oxford: Oxford University Press.

Rosenmeyer, Patricia. 2008. "Greek Verse Inscriptions in Roman Egypt: Julia Balbilla's Sapphic Voice." *Classical Antiquity* 27, no. 2: 334–58.

———. 2018. *The Language of Ruins: Greek and Latin Inscriptions on the Memnon Colossus.* Oxford: Oxford University Press.

Roskam, Geert. 2017. "On the Multi-Coloured Robes of Philosophy: Plutarch's Approach in *On Isis and Osiris.*" In *Platonismus und Spätägyptische Religion: Plutarch und die Ägyptenrezeption in der Römischen Kaiserzeit,* edited by Michael Erler and Martin Andreas Stadler, 364: 199–218. Berlin: De Gruyter.

Roullet, Anne. 1972. *The Egyptian and Egyptianizing Monuments of Imperial Rome.* Leiden: Brill.

Rowlandson, Jane. 2013. "Dissing the Egyptians: Legal, Ethnic, and Cultural Identities in Roman Egypt." *Bulletin of the Institute of Classical Studies. Supplement,* no. 120: 213–47.

Ruffini, Giovanni. 2006. "Genealogy and the Gymnasium." *Bulletin of the American Society of Papyrologists* 43: 71–99.

Ruffini, Giovanni, and William V. Harris, eds. 2004. *Ancient Alexandria between Egypt and Greece.* Leiden: Brill.

Rutherford, Ian, ed. 2016. *Graeco-Egyptian Interactions: Literature, Translation, and Culture, 500 BC–AD 300.* Oxford: Oxford University Press.

Ryholt, Kim. 1997. *The Political Situation in Egypt during the Second Intermediate Period, c. 1800–1550 B.C.* Copenhagen: Museum Tusculanum Press.

———. 1998. "A Parallel to the Inaros Story of P. Krall (P. Carlsberg 456+P. CtYBR 4513): Demotic Narratives from the Tebtunis Temple Library (I)." *Journal of Egyptian Archaeology* 84: 151–69.

———. 2004. "The Turin King-List." *Ägypten und Levante* 14: 135–55.

———. 2012. *Narrative Literature from the Tebtunis Temple Library*. Copenhagen: Museum Tusculanum Press.

———. 2019. "Libraries from Late Period and Graeco-Roman Egypt, c.800 BCE–250 CE." In *Libraries before Alexandria: Ancient Near Eastern Traditions*, edited by Kim Ryholt and Gojko Barjamovic, 390–472. Oxford: Oxford University Press.

Said, Edward W. 1978. *Orientalism*. New York: Vintage.

Sandy, Gerald N. 1978. "Book 11: Ballast or Anchor?" In *Aspects of Apuleius' Golden Ass*, edited by B. L. Hijmans Jr. and R. Th. Van der Paardt, 123–40. Groningen: Bouma.

Savvopoulos, Kyriakos. 2010. "*Alexandria in Aegypto*: The Use and Meaning of Egyptian Elements in Hellenistic and Roman Alexandria." In *Isis on the Nile: Egyptian Gods in Hellenistic and Roman Egypt: Proceedings of the IVth International Conference of Isis Studies, Liège, November 27–29, 2008*, edited by Laurent Bricault and Miguel John Versluys, 75–85. Leiden: Brill.

Schepens, Guido. 1997. "Jacoby's *FGrHist*: Problems, Methods, Prospects." In *Collecting Fragments [Fragmente sammeln]*, edited by Glenn W. Most, 144–72. Göttingen: Vandenhoeck und Ruprecht.

———. 2010. "L'incontournable Souda." In *Il lessico Suda e gli storici greci in frammenti: atti dell'incontro internazionale Vercelli, 6–7 novembre 2008*, edited by Gabriella Vanotti, 1–42. Tivoli: Tored.

Schlam, Carl C. 1992. *The Metamorphoses of Apuleius: On Making an Ass of Oneself*. Chapel Hill: University of North Carolina Press.

Schmid, Wilhelm. 1887–1897. *Der atticismus in seinen Hauptvertretern von Dionysius von Halikarnass bis auf den zweiten Philostratus*. 5 vols. Stuttgart: W. Kohlhammer.

Schmitz, Thomas A. 1997. *Bildung und Macht: zur sozialen und politischen Funktion der zweiten Sophistik in der griechischen Welt der Kaiserzeit*. Munich: Beck.

Schneider, Richard, ed. 1878. *Apollonii Dyscoli quae supersunt: Vol 1. fasc. 1: Scripta minora*. Leipzig: Teubner.

Schofield, Malcom. 2014. "Archytas." In *A History of Pythagoreanism*, edited by Carl A. Huffman, 69–87. Cambridge, UK: Cambridge University Press.

Schorn, Stefan. 2014. "Pythagoras in the Historical Tradition: From Herodotus to Diodorus Siculus." In *A History of Pythagoreanism*, edited by Carl A. Huffman, 296–314. Cambridge, UK: Cambridge University Press.

Schott, Siegfried. 1950. *Altägyptische Festdaten*. Mainz: Verlag der Akademie der Wissenschaften und der Literatur.

Schwartz, Jacques. 1949. "Ti. Claudius Balbillus (préfet d'Égypte et conseiller de Néron)." *Bulletin de l'institut français d'archéologie orientale* 49: 45–55.

Schwyzer, Hans-Rudolf. 1932. *Chairemon*. Leipzig: Harrassowitz.

Segal, Charles. 1969. "Myth and Philosophy in the *Metamorphoses*: Ovid's Augustanism and the Augustan Conclusion of Book XV." *American Journal of Philology* 90, no. 3: 257–92.

Sethe, Kurt. 1908. *Die altaegyptischen Pyramidentexte nach den Papierabdrücken und Photographien des Berliner Museums*. Leipzig: J. C. Hinrichs.

———. 1928. *Dramatische Texte zu altaegyptischen Mysterienspielen, I: Das "Denkmal memphitischer Theologie" der Schabakostein des Britischen Museum*. Leipzig: J.C. Hinrichs.

Sfameni Gasparro, Giulia. 2018. "Anubis in the 'Isiac Family' in the Hellenistic and Roman World." *Acta Antiqua Academiae Scientiarum Hungaricae* 58: 529–48.

Sharpe, Samuel. 1870. *The Decree of Canopus in Hieroglyphics and Greek*. London: J. Russell Smith.

Shumate, Nancy. 1996. *Crisis and Conversion in Apuleius' Metamorphoses*. Ann Arbor: University of Michigan Press.

Simpson, William Kelly, ed. 2003. *The Literature of Ancient Egypt: An Anthology of Stories, Instructions, and Poetry*. New Haven: Yale University Press.

Skutsch, Otto. 1968. *Studia Enniana*. London: Athlone Press.

——. 1985. *The Annals of Q. Ennius*. Oxford: Oxford University Press.

Smallwood, E. Mary. 1961. *Philonis Alexandrini legatio ad Gaium, Edited with an Introduction, Translation, and Commentary*. Leiden: Brill.

——. 1967. *Documents Illustrating the Principates of Gaius, Claudius & Nero*. Cambridge, UK: Cambridge University Press.

Smelik, Klaas, and Emily Hemelrijk. 1984. "'Who Knows Not What Monsters Demented Egypt Worships?' Opinions on Egyptian Animal Worship in Antiquity as Part of the Ancient Conception of Egypt." *Aufstieg und Niedergang der römischen Welt* 2.17.4: 1852–2000.

Smith, Steven D. 2014. *Man and Animal in Severan Rome: The Literary Imagination of Claudius Aelianus*. Cambridge, UK: Cambridge University Press.

Sonnabend, Holger. 1986. *Fremdenbild und Politik. Vorstellung der Römer von Agypten und dem Partherreich in der späten Republik und frühen Kaiserzeit*. Frankfurt am Main: P. Lang.

Sonnino, Maurizio. 2016. "Per Lia: tra Omero e Giulia Balbilla, sul filo della memoria." In *Σύγγραμμα πολυμαθές: studi per Amalia Margherita Cirio*, edited by Luigi de Cristofaro and Maurizio Sonnino, 7–17. Lecce: Pensa Multimedia.

Sorek, Susan. 2010. *The Emperors' Needles: Egyptian Obelisks and Rome*. Exeter: Bristol Phoenix Press.

Stadler, Martin Andreas. 2008. "On the Demise of Egyptian Writing: Working with a Problematic Source Basis." In *The Disappearance of Writing Systems: Perspectives on Literacy and Communication*, edited by John Baines, John Bennet, and Stephen Houston, 157–81. London: Equinox.

Stein, Arthur. 1933. "Balbillus." *Aegyptus* 13: 123–36.

Stein, Arthur, Edmund Groag, Leiva Petersen, Klaus Wachtel, Matthäus Heil, Werner Eck, and Johannes Heinrichs. 1933–2015. *Prosopographia Imperii Romani saeculi I, II, III*. 9 vols. Berlin: De Gruyter.

Stephens, Susan A. 2003. *Seeing Double: Intercultural Poetics in Ptolemaic Alexandria*. Berkeley: University of California Press.

Stewart, Charles, ed. 2007. *Creolization: History, Ethnography, Theory*. Walnut Creek, CA: Left Coast Press.

Strauss Clay, Jenny. 2020. "Typhoeus or Cosmic Regression (*Theogony* 821–880)." In *Classical Literature and Posthumanism*, edited by Giulia Maria Chesi and Francesca Spiegel, 133–40. London: Bloomsbury Academic.

Struck, Peter T. 2004. *Birth of the Symbol: Ancient Readers at the Limits of Their Texts*. Princeton: Princeton University Press.

Strudwick, Nigel, ed. 2005. *Texts From the Pyramid Age*. Atlanta: Society of Biblical Literature.

234   WORKS CITED

Stuart Jones, H. 1926. "Claudius and the Jewish Question at Alexandria." *Journal of Roman Studies* 16: 17–35.

Swain, Simon. 1996. *Hellenism and Empire: Language, Classicism, and Power in the Greek World, AD 50–250.* Oxford: Clarendon Press.

Swetnam-Burland, Molly. 2007. "Egyptian Objects, Roman Contexts: A Taste for Aegyptiaca in Italy." In *Nile into Tiber: Egypt in the Roman World*, edited by Laurent Bricault, Miguel John Versluys, and Paul G. P. Meyboom, 111–36. Leiden: Brill.

———. 2015. *Egypt in Italy: Visions of Egypt in Roman Imperial Culture.* Cambridge, UK: Cambridge University Press.

Tacoma, Laurens Ernst. 2006. *Fragile Hierarchies: The Urban Elites of Third-Century Roman Egypt.* Leiden: Brill.

Takács, Sarolta A. 1995. *Isis and Sarapis in the Roman World.* Leiden: Brill.

Tarrant, Harold. 1993. *Thrasyllan Platonism.* Ithaca: Cornell University Press.

Tarrant, Richard J., ed. 2004. *P. Ovidi Nasonis metamorphoses.* Oxford: Oxford University Press.

te Velde, Herman. 1977. *Seth, God of Confusion: A Study of His Role in Egyptian Mythology and Religion.* Leiden: Brill.

———. 1980. "A Few Remarks upon the Religious Significance of Animals in Ancient Egypt." *Numen* 27, no. 1: 76–82.

———. 1986. "Egyptian Hieroglyphs as Signs, Symbols, and Metaphors." In *Approaches to Iconology*, edited by H. G. Kippenberg, L. P. van den Bosch, L. Leertouwer, and H. A. Witte. Leiden: Brill.

———. 1992. "Some Egyptian Deities and Their Piggishness." In *The Intellectual Heritage of Egypt: Studies Presented to László Kákosy by Friends and Colleagues on the Occasion of His 60th Birthday*, edited by Ulrich Luft, 571–78. Budapest: La chaire d'égyptologie de l'Université Eötvös Loránd de Budapest.

———. 2002. "Seth." In *The Ancient Gods Speak: A Guide to Egyptian Religion*, edited by Donald B. Redford, 331–34. London: Oxford University Press.

Thackeray, Henry St. John. 1926. *Josephus: The Life. Against Apion.* Cambridge, MA: Harvard University Press.

Theander, Carl. 1951. *Plutarch und die Geschichte.* Lund: C. W. K. Gleerup.

Thesleff, Holger. 1961. *An Introduction to the Pythagorean Writings of the Hellenistic Period.* Åbo: Åbo Akademi.

———. 1965. *The Pythagorean Texts of the Hellenistic Period.* Åbo: Åbo Akademi.

Thissen, Heinz-Josef. 1998. "'Apocalypse now!': Anmerkungen zum Lamm des Bokchoris." In *Egyptian Religion: The Last Thousand Years; Studies Dedicated to the Memory of Jan Quaegebeur*, edited by W. Clarysse, Antoon Schoors, and Harco Willems, 1043–53. Leuven: Peeters.

———. 2002. "Das Lamm des Bokchoris." In *Apokalyptik und Ägypten: eine kritische Analyse der relevanten Texte aus dem griechisch-römischen Ägypten*, edited by A. Blasius and B. U. Schipper, 113–38. Leuven: Peeters.

Thom, Johan C. 2013. "The Pythagorean *Akousmata* and Early Pythagoreanism." In *On Pythagoreanism*, edited by Gabriele Cornelli, Richard D. McKirahan, and Constantinos Macris, 77–102. Berlin: De Gruyter.

Thomas, Richard F. 2001. *Virgil and the Augustan Reception.* Cambridge, UK: Cambridge University Press.

WORKS CITED   235

Thompson, Dorothy J. 1988. *Memphis under the Ptolemies*. Princeton: Princeton University Press.

———. 2003. "Athenaeus in His Egyptian Context." In *Athenaeus and His World: Reading Greek Culture in the Roman Empire*, edited by David Braund and John Wilkins, 77–84. Exeter: University of Exeter Press.

Tilg, Stefan. 2014. *Apuleius' Metamorphoses: A Study in Roman Fiction*. Oxford: Oxford University Press.

Tober, Daniel. 2017. "Greek Local Historiography and Its Audiences." *Classical Quarterly* 67, no. 2: 460–84.

Tomber, Roberta. 2012. *Indo-Roman Trade: From Pots to Pepper*. London: Bristol Classical Press.

Tracy, Jonathan. 2014. *Lucan's Egyptian Civil War*. Cambridge, UK: Cambridge University Press.

Tran-tam-Tinh, Vincent. 1964. *Essai sur le culte d'Isis à Pompéi*. Paris: Éditions de Boccard.

———. 1983. *Sérapis debout: corpus des monuments de Sérapis debout et étude iconographique*. Leiden: Brill.

Trivedi, Harish. 2007. "Translating Culture vs. Cultural Translation." In *In Translation—Reflections, Refractions, Transformations*, edited by Paul St-Pierre and Prafulla C. Kar, 277–87. Philadelphia: John Benjamins.

Tsing, Anna Lowenhaupt. 2005. *Friction: An Ethnography of Global Connection*. Princeton: Princeton University Press.

Ulrich, Jeffrey P. 2020. "Hermeneutic Recollections: Apuleius' Use of Platonic Myth in the *Metamorphoses*." *Classical Philology* 115, no. 4: 677–704.

van der Horst, Pieter Willem. 1981. *Chaeremon: Egyptisch priester en antisemitisch Stoicijn uit de tijd van het Nieuwe Testament*. The Hague: Boekencentrum.

———. 1982. "The Way of Life of the Egyptian Priests According to Chaeremon." In *Studies in Egyptian Religion: Dedicated to Professor Jan Zandee*, edited by Matthieu Heerma van Voss, D. J. Hoens, Gerard Mussies, Dirk Van der Plas, and Herman te Velde, 61–71. Leiden: Brill.

———. 1984. *Chaeremon, Egyptian Priest and Stoic Philosopher: The Fragments Collected and Translated with Explanatory Notes*. Leiden: Brill.

———. 2002. *Japheth in the Tents of Shem: Studies on Jewish Hellenism in Antiquity*. Leuven: Peeters.

———. 2003. *Philo's Flaccus: The First Pogrom*. Leiden: Brill.

Van der Stockt, Luc. 2012. "Plutarch and Apuleius: Laborious Routes to Isis." In *Aspects of Apuleius' Golden Ass. Vol. III: The Isis Book*, edited by Wytse Hette Keulen and Ulrike Egelhaaf-Gaiser, 168–82. Leiden: Brill.

van Dommelen, Peter. 1998. "Punic Persistence: Colonialism and Cultural Identities in Roman Sardinia." In *Cultural Identity in the Roman Empire*, edited by Ray Laurence and Joanne Berry, 25–48. London: Routledge.

van Mal-Maeder, D. 1997. "*Lector, Intende: Laetaberis*. The Enigma of the Last Book of Apuleius' *Metamorphoses*." In *Groningen Colloquia on the Novel VIII*, edited by Heinz Hoffmann and Maaike Zimmerman, 87–118. Groningen: Egbert Forsten.

van Minnen, Peter. 2002. "Αἱ Ἀπο Γυμνασίου: 'Greek' Women and the Greek 'Elite' in the Metropoleis of Roman Egypt." In *Le rôle et le statut de la femme en Égypte hellénistique, romaine et byzantine: Actes du colloque international, Bruxelles-Leuven, 27–29 Novembre 1997*, edited by Henri Melaerts and Leon Mooren, 337–53. Leuven: Peeters.

van Schoor, David. 2011. *"Nec me mea fallit imago*: Ovid's Poetics of Irony and Reflections of Lucretius and Pythagoras in the *Metamorphoses.*" *Acta Classica* 54: 125–47.

Vandier, Jacques. 1962. *Le papyrus Jumilhac.* Paris: Centre national de la recherche scientifique.

Vandorpe, Katelijn, ed. 2019. *A Companion to Greco-Roman and Late Antique Egypt.* Medford, MA: Wiley-Blackwell.

Vandorpe, Katelijn, and Willy Clarysse. 2019. "Cults, Creeds, and Clergy in a Multicultural Context." In *A Companion to Greco-Roman and Late Antique Egypt*, edited by Katelijn Vandorpe, 405–27. Medford, MA: Wiley-Blackwell.

Vanotti, Gabriella, ed. 2010. *Il lessico Suda e gli storici greci in frammenti: atti dell'incontro internazionale Vercelli, 6–7 novembre 2008.* Tivoli: Edizioni Tored.

Vassileiou, A. 1984. "Crispinus et les conseillers du prince (Juvènal, *Satires,* IV)." *Latomus* 43, no. 1: 27–68.

Vasunia, Phiroze. 2013. *The Classics and Colonial India.* Oxford: Oxford University Press.

Verbrugghe, Gerald P., and John M. Wickersham. 1996. *Berossos and Manetho, Introduced and Translated: Native Traditions in Ancient Mesopotamia and Egypt.* Ann Arbor: University of Michigan Press.

Vergote, Jean. 1941. "Clément d'Alexandrie et l'écriture égyptienne: essai d'interprétation de *Stromates* V 4, 20–21." *Chronique d'Egypte* 16, no. 31: 21–38.

Vernant, Jean-Pierre. 1986. "Corps obscur, corps éclatant." *Le Temps de la réflexion* 7: 19–45.

Vernus, Pascal. 1986. "L'écriture hiéroglyphique: une écriture duplice?" *Cahiers Confrontation* 16: 59–66.

Versluys, Miguel John. 2002. *Aegyptiaca Romana: Nilotic Scenes and the Roman Views of Egypt.* Leiden: Brill.

———. 2017a. "Egypt as Part of the Roman *Koine*: Mnemohistory and the Iseum Campense." In *Entangled Worlds: Religious Confluences between East and West in the Roman Empire the Cults of Isis, Mithras, and Jupiter Dolichenus*, edited by Svenja Nagel, Joachim Friedrich Quack, and Christian Witschel, 274–93. Tübingen: Mohr Siebeck.

———. 2017b. *Visual Style and Constructing Identity in the Hellenistic World: Nemrud Dağ and Commagene under Antiochos I.* Cambridge, UK: Cambridge University Press.

Versluys, Miguel John, Kristine Bülow Clausen, and Giuseppina Capriotti Vittozzi, eds. 2018. *The Iseum Campense from the Roman Empire to the Modern Age: Temple, Monument, Lieu de Mémoire.* Rome: Quasar.

Vidman, Ladislav, ed. 1969. *Sylloge inscriptionum religionis Isiacae et Sarapiacae.* Berlin: De Gruyter.

Vierros, Marja. 2012. *Bilingual Notaries in Hellenistic Egypt: A Study of Greek as a Second Language.* Brussels: Koninklijke Vlaamse Academie van België voor Wetenschappen en Kunsten.

Vittozzi, Giuseppina Capriotti. 2006. *L'Egitto a Roma.* Rome: Aracne.

———. 2014. "The Flavians: Pharaonic Kingship between Egypt and Rome." In *Power, Politics, and the Cults of Isis: Proceedings of the Vth International Conference of Isis Studies, Boulogne-Sur-Mer, October 13–15, 2011*, edited by Laurent Bricault and Miguel John Versluys, 237–59. Leiden: Brill.

Vleeming, S. P., ed. 1995. *Hundred-Gated Thebes: Acts of a Colloquium on Thebes and the Theban Area in the Graeco-Roman Period*. Leiden: Brill.

von Beckerath, Jürgen. 1984. *Handbuch der ägyptischen Königsnamen*. Munich: Deutscher Kunstverlag.

von Lieven, Alexandra. 2016. "Translating Gods, Interpreting Gods: On the Mechanisms behind the *Interpretatio Graeca* of Egyptian Gods." In *Greco-Egyptian Interactions: Literature, Translation, and Culture, 500 BCE–300 CE*, edited by Ian Rutherford, 61–82. Oxford: Oxford University Press.

———. 2017. "Porphyrios und die ägyptische Religion vor dem Hintergrund ägyptischer Quellen: Quellenkritik am Fragment (*De cultu simulacrorum*, fr. 10)." In *Platonismus und spätägyptische Religion: Plutarch und die Ägyptenrezeption in der römischen Kaiserzeit*, edited by Michael Erler and Martin Andreas Stadler, 267–92. Berlin: De Gruyter.

Waddell, William Gillan. 1940. *Manetho: History of Egypt and Other Works*. Cambridge, MA: Harvard University Press.

Wallace, Sherman LeRoy. 1938. *Taxation in Egypt from Augustus to Diocletian*. Princeton: Princeton University Press.

Wellmann, Max. 1896. "Aegyptisches." *Hermes* 31, no. 1: 221–53.

Wendel, Carl. 1940. "Zum Hieroglyphen-Buche Chairemons." *Hermes* 75, no. 2: 227–29.

Wessner, Paul. 1931. *Scholia in Iuvenalem vetustiora*. Stuttgart: Teubner.

West, Martin Litchfield. 1971. *Early Greek Philosophy and the Orient*. Oxford: Clarendon Press.

White, Peter. 1974. "Ecce iterum Crispinus." *American Journal of Philology* 95, no. 4: 377–82.

Whitmarsh, Tim. 2001. *Greek Literature and the Roman Empire: The Politics of Imitation*. Oxford: Oxford University Press.

———. 2005. *The Second Sophistic*. Oxford: Oxford University Press.

Wiedorn, Michael. 2018. *Think Like an Archipelago: Paradox in the Work of Édouard Glissant*. Albany: State University of New York Press.

Wildish, Mark. 2017. *The Hieroglyphics of Horapollo Nilous: Hieroglyphic Semantics in Late Antiquity*. London: Routledge.

Wilkinson, Richard H. 1994. *Symbol and Magic in Egyptian Art*. New York: Thames and Hudson.

Wilkinson, Toby A. H. 1999. *Early Dynastic Egypt*. London: Routledge.

———. 2000. *Royal Annals of Ancient Egypt: The Palermo Stone and Its Associated Fragments*. London: Kegan Paul.

Will, Édouard. 1979. "Le monde hellénistique et nous." *Ancient Society* 10: 79–95.

———. 1985. "Pour une 'anthropologie coloniale' du monde hellénistique." In *The Craft of the Ancient Historian: Essays in Honor of Chester G. Starr*, edited by John William Eadie and Josiah Ober, 273–301. Lanham, MD: University Press of America.

Williams, Gareth. 2008. "Reading the Waters: Seneca on the Nile in *Natural Questions*, Book 4A." *Classical Quarterly* 58, no. 1: 218–42.

Willrich, Hugo. 1895. *Juden und Griechen vor der makkabäischen Erhebung*. Göttingen: Vandenhoeck und Ruprecht.

Wilson, Penelope. 1997. *A Ptolemaic Lexikon: A Lexicographical Study of the Texts in the Temple of Edfu*. Leuven: Peeters.

Winkler, John J. 1985. *Auctor & Actor: A Narratological Reading of Apuleius' Golden Ass*. Berkeley: University of California Press.

WORKS CITED

Wohlthat, C. Urs. 2021. *De civitatibus Isidis: Ägyptische Kulte in der Zweiten Sophistik zwischen Diskursen, Vergesellschaftungsformen und Identitäten.* Gutenberg: Computus Druck Satz & Verlag.

Wolff, H. J. 2002. *Das Recht der griechischen Papyri Ägyptens in der Zeit der Ptolemaeer und des Prinzipats. Vol. 1: Edingungen und Triebkräfte der Rechtsentwicklung.* Munich: Beck.

Woolf, Greg. 1994. "Becoming Roman, Staying Greek: Culture, Identity and the Civilizing Process in the Roman East." *Proceedings of the Cambridge Philological Society* 40: 116–43.

———. 1998. *Becoming Roman: The Origins of Provincial Civilization in Gaul.* Cambridge, UK: Cambridge University Press.

Woolf, Raphael. 2015. *Cicero: The Philosophy of a Roman Sceptic.* London: Routledge.

Wynne, J. P. F. 2019. *Cicero on the Philosophy of Religion: On the Nature of the Gods and On Divination.* Cambridge, UK: Cambridge University Press.

Zabkar, Louis V. 1968. *A Study of the Ba Concept in Ancient Egyptian Texts.* Chicago: University of Chicago Press.

Zandee, Jan. 1948. *De hymnen aan Amon van papyrus Leiden I 350.* Leiden: Brill.

Zauzich, Karl-Theodor. 1983. "Das Lamm des Bokchoris." In *Festschrift zum 100-jährigen Bestehen der Papyrussammlung der österreichischen Nationalbibliothek: Papyrus Erzherzog Rainer (P. Rainer Cent.),* 165–74. Vienna: Brüder Hollinek.

Zhmud, Leonid. 1997. *Wissenschaft, Philosophie und Religion im frühen Pythagoreismus.* Berlin: De Gruyter.

———. 2012. *Pythagoras and the Early Pythagoreans.* Translated by Kevin Windle and Rosh Ireland. Oxford: Oxford University Press.

———. 2013. "Pythagorean Number Doctrine in the Academy." In *On Pythagoreanism,* edited by Gabriele Cornelli, Richard D. McKirahan, and Constantinos Macris, 323–44. Berlin: De Gruyter.

Zimmerman, M., ed. 2012. *L. Apulei metamorphoseon libri XI.* Oxford: Oxford University Press.

Zucker, Arnaud. 2014. "L'astronomie." In *Alexandrie la divine,* edited by Charles Méla, Frédéric Möri, Sydney Aufrère, Gilles Dorival, and Alain le Boulluec, 414–19. Geneva: Éditions de la Baconnière.

INDEX

Abydos King List, 41

Acoreus, 92, 198–204; parallels with Manetho, 204; as wise adviser and model of ancient wisdom, 199–200

Actium, Battle of, 2–3, 13, 87–93; "Actium script" in depictions of Egypt, 93–94; and Messalla Corvinus, 95–96

Aegyptiaca (category), 9–11, 42–43

—authors: agency and flexibility of, 146; as ambassadors to Rome, 13–15; Apion as exemplar of, 51–53, 55; Balbilla as, 70–71; as cultural ambassadors of Egyptian religion, 191; economic motivations of, 21; polymathy of, 79; self-conscious posteriority of, 204–5; social position of, 18–19; as translators, 123

—as bridge: between Egypt and Rome, 9, 16; between Egyptology and classics, 83; between Manetho and Plutarch, 134–35

—characteristics: dynamic tradition, 8, 50–51, 195; elastic boundaries, 10; generic heterogeneity *vs.* social coherence, 55–56; ongoing creolizing process, 82; plurality, 11, 56; precarious and metamorphic, 9; presence of philosophy, 185

—contexts: Josephus and Egyptian-Jewish tension, 14, 204; as key framework for Pythagoras, 183–85, 195; *vs.* material Aegyptiaca, 7, 13, 48–49; Roman power and, 53–54

Aegyptiaca (work of Manetho), 41–43

Aelian, on the Egyptian abhorrence of pigs, 128

Aethiopis (epic), 72

Afrocentrism, 204–6

Agrippina, 58, 67

Akhthoes, king, 129–30

Alexander Polyhistor, 181

Alexander the Great, 91; and Greece-Egypt relations, 48; his search for the Nile, 203

Alexandria, 18, 27–28; Alexandrian*, 17–19; anti-Jewish riots of 38 CE, 34–35, 58; Apion's delegation to Rome, 34–37; Caesar's banquet with Cleopatra, 92–93, 200–204; citizenship restricted, but culture multiethnic, 31; embassy to Claudius, 57–58; greatest emporium in the inhabited world (Strabo), 48; intermediary between Egypt and Rome, 13, 48–49; Library of, 66–68, 82; as sealed-off Greek city, 46; as site of creolization, 82; and sycophancy, 198

Alexandrianism: Apion's, 52; as citizenship status *vs.* intellectual tradition, 34; difficulty of defining, 17–19

Allegoresis: Greek, 59; Stoic, 158

Amenhotep III, statues of, 1–2, 2*fig.*, 73

Amenoth, 72–73

Ammianus Marcellinus, 155

Amometus, 52

Amun: etymology of Ammon/Amun, 150, 153–54, 184, 202; Libyan, 97; New Kingdom hymns to, 150–51

240 INDEX

Anaximander, 169

animal gods, Egyptian, 87–115; animals as divine medium, 118–19; and animal feasts, in Lucan, 92–93; in Cicero, 101–2; a cow is not a god, 89–93; demonization of, inaugurated by Augustus, 91; as military totems, 107–8; animal worship. *See* theriolatry

anthropomorphic *vs.* zoomorphic gods, 89, 113, 115; both criticized by the Elder Pliny, 102–3; juxtaposed by Cicero, Pliny, and Plutarch, 116; mapped to Roman *vs.* Egyptian, 93; Plutarch prefers the zoomorphic, 110–11

Antinoöpolis, 18, 111

Antinous, 15, 75, 111

Antoninus Liberalis, on Seth/Typhon, 120

Antony, Mark, 87; and the Battle of Actium, 2–3, 13, 90–92

Anubis, 3, 87–88, 91–93, 103; in Ovid, 99–100; statue of Anubis-Mercury, 111–13, 112*fig.*, 115

Anubophores, dog-faced, 88–89, 112

Apepi, abominable snake, 120, 133

Apion
—background and biography: Alexandrian, Greek, or Egyptian, 27–34, 41; birthplace in the Oasis, 29–31; citizenship of, 13, 29–31; delegation to Rome on behalf of Alexandrians, 14, 34–37, 53; the delegation's parallels with Chaeremon, 58; house-slave or pupil of Didymus, 30
—character: *Pleistonikes*, "quarrelsome," 29; shameless self-promoter, 28; slipperiness of his identity, 52; too loquacious, says Aulus Gellius, 28; unapologetic opportunism of, 46
—status: contrasted to Manetho, 42–43; ethnographer or auto-ethnographer, 27–28, 45; grammarian, 32; Homerist, 32–34, 37–39; outsider or insider, 28; symbolic exegete, 195; synthesizes Homer and paradoxography, 51; travels of, 32
—works: on dung-beetles, 31–32, 139; fragmentary status frustrating, 40, 207; Herodotean and paradoxographical, 33; *Homeric Glosses*, 34, 37; wide circulation of, 29; representation of Jews in, 29–31, 136–37

Apis bull, 3, 74, 88; identified with Osiris, 89, 113, 114*fig.*, 115; in Lucan, 200; in Ovid, 97–101; in Plutarch, 109; in Tibullus, 96

Apuleius, 16, 50, 112, 143–45; donkeys and Seth in the *Metamorphoses*, 135–38; and hieroglyphic, 180; Isis book (XI), 166–67; *On Plato and His Doctrine*, 175

Arignotus, 80–81

Aristotle: philosophical contemplation, 180; and Pythagoras' *Acousmata*, 181; in Plutarch, 174–75

Arouêris, 161–62

Asclepiades of Mendes, 52

ass: in Apuleius, 138; associated with Seth/Typhon, 121, 124–25, 127*fig.*, 129; golden, allegedly worshipped in Jerusalem, 136–37

Astrologoumena (Petosiris), 60

astrology and astronomy, 59–60, 82, 195; in Balbillus, 68–69; in Juvenal, 61–62; and the seasons in Egypt, 203; in Thrasyllus, 61–65

Athenaeus, 36; on Pancrates, 75–76, 78

Augustus Caesar, 67, 87; and the Apis bull, 3, 91; his Nubian expedition, 200; as pharaoh, 5; and the Temple of Dendur, 1–6

auto-ethnography: in Apion, 42; in Aegyptiaca, 9, 201–2; *vs.* ethnography, 27–28

Avaris, Hyksos capital, 136

Baal, 136

Baba and Babawy. *See* Bebon

ba bird, 157–58

Babylonia, 42

Babyloniaca, 7

Bakenrenef, Pancrates' epic on, 15, 75

Balbilli, 55; Balbilla, Julia, 65, 69–75, 82; Balbillus, Tiberius Claudius, 14, 65–69, 193, 199, 203, 207. *See also* Thrasyllus

barbarism and barbarization, 6, 74, 87–93; and impure speech, 80; in Lucan, 92–93, 202; overemphasis on, in scholarship, 116

Bastet, 98–99

Bebon, 124–26, 128, 151–53, 167

bee, sign of kingship, 156

beetle, sign of birth, 157

Bernal, Martin, 204–7

Berossus, 7, 42

binaries
—Egyptian *vs.* Greek, 12–13, 17, 27; anachronistic connotations of, 27; blurred boundaries between, 11–12; complicated by Roman hegemony, 13, 44, 48; ethnic fluidity in Egypt, 31; Greek language, privileged in Ptolemaic Egypt, 8; long history of cultural mixture, 47–48
—Egyptian *vs.* Roman, 4, 12–13, 87–88; Egyptian piety *vs.* Roman moral decline, 105–6; exoticization-demonization, 100; Roman anthropomorphism *vs.* Egyptian zoomorphism, 93; Roman self-positioning against Egypt, 12–13

bird-catching, signifies learning sacred texts, 190
Book of Gates, 128, 139
Book of Hours, 139
Book of Thoth, 12, 189–94
Brill's New Jacoby, 9, 14
Busiris, 177

Caligula, 13–14, 32, 35, 53, 205
Callimachus, *Aetia*, 98
Cambyses, 74, 200, 203
Campus Martius, 88, 163
Cancer (zodiac sign), painful to snakes, 64
canon formation, 14–15, 171, 206, 208
Canopus, 91
Canopus Decree, 187
Cassius Dio, 3–4, 62, 91
Celer, Maecius, 94
Chaeremon, 14–15, 52, 55–62, 74, 147; and the *Book of Thoth*, 189–92; compared to Thrasyllus, 65; on expletive conjunctions, 57; hieroglyphic etymologies, 154, 160–61, 164; *Hieroglyphica*, 57, 154–58, 180; philosopher-priest and sacred scribe, 59, 154, 185–88; Stoic death, 58–59; tutor to Nero, 15, 58–59, 197, 204
Charon of Naucratis, 52
Cicero, 111, 202; *De Legibus*, 102; *De Natura Deorum*, 104–6; on Pythagoras, 176, 178; *Tusculan Disputations*, 101–2
citizenship: Alexandrian citizenship, 21, 34–37; Josephus, on Apion's, 31; Roman citizenship, 21; and status in Roman Egypt, 11, 28; tripartite system of citizenship in Roman Egypt, 28
Classics: boundaries of, 207–8; and Egyptology, 5, 41–43, 83, 89; normative definition of, 10
Claudius's letter to the Alexandrians, 14, 57–58, 67
Cleopatra VII, and the Battle of Actium, 2–3, 13, 89–93
co-authorship of citing and fragmentary author, 39, 125
colonialism: ancient and modern, 19–21, 44; internal Ptolemaic *vs.* external Roman control, 20
Commagene, 70, 79
Commodus, Emperor, 113
Contendings of Horus and Seth, 106, 152
Cornutus, 59, 158
Cosmas Indicopleustes, 11
Cotta, interlocutor of Cicero, 104–6
cow: as bestial, 89–93; and Io-Isis, 95; murdered by Cambyses, 74

crabs, as cure for snake-bite, 64
creolité, French Caribbean, 19, 45
creolization, 18–21, 45–47, 49–50, 82, 146; Glissant on, 46–47, 146, 206; inscribed obelisk as document in, 164; not a teleological synthesis, 70; as unbounded process, 52–53
Crispinus, Juvenal's, 93, 163, 198
crocodiles: associated with Seth/Typhon, 121, 124–25; and Edfu/Apollinopolis, 134; magicians ride on, 80; one killed king Akhthoes, 129–30; on Roman coins, 91; worshipped in Egypt, 101, 105
cultural change, theoretical apparatus of, 18–19
cultural mixture, 15, 81–83, 208; and colonization, 18; *vs.* cultural purity, 16–17; Egypt and, 5–6; *vs.* juxtaposed diversity, 45–46; Memnon as patron of, 75; as process, 47; of the Seth/Typhon myths, 120–21; as theoretical framework, 45; unending, 47–48
cultural priority, questions of, 174–75
cultural purity, 45–46, 50
cultural representation, 116, 145
cultural translation, 12n31; and Aegyptiaca, 17; in Ovid, 117; in Manetho, 148–54; as a theoretical framework, 9, 12, 116–17, 192, 204; and translation of Egyptian terms into Greek, 192
cynocephalia, "dog-head" herb, 39–40, 200

Decius Mundus, 169
decline, rhetoric of, 44
Dedi, Egyptian magician, 80
Delta, Nile: as location of Elysian Fields, 39; authors from, 52
Democritus, 64
Den, king, 129
Dendera, Temple of Hathor at, 126, 127*fig.*, 135
Dendur, Temple of, 1–6
Diana, 87
Didymus "Bronze-Guts," 30, 34
Dio Cassius. *See* Cassius Dio
Diodorus Siculus, 52, 106–8, 125, 128, 202; on Seth/Typhon, 120
Diogenes Laertius, 169, 171; *Lives of the Eminent Philosophers*, on Egyptian wisdom, 183–84, 197; *Lives of the Eminent Philosophers*, prologue of, 177–78; *Lives of the Eminent Philosophers*, scholarly views of, 177
Diospolis. *See* Thebes
Domitian, 198–99; and Isis, 94, 112–13; and the Piazza Navona obelisk, 162–66

242   INDEX

donkeys, associated with Seth/Typhon, 121, 124–25, 127*fig.*, 129; in Apuleius, 135–38
dove, sacred to Aphrodite, 109–10

Edfu, Temple of Horus at, 12, 128, 130–31, 132*fig.*, 133–34, 138
Egypt: as barbarous Other to Rome, 3–4; continuity of pharaonic and imperial traditions, 6; creators of geometry, astronomy, and arithmetic, 178; four *poleis* of, 18; prefect of, 66–67; Roman fascination with, 89; as source of Greek wisdom, 169; two lands of, 130
Egyptian language, 140, 145. *See also* hieroglyphic
Egyptologists: and Aegyptiaca, 15–16, 41–43; and Classicists, 83, 89
Eileithyiaspolis, 126, 128
Eleusinian Mysteries, 174
Elysian Fields, 39
emic, 51, 59, 82; *vs.* etic, 27n2, 72–73, 189; in Chaeremon's etymologies, 157; Manetho, 42
Empedocleanism, 206
emperors, Roman, 53; and authors of Aegyptiaca, 56
Ennius, 38
Eos, 72
Epicureanism, 104–5
epigram, verse, 70–75
epopteia, philosophy, 175
Ethiopian hieroglyphic, 155
ethnic identity and literary production, 41
ethnography: *vs.* auto-ethnography, 27–28; in the Hellenistic period, 7
etic *vs.* emic, 27n2, 72–73, 189
etymologies, Egyptian, 150–52; Manetho's, in Plutarch, 150–52; Manetho's, in Josephus, 152–53
Eucrates, 79–80
Europa and the bull, 99
Eusebius, on Chaeremon, 59
Exodus, 11, 14, 29, 53, 58, 74, 204; and the Hyksos kings, 136, 153
exports, Egyptian, 48

Fabius Pictor, Quintus, 7
figura etymologica, 150
fish, symbolisms of, 160
Flaccus, Aulus Avilius, prefect of Egypt, 34–35
form *vs.* essence in Apuleius, 166–67
forms, Platonic, 175
fragments: limitations of, 195; pointillistic *vs.* reconstructive approach to, 9–10, 76, 124;

unsatisfactory transmission of, 155, 207. *See also* Jacoby, Friedrich
friction, in postcolonial theory, 49
frog, sign of resurrection, 156–57

Gallus, Cornelius, prefect of Egypt, 67
gatekeeping, symbolism as, 180
Gellius, Aulus: on Apion, 28, 33; *Attic Nights*, 28; bookishness of, 33; inventing the "classical" period, 206; on the polymathy of writers of *Aegyptiaca*, 79
Greek Magical Papyri, 76–78
gymnasium, 30

Hadrian: his Egyptophilia, 111–15; and Pancrates, 15, 75–79; visits Egyptian Thebes, 69–70
Harpocras, Pliny's masseur, 18
Hathor, 2, 3*fig.*, 98
hawk, hieroglyph for soul, sun, god, 157
Hecataeus of Abdera, 52, 125; *On the Philosophy of the Egyptians*, 183
Heket, 156–57
Heliopolis, 11, 41–42, 78
Hellanicus of Lesbos, 152, 161
Heraclitus, 110
herbology, in Apion and Pliny, 39–40
Hermaeus, 52
Hermanubis, 111–12, 112*fig.*
hermeneutics of the Greek tradition, 139–40
Herodotus, 33, 74, 157, 169, 171, 206; and Hecataeus, 52; and Manetho, 8, 42, 149; and Plutarch, 107–8
Hesiod, *Theogony*, on Typhon, 117–18, 122
Hieroglyphica (Chaeremon), 57, 154–58
hieroglyphic, 42, 89; and animal characters, 144, 166–67; in Apuleius, 144; Caesar asks Acoreus about, 202; Chaeremon's translations of, 154–58; decipherment of, 165; exoticism of, 166; falling out of use, 146; and inaccessibility, 202; increasingly distant from vernacular Egyptian, 167; and the invention of Greek philosophy, 179–80; overlap with zoomorphism, 145; pictured and translated, 6, 132*fig.*, 133, 143, 151, 156–57, 160–61, 165–66, 190–91; pronunciation of, 156, 161, 165; Seth as determinative, 143; Seth and Khepri in, 140
hierogrammateus, 186–87, 192, 202. *See also* sacred scribes
Hierosolymus, 136–37
hippopotamus: associated with Seth/Typhon, 119, 121, 123, 124–25, 129; harpooning ceremony, 129; royal hippopotamus hunts, 130, 137; seized king Menes, 129

INDEX 243

Historia Augusta, 113
Homer: and the Alexandrian grammarians, 15, 37, 42, 53, 206; Apion summons his ghost, 38; his heroes never ate fish, 160; his homeland, 37–38; Tzetzes on the *Iliad*, 155
Homeric Glosses (Apion), 34, 37
Horapollo, 154
horoscopes, 60
Horus, 2, 3*fig.*, 106, 121–22, 161; battle with Seth/Typhon, 131, 132*fig.*, 133–34; of Behdet, 131; as hawk, 133–34, 158; temple of, at Edfu, 130–31, 132*fig.*, 133–34, 138
House of Life, 186–88, 190–91, 193, 202
human sacrifice, 126, 128
Hyksos, 131; etymology of, 153, 167; and the Exodus, 136, 153
hymns to Amun, New Kingdom, 150–51
Hysiris, alternative spelling of Osiris, 161

Iamblichus, 171, 181
ibis worship, 101, 110
ichneumon, 108
identity: and birth, ancestry, 32; different elements of, 57; disjunctive and sequential approach to, 49; essentialist views of, 49; messiness around, 18; and movement, 32; narrow *vs.* plural, 47; and place, 30–31
imperialism: ancient and modern, 20–21; knowledge as form of, 203
indigeneities, ancient and modern, 44
initiation: exclusionary, 180; philosophical, in Plutarch, 173–75
interpretatio Graeca, 122, 170, 188, 192
inventio Osiridis, 88
Io, identified with Isis, 95
Iphis, in Ovid, 99–100
Iseum Campense, 163
Isis, 2; in Apuleius, 137–38; Isis cult, 88–89, 163, 165, 169–70; from Julio-Claudian antipathy to Flavian patronage, 89–90, 112–13, 115; in Lucan, 92; in Ovid, 99–101; in Plutarch, 159, 173–74; sacrifices a Seth-donkey, 127*fig.*; in Statius, 89, 94–95
Isocrates, 177

Jacoby, Friedrich, *Fragmente der griechischen Historiker*, 9, 14, 30–31, 55, 65
Jerome, on Chaeremon, 59–60
Jerusalem, Jewish temple in, 136–37
Jews: anti-Jewish riots of 38 CE, 14–15, 34–35; and Egyptians, antagonism between, 11, 29–30; slandered by Apion, 14–15, 29–31; slandered by Manetho, 149

Josephus, 74; abuses Chaeremon, 58; *Against Apion*, 15; *Against Apion* and Manetho, 147–49; *Against Apion* and Seth, 136–37; intense dislike for Apion, 29–31; on the irony of Apion's citizenship, 35–36; role in canonization of Aegyptiaca, 14; source for Manetho's etymologies, 152–53; targets Apion, 27, 49, 81
Judaeus, 136–37
Julius Caesar, 92; divinization of, 6; in Lucan, 198–204
Juvenal, 60–63, 93, 163, 169, 199; on Egyptian animal gods, 87–89, 107, 113, 139

Khepri, scarab god, 139–40, 157
Königsnovelle, 8

Leda and the swan, 99
Library of Alexandria, 15, 22, 67–68, 82
Libyan lion hunt, Hadrian's, 75–76
Lotus, red, named Antinoeis, 75, 79
Lover of Lies. See Lucian
Lucan, 92–93, 139; *Bellum Civile*, on Egypt, 198–204
Lucian, 184; *Lover of Lies*, 79–80; on Pancrates, 76, 79–81
Lucillius (epigrammatist), 60
Lucius, Apuleius' *Metamorphoses*, 137–38, 143–45
Lucretius, *De Rerum Natura*, 60
lunar cult, 200
Lyceas of Naucratis, 52
Lysimachus, 52

magic spells, 76–77
Manetho, 11–12, 41–43; compared to Hecataeus, 52; as cultural authority, 7–8, 124; on Exodus, 14; as foil to Herodotus, 8; kings list, 8, 129–35; as language expert, 147–54; and later Aegyptiaca, 8; *On Natural Things*, 183; parallels with Acoreus, 204; Plutarch's source for Seth animals, 123–29; *On the Preparation of Kyphi*, 43; and Pythagoras as binary stars, 183–85, 195
Martial, on Chaeremon, 58–59
Memnon, statue of, 69–75; defaced by Cambyses, 74
Memphite Theology, 106
Menes, king, 129
Messalla Corvinus, 95–96
Metamorphosis: animal, in the Edfu Seth/Horus myth, 129–34; and Egyptian animal-gods, 95, 100
metempsychosis, 99

244 INDEX

Metropolitan Museum of Art (New York), 1–4
Middle Platonism, 50, 122, 173; and Neo-Pythagoreanism, 176
Minerva, 87
mixedness. *See* cultural mixture
Moses, 11, 29
Museum of Alexandria, 15, 22, 67, 75, 78, 82, 204

natural philosophy: in Chaeremon, 187–88; and hieroglyphic symbolism, 155–56; in Lucan, 200–201, 203; and Seth/Typhon, 120, 125
Naucratis, 18, 27, 36; and Greco-Egyptian culture, 52
navigium Isidis, 88
Nechepso, 60, 63
Nephthys, 127*fig.*, 161, 165
Neptune, 87
Nero, 56, 67–68, 93, 198–99; and his tutor Chaeremon, 15, 58–59, 197, 204; comet portends death, 68; his Nubian expedition, 200
Nicander: *Heteroioumena*, 98; on Seth/Typhon, 120
Nile: Acoreus on, 200–201, 203; Nilescapes, 89; Nilometers, 200; in Tibullus, 96
Nubian expeditions, 200
Nut, Egyptian goddess, 122, 161

obelisks
intra-textual *vs.* extra-textual significance of obelisk's inscription, 164
Piazza Navona obelisk, 112–13, 162–166
transport to Rome, 4, 49
Octavian. *See* Augustus Caesar
Olympian gods: artistic portrayals of, 104–5; fugitives from Typhon, 98–99, 107, 117–18, 120
On Isis and Osiris, 16, 43, 106–12, 130, 191–92; on Egyptian etymologies, 150, 158–62, 168; and the Horus falcon, 133–34; Manetho as source for Seth animals, 123–29; multiple readings of, 172–73; on Seth/Typhon, 119–22; programmatic opening, 173
On the Preparation of Kyphi (Manetho), 43
orientalism: and Bernal, 204–7; retrojection of, 5; in Roman attitudes to Egypt, 51
Origen, 59
Orphism, 206
Osiris, 2, 43; coffin of, 121; compared to Messalla Corvinus by Tibullus, 95–97, 100; cosmogonic implications of the myth, 124–25; dismembered penis devoured by a

fish, 160; identified with Apis, 89, 113, 114*fig.*; and Isis, identified with the sun and moon, 128; in Ovid, 99; in Plutarch, 106, 109, 119–23, 172; syncretized with Dionysus/Bacchus, 96
osiritis, herb, 39–40, 200
Ovid, *Metamorphoses*, on Typhon, 97–101, 107, 120

Palermo Stone, 41, 129–30
Pancrates, 15, 52, 55, 75–81, 187, 207; *vs.* Pachrates, 77–80; parallels to Hermanubis, 113; physical description of, in Lucian, 80–81
paradoxography, 33, 42
Paris Magical Papyrus, 76–78
Paulina, Isis devotee, 88, 169
Peribsen, king, 121
Petosiris, 60, 65; in Juvenal, 61–63; Suda on his works, 61
Pharsalia, Battle of, 199
Philo, 14, 34–36
philosopher-priest: Chaeremon as, 59, 171; effective persona, 197; mixed authority of, 170–71, 195; Pancrates as, 171; Plutarch, Platonist and priest of Apollo, 172; reception in Rome, 197–98; semantics of, 185
philosopher-scribe, 191–92
philosophy: cultic turn in imperial age, 174; Egyptian origins of, 176–78, 197; as frame for Egyptian religious traditions, 171; priestly origins of, 172; pupil in *Book of Thoth* called "he who loves knowledge," 191; and religion, 167–68
Pierides, 97–99
pigs, associated with Seth/Typhon, 121, 128
Plato: Caesar compares himself to, 202–3; philosophical contemplation, 180; Platonic themes in Apuleius and Plutarch, 143; in Plutarch, 122, 124, 172, 174–75; and Pythagoras, 175–76, 197; Thrasyllus' tetralogies, 64–65, 206; travels in Egypt, 175–76, 202–3, 205–6. *See also* Middle Platonism
Pliny the Elder: on anthropomorphic *vs.* zoomorphic gods, 102–3; on Apion, 29, 38–39, 50; on Apion and scarabs, 31–32, 139; on astronomy, 60; on snake-bites cured by crabs, 64; on Thrasyllus, 64; on the transportation of obelisks, 4
Pliny the Younger, 18
Plutarch: and the divine, 110–11; and hieroglyphs, 180; on Pythagoras' enigmas, 181–82; on Thrasyllus, 63–64. *See also On Isis and Osiris*

INDEX 245

Poetical Stele from Karnak, 165
polyonymy, in social life and Balbilla's verse, 72
pomerium, sacred boundary of Rome, 88
Pompey Magnus, 92–93, 198–99
Porphyry: on Chaeremon, 59; on Hermanubis, 113; on Ptolemy, 60
Poseidon, 161
postcolonial scholarship and Roman Egypt, 19–20, 44
Pothinus, 199–200
Propertius, on Cleopatra and Actium, 90–91
prosopography, 10, 66, 76, 207
Proteus, 95
pseudo-Apollodorus, on Seth/Typhon, 120
Ptah and Ptah-Sokar-Osiris, 96, 125, 131
Ptolemaic dynasts, 42–43, 68
Ptolemais (city), 18
Ptolemy of Mendes, 52
Ptolemy XIII, 199
Pyramid Texts, 122, 130, 160
Pythagoras: as inventor of philosophy, 177–78, 192; as key framework for Aegyptiaca, 184–85, 196; and Manetho as binary stars, 183–85, 195; number theory, learned in Egypt, 178, 182; in Ovid's *Metamorphoses*, 99; Plato's mentor, 175–76, 197; travels in Egypt, 175–76, 195, 205–6; as world-traveler, 172
Pythagoreanism, 37–38, 64, 80, 161, 194, 206; *Acousmata* or *Sayings*, 178–81; as cult, 171

Qadesh inscription, 165
Quellenkritik, 123. *See also* source criticism

Ra, 120
Ramesses II, 165
rhizomatic philosophy, 47, 49–50
riots, anti-Jewish, of 38 CE, 14, 34–35
road, as theoretical frame, 21, 49–51, 53
robe, Osiris's, 175
Romaica, 7
Rosetta Stone, 186–187

sacred scribes, 56, 59, 79, 155, 186–87, 200, 202
Sappho, reception in Balbilla, 71
Sarapis, 91, 100, 103, 115
scarab (dung beetle), 31, 139–40, 157; and semantics of autogenesis, 144
Second Sophistic, 16, 70, 173
Sekhmet, 98
Seleucid dynasts, 42

Seleucus of Alexandria, 52
Seneca, 198–200; on Apion, 32–33, 41; on Balbillus and the Nile, 68–69; *Natural Questions*, 68, 201
Senusret I, 165
Seth/Typhon, 98, 106, 118–19; alleged father of Hierosolymus and Judaeus, 136–37; in Apuleius, 138; associated with disorder and foreignness, 126; battle with Horus, 131, 132*fig.*; and Bebon, Baba, and Babawy, 151–52; as "chaos" in hieroglyphic, 145; as determinative, 143–44; metamorphosis into ass, in Apuleius, 135–38; metamorphosis into hippopotamus and crocodile, 131; metamorphosis into serpent, 133; as opponent of Osiris/Zeus, 120; in Plutarch, 119–23; as symbol of the bestial and irrational, 126, 167; syncretism of, 119–29; worshipped by the Hyksos, 136–37
Skepticism, philosophical, 104–5
source criticism, 10
Statius, propempticon for Celer, 94–95, 100
stereotype appropriation, 170
Stoicism, 15, 56–61, 68, 158, 171; in Cicero, 101; in the Elder Pliny, 103; in Lucan, 200
stork, hieroglyph for soul, in Chaeremon, 158
Suda: on Apion, 30, 34; on Chaeremon, 57; on Petosiris, 61
Suetonius, 68, 198
sun: and moon, identified with Osiris and Isis, 128; and scarab (dung-beetle), 139–40
Swallow Wall, 63
symbolism: of hieroglyphic script, 154–55, 167–68; as object of cultural translation, 180; Pythagorean oral tradition as, 179, 181; strong impulse in Egyptian culture, 193; various meanings of, 171
syncretism: Greek metamorphosis and Egyptian animal-gods, 95, 97–100; Seth/Typhon, 106, 119–29

Tacitus, 62, 66–68
Tale of Sinuhe, 165
Tefnut, 2
Thales, 169
Thebes (Egyptian), 69, 72–73
theoria, divine, 173
theriolatry: and idolatry, 109; limitations of the phrase "animal worship," 103–4; and Typhon, 118; utilitarian and symbolic explanation, 108; *vs.* zoomorphism, 104, 108–9

theriomorphism: as ridiculing strategy, 98–99; of Typhon, 118; *vs.* zoomorphism, 103

Thoth, 2, 98, 189–92

Thrasyllus: one or two, 63–64; Thrasyllus of Mendes, 52, 63–64; Thrasyllus, Tiberius Claudius, 61–65, 68, 193, 203, 206

Thutmose III, 165

Tiberius, Emperor, 29, 60, 68; and the *Iseum Campense*, 88, 169

Tibullus, 95–97, 100, 113

Tithonus, 72

Titus, Emperor, 163–64

translation: "Greegyptian" argot, 159; task of translator (Glissant), 145–46; *vs.* transliteration, 73; of the word "translate," 148–49. *See also* cultural translation

transliteration: and emic expertise of Julia Balbilla, 73; of foreign names in hieroglyphic, 164–65; of Pachrates/Pancrates, 77

Turin Royal Canon, 41

Typhon, 97–100, 107; in Hesiod, 117–18; Olympian gods flee from, 98–99, 107, 117–18, 120; on Corinthian vases, 118; syncretized with Seth, 106. *See also* Seth/Typhon

Typhonians, burned alive, 126, 128

Typhonomachy, 98–99

Tzetzes, Ioannes, 155, 165

Vatican City, Gregorian Egyptian Museum, 111–12, 114*fig.*

Velleius, interlocutor of Cicero, 104–5

Venus, 87

Vespasian, 163–64

Vibia Sabina, 69–71

viewership *vs.* readership, 164

Virgil, *Aeneid* 8, and the Battle of Actium, 2–4, 87–93

visual poetics of hieroglyphic, 166

web, culture as, 53, 167

winks *vs.* blinks (Geertz), 123

wordplay, etymological, 151

Zeus, earless, statue of, 110

zoomorphism, 89, 113, 115, 202; and animal-shaped hieroglyphs, 145, 166–67; *vs.* anthropomorphism, in Greco-Roman literature, 102–3, 116; mapped to Egyptian *vs.* Roman, 93; in Plutarch, 110–11

Founded in 1893,
UNIVERSITY OF CALIFORNIA PRESS
publishes bold, progressive books and journals
on topics in the arts, humanities, social sciences,
and natural sciences—with a focus on social
justice issues—that inspire thought and action
among readers worldwide.

The UC PRESS FOUNDATION
raises funds to uphold the press's vital role
as an independent, nonprofit publisher, and
receives philanthropic support from a wide
range of individuals and institutions—and from
committed readers like you. To learn more, visit
ucpress.edu/supportus.